DEAD END

The Crime Story of the Decade:
Murder, Incest, and High-Tech Thievery

DEAD END

The Crime Story of the Decade:
Murder, Incest, and High-Tech Thievery

Jeanne King

M. Evans and Company, Inc.
New York

M. Evans and Company, Inc.
216 East 49th Street
New York, New York 10017

Printed in the United States of America

9   8   7   6   5   4   3   2   1

CONTENTS

PREFACE

It is often said that evil is banal. This certainly proved to be true in the case of Sante and Kenny Kimes. As this mother and son sped up the East Coast in their stolen Lincoln, Sante laughed and plotted. Above her dead smile, her eyes were devoid of humanity. Kenny, at 23, had a gleam of violence and dollar signs shining in his eyes. He took note of a good spot to dump a body. They didn't openly talk about a murder. They both knew the plan for 82-year-old Irene Silverman. This should be the last big score.

Sante and Kenny arrived in New York City on Sunday, June 14, 1998. Wasting no time, they moved in on their elderly victim, "I.S.," as they liked to call her. Using an alias, Kenny rented an apartment in Irene's multimillion-dollar townhouse, pretending that Sante was his secretary. They tapped Irene's phone and spied on her. They forged documents and kept notes on the activities in the house. They used anybody and everybody they came in contact with and stuck to their plan to take over Irene Silverman's luxurious townhouse. They had done their homework: there were no relatives and there was a sparse staff on weekends. But Irene would not be so easy for these two. Irene was a savvy businesswoman and a good judge of character. She sensed the danger. She told her friends and her staff that Kenny "smelled like jail" and that he was not to be trusted. She regretted allowing Kenny into her home. His one bedroom apartment was just down the hall from Irene's. How would she stop this stranger and the woman he was with?

Irene knew she had to kick them out. She announced this to her staff and friends on the Fourth of July. By the next afternoon the spirited millionaire had vanished. Irene would not be seen or heard from again. Also missing were her new tenant and his lady friend.

Sante and Kenny had moved out. As the local precinct's police were summoned to Irene's home, across town the New York City Police Department's Joint Federal Fugitive Task Force had arrested the mother and son grifter team near the Hilton Hotel. Sante and Kenny had been picked up on a warrant from Utah relating to the stolen Lincoln. The press exclaimed, MILLIONAIRE DISAPPEARS WITHOUT A TRACE. The bosses of the NYPD demanded that Irene be found.

The duty to find Irene fell upon the Silver Task Force. It was made up of a select team of detectives from the fabled Manhattan North Homicide Squad and a team from the crackerjack 19th Precinct Detective Squad. Downtown, the New York County District Attorney's Office assigned four of its brightest and most seasoned prosecutors to work with the Task Force on the investigation and to ultimately prosecute Sante and Kenny. Together, the detectives and prosecutors embarked on a journey that took them across America and beyond. What they found was a tale of broken lives, greed, slavery, arson, and murder. What they didn't find was forensic evidence, an eyewitness, a murder weapon, an admission, or Irene Silverman's body. Without such evidence and without a confession, would this be the last of the cons by this mother and son? Take a seat and find out.

Joel Potter   *Eugene Wasielewski*
Detective, NYPD (Ret.)   *Sergeant, NYPD (Ret.)*

Manhattan North Homicide Squad
New York City, November, 2001

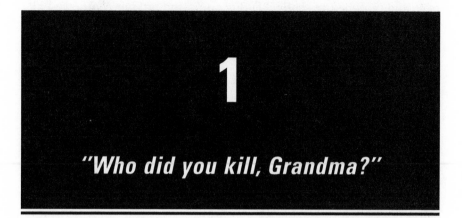

1

"Who did you kill, Grandma?"

Dawn had just broken, yet the temperature outside Stanley Patterson's trailer home on the outskirts of Las Vegas, miles away from the neon-lit casinos downtown, was a blistering 96 degrees. The worst was yet to come: by mid-afternoon, forecasters were predicting the mercury would climb even higher, to a scorching 104 degrees in the shade . . . if you could find any.

Inside the tiny one-bedroom, sparsely furnished trailer Patterson shared with his wife, the morning sun was already peeking through the slats of a rickety wooden window shade when the telephone rang, rousing Patterson from a deep sleep. Turning over slowly, he peered at the clock radio on his nightstand, which read 7:15.

To others, Vegas might be the town that never sleeps, but to

1

Patterson at that moment there was, or should have been, only one 7:15 on the clock, and it wasn't 7:15 A.M. Eyes half open, he reached over and punched his caller ID button to find out who could be calling him at this ungodly hour: it was a 917 area code phone number he did not even recognize. Shit, he thought, who the hell could this be? He pulled the receiver to his ear and managed a groggy hello.

"Hi, how ya doin'?" asked a deep, annoyingly cheery male voice at the other end of the line. "Here's mom." Even half asleep, Patterson had no trouble recognizing the voice as belonging to Kenny. Instantly, as if black coffee had been mainlined directly into his bloodstream, Patterson was jolted awake, and before he could swing his legs off the bed and without even so much as a hello, the woman Patterson knew only as Ellen was on the phone, rattling out a plan.

"Come to New York. I've got an apartment for you to manage that's owned by this old woman. She's eccentric. You've never seen anything like it. Late at night, when she gets drunk, she dances in the hallway in a frilly negligee, tiptoeing like a ballerina. It's a sight to be seen. Listen, Stan, we want you to be the super and manage the building. You'll go in there and throw out all the deadbeats. Evict all the faggots and derelicts in the building. Paint it, fix it up, and bring it up in value."

Ellen, who barked orders like a Marine drill sergeant, spat out her words in such rapid-fire fashion that she rarely left room for words from anyone else. Finally, the puzzled Patterson managed to crowbar in a question. "How do I evict everyone if the eccentric lady is still there?"

"Don't worry about her," Ellen replied. "Just live in the apartment. If someone knocks on the door, ignore all questions. Tell them to leave a card, that the building is being taken over by a corporation, and someone will get back to them."

There was more. As the cobwebs faded from his head, Patterson heard Ellen tell him that she was prepaying an electronic plane ticket for him on America West and that he should pick it up at the airport in Las Vegas. Once in New York, she instructed, he would take a shuttle bus to the Hilton Hotel and call her on her cell phone as soon as he arrived.

"Don't forget," she added, "I want you to evict these guys. There was a blond Mexican guy renting this apartment for three months for $6,000 and the landlady said it was only for one month. He demanded his money back and couldn't get it. The man had $5,000 on the dresser in his bedroom and somebody stole it from him."

Patterson had no fucking idea what she was talking about. It made no sense, but it didn't matter. From experience, he knew that he'd find out soon enough what Ellen was talking about, and it probably meant trouble.

"Don't tell anyone about this," she warned, talking even faster now, as if that were possible. "Nothing. Nada. Pack enough clothes, because you're going to be there at least a month. And one more thing, Stan, bring your toys," she added ominously.

Patterson knew exactly what Ellen meant, but before he could answer, he heard Kenny yell in the background, "Don't do that, Mom. Don't have him bring any guns. We don't want no shoot-outs in New York."

"You got it all?" Ellen asked, ignoring her son's cautioning words. "And Stan, just make sure you're coming," she ordered.

"How much is in it for me?" Patterson asked.

"More money than you could ever dream of," Ellen answered.

"I'll think about it," Patterson told her, and then he hung up the phone.

Patterson knew better than to believe Ellen's promises of Vegas-sized, jumbo jackpots. After all, he'd heard more than enough versions of the same rap before. Patterson was a construction worker/handyman down on his luck and actually could have used the work Ellen described, though the mention of bringing his "toys" did worry him. He had good reason to be suspicious of Ellen and her offer, and he couldn't help but wonder what she had up her sleeve. Whatever it was, he knew it was trouble, trouble he couldn't afford to get into. After all, he'd met Ellen and Kenny only six months ago, but less than a week ago he had learned that their antics had landed him in deep shit with the law.

At 55, the craggy-faced Patterson was well built and rather muscular. His weather-beaten face and chiseled features had that worn-out, tired look of an old cowboy. Despite his slightly receding

3

hairline, his salt-and-pepper hair made him look somewhat distinguished. Patterson had lived in Las Vegas 22 years and had worked the hotels there since 1978 as a maintenance engineer. But he lost his job in 1997, and since then, the divorced father of four grown children had struggled to make ends meet.

He first met Ellen and her son Kenny in January 1998, when he answered an ad in the *Las Vegas Review Journal* looking for someone to do home repairs and small moving jobs. Ellen had placed the ad and when he called she offered him $300 to move her belongings from Vegas to a storage facility in Sherman Oaks, in Los Angeles. Ellen was a real charmer, promising him grand trips to the Bahamas, vacations in Hawaii, and enough work to set him up for life. Under other circumstances, he might have been skeptical, but because of the hard times Patterson was going through, he wanted to believe Ellen and her promises of the good life, and so he was blinded by her glib talk and flirtatious manner.

As he sat there on the edge of the bed, the phone at his side, Patterson pondered that first impression of Ellen and recalled her superficial smile that never went higher than her immobile upper lip. He remembered her deep black eyes that stared menacingly through the Coke bottle lenses of her cheap, over-the-counter glasses and her distinctively thick black eyebrows that were plucked into gothic arches that enhanced a suggestion of demonic possession.

As for Kenny, he was a docile, dutiful, humanoid son to the woman he called "Mom" in a way that Patterson found a little creepy. Kenny, who was easygoing, had youthful, collegiate good looks, yet his smile was at times as sinister as that of Hannibal Lecter. Kenny could be personable and charming one moment, but in the flash of a second he could switch, revealing a wild temper that could send shivers up your spine. If he were ever to be played by someone in a movie, Patterson thought Sean Penn would make for perfect casting.

On January 23, as he was loading furniture and documents into a U-Haul truck for the trip to LA, Patterson mentioned to Kenny, who was hanging around watching him work, that he was a gun collector. Kenny seemed fascinated and asked to see his collection. That very day, while the U-Haul truck stood packed and ready to leave, both Ellen and Kenny accompanied Patterson to his trailer where they handled and dry-fired his guns, which included a .380 Magnum, a Smith & Wesson revolver, two .22 Jennings automatics, a .22-caliber Beretta, and a 9mm Glock pistol.

Kenny said he wanted to purchase two of the guns, because, he explained, he couldn't buy them from a firearms dealer since he was only 20 years old. Only later did Patterson learn that Kenny was actually 22 years old and that he was lying simply to see whether Patterson was someone who could actually provide him with his "toys." Despite the show and tell session, no guns were sold that day.

Almost precisely one month after moving Ellen and Kenny's belongings to Los Angeles, Patterson received a phone call requesting his services again. This time, they wanted him to drive still more of their belongings from Las Vegas to Los Angeles, to a home they had rented in the Bel Air area. They also asked Patterson to bring along two .22 Jennings pistols—and then Kenny added a particularly odd request. "Can you find a way to silence them?"

"Why do you need a silencer?" Patterson asked.

"I just want to do some shooting in the backyard, and I don't want to bother the neighbors," Kenny answered, a little too innocently for Patterson's taste.

"Take a potato, take a knife, and bore it out a little bit. It works just as good," Patterson advised, offering Kenny a tip he'd learned from an engineer.

"That's too easy," Kenny replied enigmatically.

Patterson accommodated his new employers and brought the two Jennings pistols with him during the February Los Angeles trip, and agreed to sell the guns to them for $20 apiece. Patterson gave both of them to Kenny to try out. Kenny later returned one of the pistols, claiming it didn't work, but he never returned the other one and never paid for the one he did keep. Kenny and Ellen then prevailed upon Patterson to buy two other pistols for them, a Beretta and Glock, which Patterson handed over only after they promised to reregister them in their own names. He didn't trust them and the last thing he wanted was to have them wind up being used in some crime and then being traced back to him.

Patterson heard nothing more about this odd couple until June 27. He was working on his beat-up pick-up truck outside his trailer that afternoon, when he was approached by two Los Angeles detectives, Dennis English and William Cox, along with a Las Vegas detective named Jimmy Vacarro. The detectives wasted no time showing Patterson they were playing hardball. They told him the woman he knew as Ellen had 22 other aliases, including "The Dragon Lady." They said her real name was Sante Kimes and she was a career con artist with a police record going back nearly four decades, including convictions for involuntary servitude, forgery, and grand larceny. Her son Kenneth, who was always referred to as Kenny, was her partner in crime.

The detectives made it very clear to Patterson that unless he cooperated with them, he could face serious criminal charges as the registered owner of a gun that might have been used in a murder in LA back in March. The victim's name was David Kazdin and he was a former business associate of the Kimeses, who were, the detectives explained, the chief suspects in the murder. Immediately, Patterson knew what happened to that missing Jennings pistol, and he realized the Kimeses had tricked him into supplying them with legally registered weapons.

Patterson was no fool. He was no killer either. He knew that keeping his mouth shut would do him no good and so he wasted no time admitting to the detectives about the gun transactions and he agreed to cooperate, promising to let them know the next time the mother and son duo contacted him.

On that morning of July 1, immediately after receiving Sante's call from New York, Patterson contacted the LA detectives, who then came up with an elaborate plan to arrest Sante and Kenny in New York City, using Patterson as bait.

Over the next few days, "Ellen" called Patterson at least seven more times and each time he spoke to her, Patterson immediately relayed what she said to the LA detectives. When she was sure he was making the trip, Sante, whose speech sounded as jittery as a wind-up toy, gave him final orders for Sunday, July 5. Once in the lobby of the midtown Hilton Hotel, he was to call her on her cell phone number and await further instructions.

Meanwhile, Detectives English and Cox submitted a formal request to the joint FBI/New York Police Department Fugitive Task Force in Manhattan for assistance in a homicide investigation that began in LA on March 13, 1998, and involved Sante and Kenny Kimes, who were now believed to be in New York.

The LAPD request was brought to the attention of David Stone, a 23-year veteran of the FBI and the supervisor in charge of the New York Task Force. According to the LAPD, the murder victim, David Kazdin, 63, was a former insurance claims adjuster who had investigated the 1973 theft of a tapestry filed by the late Kenneth Kimes, Sr., Kenny's father and the man Sante claimed was her husband. More recently, Kazdin ran a copy machine business near his Granada Hills home in the San Fernando Valley. Over the years, Kazdin and Kimes, Sr., became friendly enough for Kazdin to agree to be listed as owner of Kimes's Las Vegas Geronimo Way home so that some of Kimes's assets could be hidden. Kazdin was getting set to retire when his body was found in a black heavy-duty garbage bag bound with duct tape inside a dumpster behind Los Angeles International Airport on March 14, 1998. Police forensic investigators determined that he was shot with a small caliber pistol.

Technically, Sante and Kenny were wanted only for questioning in connection with Kazdin's murder, but there were sufficient grounds to pick them up and hold them on an outstanding Utah warrant issued in connection with the fraudulent purchase of a green Lincoln Continental Town Car, paid for by a bad check for $14,900. That's exactly what the detectives planned to use, so that they wouldn't tip their hand when the arrests were made.

By Saturday, July 4, Stone had briefed over a dozen agents assigned to the case, who were all ordered to report for work early the next morning. The plan called for detectives to intercept Patterson at John F. Kennedy International Airport and bring him to Task Force headquarters for questioning before sending him over to the Hilton Hotel to flush out the Kimeses.

Stone agreed to the LAPD request that the Task Force would not interrogate the Kimeses about the Kazdin case; instead he would simply hold them, pending the arrival of Los Angeles detectives, who would be dispatched to New York once the Kimeses were in custody.

DEAD END

It was a balmy 71 degrees with virtually no humidity—a rarity for New York City in July—when a weary Patterson sauntered off the red-eye flight at JFK airport. Wearing baggy blue jeans, a blue plaid shirt, cowboy tie and jacket, and cowboy boots, his head covered by a Crocodile Dundee hat, he was hard to miss. As soon as he entered the terminal, he was flanked by two agents from the Task Force: FBI case agents Wilfred Baptiste and Emilio Blasse.

"Are you Mr. Dwight?" Baptiste asked.

"Not today," Patterson replied. "My middle name is Dwight."

Patterson's use of his middle name had been a pre-arranged code set up before he left Las Vegas and would be used to initially identify him to law enforcement agents so Patterson, who had long since stopped trusting "Ellen," could be assured that those meeting him at the airport were agents and not cohorts of Sante's.

Flanking him, the agents took Patterson by the arms and hustled him to a waiting unmarked police car and guided him inside. As the car sped into the city, one of the agents asked the obviously nervous Patterson why he was wearing a bulletproof vest underneath his shirt. Knowing that Sante had asked him to bring his guns and knowing that she and Kenny were capable of murder and may have picked up weapons from another source, he replied, "I'm in fear of my life. The Kimeses may kill me."

Traffic that holiday Sunday morning was light, so the car carrying Patterson and the two agents quickly reached the giant federal building at 26 Federal Plaza, where an elevator whisked them to FBI headquarters on the 28th floor. There, in a large room, nine other agents were waiting to interrogate Patterson. After an hour,

Patterson, who was periodically glancing at his watch, reminded the agents that he needed to get to the Hilton soon, if they didn't want to arouse the suspicons of Sante and Kenny.

By 10:30 A.M., more than a dozen FBI agents and NYPD detectives had infiltrated the Hilton Hotel at West 54th Street and Sixth Avenue, staking out the lobby and exits and searching the garage for the green Lincoln Town Car that Sante had paid for with a rubber check. Hilton security was notified and the hotel's computer was searched on the possibility the Kimeses were registered there, but nothing turned up and there was no trace of the Lincoln in the garage or parked on the street near the hotel.

At precisely 11:02 A.M., Patterson, still obviously nervous, strolled over to a bank of pay phones in the ornate lobby and made the first of several calls to the Kimes' cellular phone. Each time he called, he left a voice mail message saying he was at the Hilton, waiting in the guest house phone area.

At 11:26, Sante called back. "We're on the Garden State Parkway," she announced, as the agents, who were close enough to Patterson to pick his pockets, listened intently. "We're having car trouble. It runs for 20 miles and quits. Be about two hours getting in. While you're waiting for us, find the cheapest car rental place and find out how much it will cost to rent a car. Get the number for me so I can call it when I call you back," she ordered before hanging up.

The agents and Patterson were suspicious—they doubted Sante was really having car trouble—but they could do little else but wait. Nevertheless, over the next three hours, Patterson tried a couple more times to reach Sante on her cell phone. Now the phone simply rang without being answered, which probably meant that it had been shut off.

Finally, at 3:24 P.M., when Patterson tried calling once again, Kenny answered and put his mother on the line. "The car is still acting up," she said, "but I'll see you in 30 minutes."

Patterson reported this short conversation to the agents, and a few minutes later, Detective Michael Ryan called Sante's cell phone number to confirm that Patterson was being truthful. When a male voice answered, Ryan hung up.

9

At 5:00 P.M., when the detectives and agents were considering suspending the operation for the day, a woman's voice called out Patterson's name. He turned to see Sante Kimes sashaying across the lobby. She was heavily made up and gaudily dressed in dark pants, shawl, and a wide-brimmed hat. On her arm she carried a cheap black patent leather purse, and on her right hand she wore a ring that had what looked like a diamond as big as the Ritz. As she gave Patterson a kiss and steered him to the lounge area, the Task Force agents held back, preferring to make their move when Kenny arrived.

"I'm dried out and thirsty," she announced jauntily. "Let's go get a drink at the bar."

"Where's Kenny?" Patterson asked, as he sipped his drink.

"He's taking the car to be fixed at the garage," she answered, then quickly changed the subject, as she fingered her highball, the first of three she would order. "Listen, Stan, we need to discuss this apartment you're taking over. First of all, I want you to change all the locks." She repeated what she had already told him on the phone about how a man named Manny Guerin had put down $6,000 on the apartment with another guy, thinking he was renting it for three months. "He's gone now and you can move in," she said.

About 6:00 P.M., Sante announced she was hungry and wanted to go somewhere for a snack. Later, she said, when Kenny arrived, they could have a real dinner. When the $24 tab came, she slipped Patterson $180—a $100 bill and four $20s in crisp new bills—under the table, so he could pay. "I hate drinking with a poor man," she confided.

As they were leaving the Hilton, Sante realized she had left her shawl back in the bar and went back to retrieve it. When she returned, they crossed Sixth Avenue, where a street fair was in progress, and went into the Cio Europa restaurant in the old-fashioned but elegant Warwick Hotel. They had some wine and an appetizer, for which Patterson, using the money Sante had slipped him, paid $42 plus a $10 tip. Leaving the restaurant, they strolled through the Sixth Avenue street fair where Sante bought three T-shirts and a cowboy hat.

By now, FBI supervisor Stone had a huge surveillance team set up outside the Hilton and along Sixth Avenue. Stone had assigned Detective Michael Ryan to take Sante, while other agents would nab Kenny. Stone's job would be to get Patterson away from the Kimeses so they wouldn't suspect that they'd been set up. As Sante and Patterson started walking up the avenue, one of Stone's agents alerted him to a dark-haired young man who was obviously following Patterson and Sante. Stone watched as Sante and Patterson stopped at a booth and the young man ducked into a doorway. The young man fit the description they had of Kenny Kimes. Stone signaled the other agents that the arrests were about to go down.

At this point, Kenny approached his mother, giving her a hug. He looked exhausted and, even though the evening was mild, the back of his black shirt was soaked in sweat. He turned to give Patterson a hug and felt the bulletproof vest he was wearing and knew that this was the kiss of death, but before he could do anything, Patterson had taken off his hat, giving Stone the signal to have his men move in.

With shouts of "Police! You're under arrest!" several agents grabbed Kenny and pushed him to the sidewalk. He resisted fiercely and had to be subdued.

When Patterson turned back to look at Sante, she already had handcuffs on. She tried to give her purse to Patterson, but Stone, in an effort to maintain Patterson's cover, pulled him away, pushed him up against a wall, and handcuffed him as well. When the Kimeses were out of sight, Stone had Patterson uncuffed, commandeered a taxi, threw Patterson and his luggage inside, and told the driver to take him to the airport.

Meanwhile, Kenny was cuffed and frisked by Detective Edward Murray, who removed brass knuckles and a knife Kenny was carrying. As he was being patted down, Kenny wet his pants and his urine, traveling down his leg, made a small puddle on the sidewalk.

"What's going on? What's this all about? What are you doing to my son? Leave my son alone. We didn't do anything!" Sante screamed.

Sante was placed in the back seat of a car. As Murray got into the front passenger seat, Ryan handed him Sante's black bag, taken from her at the time of arrest. It seemed unusually heavy and

Murray's first thought was that there might be a weapon inside. He opened it and instead of a pistol he saw a large amount of money on top, upwards, he figured, of $10,000.

As soon as Sante saw him staring at the contents, she screamed, "The bag isn't mine. It belongs to a friend. The money is mine. I need the money because I'm on vacation in New York." Sante blurted out, "You can never come to New York and be on vacation with less than $10,000."

Murray smiled. "Ten thousand dollars? I don't even come to New York with ten dollars, if I am lucky," he joked.

With Ryan driving downtown toward FBI headquarters, the detectives began to question Sante about her identity. "What's this all about?" she asked.

"We're acting on a Utah warrant," one of the detectives explained.

"I have a right to see the warrant," Sante argued.

"You'll see the warrant back at the office, but we need to know your name first," said the detective.

Sante wouldn't answer directly. Instead, she told them they had no right to ask her any questions. She had been a paralegal, she said, and knew they shouldn't be asking her any questions without an attorney being present.

In the meantime, special agents Baptiste, the case agent, and Emillo Blasse took Kenny to FBI headquarters in another car. When Kenny asked what the charges against him were, they said it was for a stolen Utah car.

"Okay," Kenny said. "That's no problem, we can take care of that."

"Do you have a car parked around here you'd like us to move?" Blasse asked as innocently as possible.

"Why?"

"Because this is New York and your car will be towed if it is not parked correctly," said Blasse, but Kenny didn't answer.

Kenny, still in handcuffs, was the first to arrive at FBI headquarters, shortly before 8:00 P.M. He was taken to the 28th floor and put in a normal-sized nine-by-nine foot interview room with three or four chairs, a desk, and a couple of poles for use with handcuffed prisoners.

Once again, Kenny was searched. This time the detectives came up with a number of credit cards and IDs belonging to Max Schorr, an elderly Florida lawyer, a Florida identification card with the name Manny Guerrero, and an American Express card in the name of Irene Silverman. They also found two sets of house keys, both of which were fastened together with safety pins, one large, one small. Both sets of keys were painted with red nail polish.

Detectives also found a parking stub indicating that Kenny had parked a car in a garage at West 44th Street and Sixth Avenue at 6:40 P.M. The stub was given to Stone, who, with another agent, Robert Benninson, drove to the garage. There they found the green Lincoln. In the rear window of the vehicle was a temporary paper plate license from Utah. The keys were in the ignition, the blue-tinted windows were down, and the back seat was piled from floor to ceiling with luggage, plastic bags, and papers. After checking to make sure there were no weapons or explosives in the car, Stone drove the Lincoln downtown to the basement of the federal building and left it in a secure FBI parking area.

Back at Federal Plaza, agents Blasse and Baptiste began their interrogation of Kenny, who was in constant motion.

"What's your name?" Kenny asked Blasse.

"Special Agent Blasse. What's yours?"

"Okay, Special. I'm not sure I should give you my name," Kenny replied, deliberately omitting the agent's full name.

"We have an arrest warrant for Kenneth Kimes. Is that your name?"

"What if it's not?"

"Then we'll let you go," Blasse said.

At the same time Blasse and Baptiste were trying to get information out of Kenny, Detectives Murray and Ryan brought in Sante and installed her, still handcuffed, in an interrogation room two doors down from where her son was being questioned. Like him, she was obstinate and determined to give the detectives a hard time. Instead of offering her name, she insisted on knowing Murray's name.

"Excuse me, but I'm the detective here. I'll ask the questions," he snapped.

Murray and Agent Baptiste left Blasse alone with Kenny while they inventoried the contents of Sante's black bag in her presence, listing the property belonging to her, and separating those items that she said did not.

When they pulled the cell phone from her bag, Sante immediately insisted, "The cell phone is not mine."

"Yours or not, you can't take it with you where you're going," Murray said.

As Baptiste itemized the documents in the bag, he came across a passport, bankbooks, and other documents in the name of Irene Silverman. "Who's Irene Silverman?" he asked.

"She's a friend of mine. She's a ballerina and she lets me hold her papers and documents sometimes," Sante replied calmly.

As city detectives and FBI agents took turns moving between the interrogation rooms to question the mother and son, they purposely left the doors open. Kenny and Sante began shouting at each other, asking if the other was okay. Sante issued instructions as to what questions her son should answer. This was just what the detectives wanted, as they thought it would serve their investigative interests in case either Sante or Kenny inadvertently misspoke.

When it came to reading Kenny his Miranda rights, it took the agents and detectives nearly an hour because he questioned every line and yelled down the hall to his mother asking her if he should answer, then waiting for her response before he'd speak.

"Mom, what should I do? I don't quite get this? Is it okay?"

"Yes, it's okay. Do you understand what's going on?" Sante replied.

Like a broken record, Kenny kept asking the detectives, "Can I speak to her? How's my mother doing?" And then he turned toward the open door and shouted, "Mom, is everything okay?"

"Yeah Kenny, I'm fine," she replied.

The detectives and agents were careful to reassure the Kimeses they were being arrested only on the basis of the Utah car theft warrant. Blasse read the warrant to Kenny. Dated April 9, 1998, it called for the arrest of Sante and Kenneth Kimes on communications fraud charges, relating to the purchase of the Lincoln Town Car, paying for it with a bad check for $14,900 from a frozen account registered in the name of Nanette Wetkowski. The warrant was signed by a judge in the Fifth Judicial District Court in Iron County, Utah, the area around Cedar City in the southwestern corner of the state. Bail was to be set at $20,000 once they were apprehended.

"Oh, that's all?" Kenny said offhandedly, as the detective finished reading the charges. "I'm probably the only person who's had so many agents pick up someone on this kind of charge. Sorry to waste your time," he said patronizingly. "This is all just a misunderstanding. We can clear this whole situation up. Can I post a bond or bail and just get out of here? Can the judge just tell me how much is it? We have the money," Kenny said.

"That's up to the judge. I really don't know. I'm assuming you're Kenneth Kimes," Blasse said.

"I never said that," Kenny said indignantly.

"If you're not Kenneth Kimes, then I guess we have to release you because we have a warrant to arrest Kenneth Kimes," Blasse said.

Kenny breathed a sigh of relief. "Whew! This is only about the car? If that's all this is about, I'm very happy. When I get back from Utah, I'll buy you guys a drink," he told Ryan, as he proceeded to give the agent his name, date of birth, and a mail box address in Las Vegas.

Likewise, Sante began to relax a little after seeing the Utah warrant, which listed five aliases, including Sandres Singrea and "The Dragon Lady," as well as three separate birth dates: 1934, 1937, and 1944. "Is this really only about a Utah warrant?" she asked hesitantly. When she was told that it was she seemed to perk up. "It says here that one of my names is 'The Dragon Lady.' Okay, I'll tell you my name, my real name. It's Sandra Louise Walker and I'm from Oklahoma."

At 11:00 P.M., as detectives Murray and Ryan started to walk Sante over to the New York City Corrections Department jail for the night, they passed the room where Kenny was sitting. Kenny, noticing them pass by, called out through the door and asked the detectives if he could turn off his mother's cell phone.

Hearing her son's voice, Sante shouted back, "Don't worry, we'll clear this up. This is just a misunderstanding. We have all the paperwork."

Once inside the Criminal Court Building at 100 Centre Street, three blocks north of Foley Square, Sante was taken to the Central Booking section in the basement and placed in a huge cinder-block cell with half a dozen women waiting to appear before a judge. One of her cellmates was Renee Andrews, a prisoner awaiting arraignment on a minor drug charge. Andrews gave Sante the once-over and asked, "Why you here? Who did you kill, Grandma?"

Sante reddened and glared venomously at the young woman, who backed off immediately, saying, "Only kidding, Grandma. Only kidding."

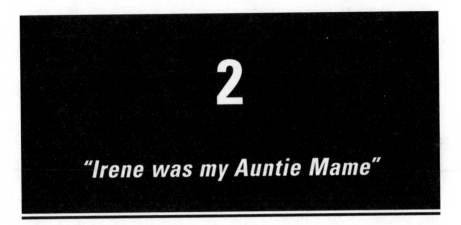

2

"Irene was my Auntie Mame"

The morning before Stanley Patterson was to arrive at JFK airport on his way to meet Sante and Kenny Kimes, Norma Eberhart Dauphin, a former actress and widow of the acclaimed French actor, Claude Dauphin, best known to filmgoers for his roles in *Les Miserables* and *Two For the Road*, stepped out of her elegant townhouse on East 65th Street on her way to do some errands. Two doors down, she noticed her long-time neighbor, Irene Silverman, standing outside her own luxurious, five-story townhouse. The diminutive woman, who was just under five feet tall and weighed less than 100 pounds, was dressed only in a bathrobe and seemed nervous and upset. Norma was concerned. Irene was usually so full of life, smiling, laughing, joking, the incarnation of the fictional Auntie Mame who, during the height of the

Depression, liked to repeat the phrase, "Life is a banquet and most poor sons of bitches are starving to death."

Norma asked Irene what was wrong. "It's my tenant," Irene complained, shaking her head. "I've got to get rid of him."

Norma knew exactly who Irene was referring to. Irene's tenant, one of many to whom she'd rented apartments to since her husband passed away nearly twenty years earlier, was a young man who said his name was Manny Guerin and who'd moved in three weeks earlier. Manny was a strange man who was constantly accompanied by an older woman whom he sometimes introduced as his secretary, Eva. You couldn't miss them. They stuck out like a sore thumb in an elegant neighborhood blanketed by posh high-rise apartment buildings and chic, expensive designer boutiques. To Norma, he looked like a little rat, with those shifty eyes of his, and the woman, who seemed as if she were joined to him at the hip, was very tacky, even slutty-looking. Norma thought he was probably her boy toy, the way they acted toward each other in public, walking arm in arm down the street. Disgusting. It was no wonder Irene wanted him out. These people were definitely out of character for the neighborhood. But then again, so was Irene Silverman.

That Irene Silverman was herself a part of this exclusive, Upper East Side neighborhood was something of a miracle. The fact is, this daughter of an immigrant Greek mother had come a long way from her rather humble beginnings in New Orleans more than three quarters of a century earlier.

On a cold, chilly February morning in 1914, Irina Meladaki, 24, along with a distant cousin as a companion, boarded a ship in Piraeus, the seaport of Athens, and began the stormy 22-day voyage across the Atlantic to America. When the two immigrants disembarked at Ellis Island, they had only $30 in gold coins between them. Three days later, when they finally reached New Orleans by train, Irina's father, who had emigrated earlier, met them and escorted them to their new home in their new country.

Within a year, Irina met her future husband, George Zambelli, an Italian-American sometime fish seller whose main occupation was gambling. Zambelli was a man who, according to those close to him, lived "on the edge of respectability." Nevertheless, Irina was smitten and she married him. In 1916, they had a daughter, whom they named Irene. Sixteen years later, during the height of the Depression, George abandoned his small family, leaving Irina and her teenage daughter to fend for themselves.

Irina was a resourceful woman and she decided that her future wasn't in New Orleans—she and Irene needed a much larger canvas to serve as the backdrop of their dreams. She packed up her bags and she and her 16-year-old daughter traveled north to New York City to make a better life for themselves. Upon arriving in New York, the two women set up housekeeping in a cold water flat on Tenth Avenue, in the midst of the notorious Hell's Kitchen section of the city, characterized by crumbling tenements, decrepit factories and a high crime rate.

Hell's Kitchen, which runs between 34th and 59th streets, from Eighth Avenue to the Hudson River, has a sordid history. By 1870, the neighborhood was one of the most notorious criminal enclaves in town, home to more than 7,500 grog shops, as well as some of the worst criminals in New York. The writer Herbert Asbury named it "the most dangerous area on the American continent," and the police walked the streets only in pairs.

It was here that Irina and Irene made their home, with Irina finding work as a seamstress, eventually earning enough money sewing to have her daughter study with noted Russian ballet choreographer Michel Fokine, who created sixty ballets in his lifetime, most notably *Firebird*, *Petrouchka*, and *Les Sylphides*. Irina paid Fokine's five dollars for a half-hour lesson by sewing custom-made costumes for his private recitals.

By the time she was 17, Irene had begun her career as a ballerina at Radio City Music Hall, the largest indoor theater in the world. Throughout her life, many people mistakenly thought Irene was a Rockette, because the *corps de ballet* alternated on stage with the more famous high-kick precision tap dancers, but Irene always quickly corrected the misconception, politely informing them she was a ballerina and making it quite clear that she did not like being called a Rockette. Working four shows a day, seven days a week, Irene worked up to making $36 a week, which wasn't bad money for 1933, the height of the Depression. As the shortest dancer in the ballet troupe, Irene was so tiny she looked like a pixie and was placed at either end of the stage. In fact, friends often delighted in telling about Irene's needing a footstool when she sat in a chair in her home because her feet couldn't touch the floor.

Other than her mother, Irene's only immediate family was a distant second cousin, Despy Mallas. As a teenager, Despy recalled visiting Irene in an apartment she had across from Radio City Music Hall. Irene and her mother had worked in the couture department at Elizabeth Arden's Fifth Avenue salon and Despy was impressed that Irene Jr., as she was sometimes called, would design clothing items for Elizabeth Arden and her mother would then sell them out of their apartment.

During an evening at the Music Hall in 1940, Samuel Silverman, a handsome, up-and-coming real estate developer, spotted Irene from the audience. It was hard to miss her, as she was the shortest dancer in the ballet group, standing at the end of the stage on her tiptoes. It was love at first sight. Sam, a dashing, witty, six-footer with light strawberry-blond hair and a twinkle in his eyes, became the stereotypical Stage Door Johnny and Irene quickly fell under his spell.

After a whirlwind courtship, Irene married Sam on October 3, 1941, in a synagogue near Radio City. Irene, a Roman Catholic, once joked to a friend that with a Greek mother and an Italian father, she decided to do something about her name. "So I anglicized myself by marrying a Jew."

Sam went off to fight in World War II and Irene continued at the Music Hall until 1945, when her husband came home from the war and she retired from the grueling grind of a ballet performer. With her career behind her, Irene and Sam took off to lead the luxurious lifestyle around the world that her husband had promised her when they'd married.

One of their first stops was Paris, where Sam and Irene met Florence and Ben Barrack. Florence was the dress designer for her husband Ben's dress manufacturing firm, which catered to elegant ladies who bought at Bergdorf Goodman and Saks Fifth Avenue.

"Irene and Sam had just bought a narrow brick townhouse on the Square de l'Opera behind the Opera House," Florence recalled.

"I had heard through a mutual friend that Irene loved cooking with herbs. That was my incentive to call on her and we became lifelong friends." Irene was an excellent chef and the Barracks often marvelled at "the mouthwatering aroma of gourmet food [that] filled the air as Irene pulled out this huge tray of hearts of artichokes with cheese from the oven."

Florence thought of Sam and Irene as quintessential bohemians. Irene was kooky, which endeared her to Florence, and a special bond developed between the two women. Florence admired the fact that Irene was both an artist and a businesswoman. She was tough, powerful, and colorful. She had very strong likes and dislikes and could often be a very critical woman, a personality trait that Florence appreciated.

The Silvermans also bought a farmhouse outside of Paris in the tiny town of Seine et Oise, a very chic area, where top couture designer Jacques Fath had a nearby home. It was here that the Silvermans first introduced the Barracks to Emil and Helen Sabouraud. Emile was a French impressionist painter known for his landscapes and still lifes. The Silvermans were generous with their money, as evidenced by the fact that they later put Sabouraud's son through medical school.

The Silvermans loved to travel, and although New York City was their home, Sam was often on the road drumming up business. Eventually, Sam and Irene bought a small beachfront condominium in Honolulu and Sam got involved with local and state construction projects. Sam also worked in the real estate division of the Empire Trust Company of New York, one of the city's biggest banks. He was instrumental in financing the 800-room landmark Ilikai Hotel, now the Renaissance on Waikiki beach, made famous in the opening credits of *Hawaii Five-O*.

At the time, Sam also represented Columbia University, which was building its real estate portfolio, and he referred what he believed to be good short-term investments to them. Sam had a wide range of friends in real estate, in movie financing, and in the hotel area; he was instrumental in the Westin Hotels' acquisition of the Plaza Hotel in New York City in the 1970s. He was also financial adviser to William Forman, a pioneer in motion picture distribution and founder of the second-largest theater chain.

When the Silvermans moved back to New York City, their first apartment was a pied-à-terre on Park Avenue. A few years later, they added a brownstone in the Murray Hill district in the east 30s between Lexington and Park Avenues to their real estate holdings. By 1957, Sam felt that having a chic address would be good for his growing business, and this was enough of an incentive for the Silvermans to settle down in the six-story limestone landmark mansion with a sweeping marble staircase at 20 East 65th Street between Madison and Fifth Avenues. Aside from it being a good address, the townhouse boasted a breathtaking Central Park view from the roof garden. The mansion was set in the middle of the block on the south side of the street, diagonally across and down the street from Temple Emanuel-el, the largest Jewish Reform congregation in the world.

The Beaux Arts mansion was built around the turn of the century and had undergone several renovations since 1901, as various owners remodeled, adding extensions and altering the interior of the rooms. Following suit, Sam and Irene renovated the house after buying it, ripping out walls and gutting several rooms.

Four years before he died of lymphoma cancer in 1980, Sam transferred title of the house to Irene and, after his death, she converted most of the rooms in the house into luxury rental apartments that she rented out to interesting, well-heeled people, charging them anywhere from $6,000 to $10,000 a month.

The façade of the 25-foot-wide building had an ornamental gargoyle above the entranceway that served as protection against evil as well as a spout to throw rainwater clear of the building. More modern security innovations included the two video surveillance cameras hidden in the upper reaches of the vestibule wall that monitored visitors before they passed through to the mansion's imposing turn-of-the-century, solid oak door.

Once the Silvermans completed their renovations and redecoration, the house was impressive. In the lobby, visitors were greeted by a Queen Anne style desk. Off to the right of the foyer was Irene's mirrored office, apartment 1A, an area where she slept and where she spent a good portion of her day chatting on the telephone, reading newspapers and magazines, or working at her desk. Telephones, television sets, and office equipment, including a printer, fax machine, computer, and an electric typewriter, were crammed into the room. Her old passports, as well as $10,000 in crisp bills were always neatly arranged in envelopes in her closet, as was jewelry and memorabilia belonging to her late husband and deceased mother.

Down the black marble hallway from her office sat the bench Irene used when waiting to use the tiny two-person elevator that would take her to the upper floors of the building. Next to the elevator was the spacious apartment 1B that Irene wanted to convert into a museum to hold her mother's embroidered artwork but that she had instead rented to the young tenant she was complaining about to Norma Dauphin.

The centerpiece of the lobby was a magnificent, sweeping white marble staircase that led to the second floor, where there was a formal living room styled after Versailles, with a wood-burning marble fireplace, one of nine in the house. The room held velvet and silk brocade sofas and post-impressionist art. Old World paintings covered every wall space from floor to ceiling. Murals, life-style sculptures, and antiques enhanced the huge room, scattered with an abundance of white Chippendale chairs. A lovely wood-paneled dining room is to the rear of that floor, where there was a stunning carved wood statue of Saint Roche that Sam and Irene brought back with them from one of their frequent trips to France.

Every bedroom apartment on the upper floors that Irene rented was tastefully decorated. Some rooms displayed wood ceiling beams, while others had ornate gold molding and elegant wallpaper. The eight apartments were furnished with antiques, grandfather clocks, lots of photographs, vivid-colored paintings on the walls, and spectacular crystal chandeliers dangling from the twelve-foot ceilings.

Irene's duplex on the fourth and fifth floors was breathtaking. Every wall in the 2,500-square-foot plush-carpeted apartment was covered with modern and medieval oil paintings, including an original Renoir and signed and numbered prints of Picasso and Degas. Two ten-foot mahogany glass étagères were crowded with fine bone china and sets of crystal glasses. A life-size oil portrait of Irene in a blue and white tutu, dramatically featured on the wall between the two front windows, was the main attraction of her living room.

The highlight of the fourth floor was a terra cotta tiled terrace featuring a sculptured water fountain that was surrounded by an arbor of woodland trees, shrubs, and exotic flowers, such as white gardenias and orchids, a profusion of azaleas, lilies, amaryllis, ferns, and rhododendron and evergreens. A cozy black wrought iron table and chairs were the only furniture on the terrace.

A black spiral staircase led from a hallway to the fifth floor, where Irene's bedroom and dining area were located. The penthouse roof garden was where Irene often went to play with her cats and Georgie, her champion boxer. It was also the area where Irene exercised by placing her leg on the bar and touching her head to her knees as she did in her younger days as a ballerina.

In the summer, the rooftop was where Irene grew her favorite tomatoes in potted planters. But here, too, as a security measure, a menacing white iron barrier railing spiked and curved inward, surrounded the entire roof area and greenhouse to prevent intruders from entering the home from an adjacent roof.

Irene's mother, Irina, lived in the house with the Silvermans until her death in 1985. By this time, she had turned her sewing talent into making museum-quality needlepoint and appliqué creations. She even used to make couture boxer shorts for Sam, who was extremely fond of his mother-in-law.

A selection of Irene's mother's handiwork was generously displayed throughout the mansion, most notably her wool afghan of Picasso's *Tete de Femme*, which took her five months to copy, and a four-by-six-foot afghan of a Toulouse-Lautrec. To honor her mother, it was Irene's idea to turn what was once Sam's office in the mansion into a needlepoint museum. Coby, a pet name both mother and daughter would call each other, was selected as the official title for The Coby Foundation.

Irene and Sam loved throwing elaborate parties in their home, estimated in 2001 to be worth in the neighborhood of ten million dollars, and when Irene entertained, she did it with style and elegance. She liked anybody who was odd or offbeat and often threw costume parties at which many of her guests would show up in outrageous attire. If you didn't come in costume, Irene insisted on formal attire.

Irene was a frequent visitor on those occasions when Norma Dauphin had her show business buddies in for cocktails. "She was the life of the party and loved hearing good funny jokes," said Dauphin. "I could tell her any kind of joke and she'd laugh her head off and then turn to me and, with a dead-pan face, shake her head disapprovingly and say, 'To hear these things come out of your pretty little mouth.'"

Although she was getting on in years, Irene was an irrepressible, entertaining character. Well into her seventies, she was styled the Bon Vivant of East 65th Street, and once showed up at a black-tie dinner party with ten stunning young men. When asked about her dazzling escorts, she replied with a straight face, "I rented them for the night."

Irene was a woman who was delightful, exciting, unpredictable, and caring. "Irene was my Auntie Mame," said Zang Toi, the Malaysian fashion designer who dresses the likes of Sharon Stone, Whitney Houston, Madonna, and Ivana Trump. Ivana's daughter, Ivanka Trump, parades Toi's stunning duds down the glamorous runways of the world.

Zang had met Irene at a Christmas party given by a mutual friend eight years before Irene was murdered. The two became fast friends and, despite his hectic schedule as one of the most successful designers in the fashion jungle, Zang always found time to dine with Irene in her spacious wood-paneled basement kitchen once a week.

"She became like a mother to me," Zang said. "She had a dry wit, she was a person who was thoughtful and sensitive to others' feelings. There was a big difference between us in age, but I could tell Irene things I couldn't confide to my own mother. She was very open about my sexuality, my being gay, very open-minded, and she treated me like a son. She loved me for who I am. She embraced me with open arms, a real friend. She had charisma and presence and loved living life to the fullest."

Although to some, Irene might have seemed a little ditsy and eccentric, she had a sharp mind, especially for business. For instance, she was once dickering over the rental rate of one of her apartments with a well-known real-estate agent who wanted the place for one of his Italian clients. Irene quoted him a price of $450 a night, and when the agent slipped in the lower amount of $400, figuring Irene was probably absent-minded and wouldn't notice the difference, she gently reminded him that the cost for one night was $450.

Among her paying guests were orchestra leader Peter Duchin and his wife, Brooke Hayward, the daughter of Broadway's Leland Hayward and actress Margaret Sullavan; pop singer Chaka Khan; and Peter Jacobson, ex-husband of Fran Drescher and producer of her television series, *The Nanny*. Jacobson loved the peace and tranquility of the house so much, he often rented Irene's duplex, paying her $10,000 a month.

Manny Guerin was Irene's latest renter and, quite frankly, she was sorry that she ever took him in.

SATURDAY, JULY 4, 1998, NEW YORK CITY

On Saturday afternoon, Irene placed a call to her good friend, Helen Pandelakis, to inquire about her health. The two women had met 26 years earlier when they were classmates in an oral history course at Columbia University. As they got to know each other, they realized they came from similar Greek backgrounds. "My mother comes from Crete," Irene announced proudly, which turned out to be the same island as Pandelakis's parents hailed from. They were in touch at least once a month, even occasionally going on trips together, as they did once to see the El Greco exhibit in Washington, D.C. Now Helen was recuperating from recent angioplasty surgery, and Irene was concerned about her friend's health. After a short conversation, Irene promised to check in with her friend the next morning.

That evening Irene hosted a small Fourth of July party, complete with those All-American favorites, hot dogs and beans. Among the small group of friends was Carol Hansen, a 45-year-old graphic artist who first met Irene in June of 1996, when she was writing a magazine article about Irene and the Coby Foundation for *Embroidery Business News*. They became friends and kept in contact by exchanging cards and newspaper articles of mutual interest. Irene was putting together a Coby newsletter and Carol was helping her edit it.

Elva Shkreli, a 28-year-old fashion designer, was also a guest. She had met Irene three years earlier at a gala event at the Metropolitan Museum, when Irene had arrived on the arm of Jeff Feig, her business manager. After that, Elva and Irene became close friends, speaking or meeting each other at least once or twice a week.

During the evening, Irene, always the life of the party, entertained her friends by reading a short story she'd written about a memory from her childhood in New York. But during the evening's festivities, Irene's tenant, Manny Guerin, was still very much on the hostess's mind. From the time Manny moved into the townhouse, Irene was suspicious of him, and as a result she ordered her ten full- and part-time employees, including Mengi, her ever-faithful caretaker, "to keep an eye" on the man she called a "low-class jerk."

Mengi, whose full name was Mengistu Melesse, met Irene in 1992, when he was a delivery boy for a Madison Avenue greengrocer. An Ethiopian native, he left Africa in 1990 to escape political persecution and was staying with relatives in Jersey City, New Jersey, living on hot dogs, when Irene ordered vegetables from the store where he worked. When he made the delivery, Irene tipped him $20. Three days later, Mengi, remembering that $20 tip, returned with another delivery, along with a box overflowing with cherries, eliciting another generous tip. A few days later, Irene called Mengi and asked him to come to her home and offered him a job at double his salary. He said to her, "If you'll be like a mother to me, I'll be like a son to you." Soon Mengi moved into the house, taking care of Irene's needs, making sure the plants were properly watered and fed, and Irene introduced him to a lifestyle he could only have dreamed of. She trusted him implicitly, even sending him to the Bank of New York to cash and deposit large sums of money, and, in turn, he kept a watchful eye over his benefactor.

Irene's distrust of Manny Guerin was so intense that she'd even made notes to herself about her new tenant. In her sketchbook, she drew a picture of a man with slicked-back hair and a crooked nose, beside which she wrote, *"Not a good guess of age or weight but estimate age between 38 and 40. Weight 165 to 175. Since he arrived on June 14th, he has a man and a woman with him. They stay in the apartment day and night. The woman is almost a head shorter goes in and out 'glued' to his side—I've only seen her on the monitor— Mengi said she works the computer. Mengi spoke to her but behind a closed door."*

At one point during the party, Irene announced to her guests that she thought Manny had the "smell of jail" on him, that she didn't trust him and was going to have Jeff Feig, who handled her real estate matters, prepare a letter of eviction that she would have him mail on Monday morning. Irene went even further, saying she'd be very happy to see him go and that she had a gut feeling that he would take off without paying his bills.

A little after 9:30, while the party was still in full gear, the electric eye of one of the two monitors at the front door of the house made a ding-dong noise. "Oh," said Irene, moving toward the screen while motioning her guests to join her, "here comes our friend now. Watch how he slinks by and hugs the wall to avoid the camera and then scoots in the door." With several of the guests watching, Irene's oddball tenant did not disappoint, as he tried to evade the camera's eye, much to Irene's delight.

About 12:30 A.M., when it was finally time to call it a night, Irene, as was her habit, presented all her guests with a small gift. Carol, who Irene noted wasn't particularly fond of jewelry, received several military medals.

"Irene was my Auntie Mame"

At 11:30 A.M., as promised, Irene placed a return call to her friend Helen Pandelakis. After Irene inquired about her health, Helen suggested they take a trip to Greece. Irene, who had taken her last trip to Europe in 1986, a year after her mother died, explained to her friend that her traveling days were long over and, though grateful for the thought, she declined the invitation. The conversation ended after a few minutes with both women promising to stay in touch.

Another phone call Irene wanted to make was to Carol Hansen. Carol wasn't home, so Irene left a message on her answering machine, telling Carol that she'd had a great time at the party and thanking her not only for taking Elva home, but also for her gift of the statue of Saint Marta which, according to legend, would act as a protector of the house. "We are expecting miracles," Irene added, referring to a prayer the partygoers had made the night before, when they called upon God to see to it that her troublesome tenant vacated her house and her life.

Marta Rivera, whom Irene called Aracelis, had worked as a weekend companion for Irene for eleven years and was the only employee working that Sunday of the holiday weekend. At 11:45 A.M., just minutes after completing her calls to Helen and Carol, Irene, who was in her office on the first floor of the building, asked Aracelis to wash a few nightgowns and take Georgie, her champion boxer, for a walk on the roof.

During the next three hours, Aracelis completed several chores, including doing the laundry in the basement, walking the dog, and feeding the cats. She also made several personal calls and checked her voice mail at home before heading to the kitchen area in the basement, where she boiled hot dogs for lunch and, with the pounding rhythmic beat of merengue music blaring from the radio, cleaned the parakeet's cage.

At 2:21 P.M., Carol, who had returned home from church, got

Irene's message and returned her call. She expected Irene to pick up the phone, but instead, it was Aracelis who answered. Carol assumed Irene was napping and the two women chatted amiably for several minutes before Aracelis returned to her chores.

At 4:40 P.M., the phone rang again and Aracelis answered. It was a strange voice—Aracelis couldn't tell if it was a man or a woman disguising her voice to sound like a man—and it upset Aracelis enough that she called Carol and told her about it. Carol was concerned. "Go and wake Irene up and I'll stay on the line," she said. "And take Georgie with you."

Several moments later, Aracelis returned and told Carol that she was unable to rouse Irene.

"Go back and bang on Irene's door and yell as loud as you can." Carol said.

Aracelis followed Carol's advice, but still there was no response from Irene.

✖

It was close to 5 P.M. when Jeff Feig returned to his apartment from a lazy afternoon of meandering around the city. It had been a beautiful summer day, a fitting end to what had been a perfect July Fourth weekend. The humidity was low, there was a gentle breeze wafting through the concrete canyons of the city, and it was a pleasant 79 degrees. Jeff had spent the early afternoon downtown strolling around Union Square for a brief time before stopping at Moe Ginsberg's department store on 21st Street and Fifth Avenue, where they were having a July Fourth weekend sale. He stayed there an hour or so, then got something to eat before heading uptown on the subway, ending up at Crate & Barrel on 59th and Madison Avenue, before making his way back to his Upper East Side home.

When he checked his answering machine, there was only one message waiting for him. It was from Carol Hansen who, in an excited voice, said that Irene Silverman couldn't be located in her house. Immediately, Jeff picked up the phone and tried to call Carol back, but when he had no luck, he called Irene's house to speak with Aracelis. Speaking quickly, in a voice so animated that Feig had a little trouble understanding her, she told him that Irene was nowhere in the house and that she wanted him over at the mansion as soon as possible.

Jeff Feig had known Irene Silverman since 1993, when they met in his capacity as director of support services at Feathered Nest, a residential real estate company in the city where he prepared leases and contracts for his firm's exclusive upscale clientele. The two became good friends and Jeff began working for Irene on a part-time basis on Saturdays for about four to five hours beginning at noon, assisting her with the management of her townhouse, for which she paid him $150 a week. In fact, Feig was close enough to Irene that he spoke to her on a daily basis, and he had seen her the day before when they'd discussed sending the tenant in apartment 1B an eviction notice.

Feig knew Irene was a very wealthy woman. He knew the town-house was worth at least ten million dollars; it was free and clear of any mortgages or liens, and he knew that she always made sure to pay her substantial real estate taxes of $25,000 on time. The contents of her home alone were extremely valuable. Irene also had property in Hawaii worth $880,000, of which she received between $70,000 and $75,000 annually in income, and she had property in New Jersey worth $83,000. She also had nearly one million dollars in municipal bonds, $25,000 in various checking and saving accounts, and $17,500 in cash neatly tucked away in tissue in a lower cabinet in her apartment. And he knew that she was concerned about her new tenant.

Feig and Irene had spoken many times about her new tenant, especially when it became obvious to everyone that more than one person was residing in the apartment. Guerin had also refused to allow the cleaning staff into the apartment five days per week, as specified. In addition, Irene had expressed to Jeff her concerns about the way he would enter and leave, sneaking in and out of the building.

When Feig received the phone message from Carol Hansen, he was immediately suspicious and worried. He knew Irene rarely left the house, and when she did, she was never alone. Even if she were going to the roof to walk Georgie, she let one of her staff know where she was going to be. Whenever she made plans to go out, she made preparations well in advance and was always accompanied by someone she knew. If she went to the Metropolitan Museum, it was with Feig. If she went to the doctor, it was with Aracelis. If she took a walk around the block, she went arm in arm with Mengi.

Feig also knew Irene always carried her own personal keys with her wherever she went. In fact, all her clothes were made with big pockets for her glasses, her tissues, and her keys, and she never gave them to anyone, not even her household staff. They were painted with red nail polish, because this made it easier for her to identify the key she wanted to use.

Worried about her safety, Feig couldn't help but associate Irene's disappearance with the tenant in apartment 1B. And so, instead of heading to the townhouse, he jumped into a cab and went directly to the 19th precinct on East 67th Street between Lexington and Third Avenue, to report the situation to the guardians of New York's "Gold Coast," the wealthiest area of the country.

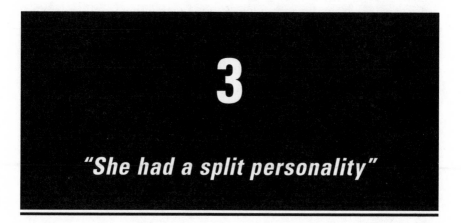

3

"She had a split personality"

Having intimidated Renee Andrews, Sante Kimes immediately shifted tactics and turned on the charm, conning her cellmate into believing she was a widow who had lost three children in a tragic accident in the Bahamas. Sante promised the young black woman that she'd be happy to put her up in a hotel she owned in the Caribbean, if only Renee would help find a bondsman to get Sante out of jail.

For years, Sante had been a compulsive letter-writer. Now, she was desperate to get a message to Kenny, who was being held elsewhere in the bowels of Central Booking, in the men's section. Sante's eyes darted around the barren cell, anxiously looking for writing paper. Finding none, she finally tore off a long piece of toilet paper resting on the concrete floor near the communal open toilet in the cell and dashed off a note to Kenny, scribbling her words of wisdom with a felt-tipped pen.

After scrawling the message, Sante placed the fragile piece of paper in the black plastic purse that she had been allowed to bring with her into the cell after her interrogation by task-force members. Sante figured that because of her lengthy record of arrests and convictions, she might not get released on bail, but Kenny stood a better chance of release, even with his one arrest in Miami. Her plan was to smuggle the cryptic message to her son when both appeared before a judge at their arraignment.

As usual, Sante was doing her best to control the situation. It had worked for her many, many times before. After all, this wasn't the first time she'd found herself in trouble with the law.

✖

On Tuesday, July 24, 1934, just before midnight, inside a dilapidated Oklahoma City farmhouse at the corner of May and Reno Avenues, 37-year-old Mary Van Horn Singhrs gave birth to her third child, a baby girl. The father, 44-year-old Prame Singhrs, was a farmer who lived with his wife and their two other children—a son, Karam, and daughter, Prema—on the edge of town at 2419 Northwest 2nd Street. A fourth child, another daughter, Retha, was born in 1939.

Prame had migrated from India, where he had had a varied careeer as a laborer, bridge builder, magician, and physician. In his early years in the United States he performed on the Pantages circuit as a magician and was an herb doctor in Waco, Texas. Later, in Oklahoma City, he eked out a meager living working both as a manager of the Dawson Produce Green House, about half a mile from what is now the state capitol complex, and as a sharecropper toiling the parched, dusty land that Woody Guthrie would immortalize in song.

Oklahoma suffered severe hardships during the Great Depression. At its height, some 13 million people were out of work and Prame was one of them. Business was bad, farm prices were low, banks failed, people lost their savings, and regions of the midwest suffered harsh water shortages, causing crops to fail as high winds stripped away acres of fertile topsoil and whipped dry dirt into dust storms so intense they wiped out farmland.

Sante's family managed to live a Calcutta-like existence for the first year of her life, but by 1935, the intense, brutal dust storms drove the Singhrs off the land. Like other down-and-outers, they joined a million other Okies who gathered their possessions and headed west in decrepit trucks to what they hoped would be the promised land—California. Official city records show that by 1935 the Singhrs and other members of his extended family had pulled up stakes in Oklahoma City, but when they reached California they learned it didn't exactly welcome migrant farmers. Those who found work in the fields were truly fortunate. Prame was not so lucky. The Singhrs hung around California until 1937, then went back to Oklahoma City. A year after Retha was born, Prame died, and his widow returned to Los Angeles with the four children.

Sante's early years are bathed in shadows. According to Sante, her mother, Mary, of Dutch stock by way of Illinois, was an alcoholic who turned to prostitution to bring in what little money there was to support the family. "I would have to say I hated my mother," Sante said later. "She was never home, and it seemed like when she was, she was drunk or had a different 'date' with her. She was hard on us kids. She'd hit us when she was drunk. I just remember being starved and hungry all the time, and there was never any money. We didn't even have a refrigerator, just a little hot plate that we used to warm soup and things like that. I blocked a lot of it out from that period of time. I know I should be able to remember more, but I was always so miserable that I have always made a conscious effort to forget those times."

Sante's daily escape from the family's dirty, dingy rooms was to wander the streets in a rundown section of Los Angeles. Wearing worn clothing and never knowing where her next meal was coming from, Sante took to panhandling. A vagabond waif, she made a heartrending appeal to passersby, crying out for small change to buy food. Later, her mother also instructed her on how to steal.

When she was ten years old, a shopkeeper caught her stealing cheese and called the police. By then, Sante had already learned how to manipulate men, and she expertly spun a heart-wrenching story about her sad life. According to Sante, the police officer was so touched by her story and by the conditions in which she lived that he wound up befriending her. He took her to parks and movies and, according to Sante, he began doing something else: molesting her on numerous occasions over the next three or four months. "All I can remember is that he was a very nice man who was very kind to me, except for wanting to fondle me. I knew it was wrong and it bothered me quite a bit, and I went to some friends to get help."

Looking, no doubt, to gain sympathy and be viewed as a pitiful victim, she confided her predicament to Dorothy and Kelly Seligman, a middle-aged couple who ran a small coffee shop where Sante spent much of her time. For more than a year, the Seligmans took Sante under their wing and often fed her, making sure she had breakfast. Sante also claimed that the Seligmans confronted the police officer and threatened to inform his superiors; she said she never saw him again.

Several months later, the Seligmans asked Sante's mother for permission to send Sante to Mrs. Seligman's sister, who lived in Carson City, Nevada, a historic frontier town surrounded by the rugged beauty of the High Sierra Mountains near Lake Tahoe. Mary Van Horn readily agreed, and within days, a freshly scrubbed Sante in pigtails boarded a bus for the 445-mile trip from Los Angeles to her new home with Edwin and Mary Chambers.

Mary Chambers was a former scriptwriter for Paramount Studios and Edwin was a colonel in the U.S. Army, attached to the Nevada National Guard. Like Sante, he was an Oklahoman, born in Shawnee. The Chambers, who were in their 40s, had already adopted another child, Howard, who was four years younger than Sante. When Sante turned 11, the couple also formally adopted her. "It was the most important thing that ever happened to me. I went from nothing to everything. I had my own room and new clothes and very nice parents," Sante recalled later.

Sante described the pipe-smoking Mr. Chambers as very charismatic. "He was the handsomest man I ever met. He was almost like an Englishman, tall, very immaculate in his dress, and proper in his manner. He was like Walter Pidgeon, only better looking."

In her new home, Sante began living a Lolita-like existence. Later, she claimed that her adoptive father raped and molested her. At first, she maintained that he limited his actions to fondling, but as time went by, he had regular sexual intercourse with her. "I knew it was wrong. I didn't like it, but I was starved for affection," she explained.

As with any story Sante tells about her past, there is much room for disbelief. For instance, years later, in recalling her time spent with the Chambers family, she admitted she "actually loved having sex" with her adoptive father. "I matured at an early age and looked years older than I was when I was 12 or 13. I was aware that older guys looked at me and, looking back on it, I can see where my father took advantage of things. I never told anyone for years, probably because I was starved for attention and, it's hard to explain, but I really liked him." It should be noted that when Sante made the accusations, Chambers had been dead six years, having died of a stroke in 1980 at the age of 81. His wife Mary had died in 1969.

"I know it sounds like a terrible thing to say, but I've had mixed feelings about this all my life. I'm mixed up to this day on my feelings about this because I really loved my father. He was incredibly handsome and so perfect in many ways. I told my adoptive mother after four or five years, and the news turned the family into a bad situation. She never forgave her husband or me, and they often quarreled after that. I ran away several times because she got very strict with me and totally changed the way she acted toward me.

"I can understand how she must have felt. If my father tried to stick up for me, she attacked him for protecting me. Right after I graduated from high school, she told me she wanted me out of the house and called me a tramp. I feel terrible for what I did to her. She treated me with love and I hurt her."

The alleged repeated sexual abuse by her adoptive father was a source of shame and confusion for her, Sante said, and while her adoptive mother knew about the incidents, the abuse was never reported to the police or other authorities. Sante claimed that Mary Chambers preferred to ignore what was going on in her home. What may have triggered her adoptive mother's indignation about Sante's behavior, however, was Sante's arrest when she was 16 years old for shoplifting lipsticks at the five-and-ten store, a charge that was later dismissed.

Edwin Chambers retired from the military as a brigadier general and he and Mary moved to Rancho Cordova, a suburban village on the outskirts of Sacramento. On September 29, 1971, in the only interview he is known to have given about Sante, Chambers disclosed that he was quite bitter about his adopted daughter, whom he had not seen for several years. "We had a parting of the ways situation before she moved to Southern California," is the way Chambers expressed his relationship with Sante.

Sante claims she left home soon after graduating from Carson City High School on June 6, 1952, where, according to the school registrar, she attended under the name of Sondra Louise Chambers. While at Carson High, Sante or Sondra Louise maintained a B average, although she did manage to get a few As, was a cheerleader and a member of the 4-H Club, as well as singing in her school chorus. She was also named a representative of the Nevada Girls' State convention and participated in the Girl Scouts. She attended church regularly and was a Sunday school teacher. She graduated 12th in her class of 42, and her school records indicate that she was in good scholastic standing, had a fairly good attendance record, and had developed good leadership skills.

Her best and closest friend at Carson High was Ruth Thom Tanis, who once described Sante as "an exciting person, a person that's informed and knowledgeable and caring." Like Sante, Ruth also left home when she graduated, and the two were roommates for a while when they attended business school in Reno. They also took a secretarial course that taught Sante the clerical skills she used when she later found work in Sacramento as a secretary.

When Tanis married in 1957, she and Sante went their separate ways, but they stayed in contact. Unbeknownst to Tanis, Sante used her name on forged deeds and off-shore banking accounts over the years. When asked if she had ever had any business dealings with Sante or allowed her to use her name, Tanis said emphatically, "No. No way. Not in any fashion." She said she'd heard that an R. Tanis was the president of some business involving Sante, but that she'd never given Sante permission to use her name. "I never had any business dealings with Sante Kimes." Tanis died of cancer in late 1998.

Sante claimed that, with her father's financial assistance, she entered the University of California at Santa Barbara in 1962 and studied journalism for two years. But the university can provide no record of her attending the school. She told others she was a student there for four years in the mid-1950s, but the registrar's office does not have any record of that either, not under any of her many known aliases.

Over the years, in all her interviews with authorities and officials in the prison system, the one person Sante had never mentioned is Lee Powers, a former Carson High classmate whom she conned into marriage in 1956 by claiming she was pregnant. Less than a year later, she divorced the Santa Ynes, California, high school teacher and renewed her relationship with Edward Walker, another classmate she'd known since sixth grade. Walker, an architect who now makes his home in Carson City, thought of Sante as "an intelligent girl who did very well in school. She was attractive and was a cheerleader. She dressed very well. She was always very neat in appearance. The Chambers provided for her very well. During the time she was in school, she didn't have many friends. It seemed like she was afraid to trust people and was afraid to let people get close to her. I think that extended even to her stepparents. They were warm people, but although she liked them, they didn't have the closest relationship. She never talked about her early life."

Walker and Sante went together during their senior year and continued dating through college. "We were very serious about the relationship, but then she went to a California school and I went off to college," Walker remembers. One day, he received a call from his former girlfriend. "Sante was like a wild woman on the phone, chewing me out for not going to a California school after graduation. Wow, does she have a real hot temper. After that, she just disappeared, and in 1956, I found out she had married Lee Powers. About a year later, I got a letter from her saying she was sorry she had gone off and gotten married and that it was a mistake. Two months later, she showed up on my doorstep, and in November 1957, we were married and moved to Sacramento."

Sante didn't work for a while after marrying Walker but then, in an effort to make the marriage successful, she got various sales jobs at which, according to Walker, she excelled.

As time passed, Walker began to notice Sante's behavior becoming unpredictable, somewhat erratic. "It was like she had a split personality. She was attractive and intelligent, but sometimes she was just totally out of control and couldn't help herself. I'm convinced she did things without much deliberation. I guess you could say it was situational. It's almost like she doesn't know who she wants to be. In high school, her name was Sandy. Then, after she got out of high school, she changed it to Santée with an accent. Now she spells her name S-A-N-T-E. Like I say, it's almost as if she has several personalities. She is just a very driven person."

Walker said his wife had "an absolute paranoia of being poor. She has always been absolutely obsessive about it. This led to problems between us, because she felt that I wasn't bringing in the money fast enough, and she was always pushing me to get up the ladder faster."

Sante's profiligate behavior began to show itself about three years after she and Walker were married. During the 1960 Christmas holiday season, Walker recalled, "She went out and spent about $13,000 on gifts for everybody. I was shocked. That was the equivalent of a year's wages or more back then, and she blew it just for Christmas gifts. We paid off all the debts, because most of the items she bought had been given away. It took a long time and caused real problems."

On December 18, 1960, a mysterious (and suspicious) fire broke out in the kitchen of their home at 4931 Hemlock in Sacramento, partially destroying their furnishings and causing structural damage to the property. A second suspicious fire at another home they owned "just blew up," Walker recalled.

Sante's bizarre behavior escalated further two months after the earlier fire. "It was Sunday, February 12, 1961. After dinner that day, we went to the shopping mall in Sacramento and she disappeared in the store. When I couldn't find her, I went to the manager to find out that Sante was arrested for shoplifting a hairdryer." Sante was 26 years old when she was arrested under the name of Sandra Louise Walker. Charged with petty larceny, this officially marked the first time she was taken into custody as an adult. Walker bailed her out, and three days she later pled guilty and was fined $131.25.

"I just couldn't believe it," Walker recalled incredulously. "We had plenty of money to buy a hairdryer or almost anything else, but for some reason, she just took it."

When he asked Sante why she did it, she explained innocently, albeit nonsensically, "I wanted to save money."

Walker began to see other disturbing sides to his wife's character. "She had a very obsessive personality . . . and was very preoccupied with cleanliness. The house had to be a showplace every day, and she was always dressed like she was getting ready to pose for modeling pictures. She didn't even like me to lounge around in Levis or informal clothes. She wanted me to be completely neat at all times. You couldn't relax around her, we had no home life," he said.

As time went on, Sante's criminal compulsions got worse. Walker's troubles with Sante began to intensify in late 1961, when he started to build three residential homes about 20 miles northeast of Sacramento near Roseville for millionaire land developer Everett Earl Wagner. Sante ingratiated herself to Wagner and went to work handling the books for the project, but when contractors on the job began complaining to Walker that bills weren't getting paid, he went to the bank, where he learned that there was not sufficient money in the account. When Walker confronted his wife about Wagner's failure to see that funds were available, the two quarreled and she convincingly defended the developer's oversight.

Walker ultimately sued Wagner in civil court in January 1963, and ten months later he was awarded $8,774.96 for his architectural and contractual work on the project. But he was obviously kept in the dark as to what was really going on between his wife and Wagner. It wasn't until February 1963 that Walker came to believe that she had been carrying on a hot love affair with the land developer at Walker's Winding Creek Way office in Fair Oaks, inside the very homes he was building for the last two years.* Given Sante's craving for money, it's more than likely that she socked away the project money for the contractors.

When Wagner's wife, June, filed divorce papers that February, she branded Sante a home-wrecker and accused her husband of "committing adultery with one Santée Walker."

---

*Wagner denied in court that the affair had ever happened.

41

With the two families at war with each other, matters got worse when Sante and her husband sued the land developer for $110,000, alleging he "assaulted, beat and bruised" them during an altercation on March 18 at 11:30 P.M. in Sacramento County. The outcome of the litigation was not reflected in any of the court papers, but when the Walkers moved from their 8455 Winding Way home in Fair Oaks to Southern California, neighbors said they "left plenty of gossip in the area."

Whether it was the scandal of the Wagner's divorce that made page one headlines in the *Sacramento Bee* highlighting Sante's role as a femme fatale, or merely the Peyton Place atmosphere of the small community, another bit of fodder was Sante's pregnancy. Kent Walker was born on September 27, 1963. When Ed Walker got to her hospital room, he found Sante in the arms of Everett Earl Wagner.

"After she went home from the hospital, Sante started to stay out late more and more," Walker recalled. "One night I went looking for her and went into a nearby club and found her kissing Wagner again. We got into a fight and she told me that Wagner was the baby's real father." Later, Sante denied her statement and told Walker he was the real father and that she was only having an affair with Wagner.

However, in statements made later to her federal probation officer and a court-appointed psychiatrist, Sante again claimed that Kent was not the offspring of Walker but was the son of a deceased businessman 20 years her senior from Southern California with whom she had "a long-term affair." The story she told was that she saw the man for years and while he never took responsibility for their child, he helped her financially. After the Walkers moved to Los Angeles, Sante said she continued meeting with her lover.

Sante described her relationship with Walker in court papers "as more like that of brother and sister than that of husband and wife," saying "that they almost never had sex and that they both pursued their individual careers with little focus on maintaining a conventional marriage."

Today, Walker agrees with his ex-wife's assessment of their 12-year marriage, saying that while Sante was always a good mother and a good provider when she worked, there was another aspect of their marriage that was unusual. "It was almost like a business partnership rather than a marriage. She always wanted to talk about business and it was like, when we got together, we had these meetings rather than a normal family-type of relationship," he said.

Although her assignations with her paramour were a rude awakening for Walker, he didn't throw her out of the house, and despite any misgivings he may have harbored, they continued living together.

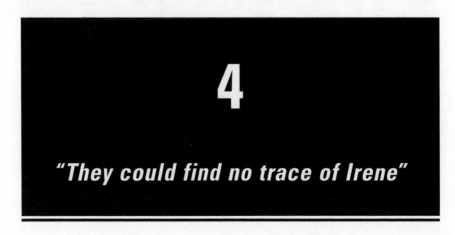

4

"They could find no trace of Irene"

JULY 5, 1998

After Jeff Feig reported Irene's disappearance, the police suggested he return to the mansion, telling him he had to personally search the building before they could conduct a large-scale manhunt.

When Feig arrived at Irene's house, Aracelis was waiting for him inside the lobby area. None of the other renters were around. Peter Jacobson, a producer at CBS-TV, had been at the gym until 1:00 P.M., then home until 3:30 or 4:00 P.M., after which he spent time in Central Park until 8:00 P.M. John Kirtley, who owned an investment firm, was in Germany that weekend. Dr. Ronald Castellino, a radiologist at Sloan-Kettering, was away for the holiday weekend. All three of these men rented one-bedroom apartments on the upper floors of the building.

Feig and Aracelis began their frantic search of the building. They started with the ground floor, or basement level, then the kitchen. They searched the basement's first-floor apartment 1A; the second floor, where there was a one-bedroom apartment and huge living room; the third floor, where there were several one-bedroom apartments; the fourth- and fifth-floor duplex, which served as Irene's apartment; and the sixth-floor roof garden.

Feig and Aracelis searched 1A. She wasn't there. However, in the bedroom, Feig noticed that the closet was unlocked and the door was open. When he ventured inside, he found that the closet was in disarray. He knew this was totally out of character for Irene, who was a meticulous organizer. He also knew that Irene kept her money in the closet, and there was usually a substantial amount of it, fanned out like a deck of cards standing up against the closet wall. But there was no money there.

Next, Jeff and Aracelis went up to the roof and worked their way back down to the basement, looking in every single apartment except 1B, which Manny Guerin occupied.

When their search was over and they could find no trace of Irene, Feig returned to the 19th precinct and was informed that a squad car had been dispatched to the house. At 6:00 P.M., when the patrol officers on the scene notified the desk sergeant that they could not locate Mrs. Silverman, the 19th detective squad was called into the case.

On duty that Sunday for the 4:45 P.M. to 1:00 A.M. shift were three of the four Tommy's assigned to the squad: Tommy Hovagim, Tommy Ryan, and Tommy DiDomenico. For that holiday shift, Ryan and DiDomenico were to handle burglaries and Hovagim was to deal with any robbery that would occur during the shift.

Figuring that the city had pretty much emptied out for the holiday, Tommy Hovagim, 35, a 14-year police-force veteran though a rookie detective, was expecting a quiet evening at the precinct. When he arrived at the station house, he and the others on duty decided to order an Italian dinner from Arturo's, and it was Hovagim who went to the restaurant to pick it up. As the detectives were about to sit down to eat, Tommy Ryan took a call from the desk sergeant reporting an elderly woman missing. Ryan and

DiDomenico went over to the mansion while Hovagim kept the food warm, figuring the call would turn out unfounded and the other two Tommys would be back in the squad room shortly to resume the meal. Three days later, the food that had been kept in the refrigerator was thrown out. "After that," DiDomenico said later, "we figured it was a jinx and since then we have never ordered food in again on a holiday weekend."

Once at the townhouse, Ryan immediately put in a call to the Emergency Service, because they were equipped with special tools that were going to be needed to conduct a thorough, detailed search of the building, including opening vents and climbing shafts. The detectives then proceeded to search the house. On the desk in Irene's office in 1A, they found the pencil sketch of Manny Guerin as well as the brief description she had made of him.

Meanwhile, back at the squad room, Hovagim manned the phones and spoke with Aracelis. From this brief conversation, Hovagim learned that Irene employed a staff of ten full- and part-time workers. Aracelis described Irene as being just five feet tall, with red hair, wearing red-colored framed glasses, and as being extremely agile for her age. She also gave Hovagim a description of the elusive and suspicious missing tenant known to the staff as Manny Guerin. When Hovagim was finished taking Aracelis' statement, he, too, headed over to the Silverman mansion.

At 6:30, just as Hovagim was pulling up to the mansion in a squad car, Carol Hansen arrived at the house. By this time, Ramon Casales, the building superintendent, who had worked for Irene over 20 years, was also on the scene. Both Carol and Ramon felt that Irene might be in apartment 1B and suggested to the detectives that they search the room, but the police were hesitant about entering what was essentially an occupied apartment without a search warrant. As superintendent of the building, Ramon told the detectives that he "knew where every little screw in the building is" and said he would take responsibility for opening the apartment door. After all, it was an emergency, he argued. Hovagim and Ryan followed Ramon and Carol into the tenant's apartment. They went in through the hallway, down some steps to the foyer. They checked in the bedroom and saw that the bed was made and Carol noticed what she thought looked like a slight indentation, as if someone had lain there. She pointed this out to the police and they told her not to touch anything.

Across from the bed on top of a cabinet near a television set, Carol observed a sealed rolled of duct tape. In the kitchen area, in a dark-colored garbage pail, she saw one of the most significant pieces of tell-tale evidence: "Balls of duct tape which alarmed me," Carol said later. Missing from the apartment was a beige comforter that belonged in apartment 1B. Other than finding a letter opener that looked like a knife, a jacket and shirt in the closet, and a plate of cooked bacon, there were no signs of Manny Guerin or his assistant, Eva.

5

"She had the largest breasts and most active tush"

By mid-1965, Sante and Ed Walker were living in Burbank, where she had started her own business. Calling it the Sante Building Advisory, Inc., it was the first time she would ever use her given name in any business venture.

On the surface, it seemed as if Sante had everything she could want, compliments of an indulgent husband who provided her with an opulent lifestyle—but everything wasn't good enough for Sante. Despite the fact that Walker seemed to give in to every one of her whims, including the construction of a showcase house for her business in the Laurel Canyon area of Los Angeles, just outside of Studio City, she was far from the ideal wife.

"She made my life hellish," Walker recalled. "It was a living nightmare. I came home one night to find no Sante in the house, just the baby-sitter. Finally, she called to say she had been arrested for ten credit-card frauds. That wasn't all. My checking account was overdrawn three times, and when I went to the bank, I learned she had been forging my name to checks."

What unfolded next must have seemed like a living nightmare to Walker. He returned home from work one day and found the Los Angeles Police Department in his house. They had raided the place. "I was flabbergasted. I came to find out she had been charging items to other people's accounts and had bought coats, shoes, and various kinds of clothes, and to top it all off, she stole an automobile in Beverly Hills." In the span of just five days, from December 29, 1965 to January 3, 1966, Sante managed to rack up three additional arrests.

On May 2, 1966, Sante was convicted again, but amazingly she got off with a three-year probation and a paltry $200 fine that Walker obediently paid.

A few months later, while still carrying on her illicit affair with Wagner, Sante, who couldn't seem to leave well enough alone, strayed again, as the hapless Walker caught her with yet another man. Finally, Walker threw in the towel and moved into an apartment in Palm Springs, two hours southeast of Los Angeles. Kent was left to live with his mother.

As a result of what she probably considered an unwarranted abandonment, Sante became increasingly irrational. Time and again, she made the two-hour, 114-mile trip back and forth between Studio City and Palm Springs, evidently trying to draw Walker back into her web. One night, while Walker was relaxing in his living room watching television, he heard the sound of glass breaking in his bedroom. Startled, he rushed into the room to find that Sante had broken the window with a rock or brick and there she was, climbing into his apartment through the window as if it was the usual way to enter. Walker was at the end of his rope and was running out of patience. "We had a major league fight," he recalled.

The couple finally separated for good on May 1, 1967, and Walker returned to live in Carson City. One day, in late November, Sante called him and, with a sense of urgency in her voice, told him that Kent had been bitten by a rattlesnake and was very sick. "I panicked and took the next flight to Los Angeles, and when I stepped off the plane, I was served with the divorce papers," Walker recalled. The grounds, in what must have seemed to be a sick, ironic joke, was extreme mental cruelty.

But Sante wasn't finished. Along with the divorce papers, she served him with another demand: she wanted him to pay her $1,400 a month. When Walker balked, she handed him his copy of the agreement, already signed, and smugly walked away triumphantly. Walker was surprised, since he had no recollection of signing any such paper. The truth was, he hadn't. Using a skill she'd picked up along the way, Sante had simply forged his name on the document. This was a talent she would put to good use over the years. When it came to forgery, Sante was a master. Her modus operandi was to obtain the letterhead of an organization, place a blank piece of white paper over the typewritten body of the letter, being careful not to obliterate the signature of the sender and then take it to a copy machine store to be duplicated. She would then proceed to run off as many copies of the letterhead as she needed for whatever criminal purpose she was involved in at that particular moment.

Sante was eventually granted an interlocutory decree on January 9, 1968. At the hearing, the court minutes disclose that she and another man with whom she had a "close relationship" were both sworn in and testified against Walker. Sante was granted $300 a month in child support and $700 a month in alimony; a 40 percent interest in Skyways Enterprises, which also included the Fountain Hotel in Palm Springs that they jointly owned; and a 50 percent interest in her Hi Welcome to California, Inc., venture, which was only a paper corporation organized to build the Walkers' Studio City home on Laurel Canyon Boulevard in 1963.

A final divorce decree was awarded on December 8, 1969, but not before there were more charges and countercharges lobbed back and forth between the errant couple. Sante claimed Walker was in contempt, because he was $14,000 in arrears to her and $6,000 for Kent's support, that he drove a new Lincoln Continental, dined at the finest restaurants in Palm Springs, wore very expensive clothes, and lived with other women in both Nevada and California.

In turn, Walker accused her of dishonesty—as if that were something new—claiming that while he was in Nevada, Clyde Wainwright, yet another well-heeled man with whom Sante had hooked up after they split, contacted Walker in August 1968 and informed him that Sante was very ill and that his presence was badly needed in California. When Walker arrived in Palm Springs, he found that he had once more been duped; this time he was served with the support contempt summons.

In his court filing, Walker further contended that his income was only $5,000 a year and that he "could not make the outrageous support payments." He alleged that although he and Sante were technically separated, they lived in the same house that, incredibly, Wainwright also shared. Wainwright not only paid the household bills but also had allegedly hired Walker to do work for him.

Finally, in a stipulation signed by both parties, Walker agreed to make support payment of $1 a month to Sante and that child support payments would be based on a percentage of his monthly earnings.

Even after the divorce, Walker still couldn't disentangle himself from Sante's web. When Sante saw that she couldn't squeeze another penny out of her ex-husband, she embarked upon a bitter custody fight over Kent that was, according to Walker, "a living nightmare." She also reverted to old habits and forged his name to several divorce papers that granted her various visitation and custody privileges. In addition, Walker, who must have dreaded the appearance of the postman each morning, continued to get bills in the mail that Sante had run up in his name for vacations, clothes, and long-distance phone calls.

In the meantime, Walker was not her only target. She forged the name of Robert Prescott to a conditional guarantee of a sum of $47,000 on the construction of a Palm Springs home, which she claimed was the residence of Dorothy Seligman, the sister of Sante's adopted mother, Mary. Prescott, who had supplied the money for the construction of the home, sued the Walkers in civil court. The Riverside County district attorney declined to prosecute the Prescott matter criminally.

Once Sante was free of Walker, she took up with her new boyfriend Wainwright, who made a convenient partner for other swindles, including allegations they misused funds and removed valuable fixtures and furnishings from a hotel in which they once had a partial interest.

As if Sante needed any more help in furthering her criminal skills, she apparently learned the fine art of real estate scams, impersonations, and opening bank accounts with stolen identities from Wainwright who, like Sante, had a host of aliases. At six-foot-one and weighing 190 pounds, Wainwright was Sante's ideal man: tall, dark, handsome, and perhaps most importantly, a very smooth operator. He had brown hair, hazel eyes, and was born in Arkansas on October 25, 1909, making him a quarter of a century older than Sante. He spoke with a delicious soft southern drawl that simply swept her off her feet. Of course, the fact that he had some money and was a much older, sophisticated man didn't hurt his chances with her.

It wasn't long before the two became lovers and began an on-and-off relationship that was to last into the early 1970s. Not to say that it was monogamous, at least on Sante's part. At the same time she was having a relationship with the elderly Wainwright, she was also having love affairs with two other men.

Soon after they began living together in July 1968, Wainwright, who evidently lacked some of the subtlety of his cohort, who used a pen to rip people off, rented a U-Haul truck and pulled a burglary in the Los Angeles area.

During this same period of time, he and Sante bought a home in Palm Springs. They opened a joint bank account at the City National Bank, Commonwealth Branch, in Los Angeles and began to pass several rubber checks in the Palm Springs area. The scheme was simple. Sante would stroll into a store with Kent in tow, tell the shopkeeper she was Wainwright's housekeeper, pick out what she needed, and then Wainwright would come in and pay for the merchandise with a rubber check.

Even though Sante was with Wainwright, she was still in Walker's life, in part because they shared a son. During the 1969 Christmas holidays, Sante showed up on the arm of Wainwright to pick up Kent, who was visiting with his father, and Walker graciously offered to take them all out to dinner. Sante, Wainwright, and Kent piled into one car and Walker followed in his automobile. At one point, Sante pulled her car off to the side of the road. Thinking there might be a problem with her car, Walker pulled in behind them.

"Sante got out and pulled a gun on me and started yelling and screaming and ranting and raving. She fired three times at fairly close range before I realized she was firing blanks," Walker said. "At that point, Wainwright got out of the car, took out a shotgun from the trunk, and he began firing at me."

After Walker successfully grabbed both weapons from them and tossed them away, Sante and Wainwright jumped into their car and drove off with Kent into the desert sunset. Walker, in trying to come up with some semi-rational reason for this bizarre episode, now believes that Sante was in big trouble with somebody, thought that he had been talking to someone about her, and she was trying to scare him.

✖

It was late 1969, and Sante was in the process of dumping Clyde Wainwright. Her divorce from husband number two, Ed Walker, was final and she was on the prowl for a new trophy to pay her bills.

Sante had been manipulating men since her early teens and knew how to set a trap for a millionaire. She was a master strategist and knew just what to do when she eyed a feature story in *Millionaire Magazine* about a single, self-made affluent man and his lifestyle—Kenneth Kimes, Sr.,. Once she took a look at the magazine's photograph of the six-foot-two, fair-skinned Kimes, with his mink-brown curly hair and gray-blue eyes, she knew who her next target would be.

Kimes owned a string of motels along the California coast, including the Mecca Motel, across from Disneyland in Anaheim. According to the article, he was worth in the neighborhood of $12 million to $15 million.

After seeing his picture and reading the article, Sante moved quickly. Following leads from the article, she strolled into a local liquor store in the prestigious Rancho Mirage area near Palm Springs, the so-called Playground of Presidents, one of the wealthiest communities in the country. Her visit was not accidental: she had learned that the owner of the store knew the Kimes family. Engaging the owner of the store in conversation, she somehow managed to get the woman to set up a meeting with Kimes's younger sister, Hanna, and Ken himself, who at the time was building an addition to his 150-room hotel in Palm Springs. Once the meeting was set up, Sante took over, incorporating herself into his life by creating a comfort zone for Kimes.

In recalling the day that Sante invaded his life, a friend explained that Ken Kimes was "not exceedingly social and he was only comfortable within his family. But if his sister was present, he was at ease." Sante knew that the best way to set up her victims was to have them in situations where they felt protected.

The fact that Sante had competition from other women didn't seem to deter her. It seemed that Kimes liked keeping several women on a string, if for no other reason than to assure his freedom. "He had managed to escape their clutches, so he felt confident that no one was going to get to him," recalled a cousin. "One thing for sure, Ken was very protective about his business matters."

By the time Sante was snugly secured into the picture, Kimes's daughter, Linda, was 22 and working in her father's office. She was not a fan of Sante's. One of the bookkeepers once overheard her ask her father, "Who is this woman with all this synthetic, long, straggly, black, fake hair that is shedding all over you?" He responded that she was "a gorgeous pin-up girl from a dating service, who worked as a model."

"Model for what?" Linda asked.

"Well, I don't quite know. They're shooting a calendar thing or something," he replied awkwardly.

Linda wasn't buying any of it. "Oh, Dad, please give me a break. No, this isn't a model. It's, you know . . . don't you mean, she's what some would call 'white trash.'"

"Don't worry," he added, "nobody can get at me. I'm in control."

But Sante, who had her eye on Kimes's millions, aimed to change that.

Sexual fantasies were not Kimes's only weakness. He had another. He was a self-made man who had started as a poor Oklahoma dirt-farmer, and he had something of a Pygmalion complex. He believed that he could help all the poor, depraved people around him. Most of his former girlfriends had been women with problems. Sante fit the description: she was a single woman with a young son to raise. "He thought he could change things," a cousin said about Kimes's relationship with Sante, "but you can't take a person like that and put her in a fine environment and really change her. All you do is feed her frenzy for more control and more opportunities to flaunt her newfound wealth and position."

Sante was sharp when it came to learning how to refine and remake herself. She had to have the biggest diamonds, the most luxurious fur coat, the biggest hair, and as a Kimes family member said, "she had the largest breasts and the most active tush." To succeed in her scheme, she read books and magazines on how to order the finest food and the best champagne. When she found out that Sophia Loren drank Veuve Clicquot, she became a connoisseur of fine champagne. If she read about some movie star dining at a to-be-seen place, such as the Brown Derby, still one of the "in" spots back in the 1970s, she'd make sure to learn what they ordered and, before too long, she would make reservations there for her and Kimes and order the same.

As time passed, those closest to Kimes began to observe that he was beginning to slowly lose control. Sante was constantly pumping everyone she could for information about him. Whether it was his favorite color, fragrance, flower, food, it didn't matter, just so it added to the dossier she was building. The goal was to know every button to push, because Sante wanted to give Kimes a steady diet of every pleasure point in life. Even sex wasn't enough. Make everything smell like gardenias because he liked the scent; always wear white because it looks so elegant and made her look royal. Feed him steak and potatoes, and go to places like Chasen's or Scandia and demand that his food be prepared medium rare.

"She wanted to completely inundate him with all the pleasures she could. She was very smart. She was the epitome of that book written by Helen Andelin in the 1970s, *Fascinating Womanhood*, that offers practical advice on how to awaken a man's deepest feelings of love," Hanna Kimes said.

"She read 'em all and wrote a few lines in between," a Kimes cousin said of Sante. "She just made him her number one project. She's a professional and her profession was to manipulate, to scam, and she did the ultimate job on Ken. Once she succeeded, she was empowered because she had money, she had presence, importance. All she had to do is keep him on a pedestal and she could stand on it next to him. She was very smart. She quit trying to put herself on a pedestal and just put him on one at all times in an adoring sort of way with that sugary sentimental language of hers, acting like he was the most brilliant genius she had ever met."

In fact, Kimes wasn't much of a business genius. He was a real-estate investor who had several companies that were in the business of development, building, and property management. In his career, he had built custom homes, apartments, and a string of motels and strip shopping centers. He was best known for building motels, most of which were sold during the building stage, and he managed a few for a period of time until they were sold. He also purchased land for his own portfolio, later developing some of the properties that he held for a time and then sold. In a few cases, he bought a parcel of land that was already developed and operated the existing business with an eye to redevelopment in the future. In short, what he had was simply good business smarts, a lot of luck, and great instincts on opportunities for land development.

Kimes had a tendency to ignore important things that might seem obvious to others around him. "Apparently he was completely naïve about the kinds of ploys Sante was using, particularly sexual fantasy," according to a former business associate. "It was his Achilles heel. Sante knows—that is her masterpiece. She did it right."

While in hot pursuit of her wealthy paramour, the 37-year-old Sante, who seemingly could not shake her penchant for playing fast and loose with the law, managed to get herself arrested by the Santa Ana police for forging credit cards and stealing another automobile. She was indicted on six counts of credit-card forgery and one count of grand theft auto. However, by the next year, the cases against her were miraculously dismissed "in the interest of justice," and once again Sante seemed to be Teflon-coated as far as the law was concerned.

Although Kimes was intrigued by this woman with the dark hair who pursued him over a two-year period, he was also suspicious enough to hire three private detective agencies to shadow her. Their job was to provide him with detailed daily reports of her activities and whom she spent time with. Not to be outdone, Sante, using the name Lorrie Jacobs, hired licensed private investigator Gene Finneran in Anaheim, California, in March 1972 to spy on Kimes and report on his comings and goings. But when she failed to pay the detective for his services and expenses, and began to avoid his phone calls and visits to her Newport Beach apartment, Finneran threatened legal action.

"If I do not hear anything concerning my time and effort in this matter, I will be forced to file a complaint for fraud with the D.A. office and subpoena telephone records to prove the origin of calls to my home requesting the work under false pretenses." Finneran wrote her, adding as a postscript, *"I will have to take the matter up with the District Attorney and your husband* [after a thorough, exhaustive search through surveillance and court records, it is doubtful that Sante and Kenneth Kimes, Sr., were ever married] *to see who might request such a check conducted on his activities."*

Despite what Kimes may have learned about Sante's unorthodox lifestyle, he ignored all the warning signs. "Even as a child, when things were happening in our family," said his daughter, Linda, "my dad would be passive and my mother would take the lead. He would avoid things, rather than handling them as the leader of the family."

Indeed, he avoided confrontation with Sante by ignoring it when she began using his last name. Kimes was very well aware of the fact that common-law marriage was not legal in any state they lived in. And in those days it really wasn't socially acceptable to live together and have children out of wedlock, especially for people of his generation and upbringing. More than likely, Kimes allowed her to use his name and Sante began passing herself off as his wife. This much is known: during a psychiatric evaluation in connection with a later crime she was accused of, Sante claimed to have married Kimes in 1971 in Mexico City.*

The relationship between Kimes and Sante throughout the years they were together was stormy, at best, with Kimes refusing at times to have anything to do with her and refusing to speak with her on the telephone. Sante, in turn, would write long syrupy letters, pleading with him, as if she were a teenager, imploring him to at least talk with her:

> *Ken—Please, please stop this and at least talk to me. What did I ever do to you to warrant this? If you have a heart, and I always thought you did, please talk to me. I am so low and blue I just want to die. Can't you replace a little faith and at least talk with me? Even if you never cared a bit about Kent's and my life, can't you at least talk to me and remember the thousands of times I loved and cared for you? Know this, everything that has happened . . . is because I loved you and wanted to be near you. Does it make you happy to know I am calling hundreds of times and crying and waiting at home? Not even you could do that. I have in no way done anything unfaithful to you. Please know that. I have simply sunk lower and lower with money and business problems because you were the most important thing in my life.*

Sante goes on to plead that the only way she can:

---

*Later, however, she told a probation official the marriage took place in Tijuana, Mexico. She has also stated she first married Kimes on April 5, 1974, and that they renewed their vows in Las Vegas on April 5, 1981, at the World-Famous Chapel of the Bells. More recently, she again contradicted herself and lied about her purported marriage to Kimes in a handwritten letter, swearing "under penalty of perjury," she wrote, that she married him on April 5, 1984. The only evidence of a supposed "marriage" for any of the dates is a certificate that has surfaced that a marriage took place between her and Kimes on an April 5, 1981, license. A noted forensic handwriting expert, hired by Linda Kimes, who was appointed the administrator of her father's estate, has examined Kimes's signature on that marriage license and informed the California court that it is a forgery.

go on living or surviving is having you at least call or at least be a friend. Please talk to me before you completely destroy me with sadness and heartbreak. I have been terribly sick at my stomach and can't even touch a drink. I am worried that I might be. . . .*

Melodramatically, Sante doesn't finish the sentence, leaving it to Kimes's imagination to guess what is worrying her.

Friends of Kenneth Kimes who went out with him and Sante often found it to be socially embarrassing, because she inevitably made a scene. An elderly cousin of Kenneth Kimes described Sante as having "a monster mentality. She had to act like she was in charge of everything, be demanding, send things back, had to tell them the cork was bad on the wine. She had to do it to make people kowtow to her. She needed to be attended to. You just couldn't order plain food off the menu without Sante having a fit and making the waiter send it back without Ken tasting it. 'He won't eat it that way! Send it back! It's not right!' The cocktail doesn't have enough ice in it or too much in it. Poor Ken didn't say anything. He just kept sitting there and did exactly what he did when he was a child, but it was so exaggerated."

"Doesn't this embarrass you when she is standing there screaming and having a hissy fit?" the cousin asked Kimes.

"Nothing embarrasses me. I can buy this restaurant and sell it back if I want to," he replied.

One night when Sante was dining with Kimes at a restaurant in Santa Ana, she got onto the subject of communism. A business associate at the table said that there was nothing bad about communism. Sante stood up in the middle of the room and started screaming that the man was a Red, a menace to society. "Ken became confused at her outburst and sided with her," the cousin said.

---

*This treasure trove of letters and Sante's inner thoughts to Kimes and her oldest son, Kent, and others, including a 30-page handwritten *apologia* about her slavery and mink trials, was found inside a piece of luggage abandoned at the curbside of her boarded-up former Las Vegas home at 2121 Geronimo Way in March 2000. The house was partially gutted by an arson fire in January 1998.

As a close family friend observed, Sante was relentless in her quest to become part of Kimes's everyday life. "Sante didn't expect to be admired for anything above the eyebrows, but for something below the bellybutton," is the way it appeared to Kimes watchers. "She knew how to pour on the favors in order to stay involved. What she also did was to keep the family intact, initially, because otherwise he would have felt vulnerable. If she was having a party and if she already had his sister saying, 'Yes, she'd love to come,' then what she would do is drop names of some notable people she had invited—real or imagined—and that would add to the intrigue, and then Kimes would go to the party. He was eager for the sexual fantasies that she was fulfilling for him, but he also wanted the limelight and enjoyed rubbing elbows with the rich and famous."

No matter how many times the couple split up, Kimes always took Sante back, until the next time she got in trouble. He didn't have to wait long. Early in their relationship, in 1972, when she was 38, Palm Springs police picked her up on charges of stealing and charged her with petty and grand larceny. Then in Newport Beach, a couple of years later, she again got into hot water when a police officer saw Sante driving her white LTD Ford sedan and recognized the license plate number as the same number received over the police radio as wanted in connection with the theft of a statue with a feathered headpiece from a local art gallery. The officer pulled her over at a traffic stop and she got out of the car in typical Sante style, as if nothing was wrong, and approached the officer with not a care in the world.

"Officer, I want to make a report of a strange man who assaulted me in front of the bakery in Corona Del Mar. He wouldn't take his hand off my car and I am afraid," Sante said rather righteously.

Obviously used to getting her way with men, Sante was devastated when the officer placed her under arrest and charged her with grand theft. After waiving her rights, she gave the officer permission to look inside the trunk of her car, and there was the stolen statue, as well as a white jacket with rhinestone buttons and sequins that still had a $92 price tag and size intact attached on it.

A short time later, the victim of the art theft crime positively identified Sante. Besides the stolen jacket, police also found about

20 miscellaneous small objects under the right front seat of the car, all with the price tags still on them. None of the items were in bags, and they appeared to police to be brand-new. Police could not find cash receipts for any of these items.

The Newport Beach arresting officer wrote in his report: "The defendant reportedly changed her statement several times, tripping herself up on details, but never failed for words or excuses in an attempt to explain her innocence." This, of course, was vintage Sante, and it was never more obvious than when she was dealing with Kimes.

> *Ken—if the bail is put up, then I can go to Palm Springs myself. I won't have to be afraid or hide anymore. Otherwise, the police will take me there and I'm finished. If you get me out today, I can get my own attorney and win. Please Ken—every minute counts. In here, I'm dead. As soon as I'm out, I have excellent chances of getting completely off with a good attorney. Please save my life. I will make you proud of me forever.*

She scribbled this penciled letter to Kimes on a 6-by-12-inch torn brown grocery bag. Then, taking a line from a key scene in *Gone with the Wind*, she signed off on the letter dramatically, *"As God is my witness . . . I love you, Your Sante."*

For Sante, begging Kimes for bail money was as routine as putting on makeup. The letters, always written in pencil, echoed very much the same tone:

> *Please, oh please, help me . . . if you will just get me out of here. I will be able to get more help and get an attorney and [will] do anything to get money to pay you. I have no chance if the bail is not put up. It makes the difference between life and death. I swear I will work and not expect a penny or anything else. The whole thing is getting out and getting good help. Otherwise I could go to prison. You can have the house. Sell my furs. Just anything. Don't leave me alone. I swear I will be what you want and forever.*

Sante signed this missive, *"Your girl."*

By then, Sante had developed a standard stump speech that she would use for the rest of her life when arrested. It would begin as the booking process got underway at the station house: she'd become hysterical, accuse police of persecuting her, insist she was being framed, and that several police officers had assaulted her and denied her Constitutional rights.

In the gallery theft, she was convicted of stealing valuable art but got off with two years' probation. Interestingly enough, she used the name Santee Singhrs and gave a date of birth of July 24, 1944, shaving ten years off her age.

Sante loved the status and perks that came with being on the arm of Kimes, but the relationship between her and her millionaire was stormy, with dozens of breakups, screaming matches, uncontrollable weeping, and even a couple of phony suicide attempts, all designed to make the gullible Kimes feel guilty. He tried to break up with her a number of times, but she always pulled some kind of embarrassing public display, some stunt or wild scene. Restaurant managers and waiters who witnessed Sante's outbursts said that Kimes would later give them a generous tip to apologize for the disruption to other patrons.

About that time, Kimes began spending a good deal of time in Hawaii, where he planned to finalize a sizeable investment in some parcels of property. When Sante heard he was flying to Honolulu without her, she panicked. She was determined not to let Kimes go off where he might replace her with some unknown rival. She didn't have the money for an airline ticket to Hawaii, so she finagled a deal with I. Magnin, the upscale Los Angeles department store. She persuaded the store to supply her with clothing by promising to put on an in-flight fashion show on the trip to Hawaii. Then she called United Airlines and conned them into a ticket by saying that I. Magnin wanted to do this in-flight show as a test. In no time at all, she had pulled another scam on both these two companies.

Sante boarded the flight with all those gowns and accessories she'd never paid for, and flew to Hawaii. Kimes was not amused when she turned up at the Sheraton-Waikiki Hotel, and he refused to see her. In a two-page letter she left for him at the hotel, she wrote:

"She had the largest breasts and most active tush"

Ken—Please honey—I just came here because I love you and I have been worried sick. Right after you left, I began getting nightmares and I just thought if I came I could at least be here— I never dreamed you would get angry—I came because I love you. Please get me enough to get home on. I can leave late tonite.

Without you, I want to not live—don't torture me when I stand by you no matter what.

Darling I love you. Please, I can't get back without your help. I came with a heart full of love—All yours. Sante.

It was neither the first nor the last time that Sante was to plead for help from Kimes. The letters indicating a breakup always had the same familiar theme. This letter, in which she pleaded with Kimes for bail money and cash for an attorney, was sent after her arrest in 1972:

I have no one else in the world. Please stand by me. I swear I will pay every cent back, anything. I am frightened to death. Please please I love you. You know I'm alone. You are all I have. I swear I will be what you want and forever your girl. Help me. Help me. I swear upon God and you and Kent that I will work my heart out and never ask for one cent. You can sell my furs, the furniture, anything. It's worth at least $15,000. I'll sign. I have to get bailed out or I am dead. Kent is alone soon. The girl taking care of him wants off this weekend. Joan doesn't know. I am very sick and frightened and numb . . .

Whenever Kimes attempted to free himself from her, Sante fought back. Once, after Kimes broke up with her and refused to see her, she stood outside his daughter's apartment in the middle of the night screaming hysterically. "I love him!" she wailed over and over, finally driving neighbors to call security.

Linda bore the major brunt of her father's relationship with Sante, according to a former co-worker. She worked with her father in his motel business and became the buffer zone every time Kimes broke up with Sante. It was left to his daughter to answer his phone and give his girlfriend the bad news. "No, he's not here," officeworkers would overhear Linda say. Not one to take kindly to such treatment, Sante would sit in her car in the parking lot, blocking Kimes's car so he couldn't leave without speaking to her.

Linda confided to friends that the family situation by then had become unbearable. "His brother, his sister, his mother, his aunt all talked to her father, trying to coach him to get away from Sante," a cousin said. "Everyone close to Ken, including business associates and neighbors, were clearly mystified that this man would allow her to continue to disrupt his life. His brothers and sisters were always saying, 'Ken, this woman is totally evil. She is bad.' And he'd say, 'I know. A person makes mistakes.' He still seemed to believe that money fixes everything. 'If she had money, she wouldn't do that,' he'd say. But that wasn't true."

As the months of this bizarre relationship went on, everyone in the Kimes family began to gradually distance themselves from what they said was an "out-of-control golddigger."

One morning, a Kimes nephew was at the Santa Ana home of Kimes's mother, Neoma, when the doorbell rang and Sante barged in unannounced. "Linda had also stopped by for coffee and was talking with my Uncle Ken when Sante showed up. She pushed past me, forcing her way into the house. She had fire in her eyes. They had apparently had another big blow-up of some kind the night before. Linda grabbed her hair and physically just pulled her right back out the door. She put her foot up in Sante's abdomen and shoved hard and she landed on her big fat ass. Linda was standing there with a handful—Sante's fake black wig that stunk of her gardenia toilet water. She threw the wig out and slammed the door. Sante was damn near bald."

Still, Sante wasn't about to give up. Shamelessly, she simply brushed herself off, got into her car, stopped at the nearest drugstore, and headed for Kimes's motel, where she broke into his private suite and spread various pills all over his office, but not before taking five aspirin and calling the paramedics at the emergency number. As a result of the fake suicide attempt, Kimes took pity on her and resumed the relationship.

The family continued to beg Kimes to dump Sante but their pleas fell on deaf ears. In the mid-1970s, Kimes had a stroke and withdrew almost completely from public view. He had limited motion on one side and was embarrassed that people would think of him as weak. "The illness gave Sante total control of him and, boy, did she work him over," a nephew recalled.

The Kimes family began to notice that he'd begun to degenerate and drift away from them. He became suspicious and started to make false accusations against his employees and others close to him. Sante's latest theme was to turn herself into the victim, so she could continue manipulating the debilitated Kimes, further cutting him off from his family. One by one, she eliminated his family relationships. The alienation between the family and Kimes widened to the point where there was now no one to talk him out of continuing his relationship with Sante, who began referring to his family as "The Creeps."

It became obvious to the Kimes family that Ken was no longer the master of his ship. "Kimes was like a dazed bystander when it came to Sante's goings-on," recalled Larry Haile, an attorney who worked for the Kimes family. "She told him she would be his publicist and help him promote himself and promote his Americanism. He liked that flag business and liked to think of himself as an Ambassador of Good Will and saw himself as a super-patriot."

Haile first met Kimes after a tapestry that was hanging in Kimes's office was stolen. The insurance company that insured the tapestry contacted Haile because they suspected fraud. According to the Irvine Police Department crime report on November 11, 1974, the suspect entered Kimes's business through the main door with a key and removed a "handmade stitched 30-inch by 36-inch" framed tapestry "with an American eagle holding the shield and American flags on each side. It was dated 1882."

The insurance adjuster who met with Haile was David Kazdin, the man Sante and Kenny are accused of murdering in 1998. Although it seemed as though Kimes was the one who had insured the item, it turned out that it was Sante who had filled out the paperwork for the claim and had obtained the original estimates that it was valued at $100,000. "Kazdin had red-flagged the claim and wanted me to conduct an examination," Haile said. Sante insisted that the tapestry was a Kimes family heirloom that had been given to Kimes by his mother, Neoma, years earlier.

As the investigation progressed, an insurance company appraiser determined that the tapestry was a fairly common object that sailors brought back from the Far East around the turn of the century. "It was oriental and sold in junk shops over there. My appraiser advised me that it was worth maybe $800, but certainly not the $100,000 that Sante was demanding," Haile said. The lawyer said that the focus of the theft was on Sante, since she had access to Kimes's office and his keys and there wasn't any forced entry to the office.

The insurer took depositions under oath from Charloette Kimes, his first wife, from whom he was divorced at the time of the theft, and from his daughter Linda, who had worked in the office. "We had also wanted to interview Kimes's elderly mother and her sister, Alice Wardchow, because we felt they could both attest to Sante's claims that the tapestry had been in the Kimes family for years. But when we tried to depose them on the value of the tapestry and its origins, we learned that Kimes and Sante had removed the women from California juris-diction rather unexpectedly and had taken them to Hawaii to prevent them from testifying in the investigation," Haile explained.

As for the tapestry, it was determined to be virtually valueless in terms of fine art, and Haile advised the insurance company not to pay a dime. Sante was furious. She dug her heels in and wasted no time attributing her problems with the law and with the insurance company to the actions of Kimes's family, which she was convinced was out to harass her.

✖

On March 24, 1975, Sante gave birth to Ken's son, Kenny. Motherhood may change some people, but not Sante. Remaining totally in character, she stiffed both the Cedars-Sinai Medical Center in Beverly Hills and the hospital gift shop by simply run-ning out without paying her bills. Nor did she pay the obstetrician who delivered her son.

Later, Sante claimed that she didn't even know that she was preg-nant with Kenny until the fourth month of her pregnancy. However, letters reveal that Sante was conscious of her pregnancy within the first two months. *"I know I am at least 2 to 3 months along,"* she wrote in a six-page letter to Kimes in which she also pleads for money for an abortion.

> *I will go to any abortionist you want—just please pay him— The longer you wait the more dangerous it is to my life. If you won't help me then I'll just have to have the baby—Don't force me to do that—[if] you don't want him. Don't make this a horrible thing—Just take me somewhere and pay the doctor and he'll do it. Please. Please call me and tell me what to do— I can go in and get the abortion this week, if you want and if you're worried about the agreement—OK, I'll do whatever you want—Don't break my heart anymore. I have to have that abortion soon. I'll sign whatever you want—agreements— anything. I love you no matter what—penniless and pregnant!*

Throughout the four letters she sent Kimes that dealt with her so-called crisis, Sante used her charms to convince him that not only was she pregnant and willing to have an abortion, but also that she should keep the unborn child. This included her willingness to sign any agreement from Kimes. Kimes, however, was incredulous and doubtful she was even pregnant.

> *If you still don't believe me, you can take me to any laboratory or doctor you wish and get the real facts if the report is not enough. Then you will know I'm telling the truth. I have done all I can except go to another doctor. Now it's up to you.*

Before signing off, she implores Kimes, *"I'll work—just pay me like your employees."**

---

*Sante also claims she had another sonw ith Kimes, Kienan, who was supposedly born in 1982. No one has ever seen this child and Sante reportedly informed various officials that she never told Kimes about the pregnancy because he had suffered the first of several heart attacks. She supposedly arranged to place the boy with a family in Texas. She has also claimed he was adopted by a Mexican family. When it suits her purposes, Sante also blames the Kimes family for the disappearance of the child, accusing them of kidnapping the infant.

Sante's relationship with the Kimes family had now deteriorated to the point where she claimed that the family plotted to kidnap Kenny shortly after he was born, because he was heir to all of Kimes's money. She claimed they tried attacking her by placing rattlesnakes in her car, and she went so far as to accuse Linda Kimes of splattering cow's blood in one of the Kimes' motel rooms in an attempt to scare her. She even blamed the Kimes family for the first fire, in 1978, at their 271A Portlock Road residence in Honolulu.

The problem with all Sante's accusations was that they were impossible to substantiate. Even her friends, like Patricia Christopherson, a retired Los Angeles County officer who claimed to have known Sante for ten years, admitted that she was prone to "exaggerate from time to time to make a point. She had an imperious way of dealing with people." She later discovered that Sante stole stationery from her husband, Grant, so she could forge a letter.

Grant Christopherson, a retired FBI agent who was chief investigator for the California State Bar Association in 1985, agreed with his wife's assessment about Sante's exaggerating, but felt it was "because she's excitable. When they put rattlesnakes in her car, she said she was so scared because she couldn't open the door to get out of the car and had to break the window."

Kimes's family, and Linda in particular, lived in deadly fear of rattlesnakes. Sante was very specific about the rattlesnakes in her car. She had used the snake scenario as a ruse years earlier when she got her second husband, Ed Walker, to fly to California from Nevada so he could be served with divorce papers after claiming her young son Kent had been bitten by a rattlesnake. "Who would want to look long enough at the reptile to figure it out?" Linda asked. Sante's cow blood story was even wackier. A former motel worker claimed that Sante came running to the front office screaming that Linda had used cow's blood to write threats to her on the wall of the room. What made the story even more absurd is that Linda actually faints at the sight of blood. And besides, how would Sante know what kind of blood was on the wall?

"Over time, we all came to the conclusion that Sante was truly

evil, constantly lying, a vile being, capable of anything, respecting nothing and no one," said one family member. "She is a monster, the incarnation of the she-devil."

✖

Sante and Kimes, Sr., celebrated the birth of their son, Kenny, by flying off to Honolulu with their newborn infant, first settling in a rented house in the Kaneoe area across the island from Waikiki. Kimes's mother and his aunt joined them in September after he bought a lavish six-bedroom wooden and stucco oceanfront home on Portlock Road overlooking Diamond Head. The beachfront residence had a swimming pool, a gazebo, and a small cottage in the back where Neoma and Alice resided. The gated property was fenced so no one could get in without going to the front door. The dense jungle landscaping, with its lush tropical ferns and birds of paradise, gave the place a creepy feeling of isolation.

Sante was determined that the insurance company not depose the women concerning the tapestry, so she was very restrictive about letting Neoma and Alice have access to neighbors and friends at the local Catholic church. Kent became a watchdog for his mother and was very involved with controlling the movements of the two elderly women.

In May 1976, other Kimes family members became concerned that the two elderly women were being held against their will. The Kimes family traveled to Honolulu and, in a scene reminiscent of a James Bond movie, met the two women in a pew of the church they attended and escorted them back to California on the next plane with nothing more than the clothes they were wearing. Later, when Alice was admitted to a health-related facility in Orange County, doctors examining her during the admission process were shocked. Not only did they discover signs that the woman had been tortured and starved, but her vagina had been sewn up with black cotton thread.*

---

*Neoma died in 1980 at age 86. Alice died in 1977 at age 72.

Neoma told family members that Sante asked Kent to keep an eye on them, after she had planted telephone bugs and listening devices throughout the house. She also told them that Sante and Kent had hired a Hawaiian detective to keep tabs on them. On one occasion when the two women wandered off on their own to visit church friends, Sante was furious. "She wouldn't have known that unless we were being followed," Neoma said and warned family members to be fearful of retaliation and to be aware of being followed and phone tapping.

The two women informed family members that Kimes was completely powerless and that he had been unable to help them escape from Sante's control. They said he could not keep anything from Sante and could not make a single move without her knowledge.

"He was completely passive and submissive around Sante," said a neighbor who lived down the road from Kimes in Hawaii. "He was simply unable to control her or intervene in her activities. Occasionally, we could hear loud arguments erupting, but it seems Sante always came out in a more powerful position. She was relentless, always nagging, ordering, manipulating, playing roles and scheming behind the scenes."

A Spanish maid who worked at the Portlock residence, and is still fearful of Sante, referred to her as *Diablo*—the Devil. The maid observed that when Kenny was a small baby and toddler, Sante was never seen to touch him. Kimes, Sr., held him and played with him; even Neoma and Alice played with him, but never Sante. It was maids and other household staff that tended to the boy and played with him, but Sante never did one thing to interact with him as a baby. "Diablo no touch baby."

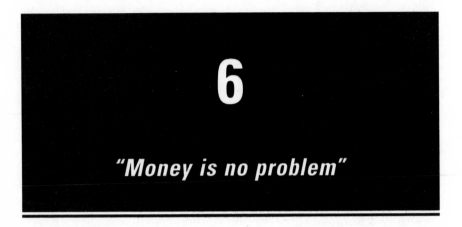

6

"Money is no problem"

MONDAY, JULY 6, 1998, NEW YORK CITY

It was just after 2:00 A.M. when Detectives Hovagim and Ryan woke Valerie McLeod, another member of Irene's household staff, at her home in the Bronx. Valerie had worked for Irene for almost ten years and, as house manager, she was responsible for showing apartments to potential renters, collecting rents, and assisting Irene in the day-to-day running of the building.

McLeod told the detectives that in the first week of April, 1998, Irene had called her on a Sunday at home and told her to expect a call from a lady named Eva who was looking for an apartment for her boss.

Valerie explained to the detectives that Mrs. Silverman "said she would rent to her just because she was a friend of Rudy Vaccari, her butcher, who she knew for over 40 years . . . and that because

71

Eva was a friend of Rudy, it was okay to go ahead and do the rental. The next day, when I came to work, Eva called me. She said she had spoken to Mrs. Silverman about a one-bedroom apartment in her building for her boss, Manny Guerin, a dress designer, who was coming to New York and needed a place to stay. I told her there weren't any available, but there was a studio, and she said okay. 'Hold the studio for me.'

"I said, 'It's $5,000 a month.' She said, 'No problem. Just hold it for me. We definitely need an apartment there. Do not rent it.'" Valerie asked Eva if there was a number to reach her, but she was evasive. "No, I'm calling from Mexico. I don't have a number. I'll call back because we're traveling."

Eva was persistent and called Valerie three more times that month just to make sure that the studio was still available. Every time Eva called, Valerie asked her for a contact telephone number, but every time Eva came up with some excuse or another to make sure that Valerie could not reach her. Since Mrs. Silverman did not have the caller ID feature on her phone, Valerie did not know that Sante was actually calling from Wellington, Florida.

In May, Eva called again to make sure Valerie had not rented the studio. This time, Valerie told her, "I believe there's a one-bedroom coming up soon. It's more expensive. It's $6,000."

"Money is no problem. We'll take it," Eva said eagerly.

Valerie asked for a telephone number and again Eva brushed off the request, saying they were in Brazil but were moving on, and so they would have to call her. "We'll be moving in on Sunday, June fourteenth," Eva said.

"I'm sorry," said Valerie, "but tenants can't move in on weekends, because the staff responsible to help tenants move in is off duty. Mr. Guerin will have to come in on Monday when I'm there."

Eva contacted Valerie another three or four times in June. During those calls she began inquiring into details about the running of the mansion, the number of people who worked there, and their duties. The unsuspecting Valerie, trying to be helpful, gave Eva the information.

Three days before Manny Guerin was to move into the mansion, Valerie, Mengi, and Noel Rodriquez, another member of the staff,

readied apartment 1B for the new tenant. The only personal items of Irene's they left in the apartment were framed needlepoints Irene's mother had created and a picture of Irene Zambelli that hung in the foyer.

Valerie told detectives that from the moment Manny moved into the apartment, Irene and all the help thought he acted very suspiciously. "He would never let anyone in his apartment to clean or water the plants. When Manny entered the building, he used to avoid the monitor camera in the lobby. Mrs. Silverman said she would occasionally see Manny's feet by the front of his apartment, standing and listening to people talking in the building." With the three-quarter-inch gap between the bottom of his apartment door and the highly polished black marble floor in the hallway, Manny's feet cast an eerie mirror shadow, giving those passing by his door a spooky feeling.

Irene adamantly refused to deal with her new tenant. "If he needed something, she wanted me handle it," Valerie explained. "So, after he moved in, I gave him my home number to call when I wasn't in the building, but he was told not to call Mrs. Silverman."

Valerie went on to describe a rather odd exchange she had with Eva. On June 20, the first day of Valerie's vacation, her phone rang. Her caller ID notified her that the call was originating from the Pierre Hotel on Fifth Avenue. "I didn't know anyone at the Pierre Hotel," she told detectives, "but when I picked up the phone and said hello, it was Eva. 'What's the matter,' I asked."

"Dear, I'm calling you because I am in Mexico and my boss just called me and told me that the lady has been saying mean things about you. Don't go back there. Don't go back there to work. She's a mean lady."

"What mean things? What did she say? What mean things did Mrs. Silverman say?"

"Oh, dear. My boss will tell you. It's very mean things."

"What?" Valerie asked.

"When you came to work there, you were very, very thin and stole food to eat and, dear, a lot of other mean things that my boss will tell you," Eva said.

Eva then instructed Valerie not to call Irene. Valerie knew she wasn't calling from Mexico, so instead she telephoned Irene, but one of the staff informed her that Irene was sleeping. The following day, Manny called Valerie at home and said he wanted to meet with her about Irene. Valerie asked if they could talk over the phone, but Manny insisted he couldn't because "all the workers at the building were talking bad things about her and he felt they might be listening to him now." They agreed to meet at the Silver Star Restaurant at 65th Street and Second Avenue, because she was curious as to what Manny had to say. When she arrived at the neighborhood coffee shop, Manny was there waiting for her, with a notebook sitting on the table in front of him. He didn't waste any time getting down to business. "Do you have Mrs. Silverman's social security number?" he asked boldly.

"No," she said, "I don't. Why do you need it?"

"Because she's been coming into my room stealing documents."

"No, Manny, Mrs. Silverman would never do that. She'd never go into a tenant's room and steal documents."

"Yes, yes. She came in my room to steal documents, and I need her social security number to check her out and see if she's done anything like this before," he said.

When Valerie insisted she didn't have Irene's social security number, Manny urged her to look in her purse to see if she had it. "No," she insisted, "I don't have her social security number and if you're so sure she came in your room and stole documents, then move," Valerie added.

"I can't move because I paid her for three months," he said.

"No, Manny," Valerie reminded him, "you only paid her for one month and she will give you back the money if you say you're going to leave."

"No, I paid her for three months," Manny kept insisting.

"Manny, it's for just one month," Valerie told him firmly.

"That bitch is lying. It's for three months."

Manny made one last stab at getting Irene's social security number by asking Valerie how he could contact Irene's former accountant, but she refused to give him the number.

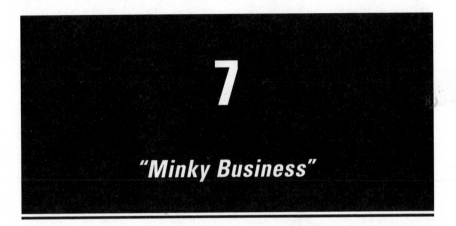

7

"Minky Business"

Putting something over on people seemed to turn Sante on. She took delight in practicing the art of stealing and scheming, as if the acts somehow certified her existence. The bigger the scam, the more alive it made her feel. Her liason with Ken Kimes only seemed to whet her appetite and dragging him along into her insane schemes only made it better.

After Sante wormed her way into Ken Kimes's life as a "public relations adviser," she and Kimes managed to make headlines in a really big way when the polished pair crashed several high-level Washington parties in February 1974.

The headline in a column by Betty Beale, the grande dame of Washington society, said it all: "The Biggest Crash Since 1929." Calling himself the "Honorary Bicentennial Ambassador of the

United States of America," Kimes and his assistant, Sante Singhres, leisurely walked into Blair House, across the street from the White House, made their way through the receiving line as if they belonged there, and shook hands with Vice President and Mrs. Gerald Ford at a diplomatic reception. As usual, Sante was heavily made up as an Elizabeth Taylor lookalike, an international, exotic, wealthy woman of the world. She was wearing a white 1900-style dress, with a diamond or rhinestone gem pasted in her ear, and topped off her ensemble with a huge white turban fur hat on her dark hair.

Their uninvited arrival into the world of international society caused quite a commotion. The Secret Service was not only embarrassed and alarmed that they had managed to violate security, but they were also puzzled as to how these two total strangers wound up inside the president's guest house.

The brazen duo weren't finished yet. After being shown the Blair House door, they went next door to the Renwick Gallery and crashed a black-tie dinner party being given by the Smithsonian. Asked to leave, they took a taxi to the German Embassy, where they were again politely shown the front door. This time Sante, thinking fast and fluttering her flashy eyes, came up with the lame explanation that she was looking for the party at the home of the Belgian ambassador, who just happened to live on the same street as the German ambassador. With no taxi in sight, the German ambassador's wife graciously offered to have them driven there. And so they were simply driven to the new address in the German ambassador's car. After they had been there barely long enough to sample the hors d'oeuvres, the host realized they were party crashers and once again they were asked to leave. Amazingly, the gate crashers rode back in style in a diplomatic car to the Statler Hotel, where they were staying.

Meanwhile, the Bicentennial Commission strongly denied Kimes's claim that he had been appointed Honorary Bicentennial ambassador, despite a letter he flaunted, claiming it was from President Nixon. The Commission ordered him not to use the fake title and also made it clear to Kimes that he had no official status with them. This didn't stop Sante from insisting to a *Washington Post* reporter that Kimes was "more than a millionaire. If somebody doesn't do what Ken is doing, the Bicentennial is going to pass us by. He is a wonderful person and a dedicated American," she said, pointing out his patriotism. She boasted that he had also organized a patriotic presentation of his flag posters, at a cost of nearly half a million dollars, and had met with First Lady Pat Nixon, who promised to place the flags in every school in the country.

Sante admitted they were "upset" about their Blair House deception and "resulting publicity," but rationalized it, as only she could, by saying that it might make America more aware of the Bicentennial. Weeks after the Blair House debacle, the White House determined that the Nixon letter was doctored—no doubt the handiwork of Sante's fine artistic hand.

Exposure didn't deter this brazen pair, and they actually made it back to Washington, D.C., and newspaper headlines, four years later. On February 3, 1980, traveling under the name of Shante Kimes, she and Kimes, Sr., whom she now always called "Papa," checked into the Capital Hilton in Washington, D.C., with their five-year-old son, Kenny, a personal maid, a nanny, and a man Friday. While at the Capital Hilton, Sante stole a man's coat from the lounge. Two days later, at the Mayflower Hotel, a five-minute walk from the White House, she was arrested for stealing four fur coats, including a white fox coat and a champagne-colored mink. Sante's arrest made the newspapers and the case took on a life of its own, becoming known as "minky business." The two-count indictment charged her with taking a mink coat belonging to Katherine A. Kenworthy, a well-to-do woman in town, and a man's coat belonging to John E. Booth.

During the investigation, Mrs. Kenworthy informed police and hotel security that while in the Towne and Country Lounge at the Mayflower Hotel, her full-length, dark brown mink coat was stolen. A woman in a white mink coat was seen taking the coat, and from the description witnesses offered, "the woman in white mink" was Sante. When police went to her room, Sante opened the door and allowed them to conduct a search. According to the arrest report, police noticed "a small piece of cloth, brownish in color, on the windowsill." The police opened the window and observed what appeared to be the coat about four floors down. The coat was recovered and Mrs. Kenworthy identified it.

John Booth said he and a friend were in the cocktail lounge on February 3, and when it came time to leave, he noticed that his black and gray tweed topcoat, a pair of gloves, and a scarf were missing. Three days later, a hotel employee, Lester Wong, informed police that he'd seen Sante and Kimes enter the lounge and take a seat at a table directly behind Booth. A short time later, Sante was seen removing the coat, which was on the back of a chair near the table; she and her male companion then walked out of the lounge. Wong confronted Sante in the lobby and asked if she had mistakenly taken the coat.

"I did not," Sante replied rather indignantly, walking off in a huff.

Wong advised hotel security about the incident, telling them that he recognized both Sante and Ken because they had stayed in the hotel in the past and had been in the bar before. A police search warrant of their hotel room turned up the plaid scarf and the topcoat, with the label removed.

Sante complained bitterly about the injustice perpetrated against her. "It was awful. They handcuffed us, frisked us, and then put us in these little green barred closets that had a toilet with no seat," she complained melodramatically.

"I've been trying to tell everyone, it was *my* coat that was stolen," she explained to a mob of reporters in the lobby of the Capital Hilton, where she flat-out denied the theft after being released from jail in the custody of their lawyer. Sante insisted she did not, as charged, place the fur coat on top of her own long white fur piece and then stroll out with both coats. Her story was that she had merely checked one of her four full-length ranch mink coats she brought with her to the nation's capital and "forgot" to pick up her checked mink when she left the hotel restaurant. When she returned the next day, the manager handed her another mink that was "not the quality of my own." Her plan, she insisted, was to file a missing fur report, when, at about 2:00 A.M., she was startled when police forced their way in their room.

"I'd been asleep and I was stark naked. They pushed me around and started searching all over the room. I said we knew nothing. It's an outrage. To think that I would need to steal someone's fur," she postured.

On July 11, 1985, after more than 15 delays over five and a half years due to continuances based on Sante's various alleged illnesses or incapacities, the case against her finally went to trial. During the six-day trial, Sante appeared in court every day, dressed to the nines in flowing white gowns and light pink outfits. Witnesses described her as a "fatter Elizabeth Taylor" or a "bad Liz." Seven days later, while the jury was deliberating her fate, Sante took off from the courthouse during the lunch break and failed to return for the afternoon session.

Meanwhile, the jury sent a note to D.C. Superior Court Judge Sylvia Bacon, saying they'd reached a verdict. With Sante not present, the guilty verdict was read in court. The judge immediately issued a warrant for Sante's arrest and set bond at $50,000.

On July 21, Sante brazenly sent a "mailgram" to the judge and to her defense lawyer, alleging she'd been involved in an accident and was hospitalized on the afternoon of July 18, which prevented her from returning to court. As if that weren't enough, she also claimed her wallet and identification had been stolen during the injury and that she was now in California.

Sante's memory of that "awful experience" was just that—a memory. It had no impact on her because any time she spent in that Washington jail cell certainly didn't convince her that crime doesn't pay.. In 1981, she was at it again when she was arrested in Las Vegas for burgling, of all items, a grand piano from a house in which she was both a tenant and a prospective buyer. The piano was recovered after it was found advertised for sale in a local tabloid. According to the Las Vegas police report, the victim advised the officer who responded to his home that he was in the process of moving and had been in and out of the house at various times all that week. The investigation revealed that Sante and her family resided in the victim's home for quite some time until the escrow closed. They had left mysteriously, without the knowledge of the victim, merely leaving a note that their clothes were still in the closets in the residence and that they would return at a future date to pick them up.

During this time, the LAPD contacted the victim in an attempt to find Sante regarding her arrest in Washington on the mink caper.

The victim informed police that she might be a suspect in the burglary of his grand piano. When the victim went to the home of Mike Connor, who had placed the ad in the paper, he positively identified the piano as his property. Connor indicated that Sante had given him the piano as a gift, as well as two silver goblets that the victim also owned. The case dragged on for a year and was ultimately dismissed.

And the beat went on. Sante found herself in still more hot water with the law when she was arrested in 1982 for stealing several cosmetic items from a local Las Vegas department store. Although that case was also dismissed, she wasn't off the hook, because other California jurisdictions had an outstanding warrant against her, on which the most serious charges were false imprisonment, kidnapping, and robbery. Bail had been set at $50,000.

Despite all these charges, she was never prosecuted. Is it any wonder that with so many of her arrests ending in probation, fines, or non-prosecution, Sante felt as though she was invincible and could beat any rap?

Not for long.

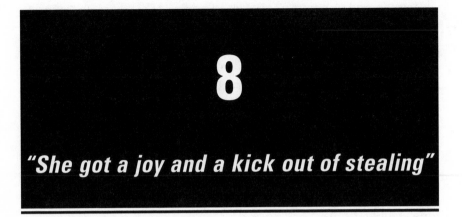

8

"She got a joy and a kick out of stealing"

Kenny Kimes hardly ever speaks of his childhood. Whether this is because it is too painful for him or because his mother has coached him to say little about his past is an open question. His mother did coach him, from his earliest days, in the art of stealing and scamming.

The Kimes' neighbors in the Hawaii Kai area of Honolulu recalled that when Kenny was a toddler, Sante would often take him out with her on shoplifting sprees, during which she would leisurely stroll down aisles with him in his carriage, engage an unsuspecting sales clerk in conversation, and scam cosmetics or jewelry or whatever was close at hand. She would then use her baby as a shield, tucking the items inside his diaper, so she could walk out of the store undetected.

Shortly after a suspicious fire at the Portlock Road residence in 1978, Sante's neighbor, Beverly Bates-Stone, who was then an interior decorator and is now a minister, offered to take Sante shopping to replace and refurnish her home. "I took Sante to my friend, Annabella, at the wallpaper store, and she found a wallpaper she really liked," Bates-Stone recalled. "I told her I would get her a 30 percent discount off the regular price, but she turned it down saying, 'Oh no. I'll just wait.' The next day I got a call from Annabella complaining that the lady I brought in returned with her maid and her little boy in a stroller, and every single roll in that bin was gone when they left."

Bates-Stone was flabbergasted. "That's impossible, Annabella. The woman is a multimillionaire." Nevertheless, Annabella was insistent and said, "Every roll of wallpaper was gone, including the one she liked."

"Sante used that baby and continued to use him, no matter how old he was," Bates-Stone recalled. "She got a joy and a kick out of stealing."

Instead of enrolling Kenny in school or even allowing him to play with other children, Sante put him under a kind of house arrest, having him tutored at home by a series of young women fresh out of college. Sante was a tough taskmaster, making sure that her son cracked the books seven and eight hours every day. She even demanded weekly reports on Kenny's progress from his tutors. "She and the tutors would have arguments, because they thought she was being too demanding of them and of Kenny," said his half-brother, Kent Walker. "They went through a few different tutors because of personal differences. I never had any tutors, but she wanted me to study three hours a day, even when I was in the third or fourth grade. She would talk to my teachers weekly."

"We thought Kenny was a retarded child," Bates-Stone recalled. "He certainly acted retarded. He never learned how to play with other children. Sante used to go around the neighborhood asking other kids to play with Kenny. He was very slow and not sharp. Kenny couldn't do anything. He couldn't even talk. He couldn't even speak English, because Sante and Ken would go on all these trips and leave the child with maids who didn't speak English," Bates-Stone said.

Bates-Stone said that she found Kenny "scary" even at a young age. "He has never been allowed to be properly schooled. He has no social upbringing. He's like a robot who was taught to say the right thing at the right time. He's not a real person. He's a clone of everything Sante taught him. He had no way of getting out of the house, no way of socializing, and no way of doing anything. She really brainwashed him from the time he was a small child," she said. "And as he grew older, Kenny imitated his mother, in words and deed."

By the time Kenny was six years old, he had become well versed in the art of petty larceny, as Sante continued her pilfering forays into boutiques and discount stores, using her young son as a protective shield. Sante wanted total control of both Kenny and Kent. Years later, as a young adult, Kent admitted that his mother had a "real hard time letting go of the reins" when he turned 18. "She wanted to control what I did. One time when I was 20 years old, I stayed out all night, and when I got back the next day, she went into an absolute tantrum. We had a big argument, and I was so mad that I moved out and didn't talk to them for six months."

Kent also found his mother and his stepfather "suspicious of others . . . almost paranoid in their suspicions of others. Mom has no midpoint on anything. Everything is to the extreme. She is very extreme emotionally. She was just overly strict and very preoccupied with neatness." Kent described "cleaning sprees where we would have to soak down the patios and scrub them with disinfectant." He felt his mother needed to be "more tolerant . . . in her approach to life," and said, "Her methods are questionable."

As if she were a female Fagin from Charles Dickens's *Oliver Twist*, Sante had big plans for Kenny, and she continued to condition her sweet little waif with her distorted values, so that he would go out into the world someday to make her fortune.

In 1985, when Kenny was only 10 years old, his mother finally went too far and, as a result, she loosened her vise-like grip, at least for a while.

9

"Greed, arrogance, and cruelty"

With the help of Kenneth Kimes's fortune and her personal philosophy of why pay for something when you can steal it or stick someone else with the bill, Sante had managed to create quite a lifestyle for herself. This included opulent homes in Hawaii, California, Nevada, and Cancun, Mexico. But even Sante couldn't be in all these places at once, so she had to make sure that she had people who could see to all her needs, which meant staffing all her homes with maids, cooks, and housecleaners.

Maria De Rosario Vasquez was 14 years old and living in Mexico City when Sante Kimes, after promising her parents she would educate the young girl, recruited her to work as a domestic at the fashionable two-story, three-bedroom condominium the Kimeses rented at the intersection of Via Mallorca and Caminto Ameca in

La Jolla, a posh suburb of San Diego, California. Sante's attempts at "education" were rather unorthodox, however, as Maria was punched, beaten, and forced to work long hours without any pay. Eventually, she was able to place a frantic collect call to relatives who alerted the FBI. The FBI raided the condo on August 3, 1985, freed the unfortunate young girl, and arrested Sante and Papa Kimes, charging them with slavery, conspiracy, and transporting illegal aliens for the past six years.

As it turned out, Maria De Rosario Vasquez was not alone. Over the years, Sante had helped herself to plenty of free maid service, including that of Dolores Vasquez Salgado, who was 14 when Sante smuggled her across the Mexican border from her home in Guadalajara in 1982. "We walked across the border on the beach, and once in San Diego, I was flown to Las Vegas to work in La Senora's home," explained Vasquez, who also said that Sante called her "stupid," "threatened me with a pistol," and once struck her "because I had burned hamburger bread." A third incident occurred in a hotel suite. "I had an allergy," Vasquez recalled. "My pressure went up and I fainted. La Senora said to go into the shower. She forced me to go in there. All of a sudden, she would steam up like that. . . . I had taken off my clothes and she told me to get in the shower. I put the water to lukewarm. She changed the water to very hot. It burned. When I moved away to a corner of the bathtub, she threw hot water on me with a little pot."

Vasquez said she often wrote letters to her parents, but Sante never mailed them. When Vasquez discovered the letters under the seat of Sante's car, Sante gave the maid a lame excuse that she had not mailed them because there were "problems" between Mexico and the United States. "She said mailmen couldn't send the letters there. Mailmen didn't speak Spanish." Although promised a salary of $150 a month, Vasquez was never paid and never given a day off. "I worked in the house from 6:30 in the morning to nine at night or to midnight." After three months toiling for Sante, Vasquez said she was taken to the Tijuana border crossing, given some money, and told to return to Guadalajara.

Another maid, Maribel Ramirez-Cruz of El Salvador, a 21-year-old illegal alien, said that Sante kept her against her will and threatened her if she talked about her "employment." Ramirez said "La Senora" hired her outside a Costa Mesa, California, employment office, promising to pay her $120 "if I worked at her house." The next day, Sante took her to Hawaii, where the hapless Ramirez remained from July to November 1984. She was given no money, no days off, and was ordered not to talk to anyone, not even to other members of Sante's household staff. "I wanted to leave, but I couldn't because they [the Kimeses and their tutors in the house] were all watching me," Ramirez said.

Ramirez said that in November she was taken to Sante's Las Vegas home. According to her testimony at the slavery trial, she was ironing one day when Sante discovered a piece of paper on her with the telephone number of another maid whom Ramirez had met in Hawaii. Sante flew into a wild rage, the young woman said, and became vicious and sadistic. "La Senora made me take off my clothes so she could search me. Then she threatened to put the iron on my face, so I covered my face with my hands and the iron burned my left hand," Ramirez said. That night she was forced to sleep on the floor of the Kimes' bedroom. "She said she was going to call some friends to put me away for good," Ramirez said.

Still another maid, Adela Sanchez Guzman, related similar atrocities during her 11-month ordeal while working for Sante. Sanchez, who was from Mexico, said that Sante went into a fury because she had talked to Ramirez. "She got mad and said she would kill me." As punishment, Sante slapped her face and head, hit her feet with a wooden hanger, and, when the hanger broke, simply changed over to a hanger made of metal. On another occasion, Sanchez said that when Sante found an address label showing where they lived in Hawaii, she took Sanchez to the bathroom, slapped her, pulled her hair, and beat her with a belt. Sanchez said that these beatings took place in Sante's Las Vegas and Honolulu homes, and that she had not been paid and was not allowed to write or telephone anyone. She testified that she escaped from the Hawaii house in December 1984 and sought refuge in a church, where a priest took the maid to police.

Shortly before she was to go on trial on slavery charges, Sante feigned a multitude of garden-variety medical complaints and was taken to the Southern Nevada Memorial Hospital by federal authorities. On December 30, still wearing her hospital gown, Sante escaped from the facility.

Sante gave varying accounts of where she spent her days of freedom, one of which had her sleeping under trees to escape the elements. In her six-page personal handwritten diary found with the other details of her slavery trial, Sante offered her own incredible explanation of her escape. She began by explaining that she was "handcuffed or footcuffed to a wheelchair, having been made sick by the shots necessary for tests she was undergoing." She wrote:

> *Joella, the guard, with absolutely no warning . . . literally pushed me to an exit and out the door. I did not willfully escape. I was in a sickened, drugged state. No matter what her reason, she pushed me out and I couldn't get back in. I ran with no clothes and I was very disoriented. I was trying to get to a phone and get help when the dog attacked me. I got really bloodied up and fell out of a tree. They say I stayed out intentionally to avoid being caught. The next day, I was sick, injured, bloody, and frightened out of my wits. I literally was frightened to death. Joella pulled the escape. I was the victim. I did not plan it or want it. The government endangered my life by hiring a crooked guard who did this for money reasons. The egg is on the goat's face. They hired Rent-a-Cops and this one was after money.*

After escaping, Sante turned up on the doorstep of a friend, Sheila Bishop, asking for help in contacting Kimes to obtain financial assistance. Sante made several calls to Kimes, and he showed up on January 2 at the Huddle Lounge, where Bishop worked, and gave her $100 for Sante. The next day, Sante appeared at the lounge, got the money, and was then captured by federal marshals and FBI agents in the parking lot of the Elbow Room Bar on East Flamingo Road, about eight blocks east of the Las Vegas strip. She was wearing a blouse and jumper and vehemently claimed she got no help from family or friends during her escape.

Sante went on trial, charged with recruiting and smuggling

young girls, as young as 14, from the ghettoes of Mexico City and El Salvador and bringing them to her homes in California, Nevada, and Hawaii. There, according to the charges, she had locked them in her walled compound like prisoners, torturing them and working them seven days a week without pay. Federal prosecutors charged that both Sante and Kenneth Kimes, Sr., were present during these trips to Mexico, when these young girls were smuggled into the country. Both were named in a 16-count Nevada indictment on August 8, 1985, which charged them with conspiracy and holding as many as seven young women as slaves by preventing them from leaving their employ.

"These were unsophisticated young women who were in the country illegally. They didn't speak English and many of them didn't know what city they were in. They were subject to physical abuse: slapping, kicking. And sometimes they were burned with a hot iron," argued Stephen Clark, one of the U.S. Justice Department attorneys prosecuting the case, in his opening statements to the jury. "This case involves greed, arrogance, and cruelty. It involves the cold and calculating use of people as if they were pieces of furniture."

In outlining the government's case, Clark said that Sante ordered the maids not to answer the door, and she forbade them to use the telephone. She instructed her other employees—tutors, secretaries and house sitters—not to talk to the maids or let them use the telephone, mail letters, or leave Sante's home. She stole their identification papers and any letters that they tried to write to their families. The victims were also kept in line with threats that, because they were illegal aliens, the police were going to come and take them away, torture them (as if Sante wasn't providing enough of that), and abuse them sexually if they tried to get away.

Defense lawyer Dominic Gentile argued that none of the maids were forced to accept the employment. "The evidence will show they were not beaten and were left alone a lot," he said. "They got all the necessities of life for compensation. If they were paid money, they couldn't have done as well." He suggested that the maids who came from "hungry and desperate" backgrounds were bending the truth to stay in the United States.

At the trial, seven of Sante's Spanish-speaking maids testified against her through interpreters, offering poignant accounts of how the seductive sociopath had lured them to the United States with promises of a good life and then brutally smashed their dreams and spirits once they got over the border.

Beverly Bates-Stone, Sante's former neighbor, also testified. When she saw that Sante's son, Kent, was in the courtroom, she became frightened. "I was scared to death that he was going to do something to me because I was testifying against his mother," she said.

Perhaps Bates-Stone had good reason to be apprehensive. Another Kimes neighbor described Kent as "a very devious child . . . always spying, listening in on our conversations. He was his mother's little soldier. Kent was Sante's stand-in and was in charge of the slave maids when it came to bossing them. He acted like a little general when his mother wasn't around. He took her orders and carried them out exactly. He would not speak in her presence unless she directly asked him a question. He was not very popular and didn't have many friends. He also resented and appeared jealous of his baby brother."

Bates-Stone has vivid memories of a young Mexican maid that she rescued from the Portlock Road house. "The girl cried and sobbed as she related how she had been sexually molested by Ken Kimes, Sr., inside the Kimes house. Sante had warned the girl that if she left, she would go to prison, because police would be informed she was illegal. She was shaking as she described the incidents," Bates-Stone said. Despite making the allegations against the Kimes family, when the maid reached the mainland, where she had family, she never filed charges against them.

One of Kenny's tutors also testified against Sante. Teresa Richards said that Sante told her to cross the border "one way or another" and bring young Mexican maids to the United States. Once at the Kimes home, Richards said they were not free to leave or contact their families. "Mrs. Kimes told me to treat the maids as if they were chairs," Richards testified. When asked by Sante's defense lawyer why she didn't leave her job, she replied she was scared and thought she'd be hurt. "I was being brainwashed," she added.

Yet another tutor, Cynthia Montano, said she got her job with the Kimes by answering an ad that promised "travel, excitement, and lots of opportunities," but like Richards, she, too, worked only for living expenses and was not paid a salary. Montano said that after a maid escaped from the household, Sante sent her to Tijuana, Mexico, with instructions to bring back "some girls as maids who wore no makeup, no jewelry, and were very subservient." When she was caught at the Mexican border with the girls in her car trunk, Montano called Sante about her unsuccessful trip. "You can't come home empty-handed. Go back," Sante ordered the tutor.

This time, Sante, who always managed to find someone else to blame for her troubles, laid the blame on her "slaves" for her problems with the law. Personal notes she wrote during the trial reveal that she accused the maids of *"walking off the property and filing a $24 million civil suit"* against them.

> *Our lifestyle and theirs would be envied by most well-off Americans. The maids' charges sound like a "repeat robot" tape. They were being told what to say. The beatings, not being able to get out—lies. Maids are saying what they are being told or brainwashed into saying. They are telling terrible closet stories. The letters are sometimes checked for stolen money and jewelry.*

Sante's 30-page personal manifesto shows how controlling and obsessed she was with contriving her own scenario as to what happened, blaming every prosecution witness for her maniacal nonsense. She also claimed the teachers were prejudiced against her.

> [because] *they could not get to us monetarily. They are lying, giving identical statements. They are obviously brainwashed. They are acting like frightened people who are in danger of the Kimes[es]. As if they were innocent little children, raped by us.*
>
> *In truth, all the teachers came to us begging for the position, gave us written contracts, swearing loyalty and protection and confidentiality. They were there to protect us from*

problems and dangers and they knew there was no salary. As teachers, they had a professional duty to protect us and instead they did not do their job of teaching or were not nice people. They tried to rip us off any way they could.

Throughout her manifesto, she blamed the tutors and the employment agency for her criminal charges.

They contend I did all the directing and no one else. The tutors ran the maids. They ran the house, not us. They should be blamed. They were in charge. They say my personality is up and down. I fly off. I have to have my own way. That's just trying to make criminal a person's personality. The only thing we are guilty of is allowing unscrupulous, money-hungry maids and tutors into the privacy and protection of our home. They had a beautiful life and could leave whenever they wanted. We did not know they were illegal. We certainly didn't know we were doing anything wrong.

Sante's strategy was to also claim that *"the employment agency gave us illegal maids, took our money, and then acted as if he didn't even know us to protect himself. I was going to turn him in if he didn't give use back a refund."* She was convinced that the only way to win the case was to have at least 35 credible witnesses. *"They are trying to steamroll us with guilty verdicts with a great number of witnesses . . . and we have to steamroll back. Seeing is believing,"* she wrote in a four-page February 20, 1986, letter to her son Kent. *"They set the battleground and attacked. We have to go in with at least as many soldiers."*

✖

Sante prepared for her slavery trial as though she were a drill sergeant organizing the troops for battle. In dozens of letters to Ken Kimes and her son Kent, Sante meticulously outlined each and every detail of her court strategy plan and how it was to be implemented. They were to oversee what defense lawyer Dominic Gentile was doing to make sure what her witnesses would say on the stand to rebut prosecution witnesses. *"I cannot stress enough the importance of reaching the witness list I have given you, my dearest precious husband,"* she wrote in an August 24, 1985, letter to Kimes from her cell shortly after her arrest. *"Study my letter closely. All of them. Do it this way,"* she urged, reminding him not to *"forget the birthday 'gifts' . . . 300 notes to each . . . for the people in the East."* She never explained who the people in the east could be, but the "notes" she refers to was obviously $300 in cash, to be given to the witnesses, emphasizing, *"They are vital to a fair trial."*

In writing the specific slavery alibi letter, Sante's approach was to draft it in such a way as to suggest to Kimes her "party line," making it easy for him to grasp her "officially correct" answers. "

> *We never transported anyone. Nor did we know if they were illegal. They told us they were legal and that was that. Even when they went to Hawaii, they went home first, got clothes, and met us at the Marriot or the airport—so we did not actually transport them. They transported themselves voluntarily—we just accompanied them. We did not force them or take them.*
>
> *We are truly innocent—all we did was provide a beautiful home full of everything anyone could want, pay the bills, and be beautiful to all, that's all we did—that's not a crime. They're after money. They entrapped us—got our own people to help them. Our civil liberties have been abused—the liberty to have people in our home—the liberty to have privacy in our homes—free from government intervention—We didn't know they were illegal. If they are trying to kill us, why not the millions of others in California who have them in their home?*

The next month, when Sante realized she was not getting out of jail on bail, she pressed Kimes to start selling property. In a September 27 letter, she said:

> *The more you sell and hide quickly, the less money is there dangling for the vicious enemies to gobble up. The more you have they can lien or attach, the more incentive they have to*

keep suing—This is our money. It always has been, so if you hide the money—they can't find it. It's not half as attractive. No money or property, no bloodthirsty devils to try to literally suck our blood out of our bodies.

In December, before escaping from the prison hospital, she wrote Kent a six-page letter marked "IMPORTANT" in which she instructed her son to *"put this document in your safe deposit box and no one should ever see it. Be very careful with it—don't even leave it in your car—Papa gets up at 3 and 4 and you know how he searches."* She further informed her son:

Papa is very sick and he is at his worst at night . . . that drinking is a serious disease—as brilliant as he is—he's a different person when he drinks. With Papa drinking and refusing to admit the truth, we are really in danger. Watch out for Papa closely. He just scares me to death when he's over drinking. There is an end to the nightmare—that's why I am being so submissive and quiet. I don't want to upset him where he goes off—it could destroy us all.

Sante then promised Kent that *"very soon my darling, you shall receive all—all there is—all I can give is yours very soon."*

With the slavery trial underway in February 1986, Sante sent Kimes an urgent six-page letter, itemizing a list of 16 points of further instructions and ordering him not to talk to certain witnesses *"until they are shown letters she has written to them. All they have to do is get up and remember they worked for us in Vegas in 1979 and 1980 and all was fine."* She also directed Kimes to purchase *"a kitchen wall phone in the Vegas house so Kent can take movies of it and of all the doors in back and driveway and mailboxes"* that would be shown to jurors as proof that the maids could make phone calls. She then orders Kimes in this note to *"My Sweetheart"* that she doesn't think he should come to court too much. *"You're supposed to be sick. Please get your hair whiter. It really helps if you look sick and tired, etc.—the jury is watching you!"*

The extent of Sante's obsession to control was absolute. For instance, she wanted Kent to perjure himself at her federal trial, even if it meant subjecting him to prosecution. In a letter to her son during the slavery trial, she penned an eight-page script for him as to what areas he should emphasize on the witness stand.

> *Kent Honey—As an eye-witness I think it would be helpful for you to bring out . . . what is being lied about and how to confront. You are the best witness we have to prove 1. The house was wide open, lots of doors and exits, both houses— Hawaii? Jump over fence. 2. They could leave anytime and did if they wanted to. 3. About half the time or more, all maids and tutors alone, free to do what they wanted. 4. Both houses had wall phones that could not be unplugged. We did ask not to call around the world for hours and that's all.*

She goes on to suggest how he should reply to questions when asked:

> *Maids treated like family, ate the same food, swam, played with Kenny, started work about 7-ish—finished about 2 and then sewing, swimming . . . How did Mom treat maids? Like a Mom—kindly, tried to teach them to do things right and look nice—Bought clothes, presents—Took them out to dinner and shows—treated them like family. Very nice, happy style of living—Had everything, lovely homes; they had own bedrooms, TV. You Kent, think the tutors took advantage of your parents. Nothing was ever enough for them. First they wanted more money, then their teeth capped, then more clothes, finally if pressed too hard or taken too much, we'd fire them—then they would be angry—they had a really soft life and unbelievable deal—they kept wanting more and more and did not do their duties.*
>
> *What was personality of your Mom? Bubbly happy, fun-loving, loved a happy home but wanted things done well. Liked a clean house. You saw letters mailed . . . they were paid . . . they usually wanted cash. Did your folks know maids were illegal? No, all maids came from agency and folks paid a lot of money to Surfside Agency. The tutors you saw were very*

self-centered and our lifestyle went to their head. A lot of maids would steal a lot—would take advantage—seemed to be very happy and loved the life we led. Most people would like to be Mom's maids—spoiled but then took advantage.

The letter rambles on and on in the same repetitive vein with constant reminders that Kent was "next in line." She also talked about his "rightful inheritance," urging him to *"get closer and closer and take over diplomatically from Papa because he's older and tired and very sick."*

In yet another letter to Kent, she reminds him again that David Kazdin was an important witness for her. She also asks her son to visit her in jail, as she will have ready *"the little preparation letters for all the witnesses—about 20 of them or 30—then take them to each witness . . . they need help and preparation,"* so they will know how and what to say when they testify, she wrote.

Sante did not testify in her own defense. Instead, her defense attorney Dominic Gentile argued that jurors didn't have to like Sante to acquit her of the charges. He suggested that there wasn't enough evidence to convict her on slavery charges because the maids voluntarily entered their employment and there was no retaliation after they left. His explanation to jurors as to why Sante was strict and secretive with her maids was that she feared that her husband's relatives, whom she referred to as "The Creeps," were trying to harm her and her young son.

In closing arguments, assistant U.S. Attorney Karla Dobinsiki called Sante "a greedy, cunning, and cruel woman" who lied to the maids, coerced them into staying at the Kimes' homes, and made promises to them that she never kept. Sante cried softly during the prosecutor's arguments and at one point yelled out dramatically, "It's all lies!"

The jury began deliberations the afternoon of February 27. As deliberations dragged into a second day, Sante, the non-stop schemer, wrote her "Papa, Love" a four-page note late that night, saying:

[If] *we lose, then we have won 2 years time for appeal which gives you time to liquidate. You have the Magic Saving*

Solution—Liquidate. You know they will win the civil suit. The money is what they are after. If you protect the money, they lose, no matter what. With the other maids coming in to sue, it's going to be in the millions. Remove the money and there won't even be pennies for them to get and it will all fade away.

Finally, after nine hours of deliberations, the slavery case jury found Sante guilty of 14 felony counts, including her escape from federal custody.

While she awaited sentencing, Sante next turned to the insurance company that carried her homeowner's policy, demanding that they cough up the millions of dollars her former maids were seeking from her in a civil suit for enslaving them.

"You can be insured if somebody trips and falls on your front step, but we don't insure people for keeping slaves," said Jeffrey Portnoy, a Honolulu civil attorney who represented the insurance company in the case. A former New Yorker, Portnoy has 25 feet of files related to Sante's slave case and also the second arson in 1990 involving the Portlock residence. Portnoy recalled that a group of lawyers were sent from the insurance company in Hawaii to take Sante's deposition while she was serving her slavery sentence at the Pleasanton Correctional Facility in California. After taking her statement under oath, the lawyers wound up at a restaurant that evening, where they were surprised to find Kent Walker, who had earlier been tailing them. When the lawyers left the restaurant, a car came swerving around the corner and forced all of them to jump out of the way to avoid being hit by the car. "It was Kent. He didn't want to hit them, he merely wanted to threaten them, scare them. If Kent has suddenly found religion now, it's because it will make a good book, but he was part of it. No doubt about it. You don't grow up in that environment without becoming part of it. He may be trying to distance himself from his mother, but I find it very ironic," said Portnoy, who has practiced law for 30 years. "She is dangerous to the point where people feel for their personal safety and property," he said.

At one point during the lengthy litigation, Portnoy said he found himself opposing not just Sante, but "scores of lawyers she had hired, including people pretending to be lawyers who did not exist," he said.

In deposing the tutors, Portnoy said they described in detail "bizarre conduct" at the house, including Kenny's temper tantrums when he didn't get his own way. They also described how Sante demanded that she be "treated like Queen Elizabeth." The household staff was not permitted to speak to her unless given prior permission. The maids were banished to small rooms when they weren't performing their duties. The tutors were brought in because Sante did not want any outside influence on Kenny, who was totally isolated.

"There is nothing anyone can tell me about Sante and what she did to Kenny as a young boy that I wouldn't believe. I have never met anyone more diabolical, more evil, more sinister, and more manipulative, and she had the money to make these things happen," Portnoy said. "The court proceedings went into the millions of dollars on a case that should have been a joke from the beginning. Sante managed to tie up this case for years in court by calling in all kinds of legal talent and ignoring court orders. With the money at her disposal, she manipulated the legal system and scared these insurance carriers into paying some money, which clearly was wrong, but at some point they had to make an economic decision to settle the matter. She made her evilness work for her."

By the time Kenneth Kimes was arrested with Sante in 1985 on the slavery charge, it was too late to help him. He had withered and lost the vigorous look he had when he first met Sante. "The muscle tissue in his body was beginning to give way, and his abuses of alcohol and the drugs Sante slipped him in his food took its toll. No longer did he look like Jimmy Stewart or have the build of a Burt Lancaster with a David Niven sort of face. His dyed hair looked awful," one of his nephews said.

When one of his brothers visited Kimes at the jail before his release on bail, he was overheard telling him that he couldn't get away from her. "Where could I go? There's no family to go to. There's nothing left," Kimes said sadly. He was right. "But don't worry, I never did marry her and I never will. I just can't get away from her," Kimes reassured his brother.

Before sentencing in the slavery trial was meted out for Kenneth Kimes, the millionaire motel mogul sent Judge McKibben a four-page letter relating his early background growing up on a 140-acre farm in the rural district of Prague, Oklahoma. Kimes told of attending school two miles from home, of his paper route, and of his subscribers, who paid him for the *Oklahoma Daily News* with chickens, eggs, butter, vegetables, and fruit. He described how he got interested in building homes after his family moved to Salinas, California, and how he saved $300 to buy a lot and build a home that cost $1,700, which he later sold for $2,700. Serving in the U.S. Army interrupted his budding building career, and after being honorably discharged in 1945, he returned to Salinas where he was attracted to the motel industry. After building his first motel in Monterey, Kimes went on to develop 50 more motels up and down the coast of California, until his motels made him a millionaire, many times over.

He also told the judge of his 15-year marriage to Charloette Taylor, which ended in divorce, and that he was awarded custody of his two then teenage children. Then he related how he was introduced to Sante Walker in Palm Springs. "It became obvious that almost every place I went, she was close by," he said. He described how his family "developed a positive dislike for her. I believe they felt that she was not sincere about my welfare, but was more concerned about her own.

"I decided that the family needed time to adjust to Sante, so I refrained from forcing her on them. As I look back and analyze the situation, my feeling is that Sante, with her motives, was trying to separate me from my family, mainly because she never had a family. She developed resentment toward them because of their closeness and love for each other. I'm sure our relationship would not have survived, except for our ten-year-old son, Kenny."

Kimes bared his soul to the judge, admitting that he did nothing to stop Sante from hiring illegal aliens. "I have spent too much time with business concerns and too little with concerns about the operation of my home." He conceded he ran the business, while "Sante took care of the home. My crime, if any, is one of omission, rather than commission, for I have never in my life knowingly broken the law."

On May 15, Judge Howard McKibben sentenced Sante Kimes to five years in prison on each count, but ordered the sentences to run concurrently. At the same time, he chastised Ken Kimes and told him that while he did not directly commit any of the acts, he did nothing to stop Sante from abusing the women. "I can't condone your activities," he said. "I think the message sent out by this court is that it will not tolerate this kind of conduct."

The judge fined Kimes $70,000 and gave him a suspended three-year prison sentence, except for a 60-day period in an alcohol treatment center.

McKibben called the case "one of the most unusual cases he had ever presided over." He said it was obvious that Sante "suffered from fairly substantial emotional disturbances. You engaged in long-standing activity of bringing in illegal aliens to the country. You have little concern for the laws of the United States and continued to violate the law."

McKibben was right on target. Sante wasted no time while in federal prison or when she was released in December 1989, in continuing the work of the devil.

10

"She's never going to let me go. It's futile."

Once Sante began to serve her sentence, Ken Kimes got rid of the tutors and enrolled Kenny in St. Viator's Catholic Elementary School in Las Vegas. Neil Huffey, one of Kenny's best friends at St. Viator's, recalled him as "just a regular boy. He was very popular in our class, even though he didn't participate in sports like so many of us. He was very inquisitive about the world. He had a tendency to throw great parties at his house while his mother was in prison. The movie *Casino* with Robert DeNiro and Sharon Stone was filmed right down the street from the Kimes residence."

Neil spent many weekends with Kenny at his home playing basketball or skateboarding. "Kenny wanted to be a good athlete but he was uncoordinated. At school, he was the class clown and always did the things in class that made you laugh. He was quite witty and intelligent. He was well versed in the history of antique cars. He never spoke to us about his mother, and it wasn't until high school years that we found out that she was in prison," Neil said. "When we asked where she was, he'd reply offhandedly, 'she's away,' as if she was at camp or at a resort."

The year Kenny graduated from St. Viator he wrote in his year-book that his favorite music group was INXS. His future plans included "to become a lawyer and an actor." His favorite TV show was *Wiseguy*. The person he admired most was "My Dad."

Kenny had virtually no contact with his mother while she was in prison. "He didn't even want to speak to her on the phone. He was ashamed of her," a neighbor said. "He often voiced his hatred for his mother."

In a two-page letter to Kenny on February 22, 1986, Sante con-stantly reminded him that she loved him *". . . more than anything and am thinking of you every second. Kiss my picture goodnite and I am with you—always. Send me silent kisses and hugs, OK? Write me a letter honey and Kent will mail it to me, please. I would love to get a letter from you. Tell me what you are doing and thinking."* Sante signed it, *"Your lovin Mom,"* and sealed it with a big red lipstick smooch imprinted at the bottom of the letter.

Six days later, Sante wrote Kenny again, a four-page letter, mailed shortly before his 11th birthday. *"It's a bad time for us right now because bad people are trying to get our money. There are a lot of bad people trying to lie so they can get our money. Don't worry, they won't. We will win—but we have to all stick together honey."* The letter drones on for pages with the same repetitive theme of sticking together, always reminding him to *"never forget how much your mother loves you and needs your love."* Toward the end of the letter she abruptly asks Kenny his weight and *"are your warts all gone?"*

With his mother temporarily out of the picture, Kenny seemed to thrive during his adolescent years. "Kenny referred to his mother's imprisonment as his 'golden years,'" said Vittorio Raho, a school-mate from St. Viator's Catholic Elementary School and now a med-ical student at the University of Nevada in Reno. "His father was a very kind guy, a good friend. We'd go over to his house and he'd buy ten McDonald's [meals]. There would be four or five of us there lazing around."

Raho recalled that while Sante was in federal prison, Kenny's father put a rush on construction of a swimming pool in back of their Geronimo Way home in time for his son's birthday. Later, Kimes took Kenny, Vittorio, and another friend on a weekend trip to Beverly Hills, where they stayed at a Rodeo Drive hotel, shopped, and ate breakfast in bed.

"Kenny had a very creative mind; he was always thinking ahead, always well prepared, but pretty much a dreamer," said Neil Huffey, who now works in Vegas as a gaming analyst for a resort hotel. "He wasn't very aggressive. He never displayed a temper. That's not the Kenny I know. He talked about his dad a lot and said he wanted to become a real estate developer like him. He had a very good relationship with his dad, and when he passed away, his whole life just crumbled."

Kimes, Sr., was devoted to his son and gave Kenny freedom and friends, lifting the social constraints that Sante had imposed on him throughout his young life. "The house was a fun house while she was off in prison," Neil said. "But it was a very strange house. What I remember most is that it was cluttered with knick-knacks, collectibles, artifacts, and lots of TVs; some worked, others that didn't. When his mother came back in the picture, everything changed."

Shortly before Sante's release from prison, Kenny had a heart to heart talk with his half-brother. According to Kenny, "Kent and his wife sat me down, and Lynn said, 'If you go back to your mother, you're going to end up in jail for the rest of your life.'"

"I have to go back," Kenny said. "No matter what I do, she's going to make me go back. You don't know my mother. She's never going to let me go. It's futile. I might as well go there now because I'll wind up there anyway."

Once Sante was out of prison and back in control of Kenny, her first order of business was to pull him out of Bishop Gorman High School two months into his freshman year and enroll him at Green Valley High School, a public school in Henderson, Nevada, a suburb of Las Vegas. "She just manipulated his every move. Kenny was very unhappy," Neil recalled.

Kenny remained enrolled at Green Valley for only one year and eventually earned his high school diploma by passing the Government Educational Development (GED) test.

"The best time of my life was when my mother was in jail," Kenny said. "It was the glory days. The house was the center of my life and headquarters to my friends who hung out with me. It was like a playhouse. We'd have pinball games and pool tables. It was a fun house and dad was very generous, very warm to my friends."

Kenny may have recognized that rejecting his mother was the right move to make, but he was not able to overcome Sante's domineering drive, and he was resigned to give in to her demands. The relentless fights between Sante and his father made an everlasting impression on Kenny. "Both drank to excess, and they would engage in these combative battles. One day, Mom threw a whiskey glass at my father and hit him in the head. It bled so much that he had to be taken to the hospital, where he needed a number of stitches to close the wound," Kenny said.

"Most of the fights were about money for Kent," Kenny explained. "Kent always wanted money and Mom wanted Dad to give him the money. She was relentless. Kent kept coming back for more money and more money. He'd be given $100,000 by Dad, and six months later, he'd come back and asked for another $200,000. And Dad would say, 'What happened to the first hundred?' And Kent had no explanation as to where it went."

Whenever Kenny bonded with a friend, Sante was right there, making sure it didn't last. "She would move to another house in another state to get me away from that person. She wanted to control everyone I hung out with. She didn't like anybody who was my friend," Kenny recalled.

Sante wanted Kenny to rely only on her and used what amounted to brainwashing tactics to create and maintain their symbiotic relationship. She once told her son that the two of them "were superior and better than everybody else. 'We're geniuses and they are pieces of shit,' she'd say. 'We're above everybody else. We're royalty. Kenny, everybody else uses five percent of their brain. We use 75 percent. We're geniuses and the rest of the world are a bunch of idiots. We're special because we use more of our brain than anyone else.'"

Kenny began his college education at the University of California in Santa Barbara, on a picturesque 989-acre palm-and-eucalyptus-lined plateau overlooking the Pacific, near the Santa Ynez Mountains. With an enrollment of 18,000 students—16,000 of them undergraduates and about 2,000 residing on campus—it was a bustling community.

The university is the same institution that Sante alleged she had attended after graduating from Carson City High School more than forty years earlier. Sante may have considered her son a genius and superior to others, but by the end of his first semester as a freshman in the fall of 1993, his grades were abysmal. He wound up with two Ds—in American Government and in Politics and Social Organization—while managing to squeak by in Human Anatomy with a C-plus.

By the 1994 winter session, after moving into the co-ed residential Santa Cruz Hall dorm at the college, Kenny's learning abilities seemed to improve. He earned a B in Music and Pop Culture, a C-minus in American Government and Politics, and a B-plus in Religious Studies.

Alan Katje, a retired California highway patrol officer, was at his desk at the UCSB campus security office working as a dispatcher in late March 1994 when he got an anxious call from Sante saying she had sent her son, a student, airline tickets for a trip to New York over the spring break and he had not received it. For some inexplicable reason, she thought the tickets might be in the office of the Dean of Students. Katje went looking for the elusive tickets and tracked an envelope addressed to Kenny to the Federal Express office in town. When he reported the news to Sante, she asked if he would do her "another favor" and deliver the envelope to Kenny "because his car had broken down." She not only offered to pay him for the service but promised him a trip to the Bahamas "as her guest."

"From the phone conversations, she sounded a bit strange, eccentric, and overprotective of her son," Katje recalled. It is also doubtful that the misplaced envelope to Kenny actually contained tickets to New York City. About six weeks later, Sante was back on the phone with a new problem. If her first request was out of the ordinary, the second request was bizarre. Kenny's roommate had come down with mononucleosis, and she wanted Katje to sterilize his dorm room.

"You are blowing this out of proportion," he told Sante, turning her down.

Having her son in college didn't deter Sante from pursuing more of her illegal schemes. During the same week in March that Sante sent Katje to look for the envelope, she and Kimes walked into the First American Title Insurance Company on State Street in Santa Barbara and asked for a property profile on a property in Santa Maria. "The funny thing is that no one in my office wanted to go to the front counter to help them, because they looked so Las Vegas," recalled Carolene Davis, the title company service manager. "She had on a white ruffled blouse, white chiffon slacks, pink rimmed glasses, long fake nails, heavy false eyelashes, a big black wig and a lot of makeup. For a man his age, he looked absolutely ridiculous in a white John Travolta-style buttoned-down shirt from the '70s and it was obvious that he dyed his gray hair black."

Carolene prepared the documents, and when she handed them to Kimes, he pulled out a wad of $100 bills to pay her. She refused to take it, however, telling him, "It's complimentary, through my company," as she handed him her business card. Sante tucked it away in her purse. She would soon have a use for Carolene.

A few days later, on March 28, 1994, Sante and Ken Kimes were outside the Wells Fargo Bank in Goletta in nearby Santa Barbara, less than five minutes from Kenny's dorm. She went inside to transact some business, leaving Kimes in the car. When Sante came out of the bank, Kimes was dead. He had died of a fatal aneurysm. To this day, the Kimes family is convinced that Sante had been spiking his drinks by feeding him a drug that further weakened his already damaged heart. Relatives and friends visiting the elderly Kimes would often see Sante giving him his "protein drink." There was only a limited autopsy, and two days after Kimes' death, he was cremated. Then Sante, with Kent's help, set about to keep his death a secret by giving Santa Barbara officials false information about Kimes, such as an incorrect social security number (the man to whom the number was actually issued was declared dead and his social security check stopped), the wrong middle name, and the incorrect name for his parents. And instead of listing his 2121 Geronimo Way home address, Kent gave a post office box address in Las Vegas.

All of this misinformation prevented the real Kimes family from knowing that Kimes, Sr., had been dead for two years. The Kimes family blame Kent, who supplied false information to the Santa Barbara coroner, for allowing Sante and Kenny to steal the Kimes estate from the rightful heirs.*

In an eight-page private letter in November 2000 to the Santa Barbara Superior Court, in which Sante protested the appointment of Linda Kimes as the administrator of her father's estate, Sante described their "30-year" marriage this way:

> Ours was and always will be, the sweetest, sexiest, [most] scintillating, wonderful marriage ever. Our incredible love affair lives on and on. What a wondrous, loving, exciting life we had! A life that even the rich and famous would envy! He was the most loving husband, and we had the greatest love affair and marriage of all time. We could not keep our hands off of each other, even after 30 years! My wonderful papa! On the last day of his life and of our incredible, wondrous love story, after 30 years of our magical love affair, he turned and embraced me, in front of everyone and he said: "I love you, Mama Kimes!" And then he died.

Kimes's death didn't stop Sante from signing his name on checks and deeds to property he owned in Santa Maria, California, including two forged deeds she filed after his death.†

---

*The Social Security Administration stopped Sante's $1,100 a month survivor benefits in June 2000, after her sentencing, and informed her that the government intended to go after her for overpayments made since the death of Kimes, Sr., in 1994.

†Sante was able to keep Kimes "financially alive" until she was caught in July 1998.

"She's never going to let me go. It's futile."

Sante wasted no time mourning Kimes's loss. In early April 1994, she was on the phone to Carolene Davis and made no mention of her sudden bereavement. "It was just a normal chitchat conversation about how helpful I had been and how 'Papa said you were so darling. You were the daughter we never had.'" Sante was off and running on what was the beginning of a long friendship with Carolene, whom she called constantly, asking her to check on property in Florida, Los Angeles, the Bahamas, and New York.

When Sante learned that Carolene and her husband, Tim, a construction worker, were planning a weekend trip to Las Vegas, she insisted the couple stay with her at her 2121 Geronimo Way home. Sante could turn on the charm when she wanted to, and that's what she did with the Davises. "She didn't take no for an answer," Carolene said. "She had Kent take us to dinner at Caesar's Palace, and the next day she took me shopping at Neiman Marcus, buying me a $300 cocktail dress that she paid for with crisp $100 bills. She was very generous. She was like my second mother. It was just too much fun being out with her."

Carolene recounted the times she and Sante went shopping. Sante would put on a pearl necklace in the store and the next thing Carolene knew, Sante was out the door, still wearing the necklace. "She had just stolen that necklace. Or we'd be at the Elephant Bar in Santa Barbara having lunch and cocktails. She'd just tear up the bill and walk out of the restaurant. Sante liked to get away with little things. It was a thrill for her," Carolene said.

"When we got into the store, people would turn and say, 'Gosh, is that Elizabeth Taylor?' It was neat. Sante had this beautiful ring on her finger that she said was a diamond and it sparkled. She always wore white and she was beautiful."

Bates-Stone, Sante's former Hawaiian neighbor, said the ring was a fake. "Sante claimed Ken bought her this ten-carat diamond, but Ken told my former husband he never bought her the ring and that it was one of those cheap knock-offs," Bates-Stone said.

Carolene was also fond of Kenny, whom she met when he was 19 years old. "He was a typical teenager. Wild, a lot of energy, raring to go to parties. He was a great kid." Yet, the Davises found that it was difficult to get close to Kenny, primarily because Sante wouldn't let them.

Carolene very much admired Sante's home. "It was a dream house. When you walked in, there was a really big living room with a piano. Upstairs there were five bedrooms and four bathrooms. There was a pink panther that greeted you at the top of the staircase. It was Sante's way of saying 'welcome.' She had satin sheets on all the beds, a big mirror. We'd sit and talk for hours in her bedroom. It was wonderful. I loved that house."

It was during Carolene's second trip to the Geronimo Way house that she finally learned of Kimes's death. "We were in her bedroom watching TV, and Sante snuggled up to me and said she wanted to talk to me. I could tell from the tone in her voice and the look in her eyes that she was so sincere," Carolene recalled.

"Sante began to cry and was so emotional before she could spit it out. She said, 'You were so fortunate to have met him. He was such a wonderful man in my life. He's gone now. He passed away in Santa Barbara.' She made me promise never to tell anyone that Papa had died, not even Kenny, who just happened to be home for the weekend from school."

A few weeks later, Kenny stopped by Carolene's house for a home cooked meal. After dinner, Carolene and Tim were sitting around the table when Kenny blurted out that his mother had been in prison. "He told us that he beat her when she came home. He jumped on her and started punching her because he was so mad at her for being home from prison," Tim said.

Sante again called Alan Katje, the university security officer, sometime in April, telling him that her husband was very sick and that he, Katje, was a godsend. "You're helping my boy. Kenny has nobody else," she said dramatically. Never again did she make any mention of a New York trip.

At the time, Sante was very convincing. It was only later that Katje began to see through her. "This is where she really started her con," said Katje. "It took me a while to learn that Sante uses and abuses people and then throws them away like yesterday's trash."

Sante went to work on Katje, setting him up so that he would let his guard down. "I think you are like Kenny's guardian angel," she told him, "He needs somebody here that he can depend on. Kenny's dad is really, really sick, and he's fallen deathly ill, and Kenny does not even know about this. I don't want him to know. It would ruin his studies."

Sante rattled on about how brilliant Kenny was. By the next phone call, Sante moved along the progress of Kimes's demise, saying he had had a stroke and was in very bad shape. She made several more calls seeking favors of one sort or another, always dangling the carrot of a Bahamas trip. Then in early June, while Kenny and the other students throughout the university were cramming for finals, Sante called Katje, purportedly from Hawaii, and asked if he would buy Kenny a $40 flight bag for his trip to Honolulu. She sadly told him that "Papa passed away."

"Kenny still doesn't know," she explained. "He doesn't even know that he's been ill. I need you to get him on a plane that will take him to Hawaii. But you can't tell him that Papa has died."

"Why can't Kenny know that his own father has passed away?" Katje asked. As usual, Sante was right there with an answer.

"If he were to find out that his father is dead, he would be so overwrought he would not be able to concentrate on his studies. It would destroy his concentration and he would not be able to finish out the school year, and it would have been wasted. When he gets to Hawaii, we'll tell him. Papa would have wanted it that way," she replied.

Kenny was puzzled that his father was not at the airport to greet him and, as he later related to Katje, when he got off the plane in Hawaii, he asked his mother, "Where's Papa?"

Sante walked him to the waiting car, opened up the rear door of the sedan, pointed to an urn resting on the floor, and calmly said, "There's Papa."

Kenny scattered the ashes in Hawaii, and a few weeks later, they returned to Las Vegas to spend the summer.

Just before the school term ended, Kenny had gotten involved in a fight with a student in his dorm whom Kenny felt was playing his stereo too loud. According to the story Kenny told Katje, the other guy burst into his room screaming at him, pushed him and hit him, and the two got into a fight, which sent the other student to the hospital with injuries. Although the student didn't want to press charges, a police report was made of the incident. At the start of the new semester in the fall of 1994, the college started a disciplinary action against Kenny, and he was kicked out of Santa Cruz Residential Hall.

"I wasn't surprised. I knew Kenny had a temper," said Katje's wife, Trish, who recalled a knock down, drag-out fight Sante had with her son at their home after she learned that he was sneaking into a dorm where he had been banned. "Kenny loved the thrill of adventure and getting away with it, and Sante kept feeding into that type of behavior. If he had been left alone, he could have been a normal kid."

Kenny's expulsion from the dormitory was very upsetting to Sante. She got heavily involved in the college disciplinary hearings, even going so far as to fly into Santa Barbara to personally confront the chancellor of the university about her son's ouster from the campus dorm.

Despite the turmoil in Kenny's life, that spring semester in 1994 actually turned out to be one of his best academically, earning him an A-minus in Introduction to Communication, an A in Introduction to Oceanography, a B-minus in an English writing course, and a C-plus in Social Organization.

In July, Sante called Alan Katje again, asking him to drive to Las Vegas with Kenny's computer, which Kenny had left at Katje's home for safekeeping before he went to Hawaii. It was the first time Katje met the mysterious voice he had come to know as Sante. "She was very flamboyant; she was dressed to the hilt in a fancy white pants suit and she looked like Elizabeth Taylor."

"Sante took me up to her bedroom," recalled Katje, "showed me a picture of Mr. Kimes with Vice President Ford, and then asked if I could get her a gun. 'I need it for protection. There's no man around,' she said."

Some time later, Katje received another call from Sante about the gun, and he agreed to bring her three firearms: a .380 semi-automatic, a .38 revolver, and a .357 Magnum heavy-duty revolver. Katje drove over to Las Vegas in late July, and Sante selected the .380 semi-automatic, giving Katje $100 for the gun. Ten days later, Sante returned the gun and got a refund.

As Kenny had no place to live, Sante prevailed on Katje for yet another favor. She asked if Kenny could rent a room in Katje's house. "Alan set a price of $450 a month, but she went behind his back, spoke to me, and I unknowingly lowered the price to $375 a month," Trish said. Sante, ever the Miss Clean, sent four guys from the Salvation Army to go to the Katje home and clean up the den where Kenny was going to set up housekeeping.

In late October 1994, Kenny became a member of the Katje household and stayed with them until April 1995. "I treated him like the younger brother I never had," Katje said. "We'd lift weights together, watch movies. Kenny was a lot of fun. He had a real zest for life. He brought a sense of joy and adventure to the house. He always had a big smile on his face. He used to pick me up and give me a crushing bear hug to show me how strong he was. He'd bring his friends over, and we'd rent action-adventure movies. He never took advantage of us. My wife and I trusted him with our children, Amanda, then 7, and Tim, 13. He baby-sat them when we were out. His only problem was that his mother controlled everything about his life. He didn't have a checking account; he had hardly any money. He always had to go to her if he needed money.

"Kenny liked to play the stock market. He owned several stocks," Katje said. "Among them, AT&T and Xerox, and he followed them quite extensively, watching them closely on the financial television news on television. He claimed he was taking business courses at UCSB and was talking about going to work at a brokerage firm and wanting to go to Columbia University in New York. He was a smart kid and had the ability if he had stayed focused on staying in school and had kept his grades up."

In November 1995, Sante decided to visit Kenny for an extended stay. After looking at several possibilities, she decided on a prominent physician's residence near the school, which would be available for six months. Without seeking permission, she pulled up to the front door of the magnificently furnished home, complete with an observation deck that overlooked the ocean, and convinced the groundskeeper that she had actually rented the property. She wound up moving into the house illegally, forging the signature of the owner on the lease. She even tried to get the security dispatcher at Kenny's college to break into the house, claiming she had changed the locks and couldn't find the keys in the house she claimed to have rented.

"I began to call her the witch woman. She used and abused me shamelessly. I'd catch her in lies," Katje said. "She claimed she needed to let the houseman into the home and kept wanting me to break into the house."

"No way, Sante," Katje told her before slamming the phone in her ear. "But she got into the house anyway, and when the owner returned and found out about a strange woman living in his house, he initiated eviction proceedings. But Sante threatened *him* with legal action, using my address to forward her mail.

"At one time, a city marshall came to my house looking for Sante to serve her with a subpoena after she had stiffed an engineer and contractor she had hired to survey the Santa Maria property," Katje added.

By the winter of 1995, possibly as the result of Sante's pressure, Kenny's grades headed south.

Although Sante treated the Katjes as friends, even family, she in fact dealt with them like any other mark. A sore spot with Katje, who was pressed for money at the time, was that Sante was always two months behind in the rent for Kenny's room. "She claimed she had cash-flow problems and gave me a story that she had gone to Hong Kong to conduct some business. And when the people there heard that her husband died, they took advantage of her and her investments went sour, causing her to lose three or four million dollars," Katje said.

After Kenny moved out of the Katje's home in April, he settled into a duplex apartment at 6795A Trigo in Isla Vista. Sante kept dropping in on Kenny unexpectedly to stay with him at the apartment, and his housemates complained about her presence.

Meanwhile, Katje said he made several 70-mile "Driving Miss Sante" trips to the Santa Maria property, north of Santa Barbara. "It was obvious she didn't know what she was doing. She came across as flamboyant, wearing this huge four or five carat ring that Kimes supposedly gave her. She told me it wasn't the real ring, because she couldn't wear the real one for fear it would be stolen. She told us it was glass.

"One gentlemen told her outright that he had no interest in her property. 'You've wasted my time. You are out to lunch,'" Katje said the prospective buyer told Sante.

Kenny's temper persisted in Isla Vista, and he had a problem with Carrie Louise Grammar, a student at UCSB. Grammar alleged that while she found Ken, as she called him, "very charismatic" and "charming," he also had an "abusive personality." The young woman accused Kenny's cat of soiling her roommate's bed linen, which cost $70 to replace. Kenny agreed to reimburse the entire amount, but when it came time to collect the money, Kenny reneged on the deal, giving her half that amount and telling her to "fuck off."

According to Grammar, Kenny went on a rampage and "came at me in a threatening manner with an infuriated expression in his face. His eyes were squinted, his jaw stuck out, his lips were pinched, and his face was red. He proceeded to angrily curse at me . . . I felt that he was going to hit me." According to Grammar, Kenny called her a "classless bitch," "a slut," a "little whore who turns tricks," and many other degrading things. On October 25, 1995, she sought a restraining order against him.

"He is very cunning," she said. "Ken only does things when he thinks he won't get caught. He is very good at not getting caught."

In his defense, Kenny claimed in a four-page sworn statement that Grammar hit him in the chest "with a clenched fist." He also swore that Grammar "started screaming at the top of her lungs for no reason in an extremely psychotic manner." The document was notarized by none other than Nevada notary Nanette Wetkowski, Sante's personal notary, who put her official stamp on such legal documents as the forged deed to the Silverman mansion, the various fake owners of the Santa Maria property, and much more. By November 17, 1995, Judge Thomas Adams issued a mutual restraining order barring both Grammar and Kenny from threatening, telephoning, or following each other's movements.

Kenny dropped out of UCSB after his spring 1996 semester. He had gotten into a "low-speed, bumper-thumper, two-mile-an-hour minor accident," Katje recalled. "There was no damage to the cars, but a couple of days later Kenny showed up in Trish's office at health services, saying Sante wanted him to be referred to a chiropractor.

When Trish explained to Kenny that a physician on staff would have to see him first, Kenny became adamant and refused. "No, I have to do what my mother tells me to do," he said sadly. "Kenny was so forlorn as he spoke, and it was obvious Sante was looking to get a big settlement from a bogus accident and wanted to sue the other driver in yet another insurance scam."

Trish was unsuccessful in convincing Kenny that he was old enough to make up his own mind and should stand up to his mother. A short time after that, Sante called Katje. "Kenny has had to drop out of school because he was seriously injured as a result of the traffic accident and in so much pain that he was unable to concentrate in his studies," she said.

Katje next heard from Kenny in March 1997, when Kenny began selling Cuban cigars that had been imported illegally.

"I've got it figured out," an exuberant Kenny said to his friend. "My business is based in the Bahamas."

When asked where in Cuba he was buying the cigars, Kenny said, "I'm meeting smugglers in back alleys of Cuba and slums."

"You could see the excitement in his face. He had gotten into this dark element and it really turned him on and excited him. He was wearing an expensive gold watch on his wrist," Katje said.

When Katje warned him that he could get his throat slit, Kenny assured him that, "I know what I'm doing. Don't worry about me." He gave Katje his web site address and a business card for "Kenny's Diamond—The Cuban Cigar Man."

Katje, an ex-Marine, a Vietnam vet, and a former law enforcement officer, could tell from the look on Kenny's face that his young friend wanted something from him. "Alan, do you still have that .380 handgun?" he asked.

"Why?"

"We want to buy it," Kenny said.

"He claimed he wanted to bring it into the Bahamas, because a neighbor had just been mugged," recalled Katje.

Katje gave Kenny a story that he had sold it and no longer had any guns. "Besides, there was no way they could get a gun into the Bahamas. It was obvious to me that they only wanted the gun for some illegal purpose."

As Kenny and Sante drove away from the Katje's home for the last time, he turned to his wife, Trish, and said, "The next time we'll be seeing the two of them will be on the news, sometime in the future, after they've been arrested."

Katje wrote Kenny a poignant letter on August 30, 1998, while Kenny was an inmate at the Tombs in downtown Manhattan shortly after his arrest in the Silverman case. In a four-page letter, Katje warned Kenny that that his mother was a hideous, evil woman.

> It is something that you have known for a long time. Trish and I both knew that as soon as you dropped out of UCSB and went off with your mom that your life was pretty much shot. God, how I wish you could have had the strength to tell your mom 'no' when she convinced you to leave school. One thing I do want you to think about and consider is for you not to stay loyal to your mother. Do not protect her and think that she is going to get you out of all of this. What did she do to you in Florida when the guards were closing in on the two of you in reference to the shoplifting incident that got you arrested? She ran away and left you to be arrested. Trish and I blame your mother for sending you down this path of destruction. So, Kenny, don't stand by your mom, and do whatever you can to help yourself. Your mom is probably going to spend the rest of her life behind bars. You still have a lot of life ahead of you. Try and salvage what you can of your life . . . your friend, Alan.

Kenny never answered Katje's letter or a second letter the Katjes sent, in which they urged him to cooperate with authorities. "The Kenny Kimes we knew does not exist anymore. That Kenny Kimes is gone, totally gone. He had become a hardened criminal. Kenny likes to think he's so tough, but there's a lot tougher guys in prison. Besides, he's got a reputation now. He's a Mama's boy," Katje said.

Sante controlled Kenny all of his life, and after she got out of prison on the slavery charge, she got her hooks into her young son again. "She turned him into the dark side and he got to like it, to the point where he became frighteningly violent and acted out," Katje continued. "She got him to kill people. She just wore Kenny down to where he ended up doing stuff he would never have thought to do. He did not have the strength and character to say no to his mother. Unfortunately, once he got involved in the dark side, he got to love it. He got his excitement from it, and it became a focus of his life, and he had become his mother's son."

11

"Maybe she's out walking her dog"

Sante met the first of her defense lawyers that Monday, when José A. Muniz showed up to represent her during her brief appearance in AR 1, the arraignment part on the first floor of the Criminal Court Building. Sante had found Muniz through a bondsman, Renee Andrews, referred to her by one of her cellmates in Central Booking.

Muniz, an experienced criminal defense lawyer, was brought up by a single mother after his father died from a heroin overdose when Muniz was eight years old. He went on to Catholic school and then to Syracuse University, where he majored in psychology before going on to New York Law School on a scholarship. Despite 15 years in criminal law, representing those accused of murder, rape, and drug smuggling, as well as "small-time con artists," meeting Sante Kimes "was an experience," he said.

Muniz was initiated into Sante's world when she innocently told him on that first meeting, "This is only about a car. The car leaked and that is why we stopped payment on the vehicle. I don't know why we're here. I don't understand why we're arrested. My son is a great kid. We just came to visit New York."

A savvy lawyer, Muniz began to make inquiries about his strange new client. He became suspicious about her story when he learned that the joint FBI/NYPD Task Force had sent a dozen men on a holiday weekend to pick her up for a $14,000 car theft.

Sante's appearance in court was delayed. When Muniz was called away to Albany, New York, on an emergency, he asked a colleague, Matthew Weissman, to oversee the routine appearance, which didn't take place until the afternoon of July 7.

The 45-year-old Weissman was a novice in the criminal court arena. A graduate of Georgetown University with a master's degree in taxation, he was a civil litigator who primarily dealt in real-estate matters. His father was at one time an NYPD police surgeon, and the family lived in Scarsdale, a posh suburb of the city. In taking on Sante Kimes, he suddenly found himself immersed in a world that he'd never seen before, which included, as he put it, "jail, criminal court and Sante Kimes."

By the time Sante was arraigned, the front pages of the newspapers and the top story on radio and television were all about the disappearance of Irene Silverman. Weissman contacted Muniz on his cell phone with the news that the case is more than just the Utah warrant. After listening to the details, Muniz warned him, "Be careful. You must always remember who you are dealing with. You are dealing with a criminal mind, and she sounds like someone who would use us to get whatever she needs and not care what happens to us."

Scores of police were fanning out on the Upper East Side, looking for Irene Silverman. They searched for clues in Central Park and combed hospital and morgue records. Residents in the area were canvassed, and people were stopped on the street and questioned as to whether they had seen Irene. That evening, deputy inspector Joseph Reznick held a press conference on the third floor of the 19th precinct, seeking the public's assistance. The police were looking not only for Irene, but the tenant Manny Guerin as well.

Reznick, who was in charge of the elite Manhattan North Homicide Detective Squad when Irene disappeared, had a fearsome reputation amongst his peers. "He's the kiss of death for anybody who's a slacker and doesn't work," said an officer who fears him. "Joe is a stern, hard-nosed task master, a no-nonsense boss. He's extremely thorough," explained retired detective Joel Potter, one of the detectives Reznick hand-picked to work on the Silver Task Force.

"Whatever word there is beyond tenacious, that's the word I'd use to describe Joe. He's a phenomenal investigator," Police Commissioner Bernard Kerik said of the 50-year-old Reznick.

At a media briefing the evening of Monday, July 6, Reznick handed out copies of a photograph of the millionaire widow and a sketch of the missing tenant that a police artist made with the help of Irene Silverman's staff.

"Right now," said Reznick, "we have an elderly woman who has disappeared very mysteriously, and an occupant of an apartment whom she rented to less than three weeks ago who has also disappeared mysteriously. We have no clue as to where they are now."

TUESDAY, JULY 7, 1998

Shortly after 5:00 A.M. on Tuesday, July 7, Detective Thomas Hackett, working a turnaround shift, was asleep on a cot in the back of the detectives' squad room at the 19th precinct. He was awakened by a call from Detective Eddy Murray of the Task Force. "I think we got your man," Murray said.

Murray had seen an early morning newscast about the Silverman disappearance and on a hunch began reviewing police teletype messages. Eventually, he got to the sketch artist drawings of Manny Guerin and compared them with the arrest photos the task force had made of Kenny Kimes. Paydirt. He and Detective Ryan went to the federal building garage, checked the Lincoln car again, then notified his superiors.

Tommy Hackett beeped Reznick, who was by then on his way to work. Reznick called back and barked, "Rush downtown and talk to the Kimeses. Take the first person that comes in on the shift and get down there." Tommy took detective Diana Rohan with him.

By the time Reznick got back to his desk, he was seething, having realized that Silverman's tenant had been in custody since Sunday evening. He really blew his top when he learned that at no time after the Kimeses were arrested did any FBI agent or police detective from the Task Force involved in their arrest on July 5 question or even investigate further why the suspects had Irene Silverman's personal property in their possession.

"I yelled at the arresting officer at the top of my lungs. 'Let me get this straight. You arrested a person that had identification on them of an entirely different person and you mean to say you didn't follow up on it?'" Reznick said. The other detectives in the 19th detective squad room ducked for cover as Reznick chewed out the officer on the phone. "As a result of this monumental foul up," Reznick continued, "we lost a day and a half in this investigation. If we had been called on the evening of July 5, this case would have been solved much faster."

By 7:30 Tuesday morning, Detective Murray had Sante taken out of Central Booking and brought back to his office at FBI headquarters in the Federal Building. It was here that Hackett, a 17-year veteran of the force, tried to enlist her help in locating Mrs. Silverman.

"Look, I don't care how Mrs. Silverman got to where she is or who did it. I just want to find out where she is," Hackett pleaded with Sante, using an interrogation technique of talking to her in a soft, soothing voice. Hackett thought that the Kimeses might have Silverman tied up someplace, and were perhaps holding her ransom. "But," said Hackett, "she was foxy. She sat across the table from me and, when I explained why I was there, she kinda folded her hands and sat up, and I thought 'this is gonna be easy.' But it wasn't. It was a game with her. Sante never slipped up at all on anything I asked. She knew exactly what she was doing."

Hackett showed Sante the front-page headline of the *New York Daily News* about the missing socialite. He even handed her the newspaper, but even after reading the article, Sante said she didn't believe that the newspaper was genuine. "You could have printed this up yourself," she told Hackett.

Hackett told her, "It doesn't have to be a murder."

"I don't know what you're talking about," Sante said. "You should really put your energy into finding this woman. Maybe she's out walking her dog," she added condescendingly.

Hackett lost his cool. Raising his voice, he shouted, "She's 82 years old. This is not some bullshit car case. She ain't out walking her fucking dog for two days."

"Maybe after I speak to my lawyer, I can tell you what you need to know," Sante replied coquettishly.

Before sending Sante back to Central Booking, Hackett took her handbag, and inside he found the toilet paper note she planned to smuggle to Kenny, as well as a mysterious handwritten piece of paper with the words "PALAZA" and several numbers following it. The message on the flimsy scrawled piece of paper read:

> *My dearest. I'm so proud of you! Fight and Win. Don't be afraid. Real Estate I.S. to be secret. In large Carmel, 20ish. Don't be followed. Store Lincoln. Later stolen. Hide all papers at Erics or Atty. Muniz. Call Larry—he can help but don't tell all. Get a room. Protect RV. Live on and to apt and here too.*

It took detectives until the third week in July to decipher the toilet paper note, which turned out to be a very important clue that led to the Kimes' conviction.

What the vague, difficult-to-understand message meant was that once Kenny got out of jail on bail, he was not to disclose their clandestine activities about I.S.—the Irene Silverman mansion scheme—to anyone. She also instructs him to look in the Lincoln Town Car for a caramel-colored suitcase containing about $20,000 in cash and that after removing the money, he is to report the car stolen. She cautions him not to be followed and to hide the important documents in the car at either Eric's—the bondman's—office or with defense attorney José Muniz. She also tells Kenny to call Larry Ledford, a jailhouse lawyer she met while in prison years earlier, for help, but not to spill the beans as to what they've been up to. She also reminds her son that, once he's out of jail, he was to get to Florida and remove important documents left in the recreational vehicle they bought with a bogus check that they stored behind the Ritz Carlton hotel in nearby Palm Beach.

Of course, what Sante was unaware of was that the Joint FBI/NYPD Task Force had already recovered the Lincoln and that it was stored in a secure area of the basement at FBI headquarters. As New York detectives delved into the case, Florida police impounded the RV and removed the documents before the Kimeses could get their hands on it in the first month of the investigation.

By mid-afternoon of July 7, at the request of prosecutors, Manhattan Supreme Court Judge Leslie Crocker Snyder signed a search warrant authorizing the police to examine the contents of the Lincoln Town Car. The job of taking an inventory and itemizing everything found in the car was assigned to Detective Ed Wallace of the NYPD Crime Scene Unit, who spent 32 hours going over the car, a search so thorough that he even itemized a dead moth found in the vehicle. Among the items Wallace found in the rear seat were an empty stun gun box, with a receipt for it in the glove compartment, and a mason jar with liquid that contained "roofies"—a date rape drug police suspected was used on Mrs. Silverman to incapacitate her. In the back seat area was a caramel-colored suitcase that contained a 9 mm Glock, 15 cartridges, $22,000 in cash, forged social security cards, and a power of attorney in Irene Silverman's name, plus unused syringes, disposable rubber gloves, 15 notebooks, a computer, more than a dozen wigs (including a red one that Sante used when she posed as Irene Silverman), stocking lace caps, mace, plastic handcuffs, a microcassette recorder, tapes, Glock and Baretta manuals, and sophisticated eavesdropping devices.

After poring over the interior of the luxury car, Wallace went to the back of the vehicle and opened the trunk. It was viritually empty, except for a large black duffel bag, large enough for the six-foot detective to fit into.

12

"Looking for Irene's killer was the ultimate hunt"

The idea that a mother and son might be capable of murder gripped the nation. The case had all the essential ingredients—mystery, intrigue, murder, socialites—and involved exciting places like New York, Las Vegas, Palm Beach, the Bahamas, and Honolulu.

The lawyers for Sante and Kenny blasted the police and prosecutors, calling the case a frame-up. They insisted there wasn't any forensic evidence: no hair, fiber, blood, eyewitnesses, not even a body. From all appearances, at least on the surface, it seemed as if there wasn't a scintilla of evidence to connect the Kimeses with the disappearance of Irene, except a strong suspicion that they *must* have been responsible for her vanishing without a trace.

It was the job of Deputy Inspector Joseph Reznick to put together a group of NYPD's best detectives to form the Silver Task Force, and it was Connie Fernandez, the deputy bureau chief of the major offense career criminal program, who was chosen to lead the team of New York District Attorney Robert Morgenthau's most seasoned prosecutors.

Seven individuals formed the heart of the 50-member Silver Task Force that crisscrossed the nation from California to Florida and from Europe to the Bahamas, delving into the bizarre world of the Kimeses.

Joel Potter was one of the seven super-specialists that made for a successful prosecution of the Kimes case. Joel and his partner, Tony Vazquez, made three trips to Las Vegas on the case, where Joel learned to gamble with whatever was left over from the food allowance of $35 a day that he got from the city. "It turned Joel into a big winner," Tony said.

Another member of the core detective team was Sergeant Gene Wasielewski, who joined the police force in February 1973 after a four-year stint with the Air Force. Seventeen years later, he was a veteran of the special victims squad, handling high-profile rape cases as well as the robbery squad. At 52, Waz, as his colleagues knew him, was a hard-nosed homicide sergeant. His six-foot-three-inch size and tenacious attitude belied the teddy bear quality that lay beneath his intimidating demeanor.

Wasielewski and Reznick selected the other key members of the Silver Task Force, including John Schlagler, 53, a highly decorated cop in the police department who had received two medals of valor for dismantling two bombs: one at St. Patrick's Cathedral in 1982 and another in 1977 before the Steuben Day parade, planted by the Jewish Defense League.

John's partner of 15 years was Danny Rodriguez, a long-time detective who had done serious undercover work. Though quiet and unassuming, he was a bulldog in the field and considered one of the best detectives the city had ever had.

Two Tommys from the 19th precinct detective squad—Hackett and Ryan—made up the rest of the inner core of the task force. The 40-year-old Ryan was nicknamed "the phone-line guy" by other team members, because he was designated to trace every phone call Sante made from jail, on her cell phone, calls in and out of the mansion, and the 800-plus calls she made from a rented Palm Beach condo. Hackett was the property man, in charge of all vouchered property, who eventually knew the origin and whereabouts of any piece of property off the top of his head. He also teamed up with Joel Potter on the California portion of the investigation.

The main function of the homicide squad is to assist precinct detectives who have the ultimate responsibility for investigating any homicide that occurs in that precinct. Manhattan North Homicide Squad has been called an elite unit in the police department. It is made up of senior, seasoned specialists, detectives who have spent at least eight years learning their skills at the precinct level, before their bosses—the commanding officers—consider them worthy of transfer to the homicide squad. "It is a career goal within the detective division," Joel Potter explained.

"The foundation of the investigation is what took place that Tuesday, July 7, and it put us in the right direction," Reznick said. "Once we connected the Kimes name with the Silverman mansion, it started the ball rolling. One of the first things we did that day was to run a 'Triple I' check on them through a state computer that ties in with 34 other states. Prior to that, we were looking for a guy named Manny Guerin who was wanted in connection with Mrs. Silverman's disappearance."

Within an hour of feeding the Kimes' names into the computer, Reznick learned of Sante's 12 prior arrests, dating all the way back to 1961, when she was charged with petty larceny in Sacramento. He also learned that she had been convicted of slavery, had escaped from custody, and that she had stolen a mink coat in Washington, D.C.

"Given the fact that we learned who these people were, it was now a matter of finding out where these people came from," Reznick said. "With the assistance of the FBI, we started backtracking, and they furnished us with information regarding their involvement [in] the Utah warrant and the murder of David Kazdin in California. We accomplished more that Tuesday than any other day during the whole rest of the investigation. The foundation of our investigation was formed, and the corner pieces of the puzzle started to come together."

Irene Silverman's disappearance dominated the media, and reporters and photographers camped outside the 19th precinct, seeking any scraps of information. Because of the media circus outside the precinct, and the fact that it was getting cramped inside the detective squad room, Reznick moved the investigation uptown to a more secluded area, where not even the media knew how to find them. In fact, it was so secret that the Silver Task Force was not even listed in any official phone book directory of the NYPD.

THURSDAY, JULY 9, NEW YORK CITY

By Thursday, investigators were aware that the mother and son con artists had asked two notaries to notarize a document that already bore Irene Silverman's signature. The first notary, Don Aoki, told detectives about a meeting on July 1, 1998, with a bedridden granny wearing a red wig and red glasses, a nightgown and a nightcap, inside a dimly lit bedroom of the mansion, who was trying to trick him into verifying a forged deed. Like the wolf impersonating the grandmother in "Little Red Riding Hood," she was half-covered with blankets and sitting in bed, Aoki said. Aoki refused to notarize the deed, because it was already signed "Irene Z. Silverman." He was then offered a one-page sworn affidavit purportedly bearing Irene's signature, stating she had signed the document on July 5, 1997, in Las Vegas, Nevada, before Nanette Wetkowski, the in-house personal notary, under a $250 monthly retainer by Sante Kimes. But again, Aoki insisted the document had to be signed in his presence.

Although unable to identify the disguised Sante as the granny in the bed, Aoki did recognize and identify Kenny as "Mr. Wynn," the man he met at the Plaza Athenée hotel around the corner from the mansion and who escorted him to apartment 1B at 20 East 65th Street.

The second notary, Noelle Sweeney, said she received a call from a woman named "Ellie" asking if she would notarize a document for an elderly client at the town house address. Sweeney told detectives that on the morning of July 2, she met "Anthony Wynn" at the Plaza Athenée and he took her to the mansion. When she entered the living room of apartment 1B, "Wynn" called out in the direction of the bedroom, "Mrs. Silverman, the notary is here." Sweeney was so captivated by the beautiful furnishings in the apartment that she did not really see Sante sign the documents or, for that matter, if her pen ever touched the paper. Sweeney did say that the woman had a "bronchitis-type cough" and was wearing a frilly Victorian nightgown and a cap that covered her whole head, and "had very dark, almost black eyes." (Irene Silverman's eyes were light brown, in marked contrast to Sante's.)

✖

While Sante and Kenny sat in a jail cell, two Los Angeles Detectives, Dennis English and Bill Cox, arrived in New York to question them about the killing of David Kazdin, found shot in the head in a dumpster behind Los Angeles International Airport on March 14. They also briefed New York detectives on what they had learned during the four months they had been chasing the Kimeses around the country.

Kazdin, 64, had put his Granada Hills home up for sale for $245,000 three weeks before he was murdered. He was killed with a .22 caliber gun, the same type of weapon as the one the Kimeses purchased from Stan Patterson. The NYPD had found .22 caliber ammunition in the Lincoln. When the LA detectives got to the city, the Kimeses wouldn't speak with them.

At their first arraignment hearing, Criminal Court Judge Thomas Barber refused to release the smooth-talking mother and son on bail. Outside court that hot July day, defense lawyers tried putting another spin on their loss in court by telling the assembled press that Sante told them she had been beaten with a telephone book during Hackett's interrogation of her on Tuesday morning at 26 Federal Plaza. "She said he did it in a way so it would not leave marks," José Muniz said.

Friday, July 10, 1998, New York City

Friday was move-in day for Reznick and the Silver Task Force. The war room for the Manhattan North Homicide Squad is in a rather unremarkable old office building at West 132nd Street and Broadway. The front doors to this ordinary building are never locked, but a key is necessary to gain entry to the elevator. There are no visible outward signs, such as the familiar round green lanterns, on the street to indicate a police precinct, and no notice that inside are detectives assigned to cover homicides from 59th Street to the upper reaches of Manhattan.

The members of the Silver Task Force had their work cut out for them. For the foreseeable future, the seven core detectives and the four talented senior prosecutors from Robert Morgenthau's district attorney's office assigned to the case—Connie Fernandez, Ann Donnelly, John Carter and Owen Heimer—would spend hours every day for months in a small, windowless 10-by-20-foot room on the sixth floor, sitting on hard, rickety wooden chairs at a round oak table. They would sift through more than five huge double-decker shopping carts crammed with evidence, including seventeen multi-colored notebooks that Kenny and Sante Kimes had filled.

Tacked to the wall, written on a plain piece of white paper, were the words of Ernest Hemingway: *"There is no hunting like the hunting of armed men, and those that have hunted armed men long enough and like it, never care for anything else thereafter."*

As the detectives familiarized themselves with Sante's and

Kenny's handwriting, they were soon able to learn that the note-books the pair kept were a virtual "to do" list detailing every aspect of the Kimes' plans. In addition, it held the names of other rich, eld-erly folks they planned to scam. The common denominator on Sante's hit list was that all the people on it owned property at the Palm Beach Polo and Country Club, a prestigious private commu-nity of luxury homes and condos in Wellington, Florida, "Where the world comes to play," and also resided in the New York City area.

The two dozen names on Sante's list read like a who's who of the social register. For example, it included Joan Bove, who, with her first husband, Lawrence Gelb, founded the Clairol company, a sub-sidiary of Bristol-Myers Squibb Company, of which her son, Richard, is chairman and chief executive officer. The widow was nearly 100 years old when she died. But when Sante—posing as "Joy Landis"—contacted Lettie Eason, the officer manager at Lawyer's Title Insurance Corporation in New York, and asked her to do an owner's search on Bove's East 69th Street residence, she got bad news. "There was no deed," Eason said. "It's a co-op, and with a co-op, a deed is not filed."

Eason explained in court, when she testified at the Kimes trial on April 7, 2000, that there "would only be a deed if the person owns the building."

Although Irene did not have any connection to the Polo Club, Sante had asked for a title search on her home. Eason faxed Sante a copy of Irene's deed, because there was a block and lot number to the mansion.

The detectives also found a green notebook belonging to Sante, in which, in her own handwriting, they found such ominous phrases as "what is Irene's background," "get her social security number," and "stun gun." Next to Irene's name were the menacing words "easy mark."

Among the other prominent socialites, bankers, stock brokers, real-estate developers, and members of the horsey crowd Sante also targeted were Muriel Siebert, who in 1967 became the first woman to own a seat on the New York Stock Exchange and who later served as New York's superintendent of banks; Amy B. Lane, managing director of corporate finance at Merrill Lynch; Jane

Forbes Clark, chairman of the National Baseball Hall of Fame and Museum in Cooperstown, New York, and a director of the United States Olympic Committee; Neil Hirsch, a polo sponsor and player; Gale Brophy, who with her husband Giles had a Kentucky Derby winner a few years earlier; and Harry Cushing, a world-renowned polo player and financial investor, son of Cathleen Vanderbilt and nephew of Gloria Vanderbilt. During the investigation, Danny Rodriguez and John Schlagler learned that Sante and Kenny had made a number of approaches to several of these targets on her hit list. The detectives believed that Sante stole the list from the security guard at the Polo Club, because they found a similar print-out of the list at the gate.

Back in April, Sante had scammed her way into a two-bedroom Polo Club condominium belonging to Amelia Elizabeth Klinger Howlett and her husband, Kevin, a stockbroker. The Howletts, of London, Ontario, were packing and heading back to Canada for the summer when Kevin Howlett met Sante and Kenny wandering around the parking lot, supposedly looking to rent an apartment; Sante was wearing white pants, a large straw hat, and a distinctive large diamond ring. Mr. Howlett brought them back to the apartment. Mrs. Howlett asked if the diamond was real, and Sante replied that it was. She then introduced Kenny as a recent college graduate from the University of California. She told the Howletts that she had investments in Cuba and children in the Bahamas, and was in the market to buy or rent a condo.

Sante, pretending to be Nan Tess Wytowski, a variant of the name Nan Wetkowski, her Las Vegas notary friend, signed the lease in the name of Wytowski. She also gave the Howlett's $2,000 cash, representing two months rent. After the Howletts left, Sante ran up $4,831.11 in long-distance charges on their telephone before moving out a month later. It became Tommy Ryan's job to track down over 800 calls listed on the phone bills that Sante racked up during her brief stay in the Howlett apartment, including calls Sante made to Irene Silverman's home while posing as Manny Guerin's representative Eva, saying she was anywhere from Mexico to the Bahamas. There were other calls to an off-shore bank and to a pharmaceutical firm, seeking to obtain a powerful knock-out drug.

"Looking for Irene's killer was the ultimate hunt"

While Tommy Ryan tracked names and numbers, Tony Vazquez and Joel Potter headed for Las Vegas to speak with Sante's other son, Kent Walker, a vacuum-cleaner salesman. Before the detectives left New York City, Kent had agreed to speak with them, provided he was handed a subpoena. When they got to Vegas, Walker upped the ante and refused to be interviewed unless he was granted nationwide immunity. Walker even had his attorney, Dominic Gentile, who had represented his mother in the slavery trial, contact New York prosecutors to demand blanket immunity throughout the United States for him. But there wasn't a prosecutor in the country who would bite at granting Walker carte blanche on any crimes he had committed.

"There is no such thing as nationwide immunity. A person seeking immunity in any jurisdiction would do so only if he thought he needed immunity for a crime he committed or participated in and was willing to discuss it without fear of being prosecuted," said Tony Vazquez.

Walker continued to play games with law enforcement in Los Angeles when detectives made several attempts to speak with him about remarks he made on nationwide television in the spring of 2001. He had said that shortly before Kimes, Sr., died, the elder Kimes told him that Sante was poisoning him. The detectives also wanted to question Walker about an alleged conversation he claims he overheard while in a car in Los Angeles with his mother and step-father regarding another murder. Walker sent a message to detectives that he would not speak with them unless granted limited immunity.

✖

An early riser, Reznick had gotten to the War Room around 5:00 A.M. that Friday, July 10, anxious to get the investigation on the road. Wasielewski was still at the 19th precinct, four miles away, maintaining what is referred to by lawyers and cops as "the chain of custody" that made it necessary to re-inventory the property Ed Wallace had earlier taken out of the Lincoln as it passed from one detective to another. "I want everybody up here ASAP," Reznick screamed into the phone at Wasielewski.

Reznick's Manhattan North office was used as the conference room for meeting purposes. When the stuff finally arrived there, he was amazed at the depth of evidence being hauled to his room. "I'm watching from my door as bags after bags—two carloads of evidence—kept coming in, and I'm laughing so hard while they're hauling the stuff in," he recalled. "I'm looking at it, saying 'holy shit, it's going to take us months to look at this stuff.' The last thing they brought up was a rolled printout of the tires. I had never seen that done before in my 28 years with the department. What our experts do is to take about 20 feet of brown paper and they ink a tire and they roll it over the paper, one tire at a time. And they are bringing it up to me, this stretch of 20 feet of tire. That was the icing on the cake. That's how meticulous and careful the detectives were in conducting this investigation."

Wearing white latex gloves, the investigators carefully unpacked the evidence in the case. They made copies of every page of every notebook. It was only when the detectives and prosecutors in the War Room started the monumental task of reading the notebooks a second, third, and fourth time that everyone on the team clearly understood what Sante's and Kenny's cryptic and ominous notes meant. There were over a thousand names in the notebooks, and they all had to be investigated, in many cases more than once.

Wallace had catalogued and photographed every item in the car and removed soil from the car grill. After Wallace checked with the FBI, prosecutor Connie Fernandez contacted the Smithsonian and Texas A & M University to determine how much dirt was needed in order to make a soil comparison, in case the Kimes' tires had swampy material on them. "We didn't have enough from the tiny bit that Wallace had taken from the tires to do anything," Reznick reported. The information gleaned from the car gave us the history of Sante and Kenny to a degree and what they were about and where they were from," Reznick said.

In the beginning, the investigation concentrated on finding Irene. Parking lots at the three airports were searched. Hospitals and morgues in the city, the outer boroughs, upstate New York, and

New Jersey were contacted to see if Irene was a patient or an unidentified DOA (dead on arrival). Interviews were conducted with employees of every self-storage facility in the tri-state area to determine if the Kimeses dumped the body in a rental facility. The FBI made flyovers using infrared sensors to detect body heat through the foliage in the swamp areas around the New Jersey Meadowlands and upstate regions. They flew along the Garden State Parkway, the George Washington Bridge, the Palisades Parkway, and the Tappan Zee Bridge. Construction sites near the mansion were checked. Owners of Dumpsters in the city were canvassed to learn the location of their Dumpster drops, and detectives took cadaver dogs with them to upstate New York, Pennsylvania, Ohio, Connecticut, and New Jersey in an attempt to find Irene's final resting place.

The detectives also checked the garage on East 64th Street, near Second Avenue, where Kenny parked the Lincoln Town Car. The garage manager, Kirk Lynch, and the parking attendant, Christopher Acuna, indicated that the car never left the garage from the time Kenny brought it in at 11:02 A.M. on June 15 until he removed the car on Saturday, the fourth of July, at 10:31 A.M., a day before Silverman's disappearance.

With the holiday in full swing, East 65th Street looked like a ghost town on the fourth of July, and the deserted street meant that the Kimeses could move their belongings to their car, parked outside the mansion, in broad daylight, with ease.

The first order of business for detectives was to piece together where they "thought" the Kimeses were on a certain date, so that they could begin to create a timeline of their whereabouts around the country. To help in this endeavor, they pasted sheets of paper on the wall, along with photos of Irene, Kenny, Sante, Stan Patterson, José Alvarez, and Shawn Little. Alvarez and Little were both homeless gofers the Kimeses had picked up during their cross-country travels in 1998.

The disappearance of Alvarez was another mystery detectives had to solve. Irene's staff told detectives of seeing a Spanish-speaking man entering the home with Kenny in the days before Irene Silverman vanished, but he was nowhere to be found. Was he an accomplice in Irene's disappearance? Or were the Kimeses responsible for his disappearance and possible death? The Cuban émigré had hooked up with the Kimeses in Florida on May 14, 1998, and they were using him as an errand boy after Shawn Little, a homeless man they found at a Nevada shelter, fled their employ and disappeared. Little's name had popped up while detectives were studying Sante's notebooks.

Kenny's laptop computer, his Sharp Memo-Master that he used to store phone numbers and addresses, and the Kimes' cell phone had to be decoded after search warrants were obtained. The police computer unit "dumped" the computer to determine what was inside his hard drive. The detectives got a two-foot stack of printouts, including scripts the Kimeses used for their alibis.

Detectives knew the Kimeses arrived in the city on June 14, 1998, the day of the Puerto Rican parade, because that's the day Kenny, posing as Manny Guerin, rented apartment 1B for one month and got a $6,000 receipt with Irene Silverman's signature on it, which he later cleverly used to forge her name to documents and deeds.

Fifteen photocopies of the original rent receipt were found among the personal property of the Kimeses. Kenny altered the forged receipts to indicate he had rented apartment 1B for three months for $6,000, instead of for one month at that figure. The copies showed that the signature was heavily over-written as part of the process of forging the deed and the other documents, and they had Kenny Kimes' fingerprints on them. Kenny's fingerprints were also found on a forged power of attorney that was recovered from the Lincoln and on the forged deed to the townhouse.

Another monumental job facing the detectives was the phone dumps, or, in police jargon, the "N-file search" at Irene's mansion. She had eleven different phones at the residence, and every phone, for every tenant residing in the building, had to be checked from June 14 to the day she vanished. The result of the dumps gave the task force stacks of computerized printouts, which allowed them to create detailed timeline charts.

Another lingering mystery to solve was the two-hour time gap between 4:30 and 6:40 P.M. on July 5 after Kenny dropped Sante off at the Hilton Hotel to meet Stan Patterson. Her explanation to Patterson was that Kenny was out fixing the car. The stamped parking stub found in Kenny's possession when he was arrested showed he brought the car to a garage at West 44th Street and Sixth Avenue at 6:40 P.M., and then walked the six blocks to meet his mother and Patterson.

Although the Kimeses could have disposed of Irene's body during the morning three-hour time gap, Reznick theorized it was also possible that Kenny used those two missing hours in the afternoon to dump Irene's body by himself, while his mother kept Patterson busy at the Hilton Hotel.

Between July 14 and September 19, more than 75 people called police with information either about the Kimeses or about seeing Irene alive and standing on a corner street. Every tip, no matter how trivial or absurd, was investigated.

Tipsters like Paula Forester, a willowy blonde who claimed to have worthwhile information, turned out to be useless. Paula initially told detectives she was a private investigator for Vincent Parco of Intercontinental Investigations in New York. She called Joel Potter one day, indicating she had valuable information for the investigation. She had been showing up every time the Kimeses appeared in Criminal Court, telling reporters an unnamed, vague friend of Irene's had hired her and wanted her to search for clues as to Irene's disappearance. But when detectives met Paula, she confessed to being a psychic pet investigator. The story she gave was that she found a Playtex glove, a scarf, and a shotgun shell on a stretch of the Garden State Parkway in New Jersey. During the first days of Irene's disappearance, she had read that police were combing the rest stops and service areas along the roadway where the Kimeses claimed they were driving when they spoke to Stan Patterson about the car trouble delay. "We vouchered the stuff and she showed us the approximate spot where it was found near the Jersey swamps, but we couldn't find anything else," Joel said. In the end, detectives were unable to link the items to the Silverman case.

Just as the investigation was winding down, Paula was back to liven up the investigation and give detectives a well-needed laugh. This time she wanted to know if either the Kimeses or Irene were into Santeria, a West African voodoo type of religion in which one of the most important rituals allegedly involves animal sacrifice. Joel and Wasielewski met her outside their office and brought her to the inner sanctum. "She showed up with a dead chicken in her hand that stunk," Joel Potter said later. "It was vile, like a DOA smell. It's stinking up the whole office, and she tells us she was in Jersey again and, according to Santeria, there's supposed to be a note, a confession to the Gods, that would have been inserted up the chicken's ass before Irene disappeared."

The detectives were looking at any lead that could help in finding Irene's killers, even if Paula's story sounded far out. Just then Reznick walked in and, when Potter briefed him that there may be a confession up the chicken's ass, Reznick threw his hands up in the air and yelled, "Get the fuck out of here!" The detectives got the dead chicken and Paula out the door fast and delegated Tommy Hovagim, who had the least seniority on the team, to take the guest of honor to a poultry shop on 126th Street and Amsterdam Avenue, where appropriate surgery was performed on the chicken's anus. Needless to say, there wasn't any note inside.

That wasn't the last time detectives or prosecutors heard from Paula. The occult expert turned up in June 1999 bearing bizarre doodles and scribbles on a discarded envelope she claimed to have found in the trash can outside Irene's home in September 1998, with the words "Silverman" and "blood" scrawled on it. The doodles appeared to be teacups and drawings of coffin-shaped boxes. She even got Laura Italiano of the *New York Post* interested in running a story on her great find. After examining what she had, detectives sent Paula on her way with the "evidence"—a crumpled return envelope for *Highlights for Children* magazine.

Other psychics came crawling out of the woodwork, claiming to know where Irene Silverman's body was buried. Tommy Hackett and Danny Rodriquez took a young psychic out to the New Jersey Turnpike, but after driving along a stretch of the highway without a peep from the back-seat clairvoyant, other than a guttural sound, Rodriquez asked her if she was getting any vibes.

"I repeated the question, and when I still didn't get an answer, I turned around and there she was, her mouth wide open and her eyes shut, and she was snoring," the detective said.

While it seemed like a waste of time going on these wild-goose chases, no matter how insignificant the lead or how bizarre it sounded, they all had to be checked out.

By the second week in July, the team of detectives had purchased a large Rand McNally laminated map to write on, so they could easily track the Kimeses. Starting with New York, they worked backward to Cedar City, Utah, where they knew the Kimeses had ordered the Lincoln Town Car, to Los Angeles, California; Las Vegas, Nevada; Palm Beach, Florida; the Bahamas; and then Louisiana.

Detectives finally traced the Kimes' trail back to the swindle of the 1998 forest green Lincoln from Utah car dealer Jim Blackner. Blackner had dealt with Ken Kimes, Sr., in the past, but he did not know that Kimes had died four years earlier. Sante and Kenny put the car agreement in the name of Aga Khan International (AKI) Corporation and signed it with the name R.C. Tanis, a name similar to Ruth Tanis, Sante's teenage friend from Carson City. The new car was delivered to the Kimeses in Los Angeles, and they gave Jim Garrett, who drove the car to them, a check for $14,963.50, drawn on an account bearing Wetkowski's signature.

On February 9, 1998, the Wells Fargo Bank froze the checking account belonging to Sante's notary, Nanette Wetkowski. Blackner found out the account was frozen when he tried depositing the check. After a series of promises to send him a new check, Sante began complaining that the trunk leaked. By the end of March, Sante demanded another car, but by then Blackner realized he was getting the run-around. He filed a complaint with Utah authorities, and a warrant was issued for the Kimes' arrest.

It was this document that eventually enabled the Warrant Squad of the Joint FBI/NYPD Task Force to arrest Sante and Kenny in New York, so that the LAPD could question the pair about the Kazdin murder.

In the four months since Kazdin was murdered, detectives Dennis English and his partner, Bill Cox, had pursued "the real-life fugitives" from Bel Air to McGee's Storage Facility in the San Fernando Valley, where nearly two dozen more incriminating notebooks were found. But the Kimeses always managed to keep one step ahead of the lawmen.

"The more we looked, the more we found, and the more we had to do, and the more complicated the case became. There was nothing quite as simple as to say that they came to New York to take over the town house. It was well beyond that," Reznick said. "It became more complex by the day."

By the end of July, based on the phone usage in the mansion, the Kimes' use of phone cards and their cellular usage, detectives had a good timeline of what transpired on July 5, based on what they learned from two phone experts. It was a high point in the investigation. AT&T engineer Gary Sutcliffe was able to accurately determine that on July 5, the Kimeses had used their cell phone, activated in the name of Tony Tsoukas, three times between 11:00 A.M. and 11:28 A.M. The records also showed that no calls were made on the cell phone between 11:28 A.M. and 2:23 P.M., almost a three-hour gap. The cell site that received those calls showed that the cellular phone user was within two blocks of Irene Silverman's home.

The one incoming call that came in during that time frame was sent to voice mail. AT&T records showed the numbers the Kimeses dialed and indicated that the calls they made were a few blocks from the Silverman mansion and not on the Garden State Parkway, as Sante said to Stan Patterson when she called to report a two-hour delay because of car trouble.

As soon as detectives found one piece of the puzzle, there was another mystery. Who was Tony Tsoukas? His identification was found in Kenny's possession when he was arrested on July 5. In early June 1998, Tsoukas, a physician, and his wife, Michelle, stayed in Carina Qureshi's apartment at the Wellington, Florida, Polo Club for a few days. The apartment was down the hall from where Sante and Kenny were staying. Since Sante planned on moving to the Qureshi apartment in the fall, she had access to their apartment. When Tsoukas went swimming with his wife, he left his wallet on the kitchen table and was unaware that his social security card and driver's license identification were missing from his wallet until detectives notified him. Kenny found the wallet, removed the cards, did not touch the money in the wallet, but used the stolen identification to open a postal mailbox drop in New York City in Tsoukas's name and to buy a cell phone and telephone service.

"Our frustration peaked before we found the Black Bag. The deed was still missing, although there was a practice copy of the deed in the car. We were getting to an exhaustion point in the investigation when we came up with the Black Bag and the forged deed inside the bag. This was a great breakthrough. The suspected motive was now documented and we had additional work cut out for us," Reznick said.

13

"That's what happens to people who get mixed up with this syndicate"

In July 1990, Sante turned her attention to a new kind of scam. She took out a million-dollar insurance policy from Federal Insurance Company, a subsidiary of the Chubb Insurance Company, on the Portlock Road house Kimes owned in Honolulu. In the application, Sante posed as a daughter of Kenneth and Sante Kimes and used the name Kiata Kines. In short, she pretended to be her own daughter.

Around the same time she took out the policy, Sante hired Elmer Holmgren to torch the two-million-dollar Kimes home. Sante first met Holmgren in 1978 when, as a claims adjuster investigating a suspicious fire at the same residence, he ruled the blaze accidental, and the Kimeses were able to collect the insurance. Holmgren was more than agreeable to setting the fire; the 59-year-old lawyer, who had fallen upon hard times in the intervening years, was desperate to make money after several business ventures and marriages had failed, saddling him with a mountain of debts.

In January 1991, when the agents from the Bureau of Alcohol, Tobacco, and Firearms contacted Holmgren, he confessed that Sante had hired him the previous August to torch the house for $3,000. He admitted to agents that he'd set the fire on September 16, shortly after midnight, and he agreed to secretly record Sante discussing the arson. A short time after becoming an informant, Holmgren disappeared after telling agents he was taking a trip to Central America with the Kimeses. He has never been heard from or seen alive since.

In the meantime, Sante pressed the insurance company to pay for the destruction of the house. They refused to pay, because their investigation revealed it was a case of arson. The company wanted to depose Sante, which was obviously something she did not want to happen. In true Sante fashion, she then began a terror campaign that included showing up at the homes of Chubb executives in New Jersey. Sante even went so far as to track down one executive in a San Francisco hotel room and then proceeded to call him at four in the morning and again at six to say she wanted to discuss her insurance claim. On another occasion, she pretended to be from ABC television and asked to use the home of a Chubb executive to film an episode of the soap opera *All My Children*. When an executive finally agreed to meet with her, she showed up and demanded to see him privately. When they met, Sante spun a wild tale about being pursued by a huge crime syndicate in Hawaii who had burned her house. She said she had a friend who also had a 17-year-old son who had been murdered and his body dismembered, and that the body parts were sent to the father. She also related that yet another friend's 12-year-old boy disappeared, never to be seen again. Not so coincidentally, the executive had two boys of his own, 12 and 17 years old. Before leaving his office, Sante ominously suggested to the executive that "that's what happens to people who get mixed up with this syndicate."

Sante claimed the Cali drug cartel wanted to kill her, because she had caused them to lose over $900,000 as a result of information she provided to the government about money laundering conducted through PaineWebber's Hawaii's business offices. She even went to the extreme of vividly describing an attack by Cali cartel members, in which they placed her in a bathtub, sliced open the bottom of her buttocks, and supposedly stood by watching her bleed to death.

Sante related this bizarre story to defense lawyers Muniz and Weissman during the Silverman case, in a strategy session in the Manhattan Criminal Court building. The stunned lawyers were flabbergasted when she physically pulled down her pants and panties to reveal the scar on her derriere, supposedly left by her drug-dealing attackers. The lawyers were doubtful of the veracity of her tale, because she further embellished the story, claiming that her German shepherd ultimately saved her life. The dog allegedly ran up the stairs, causing the drug dealers to flee rather than disposing of Sante.

During the two years she spent in New York jails, Sante often dropped her pants and would "show and tell" the story about her scar to any man who came to see her in the visiting cell area, in an effort to gain sympathy. Her lawyers believe the scar is the result of a botched liposuction procedure in Mexico that Sante said was the subject of an earlier lawsuit initiated by her against the surgeon.

Sante's constant badgering understandably unnerved Chubb executives, who obtained a restraining order against her, but not before hiring private security guards to patrol the grounds at their offices and even their homes. On one occasion, guards reported seeing a white car parked outside Chubb property and a "very large dead crow" underneath the car of one of the executives.

Eventually, Chubb agreed not to pursue her insurance claim for reimbursement for the arson fire, and at the same time they dropped the harassment suit against her.

During the period Sante was harassing Chubb executives, she met with Douglas Crawford, a Las Vegas lawyer, who was on retainer to the Kimeses. She tried to convince him that another attorney in Hawaii, who was opposing her in the insurance case stemming from the maid's civil slavery lawsuit, was actually a high-ranking member of organized crime, involved in narcotics and pornography. Crawford did not take the threat seriously, but five minutes after leaving his office one night to have dinner with Sante, the place was firebombed.

In September 1996, Syed Bilal Ahmed, an assistant general manager of First Cayman Bank, had been sent by his Qatari employer on an inspection visit to the bank's branch in the Bahamas to look into irregularities at Gulf Union Bank. The Cayman Islands is a leading offshore financial center and tax haven, with 580 registered banks serving corporations and wealthy clients from around the world. Kimes, Sr., was among the rich who stashed money at banks in the Cayman Islands, and he reportedly had close to one million dollars on deposit at First Cayman.

A colleague of Ahmed's at First Cayman and its parent, Gulf Union Bank, was dropping him off after work at the Radisson Hotel in Cable Beach, the Bahamas, on Wednesday, September 4, 1996, when they passed the entrance to a home off West Bay Street, about 200 yards south of his hotel. Ahmed had been staying in Room 507 since his arrival there on August 31, in a $105 a night room. Ahmed mentioned to his associate that it was the home of Sante Kimes and that he had plans to meet her for dinner that night about a deposit worth millions of dollars. There were also other reports that Ahmed was looking into withdrawal irregularities on the Kimes account that had been going on for about two years, ever since Kimes, Sr., died in 1994.

According to the hotel's lock report, Ahmed used his electronic room key at 6:33 P.M. on September 4. From the key report, it appears he did not use the key again, although at 9:37 that evening, the maid's key was used to turn down his bed. The next morning, at 7:34, Ahmed's key was used once. What this indicated to authorities is that either Ahmed stayed in his room all night or left the room and returned at 7:34 A.M., or that someone else using Ahmed's key entered the room at that time. At 8:47 A.M., a maid/supervisor used the key, presumably to make the bed. When hotel security entered Ahmed's room at 10:42 A.M. that same day, the room was empty, the two beds made up, and there was no luggage, personal property, papers, or anything else to indicate that a guest had been staying in the room. Ahmed had not checked out of the hotel.

The front desk clerk at the hotel remembered that a white five-foot-ten-inch male, about 30, with an American accent, approached him. The man claimed to be a guest of the hotel, Bilal Ahmed, and stated he had lost his room key and needed a replacement. The clerk refused, because he knew Ahmed personally as an employee of the bank from previous visits. Behind the young man, the clerk said, was a white female, with long dark hair, a very big woman, in her 50s, wearing a large white wide-brimmed hat. He later identified Sante and Kenny from a photo.

During the Bahamian investigation of the case, Nassau Police Chief Inspector William Daniel Moss, of Nassau's Criminal Investigation Division, tried interviewing Sante, but by then she and Kenny had fled the island. When she did call him, Sante denied meeting Ahmed the night of September 4 and stated she never had any plans to have dinner with him and had never met Ahmed at the Radisson. Sante's statement to the police was inconsistent with statements by other witnesses, who had seen them together on earlier occasions at the hotel, the Bahamian police said.

Sante and Kenny tried to set up alibis for themselves. For instance, they contacted Craig Rolle, the waiter at the Androsia Steak and Seafood Restaurant, a frequent haunt of the Kimeses in Nassau, where they had dined the night of September 4 with Ahmed. Rolle refused to go along with signing a false statement Sante sent. Next, she tried to convince Siegfried Von Hamm, the owner of the restaurant, to say that he drove her home very early that evening because her car had broken down, meaning she couldn't have been at the restaurant having dinner with Ahmed. Unfortunately for Sante, he, too, refused, pointing out that he wasn't even in the restaurant that day.

Sante wanted Alex Lavarity, manager of the Super Value market in Cable Beach, to swear that on the day in question her car stalled in his parking lot and was there for several days before being towed for repair. Lavarity, who remembered Sante because she had stiffed him for the car battery, assured detectives he did not sign Sante's prepared alibi affidavit and had never seen it. Sante also tried, to no avail, to get Reverend Irene Coakley to swear that she was with her until 8:00 P.M. on September 4 at the oceanfront home she claimed she owned, having "beverages and snacks" and sitting "out on the deck enjoying the view."

It was in the Bahamas that detectives found that the half-acre beachfront home Sante kept offering to "comp" strangers, with whom she tried to curry favors, was not even hers. Instead, it was owned by Raymond Wong, and was on the market for $3.3 million. Sante was renting the property for $1,500 a month and had stiffed the landlord for three months rent.

"Once the computer was downloaded, Joe was like an octopus. All his tentacles were spread out to every single factor in the case to cover every minute detail. 'Pursue this, pursue this,' he'd bark until they'd tied it together," Connie Fernandez said.

✖

The breadth and depth of the investigative work by the Task Force and the district attorney's office was tedious. Every name had to be itemized and cross-referenced. Boxes held lists of property, such as the empty box found in the Town Car under the driver's seat, which had held a stun gun packing a powerful punch. Imprinted on the box were the words: "knock you on your ass." A receipt in the name of Shawn Martin, one of many false names Kenny used, was found in the glove compartment of the car, showing that the stun gun cost $74.15 and was purchased from a Lake Worth, Florida, store in nearby Palm Beach on April 23, 1998. An NYPD emergency service police officer, John Cafarella, familiar with the effects of stun guns on people, testified that, when applied for five seconds to a person, it causes "disorientation and would signal pain to the brain . . . and if applied for longer than five second, a person would collapse." The empty stun gun box found in the Lincoln once held a device that would deliver 200,000 volts. Cafarella also testified that a similar device, once used by the NYPD delivered only 50,000 volts. Although no stun gun was ever found among the Kimes' property, the empty box could be used as evidence to show a jury of its existence. In fact, Sante and Kenny were very familiar with stun guns. In 1996, they took Kent Walker's daughter, Kristina, then 12, with them to the Bahamas. As the luggage was going through the scanner at the Las Vegas airport, a stun gun was found in one of Kenny's suitcases. Sante and Kenny took off faster than the jet, leaving the terrified child in tears to deal with the police. Kent and his wife, Lynn, were hardly amused.

One of the most important finds police made was that of Sante's notebooks, in which she compulsively outlined their plans to steal, cheat, and murder, whether the plot involved the Silverman mansion or the disappearance of Ahmed. From these notebooks and information found on Kenny's computer, New York City detectives discovered elaborate scripts documenting how they were going to shift the blame of Ahmed's disappearance to someone else. There were also copies of false affidavits found that were actually given to these witnesses in the Bahamas.

By far, the most incriminating evidence the police found were actual tape recordings the Kimeses made, found in the Lincoln Town Car. Presumably, the Kimeses made these recorded tapes and other secret explosive conversations for their own gratification.

Police also uncovered yet another Kimes scam, which dealt with the Santa Maria property in California (see chapter 14). Evidently, Sante and Kenny arranged for a tree specialist to be on the property Kenneth Kimes, Sr., owned. While the tree specialist was there, Kenny showed up in disguise, wearing a hazardous materials suit. He deliberately threw himself into a ditch on the property and allegedly started smothering and choking. Then Sante, using the name Gilda Alvarez Susan Alan, among various aliases, posed as a representative of Manuel Guerrero and claimed that he had contracted *E. Coli* poisoning as a result of his falling in the ditch.

As if that weren't enough, the ever imaginative Sante then convinced a lawyer to file a civil lawsuit in California against the County of Santa Barbara, seeking damages for *E. Coli* pollution on the real-estate property in Santa Maria. That lawsuit finally fizzled out, perhaps because none of the lawyers pursued it or there was no opportunity for the Kimeses to pursue the case because of their arrest in New York City.

"That's what happens to people who get mixed up with this"

Among the noteworthy items found in the Lincoln were books listing the symptoms of *E. Coli* poisoning and several letters Sante wrote, including a laundry list of illnesses that Kenny, posing as Guerrero, was purporting to suffer from.

Then, toward the end of the Silverman investigation, detectives thought they uncovered another of Sante's exploits, one that boggled the imagination. One month before the Kimeses were indicted for Irene Silverman's murder, Joel Potter and Tommy Hackett were in California conducting a number of interviews when they learned about Sante's unexpected visit to Irene DiVito, the personal assistant to Lee Iaccoca in Los Angeles two years earlier.

"Sante claimed to have important secret information about national security and needed to speak with someone who had enough clout to get the information to the president," DiVito told detectives. Sante said she was a friend of Lee Iaccoca, whom she had met in Palm Springs; that she had property in the Bahamas and was on her way to Cuba to start up a business concerning human longevity with an unknown doctor. After calling DiVito dozens of times, a meeting was arranged in a Brentwood restaurant with DiVito's associate, Rick Runyon, and with Dick Schmidt, a former government employee familiar with security matters.

"Sante started off saying she had secrets about Cuban missiles. [She] claimed to have the inside track, because she had stayed at a villa outside of Havana with some of Fidel Castro's officials, who liked her, and that they had loose lips around her and confided their business to her."

"I got very close to Castro and the other officials and went to a lot of parties with these people," Sante enthusiastically told the trio, mentioning her frequent travels to Cuba and boasting that she could obtain more inside information. "Cuba is planning to flood the United States with counterfeit money," she added.

14

"Don't ever say you're Kimes"

By the end of 1997, Sante had managed to get her hands on practically all of Kimes's millions, yet her appetite for swindling never diminished. She turned her attention to gaining control of a valuable piece of property Kimes owned in the Santa Maria area of Santa Barbara, California.

The Santa Maria scheme might have worked had it not been for the hard work of the dedicated lawyers for the Estate of Kenneth Kimes—Jill Rosenthal and Robert Eroen—who spent nearly two years of ardous and painstaking research to untangle Sante's web of fraud and deceit.

It is unclear whether Sante knew that she was left nothing in his will at the time of Kimes death. She must have known, however, that she had no legal claim to his estate. Despite all the things she had been able to persuade Kimes to do during their years together, it appears she was never able to persuade him to marry her. Kimes told one of his neighbors in Hawaii, Jacob Manley, a real-estate developer, "I'll never marry that woman. She'll take me for every dime I have. I want my money to go to my children." His will, signed in 1961, left everything to his two older children, Linda and Andrew. Sante had no legal claim to his fortune.

Rather than risk a time-consuming fight with Kimes's heirs, which certainly would have tied up the estate assets for years, Sante came up with a plan to give herself the time she needed to loot the estate by keeping his death a secret from Kimes's legal heirs, which she did successfully until late 1996.

In order to carry out her plan, she needed Kenny's computer skills. She persuaded Kenny to drop out of college so that she could begin his real education, schooling him in the cons and scams it had taken her a lifetime to perfect. She taught him how to forge real-estate documents; how to defraud insurance companies; how to take out loans against collateral they didn't own, sticking some unsuspecting third party with the debt; and how to impersonate other people. Most importantly, she taught him how to con people into believing that Kimes was still alive, giving her the opportunity to control the disposition of his fortune.

The elder Kimes had numerous domestic and international dealings. It was his habit to keep numerous bank accounts, each under $100,000 to ensure the sum would be federally insured. It was also his belief that real estate was the best investment available. Consequently, there were any number of parcels of property in his estate that needed to be located and converted into cash, which could then be squirreled away to some offshore account where his legal heirs would never be able to find it.

Poring over Kimes's business records, Sante and Kenny looked for any information relating to bank accounts, which were easiest to loot. Once they located an account number, all they needed to do was forge Kimes's name on a withdrawal slip or wire transfer instruction and they could have funds transferred anywhere in the world. To that end, it was imperative the funds not be placed in either Sante's or Kenny's names. Once Kimes's heirs figured out that he was dead and his estate had been cleaned out, they would inevitably try to trace the estate property, and any transfers to Sante or Kenny would obviously come under suspicion. To hide the funds, Kenny traveled to various offshore financial institutions, setting up secret accounts under assumed names, which were used to receive the stolen funds.

Stealing real property from the estate was more complicated. In order to convert the property to cash, it needed to be sold. But selling property takes time, and time was something Sante didn't have. The first thing she needed to do was figure out a way to get the property out of Kimes's name, which would give her time to sell it and hide the proceeds before his heirs caught on.

The main property Sante was interested in was his large parcel of real estate in Santa Maria, California. In 1959, Kimes and a business partner, John Muller, had purchased a large piece of land originally known as the Wheat Ranch Development. The land was zoned for construction of 171 private luxury homes in the mountains above a quiet town north of Santa Barbara.

Ten years later, Kimes bought out his partner, taking over the Wheat Ranch parcel, which he now referred to as the Santa Maria property. To persuade his first wife, Charloette, to sign over her interest in the property as part of the divorce settlement, he promised to leave the property in his will to their two children, Linda and Andrew, which he later did. In that deed, Kimes refers to himself "as an unmarried man."

After Kimes's death, Sante began to study the law governing real property. With the help of various people, who may or may not have known what she was up to, she quickly learned how to draft the various legal documents required to transfer, encumber, and/or sell real estate. She obtained blank forms from Carolene Davis, and she used the expertise of Alan Russell, who ultimately resigned from the California State Bar after the Bar Committee concluded he had engaged in professional misconduct.* With his help, she

---

*Russell now runs the offices of the Nevada Corporate Services in Las Vegas, a company that, according to Sante, set up the off-shore bank accounts and corporations for her.

started shifting assets, opening up foreign bank and investment accounts in the Bahamas, Bermuda, the Cayman Islands, Switzerland, and Cuba.

On April 18, 1994, less than three weeks after Kimes died, Sante recorded a Grant Deed, which was purportedly "executed," or signed, by Kimes on December 23, 1993, three months *before* he died. The deed transferred "Assessor's Parcel No. 117-330-40" to Sante Kimes "for love and affection." Unfortunately for Sante, there is no Assessor's Parcel No. 117-330-40. The large piece of land in Santa Maria that Kimes left to his children Andrew and Linda is "Assessor's Parcel No. 117-330-60." The fully developed land had a market value of over ten million dollars in 2001. Undeveloped, it is worth around three million dollars.*

By May 4, 1994, Sante had apparently figured out her mistake. Undaunted, she simply recorded another deed, again "dated" December 23, 1993, this time purporting to transfer "Assessor's Parcel No. 117-330-60" to herself. An expert would later deem Kimes's signatures on both deeds to be forgeries.

Since Sante needed to get the property out of her name, she— apparently with Russell's help—set up various bogus corporations to which she could transfer the property. Though Sante formed and entirely controlled these corporations, she was careful not to have her name associated with them in any way. In each case, she filed public records listing the names of third parties—often without their knowledge—as officers and directors. To anyone reviewing these public records, it would not be at all apparent that Sante had anything to do with them.

In order to obscure the trail as much as possible, Sante drafted a series of complicated real-estate documents purporting to encumber and then transfer the property among these various shell corporations. The fact that she was able to figure out how to create these documents without a law degree or real-estate license is a testament to her intelligence and complete lack of intimidation.

On the day after she recorded the second forged deed—the one

---

*The Santa Maria property was finally sold to a land developer in mid-October 2001, for $3.2 million.

purporting to transfer to herself the corrected parcel number—
Sante herself signed a Deed of Trust putting the property up as collateral for a $4.8 million "loan," which she allegedly received from
Aga Khan International (AKI). Of course, there was no loan. AKI
was nothing but an alter ego of Sante, an empty shell that she created to hide the property. Interestingly, AKI was not even formed
as a corporation until May 11, 1994, twenty-two days *after* the corporation purportedly lent Sante $4.8 million. Once she had created
paperwork reflecting a loan from AKI, she merely transferred the
property to AKI as "repayment" for the loan. On paper, it looked
like a perfectly legitimate business transaction.

One aspect of the transaction that would later raise eyebrows
was that the property was transferred to AKI by virtue of a quitclaim deed, a simple, no-frills way to transfer property. Unlike a
grant deed, which includes assurances and guarantees that the
seller has an unencumbered interest in the property that a third
party will not later challenge, a quitclaim deed offers no such protection to a buyer. Indeed, the only thing a quitclaim transfers is
whatever interest the owner has in the property. If the seller has no
interest in the property, that's exactly what the buyer gets: *nothing.*
Not surprisingly, most buyers are reluctant to accept a quitclaim
deed from a seller who is unknown to them. But Sante had no
problem getting AKI to accept a transfer by quitclaim deed—
because AKI *was* Sante!

When Sante first formed AKI, she named Charles Gallagher, a realtor she and Kimes knew, as president, treasurer, secretary, and sole
director on the Board of Directors. Gallagher would later admit he
agreed to allow her to use his name as a favor when she told him she
was afraid that relatives of her deceased "husband" were attempting
to "steal" her property. When Gallagher later had a change of heart
and asked that his name be removed from the corporate papers,
Sante replaced his name with several others, including her Bahamian
masseuse, James Theolosphis; the name R. C. Tanis, a name that
appears to have been loosely based on a high school chum of Sante's,
Ruth Tanis; and the name K. W. Prescott. Prescott's "signature" on the
corporate papers looks amazingly similar to Sante's own.

On November 25, 1997, Sante filed yet another list of corporate officers and directors, this time naming David Kazdin as the sole director and officer of AKI, although she used a Bahamian address for Kazdin and even spelled his last name Kazden.

But Sante wasn't satisfied leaving the property only one step away from her own name. She wanted to make it impossible for Kimes's heirs to be able to trace it back to her. Two days after executing the quitclaim deed transferring the property to AKI, Sante created another Deed of Trust—this one signed by the nonexistent E. W. Prescott, a name she presumably wanted to sign as K. W. Prescott, but in her haste she forgot Prescott's initials. In any event, the deed was signed on behalf of AKI, putting the property up as collateral for a $4.2 million "loan" from a man named C.V. Narasimhan. Of course, once again, there was no such loan. C.V. Narasimhan happens to be the name of the former under secretary general of the United Nations, a man whom Sante and Kimes had once met briefly in the 1970s.

Indeed, in a letter attached to court papers later filed by the Kimes Estate in Superior Court of California in Santa Barbara seeking to recover the property, Narasimhan told Andrew Murr, a *Newsweek* correspondent: "I have no connection whatever with any entity called Aga Khan International, or with any property in Santa Maria. I have no knowledge of either of the two documents (the deeds described above) sent with your letter . . . they were never sent to me." He further stated, "I never loaned anyone any money secured by the property in Santa Maria."

He continues, "I met Mr. Kenneth Kimes for the first time in the late 1960s when I was Under Secretary General at the U.N. Mr. Kimes brought with him a photo-montage, in full color, of the flags of all the member states of the United Nations. I accepted it from him. This was the beginning of our contact. (He did not come to me as a self-proclaimed Ambassador of the U.S. Bicentennial)." Narasimhan explains that although Kimes visited him after that initial meeting and was accompanied by a woman who called herself Sante, he stopped seeing Kimes when an insurance company representative called him and said that Kimes was using his name in connection with a questionable claim for some stolen antique artifacts. "I did not see [Sante] alone either before or after the demise of Mr. Kimes. I did not even know that Mr. Kimes had passed away or when."

He added, "Sante Kimes's statement about my being a godfather to Kenneth, Jr., born in 1975, is also untrue."

The speed with which Sante kept transferring deeds from one person to another eventually caught up with her, and she became careless. Instead of calling the corporation Aga Khan International she would often spell the corporate name *Khan* as *Kahn* on court papers.

Having muddied the waters with yet another bogus deed purportedly encumbering the property in Narasimhan's name, Sante created another Deed of Trust, this one dated December 15, 1997, supposedly encumbering the property to secure a $2.5 million "loan" to AKI from The Atlantis Group. Once again, there was no loan. And once again, the Deed of Trust was merely laying the groundwork for yet another quitclaim deed, this time dated February 4, 1998, which ostensibly transferred ownership of the property to The Atlantis Group in satisfaction of the loan. And to further spin her web of fraud and deceit, Sante's latest alter ego business entity looked perfectly legitimate.

Because Sante had organized The Atlantis Group as an off-shore corporation in Antigua, she had now managed to create a thoroughly confusing and convoluted trail that Kimes's rightful heirs would never be able to follow. But to get cash out of the property, Sante still needed to sell it, and there aren't many buyers who will plunk down several million dollars in exchange for a quitclaim deed.

Moreover, most buyers will insist upon retaining a title company to perform a title search, a review of all recorded documents relating to the property, in order to verify that the owner has full and unfettered title to the property and is entitled to sell it. The problem for Sante was that a title search could easily uncover the fact that Kimes had died weeks after purportedly transferring the property to Sante and *before* it was recorded. This would surely raise a red flag. In making inquiries regarding this, a title company might even alert Kimes's heirs to the existence of the property and the proposed sale. At all costs, Sante had to stay away from title companies. She had learned this lesson when she raised the suspicions of one of Carolene Davis's superiors.

Indeed, the only way for Sante to turn the property into cash was to find a buyer who would accept a quitclaim deed and not insist upon using a title company. The only way to attract such a person would be to offer to sell the property at such an extreme discount that the buyer would be willing to look the other way regarding all the irregularities.

When that proved difficult, Sante came up with another scheme. She would figure out a way to "trade" the property for another piece of property she would have an easier time selling. This apparently was her scheme when she went to New York and set her sights on Irene Silverman. After her arrest, a manila folder marked "FINAL DYNASTY" was found in a small black bag that Sante had stashed at the Plaza Hotel along with a forged deed that transferred Silverman's six-story, multimillion dollar town house to none other than The Atlantis Group, Ltd.

It appears that Sante's plan was to forge paperwork, making it look as though Silverman had agreed to trade her New York property for the Santa Maria property. Sante would then be free and clear to sell Silverman's property while Silverman or her estate would be stuck dealing with the claims of Kimes's rightful heirs.

Obviously, that particular scheme didn't work out for Sante, although that was the story she continued to impart to Matthew Weissman, a member of her defense team who was also a real-estate and tax attorney. Even after she was arrested, she continued to try to sell the property out from under Kimes's rightful heirs. Since Kenny—her accomplice to date in these matters—was also behind bars, she turned to her elder son, Kent Walker, for help. In a series of letters, she attempted to tutor Walker in the ways of real-estate fraud.

In an undated July 1998 letter that Sante wrote from her prison cell, she let Kent know he was to pose as a director of the fictitious Atlantis Group to find an unsuspecting buyer for the Santa Maria property. She told him that she had made arrangements to appoint him the director of Atlantis, which would give him *"authority to sell, encumber, whatever the property."* Sante also made it clear that *she* was The Atlantis Group and that *she* created the corporation for the purpose of selling the Santa Maria property out from under

Kimes's legitimate heirs, Linda and Andrew. In this letter, she also instructed Kent to call someone named Jim Hall in Lompac, California, on behalf of AKI, and indicated that her notary, "Nan" (Nanette Wetkowski), could also speak for AKI.

In an eight-page letter on July 20, 1998, Sante provided Kent with amazingly detailed step-by-step instructions on how to forge a quitclaim deed so he could sell the Santa Maria property to an unsuspecting third party for $2.5 to 3 million dollars *"in cash."*

> *We must be very secretive. Explain to your buyer to avoid any problems or attachments that we must not use any title companies or escrows.*
>
> *You and buyer work only on this. Don't involve third parties. This is urgent. They will try to stop.*
>
> *Here's what you do—*
>
> *1. Get cashier's check from Buyer. 2½ to 3 mil.*
> *2. Go to Nevada legal forms. Never go to an atty. They will complicate. You can easily do this.*
> *3. Get a quitclaim legal form.*
> *4. On the quit claim deed, type in the grantor, meaning the owner as* Atlantis Group Ltd.
> *5. If you and buyer want to save tax money, you don't have to show real sales price . . . show ½ of the real price.*

Sante then went on to have Kent call Chicago Title in Santa Maria to get the legal description of the property. She cautioned him to be secretive.

> *Give a fake name, ask for Mr. Long or whoever, charm him and ask if he can fax you a property profile. Don't ever say you are Kimes—Say you might buy property and will use their company . . . explain to your buyer because of circumstances, you must work fast and no outside anything or it will be stopped . . . your buyer is getting a fantastic deal.*

Then, sounding like the polished scam artist that she is, Sante wrote:

We can have no hang-ups. Get it thru no matter what—Treat it like a baby in an incubator—don't tell anyone—not your family. This has to be secret and fast. Your buyer has to understand this—This is the only way—no escrows or it will get attached.

About the payment, Sante pressed Kent:

Listen to me please. . . . The buyer must pay cash—no terms ever. What a deal for them . . . don't trust anyone on this.

She then explained how to record the deed. In case he was unaware of his higher elevation in the real-estate and corporate worlds, she wrote:

You, *Kent Walker have been made an officer of Atlantis Grp. Ltd.—therefore at the bottom of the quitclaim deed, you sign like this—grantor, Atlantis Group LTD, by K.E. Walker, V. Pres., in front of a friendly notary.*

Sante also told her son that *"at a corporate meeting a long time ago you were voted in. You don't want to get Kenny and I involved in any way with signature—too much red tape."* Kent was then instructed to forward the money from the buyer to the Caribbean offshore account to be deposited where *"there is no record for all who are looking to destroy and kill us."*

Fortunately for the Kimes estate, the FBI and other law enforcement agents had Kent under 24-hour surveillance after Sante's arrest and thwarted the scheme. According to conversations that authorities recorded between Kent, Kenny, and his mother, Kent told them he was followed day and night by law enforcement officers, both at his work and home, and that his telephones were tapped. He kept complaining to his brother and mother that, because of the tight surveillance both he and his wife, Lynn, were undergoing, he was in no position to help them. As a result of the FBI and law enforcement surveillance, Kimes's children were able to file a lawsuit in Santa Barbara Superior Court that precluded

Sante from selling the property. In late November 2000, the court granted a petition filed by Linda and Andrew in which they sought to "quiet title" the Santa Maria property, which meant that the court made a legal ruling that the property belonged to the estate of Kenneth Kimes, Sr., and not to Sante, AKI, The Atlantis Group, or any other entity.

A factor that lent credibility to Sante was that Nanette Wetkowski notarized all the documents; she also signed as a witness to at least five of the bogus deeds in this case. In fact, she also notarized the forged deed on the Silverman mansion. Wetkowski, who had obtained a notary license at the request and expense of Sante, regularly notarized blank documents for Sante, who would then take these documents and fill in the blanks later.

Wetkowski notarized various deeds transferring the property between AKI, C. V. Narasimhan, and The Atlantis Group, and also "witnessed" both deeds that Sante recorded after Kimes died.

Although Sante was now in jail, she was still calling the shots and wanted her New York lawyers to sell the Santa Maria property with all its encumbrances. She also asked that phony corporate minutes be prepared, removing such names as R. C. Tanis, Manny Guerrero, and David Kazdin as officers and directors of AKI and The Atlantis Group, Ltd. She wanted the lawyers to backdate and forge minutes of alleged meetings at which Kent Walker was named as the only officer.

"When I balked at doing this and tried to explain how utterly illegal it was," Matthew Weissman said, "Sante snapped at me and said, 'You are not protecting my son as you promised. You are not doing your job. If you go ahead and do what I tell you, you'll make more money than you ever dreamed of.'"

The lawyer stalled her for several months on the pretext that it was taking longer to accomplish what she wanted and alerted other members of the defense team as to her intentions.

Perhaps the most amazing scam Kenny and Sante tried to pull off involved asking Weissman to buy microphones that would transmit voice conversations within a one-mile radius of the 12th floor attorney-client meeting room at the Manhattan Criminal Court building, where they met with their attorneys. Kenny, who had clipped out pictures of the microphone he had in mind from a spy magazine, assured Weissman that the device was no larger than a thumb. The plan was to install the microphone underneath a table where the lawyer and his clients sat, where the Kimeses could later "innocently discover" it. The plan was for the Kimeses to then accuse authorities of planting the bug to snoop on meetings with their lawyers. Of course, the lawyer never purchased the microphone.

Another of Sante's hare-brained schemes was to get Weissman to prepare a power of attorney in the name of the deceased Kenneth Kimes. "Just type up the piece of paper. I'll do the rest and sign it," she said, indicating her willingness to forge Kimes's signature from her jail cell. Sante explained to Weissman that she needed the document because "it could become useful in my upcoming battle with Linda Kimes for the Santa Maria property." The request was so outrageous that Weissman not only walked out on her in the meeting but quit representing her and Kenny as a result of Sante's many demands to perform illegal acts on their behalf. He only returned a month later, after Sante assured him that she would make no further dubious demands of him for the remainder of the case.

15

"There's nothing in the notebooks that can hurt us"

Despite all the legwork the Silver Task Force did, it seemed like their investigation was at a dead end until the black bag was found.

In the purse Tommy Hackett took from Sante on July 7 was not only the toilet paper note to Kenny, but a scrap of paper with the word "PALAZA" and the number 43280. As it turned out, Sante had simply misspelled the name of the Plaza Hotel, but when detectives checked, they found there was no such tag number used on luggage at the legendary Central Park South hotel. As a result, the Manhattan South Homicide Squad was called in, and Reznick had them canvas all midtown hotels with instructions to call detectives if anyone tried to pick up a stray bag without an identification numbered ticket stub. Hotel staffers were also shown photo arrays of Sante and Kenny, to see if they recognized them as having stayed at their hotels.

After her arrest, when Sante first met with her lawyer, José Muniz, she was warned not to discuss the case on the jailhouse phone, because authorities were monitoring her calls. But Sante, who loved using the phone no matter what the risk, ignored his advice and asked Larry Frost, a private investigator hired by the defense, to meet her at the 12th floor courthouse holding cell to discuss picking up a bag she had stored at the Plaza Hotel on July 5. Before Frost could meet her, Sante changed her mind and wanted a new attorney, Mel Sachs, who had just joined the defense team, to pick up the bag.

Muniz brought Sachs into the case ten days after the arrest because of Sante's concern that Matthew Weissman lacked criminal experience and because she knew it was going to be a heavy-duty media case. For Sachs, it was a case made in media-hype heaven. A publicity hound, he never missed an opportunity to hog the television cameras with his spiel and drone on endlessly with his familiar mantra, "There's no body, no crime, no blood, no DNA, no forensics, no case."

"Mel was perfect for the case," Muniz said. "He was thrilled to get involved. He went to see the Kimeses and put on a great show for her, even doing card tricks and making coins magically disappear. Sante was sold on him. Even Mel's good friend, comic Jackie Mason, told him, 'Look, it's a good case. It doesn't matter if you win or lose. The publicity itself is worth it.'"

Sante downplayed the contents of the bag to her lawyers and kept insisting it only contained personal documents. "With your considerable charm and persuasive ability, you can get the bags," she sweet-talked the bow-tied, impeccably dressed, ever-smiling Sachs. "And by the way, you just con them a little bit," Sante added as an aside. "There's really nothing in the bag. Just some personal papers and two *Scream* masks," she said convincingly. "She never said anything about the gun," Muniz said. "She's bright. She knew if she had said 'gun,' Sachs or Frost would never have retrieved the bag.

"When Larry pointed out to Sante that he used to work at the Plaza and knew the security person at the hotel, her eyes lit up. It was finally decided that Larry would go to the Plaza."

"It's better that I go alone because I know people at the hotel," Frost explained, and he eventually did go alone.

But Sante couldn't let it go and stupidly called Frost again to discuss the bag. As her lawyers had earlier warned her, authorities overheard and recorded their conversation. "When are you going down to pick up the bag?" she wanted to know.

A Plaza bellman found the bag for Frost on July 23. With black bag in hand, Frost went to his brother's West 67th Street office, where he opened it. After removing papers, a clear plastic cosmetics bag, a bottle of vodka, two notebooks, a deed purporting to carry the signature of Irene Z. Silverman, audio microcassettes, and plastic handcuffs, he found a .22 caliber semi-automatic pistol wrapped inside a white turban. Frost, anxious to alert the lawyers about the gun, located them at Forlini's, a favorite restaurant on Baxter Street, behind the Criminal Courthouse, frequented by judges, lawyers, and the media. Before Frost could spread the latest news to them, Silver Task Force detectives were at his door. "José, I've got some police officers here. They want the bag," Frost yelled into the phone.

"Do they have a subpoena?" the lawyer asked.

"No," Frost replied.

It took detectives only a matter of minutes to notify prosecutor Ann Donnelly. She had a subpoena issued and served on the lawyers at Forlini's, where Sachs and Muniz were spinning a wild Sante yarn to *New York Daily News* columnist Juan Gonzales that Irene Silverman was a madam running a brothel on East 65th Street and that the maids at the house were actually prostitutes.

"It could have been a public-relations disaster," Muniz said. "We were trying to shape the case in a way that it wouldn't look like, we, as attorneys, were trying to break the law, or that we were trying to hide evidence or manipulate something that was evidence. On the one hand, we knew we couldn't keep it from prosecutors, but we also had to protect our clients' rights."

"What's that?" asked Gonzales, grinning mischievously and looking coy at the paper in the lawyer's hand.

"What are we going to do?" Sachs nervously whispered to Muniz as both lawyers decided to retreat to the men's room for a private conversation.

Not wanting Gonzales to write something potentially devasting, Muniz said to his colleague, "Mel, I think we should tell him."

The lawyers went back to Gonzales and he read the subpoena, laughed, and simply shook his head in disbelief. "Do you think you can write that we didn't get subpoenaed?" Muniz meekly asked.*

As the cab carrying the two lawyers sped uptown to Frost's office, weaving in and out of Friday rush-hour traffic, followed closely by a carful of detectives, Sachs' cell phone went into over-drive as he alerted reporters as to what was going down. When his battery ran out of juice, he simply grabbed Muniz's cell phone and continued his information dissemination campaign.

When they arrived at Frost's office, Danny Rodriguez, his part-ner, John Schlagler, and John Carter, another talented senior pros-ecutor, were waiting for them. Rodriguez secured the bag inside a bunch of black plastic bags; then the two detectives and Carter, a soft-spoken, gentle man, the son of a federal judge who worked diligently on Irene's case and who was sworn in as a Criminal Court judge after the trial, headed downtown to the district attor-ney's office at One Hogan Place.

It was a rather solemn occasion when the inventory began. Danny Rodriguez stood at the head of the table, wearing white plas-tic gloves. John Carter, Wasielewski, and Connie Fernandez sat on one side of the large mahogany table; Sachs and Muniz on the other side. All eyes were focused on Rodriguez as he removed the items one by one from the bag. Carter and Muniz made separate lists on legal pads during the three hours and ten minutes it took to inven-tory the contents of the bag, which turned out to be a virtual treas-ure trove of evidence against both Sante and Kenny Kimes.

Among the nearly 200 items in the bag were passports and social security cards in the name of Nanette Wetkowski, Judy Hyman,

---

*The next day, Gonzales's tabloid story read that it was the bag, not the lawyers, that was subpoenaed, and the other newspapers in the city picked up that slant.

and others; birth certificates for Shawn Little and Manny Guerrero; Sante's birth certificate; audio microcassettes; names, social security numbers and credit cards of dozens of people; wigs; a beige-colored battery-run dildo in a plastic cosmetics case; a half-empty bottle of Ketel One vodka, Kenny's favorite; and two new notebooks detailing every aspect of the Kimes' crime spree from March to July 1998. Also inside the bag, among dozens of other documents, was the grand prize: a manila folder marked "FINAL DYNASTY" along with the forged deed to Irene's mansion. It stated that Irene had sold her beloved home to the Atlantis Group for a mere $395,000, a figure Eileen Elms, a Florida real-estate title company employee, had informed Sante in April was the tax value of her home. Detectives learned of Elms from Sante's notebook in the black bag.

When interviewed later, Elms told the detectives that Sante, using the name Joy Landis, called her and claimed to be a realtor working with foreign investors. She wanted to know if there were any liens or mortgages on Irene's property and whether Irene was the owner. When Sante learned the property was free and clear of any encumbrances, she was a happy camper, because it meant it would be easier to steal.

Finally, it was time for Muniz and Carter to look at the two note-books, which appeared to be daily lists of things to do and remember. The tension in the room was high, as the two men sat next to each other, sharing the notebook as they both slowly turned the pages.

"We started with March, then April, May, and June; we got to the end, and there was nothing about getting rid of Silverman. I'm thinking great," Muniz said. "At least, they weren't stupid enough to write down that they actually murdered her or where the body is buried. Then we went through the second notebook. Same thing. Nothing. The last entry was July third. And Carter, who has a dry sense of humor, turned to me and said, 'Well, I guess we're not going to find out where the body is.'"

Because the defense would not be privy to a detailed reading of the notebooks until months later, during the discovery phase of the case, Muniz visited Sante soon after the bag was inventoried and asked her if there was anything in them that could cause trouble. "There's nothing in the notebooks that can hurt us," she confidently assured the lawyer.

But the seizure of the bag did cause legal problems for the defense. Supreme Court Judge Herbert Adlerberg had ordered that the bag be turned over "forthwith" to the district attorney's office. The defense would later take the position that prosecutors could not use anything in the bag or present it to the grand jury without a court order. Adelberg's order never precluded the prosecution from using the contents of the bag. Prosecutors went forward and used items in the bag in its presentation of the case to the grand jury, including the notebooks. After the indictment of the Kimes for murder on December 16, 1998, the defense, as part of its pretrial motions, petitioned the court to suppress all items found in the bag for the prosecution's failure to obtain a prior court order and notify the defense of their intention to use property of the bag in the grand jury. In particular, the defense wanted to suppress the two notebooks on the grounds they were protected by the Kimes' Fifth Amendment privilege against self-incrimination.

Defense lawyers advised their clients that in order to make the motion to suppress the notebooks, either Sante or Kenny would have to admit authorship or they would have no standing before the court for such an application. Neither defendant, however, would admit to writing the notebooks. But for purposes of the motion to supress the notebooks, Sante claimed authorship.

The prosecution's position was that since there was no indictment yet, the contents of the bag could be used for investigative purposes and that the defendant's rights, if any, would accrue at the time of the indictment. Perhaps most importantly, Adlerberg's order never precluded the prosecution from using the contents of the bag.

The reading of the last two notebooks kicked off a whole new investigation and confirmed what detectives basically suspected had gone on at the mansion. "Bingo," Reznick exclaimed on hearing of the latest acquisition. "It was the peak of the investigation. It solidified and verified lots of information that we had already found out. But we were still trying to put some of the puzzle together."

The night the deed was found, Reznick recalls the excitement in the district attorney's office. Among the important papers discovered in Sante's black bag was a manila envelope containing a crumpled note that Noel Rodriguez, a member of Irene's staff, had slipped under "Manny Guerrero's" door on July 2 to water the plants in apartment 1B. Irene had asked Aracelis to write the note and sign her name. It was dated and timed at 5:30 P.M. The Kimes weren't at home. In the morning, they had gotten Noelle Sweeney to notarize the forged deed. Before 3:00 P.M. they were in the Wall Street office of Chase Manhattan Bank, trying to cash a check for $8,000 in the name of Manuel Guerrero that had been sent to Chase through the Kimes' offshore bank in Bermuda. Sante and Kenny wanted Guerrero's name removed from the check, because they needed the money to pay real-estate taxes to the New York City Finance Department and to file the forged deed that approved the transfer of the townhouse to The Atlantis Group, Ltd, the shell company they set up in Antigua.

Using stolen Florida photo identification and a birth certificate and social security card belonging to Manny Guerrero, Kenny, accompanied by Sante, approached customer service representative Roseann Lombardo.

"I thought she was pushy," the Chase employee recalled, describing Sante as a woman in her fifties, wearing a big straw picture hat and with a large silver ring on her hand. "She was constantly writing in her school notebook, and she said she had a business in Bermuda and offered to 'comp' us in Bermuda."

Sante did all the talking, Lombardo said. "I thought she was keeping him because he would look at her for answers to my questions. He didn't volunteer. I didn't know that this couple was mother and son."

Lombardo never removed Manny Guerrero's name, and the checks were never cashed. In her alibi to lawyers, Sante claimed that she and Kenny were not even in New York on July 2 but were conducting "other business" in Florida on behalf of her so-called "life-time manager," Alan Russell.

The euphoria in the district attorney's sixth floor office over the note in the black bag accelerated during one of the endless late nights of preparation. Connie Fernandez re-examined the contents of the bag and looked at the back of the "watering the plant" note when she made a crucial connection, realizing that the number on the back was actually the number of the payphone in the Hilton Hotel lobby that Stan Patterson had left on her cell phone the morning of July 5.

Patterson had not arrived in the city until 8:30 that Sunday morning and did not call Sante from the Hilton until 11:02 A.M. She returned his call at 11:38. That hotel number on the back of the note established that it could only have been written by Sante on July 5 after 11:00 A.M., when Patterson left a message for her on the cell phone. Fernandez was exuberant. She turned to Wasielewski and said, "This is it. It fits our time line. We have them!"

Of course, Sante came up with a plethora of excuses about how the bag magically found its way to the Plaza check room: In her notebooks and to her lawyers, she owned up to dropping the bag off herself in June after arriving in the city. But over the months, when she realized that wasn't going to work, her alibi changed. At various times, the story went that the bag had been dropped off by Stan Patterson, Shawn Little, Jeff Feig, Manny Guerrero, José Alvarez, and finally a non-existent man by the name of Joey Lusitas, whom she referred to in her letters to Kenny as "Joey the Limp from the Bronx."

Supposedly, Joey was a friend of Stan Patterson, and he was the person who met Irene and rented apartment 1B from her. "We were just following his orders. You were just an errand boy, a college kid," Sante wrote Kenny, cluing him to the party line.

The notebooks in the black bag also revealed how Sante learned about Irene. A March entry has the name of Rudy Vaccari, the butcher extraordinaire who provides quality provisions to restaurants and who was Irene's very dear friend for 40 years. Sante got his name from Ralph Pellechia, his financial adviser, whom she'd met in 1994 at a Las Vegas Anti-Aging conference. He wanted nothing to do with Sante when she called him in March 1998. In fact, he refused to speak to her. Instead, he had his secretary, Janet Sangekar, deal with her. Unfortunately, Sangekar gave Sante Irene's name and telephone number after getting it from Vaccari's records.

By the time the Kimeses showed up on Irene's doorstep in June, Vaccari was already in Nantucket and she was unable to check Kenny's references. In her notebook of March 17, Sante writes: *"Ralph, office, O-F.—I.S. Irene Silverman, phone 212-737-3161. Vaccaro,"* "*Janet R*" referring to Ralph's secretary.

The notebooks also tied the Kimes to Florida and brought detectives to the Sunshine State. "Florida was the first of our home runs because that's where we discovered that Sante had made the more than 800 long-distance calls from the Howletts' condo," Reznick said. That phone bill led detectives to title search firms, Jean Gerber, Carina Qureshi, her ex-husband Sheik Abdus Shimveel Qureshi, Dr. Athanassios Tsoukas, José Alvarez, and many other Kimes plots.

Jean Gerber, a sweet, very proper, but perhaps naïve woman in her fifties, first met Sante and Ken Kimes, Sr., in 1993. She liked both of them and, like so many others, Sante led her to believe Kimes, Sr., was still alive as late as September 1995. The relentlessly lying "Shan-tay," as she was pronouncing her name in those days, told her that Kimes, Sr., was gravely ill and on life support.

During a May 9 visit to Gerber in Fort Lauderdale, Sante learned she planned a trip to the Bahamas. A week later, Sante used Howlett's telephone to tell Gerber she had an 82-year-old friend who was very sick and needed a medication that she could not get in this country. "Sante asked if I would go to the apothecary in the Bahamas to pick it up and that the medication cost $60," she said. Later, Gerber informed Sante that her trip had been canceled and Sante herself called the apothecary.

Investigators found it more than coincidental that Sante needed medication for an 82-year-old sick woman who would die unless she got the drug. In Sante's April notebook are entries showing that her first contact with Irene's home was in April, and that she already knew Irene was 82 years old.

Sante's penchant for knock-out drugs still needed to be investigated, because a jar that contained flunitrazepam, a hypnotic sedative, commonly known as "roofies," was found under the seat of the Lincoln. This sedative is often used as a date rape drug, and usually sells, illegally, for under five dollars a tablet. The same month the trial began, in January 2000, detectives

Rodriguez and Schlagler went to the Bahamas and spoke with the co-owner of the family-owned pharmaceutical firm, Commonwealth Drug and Medical Supply Company, that Sante called in 1998. There, detectives learned that what Sante wanted was 7.5 mg of Imovane, a controlled substance made only in France. The drug affects the central nervous system, slowing down reflexes and breathing. Its use with alcohol can impair thinking and slur speech, and overdoses of the sedative can cause unconsciousness, coma, and death. The detectives also picked up another bit of useful information: that same drug may have been prescribed for Kimes, Sr., since he had been a customer at this particular pharmacy. But because Sante didn't have a prescription for Imovane, the pharmacy refused to sell her the drug, and as Irene's Silverman's body could not be found, there was no way to determine whether the Kimeses used a drug on her before she was murdered.

Gerber's testimony at the trial was devastating to the defense. Wearing a lovely polka dot dress and looking like everybody's sweet granny, Gerber sat poised in the witness box, waiting for Michael Hardy, a no-nonsense defense attorney, to cross-examine her. Hardy faltered in his examination of Gerber and ignored the first axiom of cross-examination 101—never ask a question unless you know the answer.

Strolling leisurely over to the defense table, Hardy stood behind Sante, gently placing his hands on her shoulders, and asked Gerber in a soft voice if she had ever had any personal problems with "this lovely lady," referring to his client.

"I do have a difficulty," Gerber innocently replied.

Instead of ignoring her response, Hardy pressed on. "But in terms of Mrs. Kimes, wasn't she an absolutely reasonable, lovely person?" he asked, emphasizing the last three words.

"There was one concern," Gerber blurted out before Hardy could stop her. "She was dishonest with me. She lied to me."

With that, Hardy threw his hands up in the air, raised his voice in a biting, icy, sarcastic, and deliberate tone, and said, "Fine. I hope you enjoy the rest of your stay in New York," and sat down, never asking Gerber another question.

✖

The big push in the war room once the black bag was recovered was to find José Alvarez. From early morning to midnight, day after day, the detectives kept reading and re-reading the new notebooks until they fully understood them, placing Post-Its if they came across something they felt relevant to the case. "Look at this. It's the name of José Alvarez's father," Danny Rodriguez said one day while reading the notebook for the umpteenth time.

In a circumstantial evidence case like this, with no body and no smoking gun, prosecutors had to eliminate every reasonable hypothesis of innocence. In the Kimes case there were many: lack of a body, no DNA, blood, forensics, murder weapon, or hair fiber. Finding Alvarez became a top priority for the task force. "The Kimes were blaming him for murdering Irene, so we had to eliminate him as a suspect," Reznick said.

Believing Alvarez might be Cuban, Rodriguez and Schlagler, armed with a sketch of the missing man, spent days walking the streets of Union City and West New York, focusing their search in predominately Cuban enclaves, knocking on doors, showing the sketch to strangers on the street as they looked for the elusive Alvarez. The first break came when they were able to track his father to a trailer park in Belle Glade, Florida. Home to a large group of migrant workers, Belle Glade was about 40 miles west of West Palm Beach, just outside of the Everglades on the southern tip of Lake Okeechobee. When he was approached by detectives he was reluctant to talk, insisting that he hadn't seen his son in several months, after having a minor disagreement with him. The break in the case came after Rodriguez gained the confidence of Alvarez's stepmother, who called Rodriguez when her stepson showed up.

"When we found Alvarez in August it was our second home run," Reznick said. The detectives were still walking the hot, steamy Jersey pavements when Reznick beeped them and had them on the next plane to Florida. They landed in West Palm Beach on August 22 in the middle of a hurricane and drove to Belle Glade. Normally, it was an hour drive, but it took the detectives three hours to get through the blinding storm and the Everglades. When they arrived there, some time after midnight, Alvarez and his stepmother were waiting patiently for them at the Belle Glade police station.

It turned out that the Kimeses had hired Alvarez in mid-May 1998, after Shawn Little took off unexpectedly, concerned that the Kimeses might kill him because he knew too much about Kenny and the Kazdin murder.

The Kimeses found Alvarez through a homeless man who put him in touch with them. He fit the bill. He had a limited Cuban education and didn't speak, read, or understand the English language. Sante told him she was a 47-year-old widow and asked him to call her "Mama" and her son "Kenny." They discussed his duties, and then she had him sign a handwritten "family agreement," in English. He thought he was signing an agreement to get $350 or $400 a week for his work. "I promise to protect and help my new family at all times. I'm very happy to be here," the agreement read. Instead, the promise was for him to take care of the house and motor home for the corporation in exchange for room and board. After getting Alvarez's signature and vital information, such as his driver's license and social security number, they put him to work, ironing, washing, cooking and cleaning for them, echoing what Sante had done a decade before with her slave maids. "They always wanted me to wait on them hand and foot. She even had me wash her underpants. They treated me like a slave," he testified.

"She was always on the phone and writing in notebooks all the time. Kenny worked with a tape recorder, the phone, and the computer," Alvarez said. To disguise her voice, Alvarez told of seeing Sante use a handkerchief and placing it on the speaker part of the phone. He told detectives of finding "a small .22 caliber gun under the pillow of the bed." He said the mother and son shared the same bed together and that they were naked—a remark that at the trial caused jurors to squirm in their seats.

Alvarez was unequivocally ruled out as a suspect after detectives verified that he was working a 13-hour day at a car wash in Hialeah Park, Florida, at the time Irene was being reported missing.

Before moving out of the Howlett apartment and heading north to New York, Sante, Kenny, and Alvarez stayed one night next door in the Qureshi apartment on June 11. Sante, using the name Kate, had already become friendly with her neighbor, who confided to Sante that she was having problems getting child support from her ex-husband, Sheik Abdus Shimveel Qureshi. Sante offered to get her "good friend Marvin Mitchelson," the noted California palimony lawyer, to help her. In another bizarre twist to the Kimes saga, detectives learned that the sheik, known as Shimmy, had ties to both the Gulf Union Bank and Bilal Ahmed in the Bahamas and had once met Sante and Kenny on a plane going to the Bahamas from Florida.

To further complicate the investigation, the detectives learned that Sante had plotted to have the sheik kidnapped and held for ransom, for reasons she never fully explained to Shawn Little. He told detectives that Sante wanted him to pull off the job of snatching the sheik. In still another bizarre twist, she put through a change of address for the sheik to her Las Vegas mail drop and then had his mail rerouted to another mail drop in New York, under the name of Dr. Tony Tsoukas. Of course, the sheik never noticed these changes until the detectives investigating the Silverman case informed him. "That change of address for the Sheik turned out to have nothing to do with the Silverman case, but when we found his mail stacked in the Lincoln, we were worried about who he was and whether he was missing or dead," said Reznick.

On the way north, the Kimeses and Alvarez stopped for a night at the Starlite motel, eight miles south of Fort Lee, New Jersey, in North Bergen Township. The motel is a cheap, $26-a-night place on Tonnelle Avenue, in a heavy industrial area not far from St. Peter's Cemetery. Sante and Kenny slept together in the bed and Alvarez spent the night on the floor. The next morning, June 14, they set out for New York City but not before stealing all the sheets, pillow cases, towels, and blankets in the room. Kenny was driving. Sante was seated next to him in the passenger seat. Alvarez was in the back seat. As they drove down Tonnelle, Kenny made a right into a dirt road and stopped the car for two or three minutes in a secluded marshy area littered with dense three-foot high weeds.

"This would be a perfect place to dump a body, because the

police will never find it," Kenny told his mother. He then repeated it in Spanish to Alvarez. "I got up. I looked at it through the window and then laid down again," Alvarez said. The place had no meaning to Alvarez, and he had no idea what Kenny had in mind. "It's a place that looks deep enough to get rid of a body. You cannot find it there," Kenny said. Alvarez wasn't sure of the location but thought it could have been near the Garden State Parkway or New Jersey Turnpike. Later, detectives combed the area for days with Alvarez's help, but they were unsuccessful in finding where Kenny dumped Irene's body.

As the Kimeses made their final approach into the city through the Lincoln Tunnel, Kenny and Sante quite symbolically kissed their hands, then pushed their two fists together, touching each other's fist. "Good luck and good business," Sante warmly told her son.

Before moving into Irene Silverman's mansion, where the Kimeses continued to share a bed, Alvarez was warned several times that he or Mama couldn't be seen in the New York apartment "or they would have to pay $2,000 extra." Once inside the apartment, Alvarez's instructions were to call Kenny "Manny." The Kimeses stationed Alvarez by the apartment door and told him to look through the peephole, which Alvarez referred to as "the magic eye," watch the security camera monitor, and take notes of who came in and out of the building. The Kimeses told him they were going to buy the building, and when the transaction was done, they were going to buy some land in Canada. After four days of looking through the magic eye 12 to 15 times a day and sneaking in and out of the house with Kenny, Alvarez decided to leave on June 18, when the Kimeses were out of the apartment.

"They were bothering me and they didn't want to pay me. They had me there as a slave," Alvarez said

With no cash, Alvarez wandered around and slept in Central Park for the next three and a half days, until he ran into Kenny, who gave him $30. He used the money to take a bus to New Jersey, where he cashed a check from a chicken-plucking place he had worked for in Florida and bought a bus ticket to Miami.

As detectives continued to read the notebooks, they also listened to every cassette tape found in the Lincoln and in Sante's black bag "over and over again." It surprised them when they got "the dump" from the computer and realized they had heard the same thing on the tape a week earlier. "It made the puzzle easier to piece together, and that's when we realized the Kimeses had scripted the 'Circus Circus' scenario to Irene that was found in the notebook," Reznick said. Reznick was referring to a list of questions Sante, posing as a representative of the Circus Circus Casino had asked Silverman in an effort to trick the widow into giving up her social security number.

Within 30 days of their arrest, the Silver Task Force detectives pieced together the whereabouts of the Kimeses. "We had a line on where they were, what cities they had visited, and we started to pinpoint specific things like the purchase of the stun gun," Reznick said.

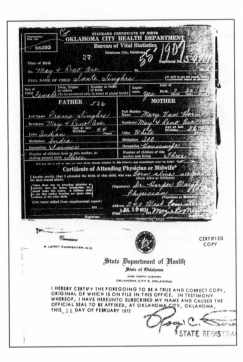

Sante Kimes, and close friend Ruth Tanis

Certified copy of Sante's birth certificate

In 1973, Sante acquired and then physically altered a Certificate of Citizenship, making it appear as though she was born in 1944, thus lopping 10 years off her age.

This picture was taken during a night out in 1986, a time when Sante was in prison for slavery. Kenny is 11 years old and enjoying the company of his indulgent father. (From l. to r.) Ken Kimes, Sr., friend, Kenny Kimes, Jr., Paul Hudiberg (cousin), and wife.

This is a true certified copy of the record if it bears the seal, imprinted in purple ink, of the Registrar-Recorder.

JAN 12 1978

Leonard Panish REGISTRAR-RECORDER
LOS ANGELES COUNTY, CALIFORNIA

REGISTRAR-RECORDER LOS ANGELES COUNTY · CALIFORNIA

CERTIFICATE OF LIVE BIRTH 0190-026458

THIS CHILD	NAME OF CHILD—FIRST NAME KENNETH	MIDDLE NAME KARAM		LAST NAME KIMES	
	SEX MALE	THIS BIRTH SINGLE TWIN SINGLE	IF TWIN OR TRIPLET	DATE OF BIRTH MARCH 24, 1975	HOUR 8:19 A.
PLACE OF BIRTH	PLACE OF BIRTH—NAME OF HOSPITAL CEDARS OF LEBANON HOSPITAL	CITY OR TOWN LOS ANGELES 90029	STREET ADDRESS 4833 FOUNTAIN AVE. LOS ANGELES	INSIDE CITY CORPORATE LIMITS YES	
MOTHER OF CHILD	MAIDEN NAME OF MOTHER—FIRST NAME SANTE	MIDDLE NAME SINGHRS	LAST NAME CHAMBERS	BIRTHPLACE OKLAHOMA	
	AGE OF MOTHER 30	SOCIAL SECURITY NUMBER UNK	COLOR OR RACE OF MOTHER CAUCASIAN	RESIDENCE OF MOTHER—STREET ADDRESS 1304 S. ROXBURY	INSIDE CITY CORPORATE LIMITS YES
	RESIDENCE OF MOTHER—CITY OR TOWN BEVERLY HILLS		RESIDENCE OF MOTHER—COUNTY LOS ANGELES	RESIDENCE OF MOTHER—STATE CALIFORNIA	
FATHER OF CHILD	NAME OF FATHER—FIRST NAME KEITH	MIDDLE NAME KENNETH	LAST NAME KIMES	BIRTHPLACE OKLAHOMA	
	AGE OF FATHER 58	SOCIAL SECURITY NUMBER UNK	COLOR OR RACE OF FATHER CAUCASIAN	PRESENT OR LAST OCCUPATION HOTEL MAN	KIND OF INDUSTRY OR BUSINESS HOTELS
INFORMANT'S CERTIFICATION	PARENT OR OTHER INFORMANT				DATE SIGNED
ATTENDANT'S CERTIFICATION	PHYSICIAN			3/24/75	620592
LOCAL REGISTRAR	REQUEST OMISSION FROM SOLICITATION LISTS	LOCAL REGISTRAR	met	APR 11 1975	

Birth Certificate of Kenneth Karam Kimes, Jr.
Sante chose "Karam," the name of her older
brother, as Kenny's middle name.

Sante Kimes, and close friend Ruth Tanis

Certified copy of Sante's birth certificate

In 1973, Sante acquired and then physically altered a Certificate of Citizenship, making it appear as though she was born in 1944, thus lopping 10 years off her age.

This picture was taken during a night out in 1986, a time when Sante was in prison for slavery. Kenny is 11 years old and enjoying the company of his indulgent father. (From l. to r.) Ken Kimes, Sr., friend, Kenny Kimes, Jr., Paul Hudiberg (cousin), and wife.

Birth Certificate of Kenneth Karam Kimes, Jr. Sante chose "Karam," the name of her older brother, as Kenny's middle name.

Portrait of Kenny Kimes, Age (TK) at a High School Dance, from the Bishop Gorman High School Yearbook

A very dapper Ken Kimes, Sr. at a black tie affair in 1964.

Postcard with the image of Ken Kimes' Mecca Motel in Anaheim, California, located directly across from Disneyland's main entrance.

4 December 1972

Dear Mr. Kimes,

My Chef de Cabinet, Mr. C.V. Narasimhan, passed on to
me the beautiful reproduction of the flags of all nations
which you have made in colour. It is an interesting
souvenir and I am most grateful to you for your thoughtfulness
in presenting it to me. I am sorry I was unable to receive
you personally in view of my preoccupation with the work of
the General Assembly and the Security Council.

With kind regards,

Yours sincerely,

Kurt Waldheim

Mr. Kenneth K. Kimes
President
Forum of Man
International Displays
2323 North Broadway
Suite 420
Santa Ana, California 92706

*Letter from Kurt Waldheim, then
Secretary General of the United
Nations, to Ken Kimes, regarding his
"flags of all nations" posters.*

*Ken Kimes, Sr., and Sante crash a party on
March 18, 1974, where they meet Vice
President Gerald Ford and his wife Betty.
During this period, Kimes identified himself as
"Honorary Bicentennial Ambassador of the
United States." (AP/Wide World Photos)*

Marriage license between Sante and Kenneth Kimes, Sr., identified as a forgery by a forensic handwriting expert in a California court of law.

Death certificate of Ken Kimes, Sr., which indicates that Kimes died of an aneurysm. False information, such as the wrong social security number, the wrong parents' names, and a P.O. box for Kimes's address, was given to Santa Barbara officials to keep the death a secret. As a result, Sante was able to keep Kimes financially "alive" for two years, which enabled Sante and Kenny to steal the Kimes estate from its legal heirs.

Kimes' former business associate, David Kazdin. Sante and Kenny are accused of killing Kazdin on March 13, 1998. His body was found inside a Dumpster at LAX airport the following day.

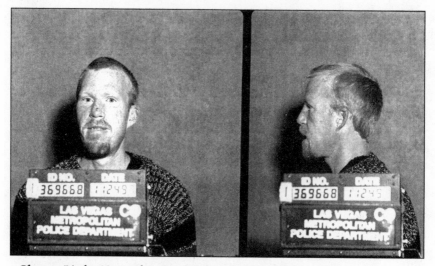

Shawn Little, November 24, 1997, an arrest photo taken before having worked with the Kimeses. Little, who accompanied Kenny to Kazdin's house on March 13, 1998, will be a key witness in the upcoming murder trial.

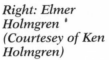

Left: Syed Billad Ahmed was a banker who disappeared in the Bahamas after dinner with the Kimses.

Right: Elmer Holmgren ' (Courtesey of Ken Holmgren)

The Silverman mansion, a five-story limestone landmark building with a sweeping marble staircase located at 20 East 65th Street between Madison and Fifth Avenues.

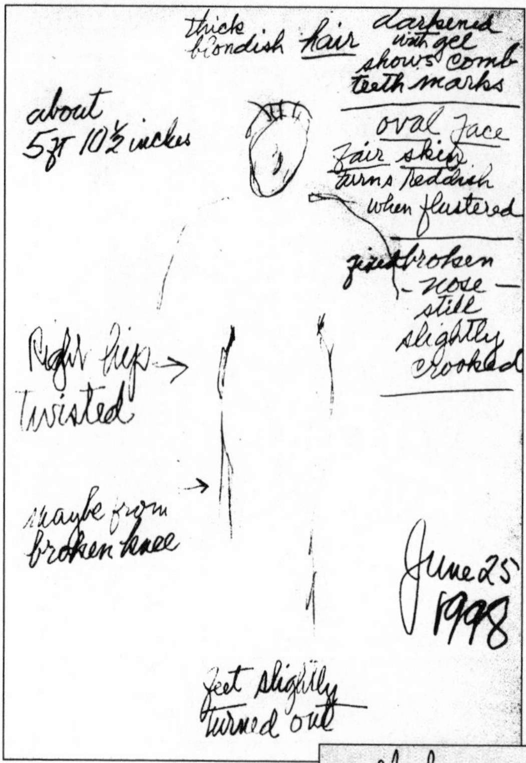

Handwritten notes (top, June 25 1998)

thick blondish **hair** darkened with gel shows comb teeth marks

about 5 ft 10½ inches

oval face fair skin turns reddish when flustered

just broken — nose — still slightly crooked

Right hips → Twisted

maybe from broken knee →

feet slightly turned out

June 25 1998

Irene Silverman made notes and even drew a sketch of Kenny because she felt suspicious of him as soon as he moved into her lavish mansion. She notes his height and approximate weight, that his nose is bent as if it had been broken, that his pale skin becomes red when he is flustered, and that his hair is done up with gel, with visible comb marks.

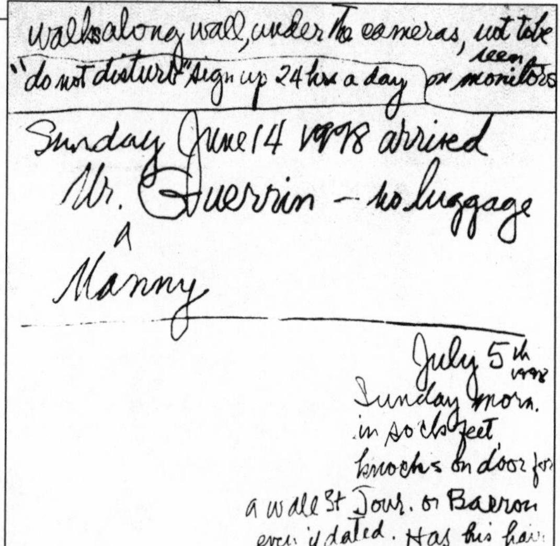

Handwritten notes (bottom)

Walks along wall, under the cameras, not take "do not disturb" sign up 24 hrs a day seen or monitors

Sunday June 14 1998 arrived
Mr. Guerrin — no luggage
a Manny

July 5th 1998 Sunday morn. in stocking feet knocks on door for a Wall St. Jour. or Barron even if dated. Has his hair washed and fluffy and looks very different — hair color still dirty blond, nose bent and deffinately hip problem but younger + more feminine.

Silverman's notes describe Kenny's odd behavior on July 5, 1998, the very day she was murdered. Kenny, sneaking up in stocking feet, asked her for a *Wall Street Journal* or *Barron's,* even if out of date. His intention was clearly to scout the area to see if she was alone. She notes his hair is washed, as though he is ready to go out.

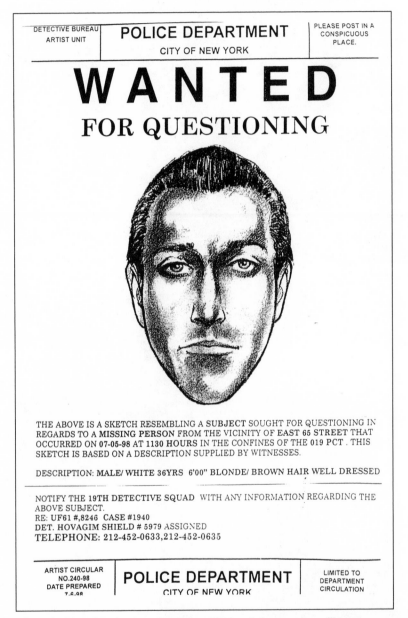

| DETECTIVE BUREAU ARTIST UNIT | POLICE DEPARTMENT CITY OF NEW YORK | PLEASE POST IN A CONSPICUOUS PLACE. |

WANTED

FOR QUESTIONING

THE ABOVE IS A SKETCH RESEMBLING A SUBJECT SOUGHT FOR QUESTIONING IN REGARDS TO A MISSING PERSON FROM THE VICINITY OF EAST 65 STREET THAT OCCURRED ON 07-05-98 AT 1130 HOURS IN THE CONFINES OF THE 019 PCT . THIS SKETCH IS BASED ON A DESCRIPTION SUPPLIED BY WITNESSES.

DESCRIPTION: MALE/ WHITE 36YRS 6'00" BLONDE/ BROWN HAIR WELL DRESSED

NOTIFY THE 19TH DETECTIVE SQUAD WITH ANY INFORMATION REGARDING THE ABOVE SUBJECT.
RE: UF61 #,8246 CASE #1940
DET. HOVAGIM SHIELD # 5979 ASSIGNED
TELEPHONE: 212-452-0633, 212-452-0635

| ARTIST CIRCULAR NO.240-98 DATE PREPARED 7-6-98 | POLICE DEPARTMENT CITY OF NEW YORK | LIMITED TO DEPARTMENT CIRCULATION |

First artists sketch, dated July 6, 1998, of the suspect, "Manny Guerrin" (Kenny's alias), identified by witnesses in the Irene Silverman case.

A family photo: (clockwise from top) Kent Walker, wife Lynn Walker, Kenny Kimes, Sante, Kent's son and daughter.

Kent and Sante at Sante's home. (Courtesey of Carolene Davis)

Sante's close friend Carolene Davis, Sante, and two unidentified gentlemen. (Courtesy of Carolene Davis)

Photos of Irene Silverman taken at her July 4, 1998, party. The photo on the left (l. to r.) is of Aracelis, Silverman, and friend Elva Shkreli. On the right is (l. to r.) Elva Shkreli, Silverman, and Carol Hanson. (photos courtesy Carol Hanson)

Closeup of keys in Silverman's hand, from a photo taken at the July 4, 1998, party. The keys were later recovered from Kenny's pocket after he was arrested.

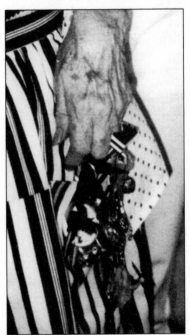

The two "Scream" masks used as evidence in the trial. The image of her attackers wearing these masks is probably the last thing Irene Silverman saw.

STATE OF NEW YORK, COUNTY OF New York ss: | STATE OF NEW YORK, COUNTY OF ss:

On the 2nd day of July, 19 98, before me | On the day of 19 , before me
personally came Irene Silverman | personally came

to me known to be the individual described in and who | to me known to be the individual described in and who
executed the foregoing instrument, and acknowledged that | executed the foregoing instrument, and acknowledged that
executed the same. | executed the same.

[signature]

NOELLE SWEENEY
NOTARY PUBLIC, State of New York
No. 30-4729331
Qualified in Nassau County
Certificate Filed in New York County
Commission Expires Feb. 28, 1999

STATE OF NEW YORK, COUNTY OF ss: | STATE OF NEW YORK, COUNTY OF ss:

On the day of 19 , before me | On the day of 19 , before me
personally came | personally came
to me known, who, being by me duly sworn, did depose and | the subscribing witness to the foregoing instrument, with
say that he resides at No. | whom I am personally acquainted, who, being by me duly
| sworn, did depose and say that he resides at No.
that he is the ;
of | that he knows
, the corporation described |
in and which executed the foregoing instrument; that he | to be the individual
knows the seal of said corporation; that the seal affixed | described in and who executed the foregoing instrument;
to said instrument is such corporate seal; that it was so | that he, said subscribing witness, was present and saw
affixed by order of the board of directors of said corpora- | execute the same; and that he, said witness,
tion, and that he signed h name thereto by like order. | at the same time subscribed h name as witness thereto.

Warranty Deed
WITH FULL COVENANTS

TITLE NO.

Irene Silverman

TO

Atlantis Group Ltd.

SECTION 5
BLOCK 1379
LOT 60
COUNTY OR TOWN New York

RECORD AND RETURN BY MAIL TO:

Atlantis Group Ltd.
1382 Third Ave. Ste 332
New York, N.Y. 10021

Zip No.

RESERVE THIS SPACE FOR USE OF RECORDING OFFICE

The two-page forged, notarized deed between Irene Silverman and the Atlantis Group. The address for the Atlantis Group is a P.O. Box in Manhattan, rented by Sante.

Standard N.Y.B.T.U. Form 8002 - Warranty Deed
With Full Covenants—Ind. or Corp.

JULIUS BLUMBERG, INC.
PUBLISHER, NYC 10013

CONSULT YOUR LAWYER BEFORE SIGNING THIS INSTRUMENT—THIS INSTRUMENT SHOULD BE USED BY LAWYERS ONLY.

THIS INDENTURE, made the ╱ day of ╱ , nineteen hundred and ninety-eight

BETWEEN

Irene Silverman, a single woman having her address at 20 East
65th Street, New York, N.Y.

party of the first part, and

Atlantis Group Ltd., having its address at 1382 Third Ave.
Suite # 332 New York, N.Y. 10021

party of the second part,

WITNESSETH, that the party of the first part, in consideration of ten dollars and other valuable consideration
paid by the party of the second part, does hereby grant and release unto the party of the second part, the heirs
or successors and assigns of the party of the second part forever, and all contents

ALL that certain plot, piece or parcel of land, with the buildings and improvements thereon erected, situate,
lying and being in the Borough of Manhattan, City, County and State of New
York, boundedand described as follows:-

Beginning at a point on the southerly side of 65th Street,
distant 95 feet westerly from the southwesterly corner of
65th Street and Madison Avenue; running thence SOUTHERLY
parallel with Madison Avenue, 100 feet 5 inches to the
center line of the block; thence WESTERLY along said center line
line of the block, 25 feet; thence NORTHERLY parallel with
Madison Avenue and partly through a party wall, 100 feet 5
inches to the southerly side of 65th Street, and thence
EASTERLY along the southerly side of 65th Street, 25 feet to the
point or place of Beginning.

TOGETHER with all right, title and interest, if any, of the party of the first part in and to any streets and
roads abutting the above described premises to the center lines thereof; TOGETHER with the appurtenances
and all the estate and rights of the party of the first part in and to said premises; TO HAVE AND TO
HOLD the premises herein granted unto the party of the second part, the heirs or successors and assigns of
the party of the second part forever.

AND the party of the first part, in compliance with Section 13 of the Lien Law, covenants that the party of
the first part will receive the consideration for this conveyance and will hold the right to receive such consideration as a trust fund to be applied first for the purpose of paying the cost of the improvement and will apply
the same first to the payment of the cost of the improvement before using any part of the total of the same for
any other purpose.

AND the party of the first part covenants as follows: that said party of the first part is seized of the said
premises in fee simple, and has good right to convey the same; that the party of the second part shall quietly
enjoy the said premises; that the said premises are free from incumbrances, except as aforesaid; that the
party of the first part will execute or procure any further necessary assurance of the title to said premises; and
that said party of the first part will forever warrant the title to said premises.

The word "party" shall be construed as if it read "parties" whenever the sense of this indenture so requires.

IN WITNESS WHEREOF, the party of the first part has duly executed this deed the day and year first above
written.

IN PRESENCE OF:

Irene Silverman

By _Irene F. Silverman_
Grantor

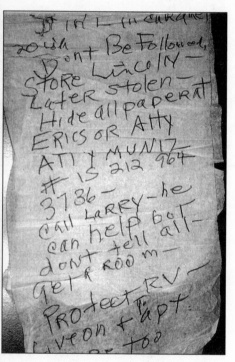

Sante, hoping to smuggle new
instructions to Kenny while
awaiting arraignment on their
arrest, scrawled a hasty message
on toilet paper.

Sante's attorney, José Muniz with Matthew Weisman, in a bold press conference outside the Silverman mansion, demanding entrance. During the press conference, they placed the blame for Silverman's dissappearance on her staff. (Ozier Muhammad/NYT Pictures)

Trial portrait (from l. to r.) Mel Sachs, Kenny, Michael Hardy, Sante, Judge Rena Uviller, Court Stenographer, author Jeanne King taking notes, Connie Fernandez, John Carter. (courtesy of Christine Cornell)

The prosecutorial team, detectives, and legal aides. Lead prosecutor Connie Fernandez is in the back row at the extreme right. Front and center is Joseph Reznick, NYC Chief of Detectives, Bronx County.

16

"I'm gonna blow your fuckin' brains out"

Blank checks found in the Lincoln Town Car sent Detectives Tommy Hackett and Joel Potter to the Bel Air home of Daniella Scaramuzza, a well known Italian photographer who was renting the house from Dr. Muzaffer Aslan. Sante had moved in to the house on February 24, 1998, after asking Stan Patterson to haul still more of her personal belongings from Las Vegas to a storage facility in Sherman Oaks. She also asked him to bring certain other items over to the 3221 Elvido Drive house off Mulholland Drive.

In all, Patterson made four trips for Sante, the last on March 21, when he drove her motor home from Las Vegas to the International House of Pancakes on Ventura Boulevard in the San Fernando Valley area of Los Angeles. With him in the rose-colored 1985 Ford motor home was Judy Hyman, a woman he knew only as Nadine. Sante found her at the homeless shelter in Vegas and hired her as her maid. Also riding along with them was Dawn Guerin, who worked as a receptionist at Nevada Corporate Services, the same firm as Alan Russell, whom Sante claimed she had hired to set up her offshore accounts and was supposedly doing legal work for her for a year. Dawn, a former marine, began working for Sante as a part-time gofer and, though married, Sante told her lawyers that Dawn had developed a crush on Kenny.

Sante had found her latest home by answering an ad in February that Scaramuzza had placed in a newspaper looking for a room-mate. The four-bedroom L-shaped ranch-style house, complete with a kidney-shaped pool, sits on a hillside along millionaire's row in the Bel Air Estates section of Los Angeles. Pumping her image and worth up to the sky, Sante claimed to be a millionaire philan-thropist. Using the names Sandy and Manny Guerrero, Sante and Kenny showed up at the photographer's home on move-in day accompanied by Robert McCarren, whom she introduced as her deaf and dumb butler, Robert Carro. Like all of the other ne'er-do-well types that worked for Sante, she found McCarren in a home-less shelter in Las Vegas.

Scaramuzza, a savvy woman in her mid-30s, was suspicious of her new roommate from the start and became apprehensive as the month wore on when she observed the supposedly mute McCarren speaking to the Kimeses. Later, when she cornered him away from the Kimeses, she pressured him to talk, and he warned her that the Kimeses were "bad people" and were taping her conversations. "Don't talk to me no more. They will hurt me," McCarren said.

Sante figured she had an easy mark in Scaramuzza, but when she discovered she didn't actually own the home, she set her sights on the real owner, Dr. Muzaffer Aslan, and told him she was inter-ested in buying the house. Sante and Kenny met with Aslan to dis-cuss the sale, provided they could first rent it on a month-to-month basis, minus Scaramuzza, of course. They agreed on a purchase price of $800,000 and, being a professional swindler, Sante came prepared with an agreement. Dr. Aslan signed the contract, and then Kenny excused himself to go the bathroom. Instead, Kenny went out and made copies of the contract. When he returned,

Aslan asked if they had a check with them, but Sante went into her usual stalling tactics, placating the doctor with, "We'll do the money dealing later."

When Aslan asked for the documents to be returned pending payment, Kenny gave him a copy, while the actual signed agreement remained in his pocket.

By March, Scaramuzza had enough of the Kimes' peculiar behavior and asked a friend, Jill Gardner, "a tough cookie who drove a motorcycle," to size up the situation. Gardner, accompanied by her rotweiller and a .357 magnum, began nosing around in the garage, where the Kimeses had stored some property. She found bogus counterfeit labels of name-brand designer clothes and perfume, notebooks, sheets of practice handwriting with signatures written over and over again, and drafts of letters introducing Sante to bank officials. Gardner called her friend, John Doty, a private eye, and told him about the strange goings-on at the house. He checked the Kimes' Lincoln parked nearby and traced the car registration to Utah dealer Jim Blackner of Parkway Motors, who informed Doty that the car had been sold to Sante Kimes, but that it had been paid for with a bum check.

Doty, who had once served as a paralegal for Larry Haile, the former lawyer for Linda Kimes, contacted Haile for help. Doty showed Haile the two notebooks Gardner had surreptitiously removed from the garage and then mentioned Sante's name. "This is an extremely dangerous woman," Haile told Doty, and he urged them to get the Kimeses out of the Bel Air home. That night, Scaramuzza went with a friend to Radio Shack, where she bought a microphone and tape. While the Kimeses made an overnight trip to Vegas on March 8 to bring Shawn Little to Los Angeles, Scaramuzza used the opportunity to secretly install the recording device behind a vent in their bedroom, in time to record the little drama that took place the following night. The recording, along with McCarren's later written statement, proved valuable.

It was after midnight on March 9 when the Kimeses returned from the 300-mile, five-hour trip to Vegas with Shawn Little. Little had been told to share the same bedroom with McCarren. But first Kenny ordered McCarren into the bedroom *he* shared with his mother. "You're talking to Daniella, telling her our business. You're not going to get this family in trouble," Kenny said. He started swearing at McCarren and then grabbed him around the throat, choking him. McCarren fell back on the bed and tried removing Kenny's hand from around his throat, but Kenny was too strong for the fragile 62-year-old, and he began gasping for air.

Kenny finally loosened his grip as a frightened McCarren continued to deny that he'd talked to Scaramuzza. Nevertheless, Sante pounced on him like a wild animal. "The only way you'll listen to us is by fear," she said threateningly. And then, turning to Little, she said, "You have my permission to beat him up. He's been talking to Daniella. I know he has."

It was now apparent to Little that he was about to earn his keep with the Kimeses as their muscle man. He went over to the slightly built McCarren and hit him on the left side of his face. McCarren's glasses broke. He fell to the floor, his back hitting against a chair. "I can break your jaw," Little snarled.

"That's just a sample of what you can get," Sante chimed in.

At that point, Kenny walked over to the closet, retrieved a gun and held it in front of McCarren's face, right up to his nose. "I'm gonna blow your fuckin' brains out," he said to McCarren.

"I can shoot you. I could just say you were threatening me," Sante piped up. "Don't talk to Daniella. You understand me."

As McCarren struggled to get up off the floor, Sante began kicking him in the leg and then stomped on his foot with her shoes, shouting, "You fuckin' son of a bitch." With that, she walked over to the desk pulled open the drawer, took out a knife, held it close to his mouth, and menacingly threatened to cut out his tongue if he continued to talk to Scaramuzza.

On Friday, March 13, Kenny took Little with him when he went to pay a "courtesy" call on David Kazdin at his Granada Hills home in the San Fernando Valley. They were going, he confided to Little, "because he's been dissing my mom."

Although he'd never signed the loan papers, on January 23 Kazdin learned from the mortgage lender, Ocwen Federal Bank in West Palm Beach, Florida, that he was responsible for paying a 30-year $280,000 loan with a variable interest rate of 9.37%, taken out on Kimes' Las Vegas home in Kazdin's name a month earlier. The loan document, of course, was a forgery. Years earlier, as a favor to Kimes, Sr., Kazdin allowed himself to be listed as the owner of their Geronimo Way home in Las Vegas, primarily because Kimes felt his wealth made him vulnerable to frivolous lawsuits. When Kazdin asked Kimes, Sr., to remove his name as owner of the property, he understood his friend had taken care of it. When he found that his name was still listed as owner, Kazdin was furious. He planned to retire to Florida, and the thought of starting to make mortgage payments at his age frightened him. He reached out to find Sante. In February, while Sante waited in the Lincoln parked down the street from Kazdin's home, she sent Nanette Wetkowski up to his door as her emissary. "You are responsible for the loan," she warned Kazdin, suggesting he not make waves.

When Kenny and Little left the Bel Air house that morning, both men had with them an extra pair of clothes. In the trunk of the Lincoln, Kenny had also packed a box of heavy-duty 42-gallon black plastic bags, duct tape, and black Nike gloves.

When they reached Kazdin's home, Kenny told Little to remain outside the house while he went inside. Next, Little heard gunshots from inside. Kenny came to the door, a gun in his hand. He signaled his accomplice to come into the house. "Get in here," Kenny ordered, also telling him to get the stuff out from the trunk.

When Little came into the house, he found Kazdin lying sprawled on the floor, blood seeping from a wound in the back of his neck. While Little stared immobile, Kenny donned a pair of black Nike gloves and tossed the second pair to Little. Kenny ordered Little to make sure to wipe away any fingerprints or any other evidence that could lead police to him. The two men lifted Kazdin's six-foot-three, 175-pound body and placed him inside four doubled-up heavy-duty plastic bags. Then they duct-taped the bags, cleaned up the floor, and changed their clothes.

Outside, the two men stuffed Kazdin's body in the trunk of his green four-door XJ6 Jaguar. Kenny tried closing the trunk with his foot, leaving the imprint of his $100 Doc Martin black and orange stitched dress shoe. The significance of the shoes and imprint is key to the Kazdin murder case, because the trunk of that particular year's model slanted downward, which permitted Kenny to close the trunk with his foot, resulting in the imprint left on the sedan. Foolishly, Kenny insisted that his New York lawyers buy him the exact same shoes, after Los Angeles detectives took the ones he wore when he was arrested in July 1998.

After leaving Kazdin's home, Little drove the Jaguar and Kenny followed in the Lincoln as they made their way to the 405 freeway, heading south toward Los Angeles International Airport. When they neared the Sepulveda Boulevard Latiera exit by the airport, they got off and circled around until they found a deserted side street, where they discarded the plastic bag of clothes. Kazdin's final resting place was nearby, inside a Dumpster in an alley behind the airport. The next morning, at 10:35, a homeless man looking for recyclables found Kazdin's body.

While all this was going on, Sante's alibi appeared to rest with Carolene Davis, who insisted that Sante was at her Santa Barbara home almost 90 miles and two hours away, and not at the Bel Air residence. Davis claimed to clearly remember Friday, the thirteenth, because she was at home recuperating from cancer surgery. "Kenny dropped Sante off in the early mid-morning, around elevenish. The soap operas were on, and Sante was telling my mother that she was dating this wealthy billionaire, Sheik Qureshi, and that his bad breath was gagging her. Around five o'clock, Sante called Kenny to pick her up. 'Hurry up. I want to get out of here before Tim gets home. Where are you?' she told him. She wanted to be out of the house before my husband came home, because he didn't like her. It was close to eight o'clock at night, though, before Kenny showed up. When he walked in, Kenny had the biggest adrenalin energy and fire in his eyes. He certainly didn't smell of alcohol, he just acted like he had conquered the world."

Police believe they have "irrefutable evidence to dispute Carolene's statement," according to Detective English. Sante was at the Elvido Drive home the day Kazdin was murdered. According to English, Davis may be confusing the date of the visit with another day later that month when Sante and Kenny bid farewell to her before beginning their 2,800 mile trek to Palm Beach by way of Las Vegas and Louisiana.

Los Angeles detectives are confident about Sante's whereabouts on March 13. They have an eyewitness that puts her in the Elvido Drive residence. And they not only have the Scaramuzza tapes of the threats made to McCarren on March 9, when the photographer set up the recording device in Sante's bedroom, but written statements of eyewitnesses McCarren and Little.

On July 7, 1998, when Reznick was briefed by the Joint FBI/NYPD Warrent Task Force on details of how Kazdin's body was disposed of in California, he sent Wasielewski and Vazquez back to the Kimes' apartment in Irene's home, where they found an unopened 50-foot clothesline, an unused roll of duct tape, and a wad of duct tape in the kitchen trash can that had Kenny's fingerprints on them. On a dresser in apartment 1B they also found a box of True Value black heavy-duty construction quality 42-gallon plastic bags that originally held 12 bags. Five of the bags were missing, and not one bag of that quality was recovered from the Lincoln. Detectives theorized that the Kimeses used four bags for Irene's body and the fifth was used to dispose of any telltale evidence.

Using fingerprints, Kazdin's body was identified on March 14. Twelve hours later, Los Angeles detectives English and Cox met with Kazdin's two grown children, Linda and Steven. "We were told that the Kimeses were two individuals we may want to look at as possible suspects," English said.

A week after Kazdin's body was discovered, Dawn Guerin and Judy Hyman were riding in Sante's motor home, arriving with Stan Patterson in Bel Air at two in the morning. Patterson parked the RV in the IHOP parking lot and spent the night in the van with the two women. Later that morning, Kenny picked Patterson up and drove him to the airport to go back to Las Vegas. Hyman and Guerin went to the house on Elvido, where they met Shawn Little and McCarren. The next day, Sunday, March 22, Sante and Dawn were out drinking when Kenny called his mother on Guerin's cell phone around one o'clock and told her to hurry back to the house, because the police had been there wanting to speak with Scaramuzza, who had earlier filed a complaint about Sante and her mixed bag of houseguests. Sante was pale when she handed the phone back to Guerin. When they got to the house, Sante had everyone pack up her stuff. "We're leaving. Take all pieces of paper, so no one can trace us," she said. Kenny ad-libbed a little by grabbing Scarmuzza's silverware on his way out the door, then shoved everything in the trunk of the Lincoln.

But in their haste, the Kimeses left behind crucial papers that linked them to David Kazdin's murder: his driver's license and passport, documents they could only have in their possession *after* David Kazdin was murdered, because he most certainly wouldn't have relinquished them while he was alive.

The Kimeses dropped McCarren and Judy Hyman at the motorhome in the IHOP parking lot, and Sante instructed her to watch him while she went with Dawn and Kenny to a nearby restaurant.

"Don't let him out of your sight," Sante told Hyman. "I'm punishing him by not giving him cigarettes because he stole $200." Then she turned to McCarren and warned, "We'll be watching you."

After the Kimeses left, McCarren convinced Hyman to let him step outside for some fresh air. As soon as he did, he ran inside the IHOP restaurant and called the police. Hyman honked the horn to alert the Kimeses, who were across the street. While McCarren was on the phone talking to police, Kenny came inside, sneaked up behind him, and slammed the receiver down. McCarren began yelling for help, and Kenny fled with the others in the motor home.

At this point, Judy Hyman left the Kimes fold and they made no effort to stop her. Her replacement was Roberta Inglis, a homeless woman in her 40s that Sante picked up from the same Salvation Army shelter where she had dug up Hyman.

The same night McCarren escaped from the Kimeses, Dawn returned to Las Vegas and didn't see Sante and Kenny again until March 31, when they showed up at her home to pick up two guns Dawn and Patterson had purchased for them with a $740 moneygram Kenny sent her under the name of Ken Johnson. However, Patterson at first refused to hand over the Glock 9mm and Beretta .22 caliber guns he had bought them unless Sante went with him to the police station to register the weapons.

"You know we can't do that," she argued. At the same time, Sante accused Patterson of owing her money, because he had damaged the motor home when he drove it to Los Angeles, and so Patterson left grudgingly without the guns.

Before Kazdin was murdered, Patterson had provided Kenny with two .22 caliber Jennings pistols. Kenny returned one of them, claiming it didn't work. The other gun has never been found, and detectives believe that pistol to be the murder weapon that killed Kazdin.

Two and a half weeks after Kazdin's murder, California detectives met with McCarren. He told them how he had answered an ad at the Salvation Army in Las Vegas in November 1996 and began working around the Kimes Geronimo Way house as a groundskeeper, housekeeper, and maintenance man. His instructions were that if anyone came looking for Sante and Kenny, he should say he'd never heard of them. The last time he was at the Geronimo Way Las Vegas house, he told them, was on January 26, 1998, when Sante and Kenny asked him to go with them to California. McCarren was excited, because they had never asked him to go anywhere with them before. When he arrived in Los Angeles, the Kimeses put him up at the Royal Westwood Motel in West Los Angeles and told him not to leave his room. They took off and returned the morning of January 31, the same day of the Geronimo Way arson fire. About two or three weeks earlier, McCarren recalled seeing Kenny and a couple of other young men he didn't know move furniture out of the house, including two curio cabinets, a grandfather clock, chairs, carved elephants, bedroom sets, two dressers, two end tables, pictures and files, fax machines, and other assorted items. A day later, the Kimeses told McCarren there had been an electrical fire at the house. At the time, McCarren didn't know why they were moving the furniture out, but after the fire he believed the items were taken out because the Kimeses knew the house was going to go up in smoke.

Mike Patterson, chief fire marshal in Las Vegas, was called to the Kimes' house in the early morning hours of January 31. "Our canine alerted to fourteen different places where flammable liquid was poured. When we checked the owner of the house, it came back as Robert McCarren. Later, we learned McCarren was simply a front for the Kimeses. We wanted to talk to the Kimeses, but we couldn't find hide nor hair of them."

In February, Kenny drove McCarren from Las Vegas to the Marriott Hotel near the Los Angeles airport, where he was to meet the insurance adjusters about the property loss surrounding the Las Vegas fire. McCarren objected to posing as David Kazdin for the meeting, but the Kimeses threatened him and demanded he do what they asked. "You don't know how lucky you are that you weren't inside the house when it burned up," Sante said.

For three days, Sante and Kenny coached McCarren on what to say to adjusters Frank Candido and Lynette Caldwell. On the day of the meeting, McCarren was fitted with a small tape recorder and taped the conversation. While McCarren was talking to the adjusters, Kenny circulated around them, keeping an eye on him. They kept him for nearly four hours, then Kenny drove McCarren back to Vegas.

By April 6 the Kimeses, Shawn Little, and Roberta Inglis were on Highway 10 heading east to Palm Beach. Kenny and Sante were in the Lincoln; Little and Roberta in the RV. They communicated with the Lincoln by walkie-talkie. The Kimeses cautioned them: if police stopped them, they should not say they were with the Lincoln and they should never give their names to authorities. They made a few stops in New Mexico and then drove on into Texas, where they made several more stops.

During the trip, Roberta observed Sante stealing groceries out of the stores they went into. Roberta kept quiet and said nothing to Kenny or Sante about her shoplifting until they reached Louisiana and stopped at a Goodyear repair shop in Baton Rouge for repairs on the RV, at which time Inglis confronted Sante in the parking lot. "I don't like what's going on. I've seen you stealing," Inglis said, after which she asked for her back wages of $1,200 a month.

"No," Sante snapped, turning her back on the woman. "You're on your own. Get your stuff out of the car."

Inglis was left stranded on the highway in Baton Rouge and wound up in another homeless shelter. Danny Rodriguez and John Schlagler found her on October 27, 1998, and she told them of her ordeal at the hands of the Kimeses.

It seemed that as soon as detectives resolved one problem, another poser would come up to be solved. And so another team of detectives was sent out of town, this time to Louisiana and a stolen motor home. In the process, detectives spoke to a witness who said the Kimeses almost killed her.

In the words of prosecutor Ann Donnelly, "it was an extremely involved scheme" that Sante concocted while in Louisiana, and it unfolded during a Sandoval hearing days before the case went to the jury on May 15, 2000. At a Sandoval hearing, a judge determines whether the defendant who wishes to take the witness stand in his or her own defense can be questioned by the prosecutor on cross-examination about prior crimes or other bad acts. The prosecutor then uses that testimony to impeach the defendant's credibility as a witness. It is the duty of the judge to balance the prejudice the introduction of such testimony causes against its probative value. The idea is that prosecutors should not use the defendant's prior bad acts to persuade the jury that the defendant is guilty just because they might have a propensity to commit other crimes that are not before the jury.

In late March, before heading to Florida, Sante, using the name Judy Hyman, telephoned the Dixie Motors dealership in Baton Rouge, Louisiana, and made arrangements to buy a Vacationer RV on behalf of Nanette Wetkowski. She claimed to the sales representative that the buyer was a corporate officer of AKI. The terms of the sale were to be cash, and they were to trade in Sante's 1985 motor home. Sante arranged to have the RV delivered to the Ritz Carlton Hotel in Manalapin, Florida, ten miles south of Palm Beach, where she and Kenny were to meet Mary Ella Von Kreuger, the sales representative. To satisfy the dealer's requirement that the check be certified, the Kimeses simply obtained a rubber stamp at a stationary store that said "certified" and stamped the check (that had the name of Lorenzo Carpeneto), which Sante had stolen from Scaramuzza's Bel Air home. The certified rubber stamp was among the property found in the Lincoln.

When the sales representative met with the Kimeses, they told her that Wetkowski was sick in her hotel room, but they wanted to show her the contract. Kenny took the contract out of the hotel area where he placed another bogus, computer-generated stamp on it. In the middle of the contract, in small print, it stated that the seller agreed to finance the purchase of the RV. Kenny placed the certified stamp over the fine print, forged Nanette Wetkowski's signature to the contract, put it together with an $80,000 forged check, and returned to the sales representative.

The Kimeses also created a forged title for the RV. The two drivers, who had accompanied Von Kreuger from Louisiana, left for Baton Rouge with the trade-in vehicle after they were duped by Sante into believing that Von Kreuger wanted them to leave without her.

It was while Sante was fumbling inside her purse that Von Kreuger noticed she had a handgun in her bag. At the same time, she realized her two co-workers from Dixie Motors had left. Von Kreuger panicked and was concerned for her safety. The Kimeses offered to drive her to the Palm Beach airport. As she opened the rear door of the Lincoln and was about to sit down and close it, she saw a stun gun on the floor behind Kenny, who was seated in the driver's seat. Von Kreuger was alarmed, especially after Sante insisted she sit in the front passenger seat next to Kenny. Knowing that Sante had a handgun and access to the stun gun on the floor caused Von Kreuger to sit sideways in the front seat, keeping an eye on both the driver and the back seat passenger.

On the way to the airport, the Kimeses persuaded Von Kreuger to go to dinner with them. At the restaurant, Kenny distracted Von Kreuger at the table while Sante went to the phone area and returned to inform Von Kreuger that Nanette Wetkowski was on the phone and wanted to thank her for the Vacationer RV. When she picked up the phone, the line was dead. Sante went through the motions of redialing but to no avail. The two women returned to the dining table, and Von Kreuger noticed that Kenny was doing something to her strawberry margarita.

"Oh, I've just gotten you a refill," he obligingly said with a smile.

Von Kreuger remembered that she had not even touched the drink when she went to take the bogus call. She never touched the drink and was glad when the meal was over and she was taken to the airport.

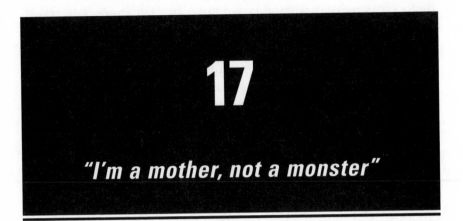

17

"I'm a mother, not a monster"

From the moment José Muniz and Matthew Weissman came on board to defend the mother-and-son grifter team, Sante Kimes's perpetual involvement in directing the defense plagued them. For instance, they advised her not to write continuously, or at all during the trial, in order to combat the image that the prosecutors intended to present of her habitually writing in the notebooks. She failed to heed their recommendation, to the point that when the notebooks were first presented to the jury, the panel looked over at the defense table to observe Sante with her head down, scribbling furiously.

Perhaps the biggest hindrance and obstacle to the defense was not anything that happened at trial. It came in the way of a protective order granted first by Justice Herbert Altman, then affirmed by the presiding trial judge, Rena Uviller. The breadth of this order was so wide that it basically stopped the defense's ability to properly prepare and conduct an investigation. As a result, the protective order precluded any contact by the three defense investigators—Larry Frost, Les Levine, and Cici McNair—and the Kimeses with any prosecution witness.

"What the order effectively accomplished was that the defense could not interview prospective prosecution witnesses in order to ascertain what they would say at trial," defense attorney José Muniz said. "Second, all documents that the prosecution turned over to us had the names and addresses of these prospective witnesses redacted. That also included redacting names and addresses in the notebooks, so that when the prosecution finally turned over copies of the notebooks, there were pages and pages that were blank."

The defense attorneys argued unsuccessfully before both judges that such information would be helpful to the defense prior to trial. In turn, the prosecution advised the court that Les Levine had been convicted of a felony, specifically with bribing a witness in an unrelated case. In his order, Judge Altman also mentioned Levine's alleged misconduct, which had occurred before Judge William Wetzel. In that case, Levine, or one of his investigators, allegedly identified themselves as police officers to a potential witness who was to testify at the trial of Oliver Jovanovic, a Columbia University doctoral candidate charged at that time with kidnapping and sexually abusing a Barnard College student he met in an Internet chat room, an accusation that Levine denies. "The prosecutors in the Kimes case didn't give us an inch and broke our balls from day one. If the defense ever did what the prosecution did to our defense team, they would have wound up in jail," Levine complained.

Notwithstanding his bitterness, Levine admits that the Kimes case was almost impossible to win from the day they were arrested. "The direct and circumstantial evidence against them in this case was overwhelming."

When José Muniz first met Sante in a holding cell on July 6, he wasn't even sure of her real name. Was it Kimes? Kline?

"Sante's performance was incredible. It was the best bullshit story we had ever heard," Matthew Weissman said. "She was completely disheveled, with her thinning hair, and she had on dirty clothes. She kept telling us a tall tale about how the case was a civil matter about a defective car, a car that leaked in the trunk, and that it was so unfair for her and her son to be in jail for such a small, innocuous civil matter."

Muniz soon found that trying to get a straight story from Sante was next to impossible. "What you're hearing is all lies," she told the lawyer. "We didn't kill her; she was a friend. We were acquainted with her. She was a crazy old lady. It was a whorehouse. She had a wild party the night before she disappeared. Her friend asked me to take over this whorehouse, because Irene wasn't running it properly. He's a connected guy involved with the Mafia, and he wanted me to come to New York and take over managing the house of prostitution, because Irene wasn't running it properly."

That was Sante, trying to convince her lawyer that she and her son were innocent and being framed. "Whenever we met, she would go into detail about how Irene Silverman was a madam and wore crotchless panties and that her employees were prostitutes. And when I asked how she knew about crotchless panties, she had a ready answer: 'That's how I made a living on the streets of Los Angeles in my early twenties. I had to live, you know.'

"She seemed obsessed about telling us that Irene walked around in flimsy nightgowns all day long and that there were Cubans and other strange men in the house who may have been responsible for her disappearance." As time went by, Sante included Stan Patterson in the invented picture, saying he was responsible for everything and that he set the Kimeses up.

When Sante saw that her lawyers weren't buying her story, she hinted she had cooperated with the government in saving the life of an assistant United States attorney in Nevada, and they were using her.

The next worry for her lawyers came when they realized the Kimeses had money stashed in offshore banks. "After we got paid a retainer from a Bermuda bank, my first thought was that the money might not have been legitimate. We had no way of knowing whether the money was from the proceeds of a crime. I surely couldn't know what they had in foreign banks," Muniz admitted.

The notebooks found in the black bag led investigators to Bermuda, where they confirmed that the Kimeses had opened a corporate account in 1998 at Lines Overseas Management (LOM) under another false identity, John Kline, and made deposits under that name. "The transactions were all done on the Internet and by fax so that Kenny and Sante never had to appear at the financial institution," Reznick said.

It was during the cross-examination of Sonja Baptiste, a broker's assistant at LOM, that the defense team almost came to a parting of the ways. Mel Sachs blundered and implied in his questioning of the woman that Kenny did nothing illegal in opening the off-shore account. By asking Baptiste the question, Sachs opened the door to illegal acts Kenny committed in his dealings with LOM, such as using a phony name and continuing to use that phony name even after his arrest in New York City.

Michael Hardy and José Muniz were on their feet, seeking a mistrial, arguing that Sachs had committed a grave legal error. The judge swiftly had the jury removed from the courtroom and warned Sachs he had "better watch it" as he continued to put his foot in his mouth. Eventually, Sachs realized the seriousness of his persistant line of questioning and withdrew the questions posed to Baptiste, and the judge struck that phase of the testimony from the record.

Prosecutor Owen Heimer indicated to the judge he was prepared to show that the funds Kenny deposited in the LOM account were the proceeds of a crime. Investigators said the money was stolen from Los Angeles businessman David Kazdin. Heimer further indicated to the judge that he wanted to present to the jury fax correspondence to LOM signed by Kenny using the name of John Kline that he wrote on Matthew Weissman's legal letterhead.

When Heimer asked Baptiste about when her company learned that John Kline was not John Kline, she replied that LOM became "suspicious when we received a fax from a lawyer requesting money for a name that we didn't recognize."

That's when the fireworks in the courtroom began again. The implication now was that Weissman facilitated an illegality by giving Kenny his personal letterhead so that he could transfer thousands of dollars from the secret bank account to the lawyer's bank account. There were even suggestions bandied about in the courtroom that Weissman could lose his license at worst or be reprimanded at best.

As a result of the Sachs and Weissman fiasco, Hardy and Muniz sought to sever Sante's case from that of her son, because the information was unduly prejudical to her. The judge denied the application and a frustrated Hardy protested, informing the court "that I may call Kenneth Kimes as a witness." A few minutes later, Sachs made a similar motion to sever the case, claiming Kenny would be tainted "with a broad brush" that prosecutors were using to damage Sante's defense. Judge Uviller denied that motion, too, and the lawyers were left to cool their heels and kiss and make-up.

During this legal maneuvering, Sante continued sending Kenny a barrage of letters giving him the party line, to make sure that their concocted stories jibed. "Yeah, Mom, that's a good idea," he'd write back to Sante. This routine was very evident when the lawyers would meet with them on the 12th floor of the courthouse in an area where attorneys consulted with their clients. "The Kimeses would always leave us and walk to the end of the cell corridor, out of earshot of us. They would constantly talk among themselves to get their story straight," Muniz said. "We'd look at each other and wonder, 'what the hell is this?' They're figuring out what to tell us and what not to tell us. And at the same time, they'd be kissing and holding hands."

Kenny's position was to continually ask his mother what she thought about everything, the lawyers said. "He was always waiting for her to supply him with what the party line was going to be," said Muniz.

As part of the overall defense strategy, the lawyers felt it important that the Kimeses see each other as often as possible, "because the police are going to try and break you," Muniz told them. "We had them coming to court three times a week so they could see each other, because I knew they would try and work on the kid. Sante would be a hard nut to crack, but Kenny was a weakling and needed to see his mother and be re-assured by her. Besides, she depended on him for financial stuff in terms of him taking care of the numbers. But she made the decisions and he had to get her approval."

Nine days after Irene Silverman vanished, the lawyers went to the lavish mansion and, during a sidewalk news conference in front of the building, they accused the police of concealing evidence that might clear the Kimeses. Muniz and Weissman were rather aggressive, and some reporters thought it obnoxious and in poor taste to be holding a news conference to trash Irene and point the finger at her devoted staff as the people responsible for her disappearance.

"As far as we were concerned, the case was simple. Kenny was still a tenant of that apartment with a three-month lease, and we, as representatives, have a right to enter," Muniz explained. "Sante told me early on in the case that there was no such thing as bad publicity," and he went on to say that it was his client who insisted that the bizarre press conference go forward at the mansion.

The lawyers certainly didn't win any brownie points with skeptical reporters assembled on the crowded sidewalk, even when the television cameramen persuaded Weissman to accommodate them by banging on the wrought iron doors demanding to be let into the building like the big bad wolf. The lawyers were rather forceful in their position to the media and charged that the police were leaking stories and smearing their client's character by depicting them as grifters who preyed on elderly well-to-do people. Sante had advised her lawyers before they embarked on the outing: "Any publicity we can get on this case is good, even if it says I'm a murderer." Sante truly believed her own hype.

Because there wasn't any real defense, the strategy for the lawyers was to attack the victim. Matthew Weissman assailed Irene unmercifully, trying to turn the tables by making it seem that Irene deserved to die. "She's a tough lady. She treats her help very abruptly. She's hard on her employees. She has arguments with them. She's not the lovely eccentric old lady who's devoted to the arts and other things," he asserted.

"Sante's theory was that if you don't respond to what is being put out there, then they only hear the prosecutor's side. Us saying something, even though the media was recording it in a negative way, was good because they still got a positive reply out. And that's why she pushed us into things we didn't want to do, such as her appearance on *60 Minutes*," Muniz explained.

Throughout July, the lawyers for the Kimeses categorically denied their clients' involvement in Irene's disappearance or even that of Bilal Ahmed, the Bahamian banker, or any connection to David Kazdin. "They believe they may have been set up by Stan Patterson. The gun and ammo found in the car belonged to him. They're not murderers," Muniz declared.

At the very beginning of the case, Sante asked Muniz if he thought it would be best to agree to be extradited to Utah on the bad check warrant for the car. "They weren't leveling with us, and deep down inside they knew it wasn't just the Utah warrant," the lawyer said. Muniz was honest with her: "It all depends upon what is waiting for you out there. I don't think it's that Utah warrant. It sounds much more serious," he told her, choosing his words carefully. "She was very concerned that the cops would break Kenny down and he would talk," explained Muniz.

Eventually, when it came out about Kazdin's murder and the disappearance of the others, it started to make sense to Muniz. "That's basically what they want you for out there," he told Sante. "If you get extradited, they are going to have access to you, which means the authorities could question you because you won't have a lawyer with you until you reach Utah. They'll probably hold you over in Utah and eventually extradite you to California."

The Kimeses were also aware of the death penalty in California, and in the end, Sante made the decision that it was better to stay in New York and fight the Silverman case, which had no body, DNA, blood, or hair fibers.

"The issue," explained Muniz, "then became one of trying to beat the Utah warrant here—fight extradition and try to beat it and force the prosecutors' hand so they would present a weak case to a New York grand jury. We really went after the prosecutors. We did motions. We appealed bail. We put all this pressure on them, and I think that is one of the reasons they presented the first indictment for the credit card fraud case at the end of July. That was just enough to hold them here a while longer while the investigation by the Silver Task Force moved forward into Irene's disappearance. Part of our strategy was to rush prosecutors into making mistakes in the grand jury presentation."

On July 31 Sante and Kenny Kimes were indicted on credit card fraud, a move that allowed authorities to detain the pair while detectives continued to investigate and gather evidence against them in the disappearance of the missing millionaire widow.

In a 17-count indictment with multiple counts of forgery and criminal possession of a forged instrument, Manhattan District Attorney Robert Morgenthau said that in the three weeks the Kimeses were in Irene's home, the pair had racked up $670 worth of charges on a MasterCard registered to Max Schorr, who, at 92 years old, was the oldest practicing lawyer in Palm Beach, Florida. The Kimeses used his date of birth and social security number to get the card mailed to them, and both mother and son used the card at luxury restaurants at the Pierre and Park Lane Helmsley hotels and at other trendy spots over a four-day period in June 1998.

No sooner were the Kimeses indicted than their attorneys called reporters, saying the charges against them were "flimsy." Morgenthau shot back and disputed the remarks. "Forgery is a serious crime. I do not consider that a flimsy charge," he said.

Sante's first stop on Monday, June 15, the day after she arrived in town, was at the Chanel Boutique at East 57th Street and Fifth Avenue. She breezed into the salon wearing a light cream camisole, flip-flop mules, a huge white hat, and her large "diamond" ring. Salesperson Jane Duval thought "she was very Florida. She had a lot of cleavage." In fact, the busty 44 DD Sante would often brag to lawyers and visitors at the jail that she carried her breasts as if they were gold medals. Sante bought two Shaker talc powders at $35 apiece and Essential Bath Oil at $35, charging the three items to Schorr's credit card. She then made a proposition to Duval: if she could find her a 1.7-ounce bottle of Fracas parfum that cost $60, Sante promised to give her "two weeks at any of my hotels in the Bahamas." Never mind that Sante didn't own hotels in the Bahamas or anywhere else for that matter. The gardenia fragrance was supposedly what Sante used to lure Kimes, Sr., into her nest when she first met him.

During the third week of July, Max Schorr learned his name was being misused. A Las Vegas bank called him to say that someone had requested a $20,000 line of credit on his MasterCard. Schorr was totally bewildered, since he had never had a MasterCard and had never applied for one. The bank official told Schorr that the person requesting the expanded credit line was believable and knew lots of personal data about him, including his mother's maiden name.

In an undated letter to Schorr, Sante apologized to him from jail, seeking forgiveness for her son's indiscretion. "He's so innocent and has never been in trouble before. We didn't use the card with the intent to defraud you. Stan Patterson gave us the authorization to use the card," she said. Sante went on to explain how she had "this horrifying problem because of my government cooperation . . . and then I fell into the hands of Stan Patterson. . . . I truly believed you were his uncle." Her bleeding heart letter ends with her offering to repay Schorr for using the card and begging him "to open your heart and drop these charges . . . for the sake of my young son, a student who is full of goodness." Sante's lawyers refused to allow the letter to be mailed to Schorr, explaining that by sending him the letter, she was admitting the fraud.

At the Kimes' arraignment on the fraud charge, Sante appealed to Jane Rosenberg, the courtroom artist sketching her, for a kinder, gentler look. "Please don't make me look like a monster. I'm a mother, not a monster," she said. Christine Cornell, the other artist sitting alongside Jane in the jury box, also tried to make Sante look better. "I felt more compassionate for her."

Judge Herbert Adlerberg was hardly swayed by the defense arguments that the Kimeses, in custody almost 30 days, should be released on bail. Adlerberg denied the bail on the basis that they had not yet been fingerprinted on the fraud charges. When Mel

Sachs continued to complain about his clients' rights, he and the judge got into a testy exchange. "You're really playing to the gallery," the judge snapped. "You look it up," Adlerberg shouted, slamming a hardbound copy of New York State's Criminal Procedure Law onto the bench.

Seeking bail became something of a joke as the summer of 1998 wore on, and the jail doors remained locked. Thirteen times, judges denied bail requests on the grounds that mother and son were a flight risk and had no ties to the city. Every time Sachs and Muniz were in court, they'd plead to have the Kimeses released on bail. It was always the same story: Kenny was a high school honor student (lie), a two-year hospice volunteer (no proof), a budding Internet web-page designer (maybe); he's worked at Merrill Lynch (no proof). And Sante? Why she was just a retired housewife with arthritis (no proof), a Salvation Army volunteer (it's where she finds free servants), and all she wants is to write children's books as a career. "The world wants to know why the Kimeses have not gotten bail," Muniz argued.

"Defense attorneys would like you to portray these two individuals as a choirboy and a housewife. But that's not true," Carmen Morales, an assistant district attorney handling the extradition aspect of the case in the prosecutor's office, told the judge.

With prosecutors freezing the Kimes' bank accounts in the Cayman Islands and Bermuda, Sante was short on cash to pay lawyers. Sante promised the investigators a piece of the Santa Maria property as collateral to ensure they would eventually be paid a fee for their services. It was an empty promise, since Sante didn't even own the property. But her lack of money didn't stop her from demanding they hire investigators to back up the varied alibis she had concocted to prove she and Kenny were innocent.

In attempting to have the defense team seek out witnesses who'd seen them on July 5, Sante was trying to defend herself as she had during her slavery and mink-caper trials back in the 1980s. She confided to her lawyers in New York that she had used her older son, Kent Walker, to seek out candidates who could be witnesses. Just as she did in the slavery case, Sante produced a long list of witnesses who she claimed would be prepared to state under oath that they were with her during the relevant time period. The two investigators who came on board during those first weeks of the Silverman case were Larry Frost and Cici McNair, the latter a good-looking, tall brunette who hardly looked like a private eye.

The first order of business was for them to check various Manhattan bars and restaurants that the Kimeses claimed they frequented on July 5. McNair felt it would be easier to float in and out of these trendy spots, such as Nosidam, Ferrier's Terramare, the Plaza, Harry Cipriani's, and the Hilton, if she was appropriately dressed, so she wore a slinky black and white silk dress, black patent high-heeled sandals, and a big straw hat, while Frost wore a business suit and tie.

The task of searching for alibi witnesses wasn't easy. They couldn't exactly use the "wanted style" pictures of the pair the police put out to push anyone into remembering if they had ever seen Sante and Kenny, so McNair came up with the idea that her out-of-town aunt had lost a diamond earring two Sundays before—and had anyone found it? Had anyone remembered her? McNair would describe her "rather dramatic aunt" in her white ruffled chiffon blouse and black jacket (Sante) and her "cousin" (Kenny) as six feet tall, slender, handsome, with brown hair and green eyes.

Sante had provided Frost with a list of witnesses, every one of whom, she assured him, would certainly confirm that they had seen, served, or had a conversation with the Kimeses. It included a bartender named Michael, a waitress named Linda, a maitre d' with dark hair named Richard, but no one remembered that Sante and Kenny drank champagne, or had brunch there on Sunday, July 5.

Sante sent McNair and Frost on one wild goose chase after another. But when Frost retrieved her black bag, as she had instructed him to do (with disasterous results), she lashed out and accused him of being a traitor. She decided she liked McNair and wanted her to stay on the case, so she pushed to have her work with Les Levine, a private investigator that attorney Mel Sachs brought into the Kimes case.

Levine, a private investigator for more than 20 years, had worked with some of the leading defense lawyers in town, includ-

ing Ben Brafman and Johnnie Cochran, whom Sante unsuccessfully sought to hire for her team. He was well known to the media
and had investigated several high-profile cases, such as Peter
Gatien, the nightclub owner accused and later acquitted of running
a vast drug conspiracy; Marv Albert, the sportscaster accused of
sexually assaulting a woman; and former cop Justin Volpe, accused
of sodomizing Abner Louima in a Brooklyn police precinct.

"That first July was filled with nothing more than a bunch of
dead ends and was typical of what was to come for the next two
years," said investigator Cici McNair. For months, she met with
Sante and Kenny for hours at a time, several times a week, during
which time she would be given dozens of names of people who
would "save" them.

Trying to find alibi witnesses for the Kimeses was like searching
for a needle in the haystack, only without the needle being there.
Sante sent the investigators on the trail of a Russian waitress who
worked at a hotel. Unfortunately, she and Kenny could not agree
upon the actual name of the place. "The Russian waitress will certainly remember us on July 5," she told McNair. "She was stocky,
with bleached blonde hair." The waitress was the key to everything,
Sante assured the investigator. "They became obsessed with the
idea that when she was found, their troubles would be over,"
McNair said, recalling a visit to a midtown hotel where she discovered that a Russian waitress had once worked at the Plaza
Athenée.

"Les and I talked to a bartender at the hotel and were told that
no Russian waitress had worked there in July of 1998 and no
Russian waitress worked there now. No one at the bar that summer
remembered the Kimeses," McNair said. When she reported the
news to the Kimeses, they claimed it was "a cover up . . . they don't
want her to talk to you!"

McNair made calls to Bahrain on several mornings at 3:00 A.M.
to find the Kuwait Airways flight attendant who had been Kenny's
girlfriend and who had visited him at Irene Silverman's mansion in
late June. When McNair reported to the Kimeses that Deborah
Montagner did not work for the airline, Sante again screamed
"cover up!"

Of course, Silver Task Force detectives were also having a difficult time locating 27-year-old Debby. They also tracked her to Bahrain, waking people in the middle of the night, then to the Italian Embassy in Rome and the Sudan before finding her in England.

Debby had met Kenny and his mother during a 1996 flight to the Bahamas. He was using the name Kenneth Diamond and told her he was involved in buying and selling Cuban cigars. At the Silverman trial, she described a 12-day visit she had with him in the Bahamas when "they became intimate" and testified about a June 18 rendezvous in New York City, during which he bought her lunch at the landmark Hurley's restaurant, using Max Schorr's credit card to pay for the meal.

Sante and Kenny were very demanding of McNair. It was not unusual for them to call their lawyers and investigators dozens of times a day or at night at home, and these calls seemed well-orchestrated, despite the fact that mother and son were not supposed to be able to communicate with each other. Sante and Kenny devised a way of communicating that bypassed the Corrections Department, which routinely monitors and tape records phone calls of inmates. Since calls to lawyers are privileged, Corrections is not privy to these calls. When the Kimeses learned that Sachs and Muniz used the same answering service on their office phones, they cleverly began calling their prospective offices shortly after five o'clock every day. When the answering service picked up a call from Sante, it was pre-arranged that the operator would patch the call to Kenny, thus allowing them to speak privately without worrying that their conversation was being recorded.

There were so many things the Kimeses wanted from their lawyers and investigators: phone calls made on their behalf, people found, letters read to witnesses. "Sante never stopped writing letters, and it didn't take long for Kenny to begin making his own lists," McNair said.

The investigators found that many of the alibis were half-truths. A person fitting the description *did* exist and on occasion did remember Kenny or Sante. "The tall, thin Hispanic girl named

Luisa always served me. I came in every day and she saw me, as usual, on that Sunday. I bought coffee and a pastry for Mom. She'll remember! She knows me! I was there!" Kenny would tell McNair.

Yes, Luisa was there. And yes, she *did* remember a young man fitting Kenny's description coming in sometimes, but not on Sunday, July 5. The shop "has never been open on Sunday. Not ever," the manager told McNair, who valiantly kept searching for other potential witnesses. "Even if seventy-two people didn't exist and couldn't say they had seen the Kimeses on that day, maybe the seventy-third person had seen them. If I could find that person, maybe he would talk to me and tell me something that would help the defense," said McNair.

As the summer of 1999 dragged on, Sante insisted that Cici McNair take a letter—one of hundreds she gave the investigator— that was to be delivered to a certain horse-and-buggy carriage driver in Central Park. Sante claimed she and Kenny had taken a ride on the afternoon of July 5 the year before. McNair was given a description of the driver and that of a "gray horse," and told "the driver will remember me because we talked and I told him that I grew up on a ranch. He'll tell you he remembers me and Kenny on July the fifth. He'll remember us because we had such a great time!"

McNair and Levine thought the request was absolutely absurd. Thinking the driver could shed light on the events of July 5 was comical. Did he just happen to look at his watch when he supposedly took the Kimeses for a ride around the park? But Sante was relentless about the importance of the carriage driver. On the day McNair finally decided to look, the carriages and the horses were confined to the stables, because the temperature had risen to over 90 degrees. Late that night, McNair faxed Levine: "You know I would do anything for the client, but I can see it coming. Sante's going to insist I find *that* horse and I draw the line at interrogating animals."

There was one person who claimed he remembered Sante and Kenny in "great detail" that critical afternoon. The alibi witness swore that he could vouch for their presence during the critical hours on July 5. However, the entire defense team was very suspicious of his superhuman memory, particularly since it involved an incident eighteen months earlier. This man, a bartender at the

Palace Hotel, was not located until right before the start of pretrial hearings in December 1999. What made the antennas go up for the defense team was that just before this witness came forward, Sante had sent a young girl to Matthew Weissman's office with an authorization from her that the lawyer was to give her $200. All the attorneys were notified of Sante's largesse, and when the lawyers questioned Sante, she could never give them a credible explanation either as to why she wanted this woman to have the money or why this man suddenly came forward at this late date and not earlier.

"A tape was made of his statements, but Levine kept it under wraps, because he didn't want prosecutors to learn of its existence. It was obvious to the defense team that the guy was a plant and would have been indicted for perjury had he testified," Weissman said.

After a lengthy defense investigation, Levine was convinced that everything Sante said was a lie, because no one could corroborate anything she said about their activities on July 5, 1998. Ultimately, Sante blamed José Muniz for the lack of defense witnesses and turned on him.

In the fall of 1999, Sante and Kenny began to insist that investigators go to Las Vegas to shore up their alibis regarding the Kazdin murder. It was important they find witnesses who would say they remembered seeing the pair in Vegas from March 12 to March 16, 1998, when they were actually in Los Angeles. "It's to save my innocent son. The truth is there," Sante rattled on week after week. Defense attorneys and investigators were opposed to the trip, but Sante prevailed, getting Cici McNair to go to Las Vegas on January 3, 2000, paying for the flight and hotel out of her social security check.

For four days, McNair drove all over the desert, made hundreds of phone calls, lived in a rented car with the map spread out on the front seat, swigging Diet Coke and eating Oreos. The first night in Vegas, she stayed up until after midnight to check on a witness who worked as a croupier on a midnight shift at a casino. Another day it was a stakeout at five in the morning in the suburbs to find people Sante claimed knew her and would vouch for her being in Las Vegas during the crucial days in March. But the minute McNair mentioned the name "Sante Kimes," the door would slam or the phone banged down. McNair poured through telephone directories and yellow pages to find Kenny's friends who "worked in a bookstore near a famous gym." When she finally located a Borders or Barnes & Noble in a shopping mall with a Gold's Gym, she figured she had scored, only to find out the friend who had worked there was gone.

"Trying to track down people in their twenties, who'd been in a place two years before, was impossible," McNair said.

Sante was insistent that the Lincoln had been brought to Signature Lincoln for repairs. But after McNair got their accounting department to dig through invoices that might lead to a repair bill that could prove the car was not in Los Angeles on March 13 and 14 of 1998, no such order for the car was found.

The most bizarre of the wild goose chases occurred when McNair went looking for a woman who worked at certain 7-11 convenience store which was, according to Sante's scant description, "catty-corner to a gas station" on Flamingo Road. Sante was convinced, she told McNair, that the woman "would certainly remember me, because I had gone to the store to get birthday candles for my son's birthday and bought Fritos on March 14."

The entire trip netted the Kimeses a big nothing. Kenny was disappointed on hearing the news of McNair's report, but Sante was certain that everyone who refused to talk to her had "been intimidated by the cops" and "gotten to." All Sante and Kenny wanted to know was when McNair could go back to Vegas to continue the futile search for witnesses who could help exonerate them.

18

"We're being killed by the press and the cops"

Michael Hardy, a civil rights lawyer and chief adviser to the black activist Rev. Al Sharpton, and his young associate, a lawyer named Eric Seifert, joined the defense team in July 1999, which meant that Sante was now playing to a new audience. Suddenly, they became her new "saviors, my guardian angels." According to Sante, Hardy was going to use "a secret defense" to get them out of jail. Of course, there was no secret defense. "It was something in her head," said Hardy, who found his new client "very engaging, very bright. But I thought she had a complete misunderstanding of her situation and what she was confronted with in terms of facing these charges. To this day, I believe that Sante Kimes did not have anything do with the murder of Irene Silverman."

No matter how many lawyers she had working for her, Sante still maintained a tight control on her defense strategy and refused any suggestions Muniz and Sachs made that her case should be severed from Kenny's. "It's a joint defense and that's it," she told the lawyers back in 1998. She also angrily refused any proposals made by these lawyers to push for a psychiatric defense for either her or her son.

There are only a few decisions a client must make: whether to plead guilty or not guilty, whether to go to trial with a jury or waive a jury and have a judge decide the case, whether to testify, and what sort of defense should be presented. In taking an attorney's advice on whether to have a joint defense or whether to claim to be psychiatrically impaired, the area is very murky. Kenny might have had a good shot at a psychiatric defense based on the fact that his mother dominated him and he was constantly under psychological duress. Decisions such as tactics and strategy are almost always left to the lawyer, who is obligated to consult with his client. But ultimately, if there is a disagreement, the client can discharge the attorney, and that gives the client an enormous amount of power.

"In the case of the Kimeses, both were adamant, and no amount of persuasion could dissuade them that it was the wrong route to take," Sachs said. "They were absolutely vehement about going to trial together and maintained that inflexible position, insisting that they didn't have anything to do with the disappearance of Irene Silverman."

Michael Hardy sought a second request for severance, but that too was denied. In his opinion, the primary mistake made early on in the case was the decision to retrieve the bag from the Plaza Hotel. "It would have been better for the bag to have been left behind where it was. Either it would not have been found or the police would have found it and would have been unable to connect it to the Kimeses," he said. But it was Sante who insisted the bag be picked up and talked about it on the jailhouse phone while aware she was being recorded. She even went to the extreme of calling her son, Kent Walker, to ask him to fly to New York and retrieve the bag.

Of the entire defense team, it seems only Hardy stood up to Sante and knew how to rein her in. She respected him the most and often voiced concern that he'd quit the team if she didn't listen to him.

In a 27-page decision on September 13, 1999, State Supreme Court Judge Herbert Altman paved the way for the trial to get started in January 2000, by ruling that prosecutors had presented sufficient circumstantial evidence to a grand jury to support "the inference" that Sante and Kenny "caused the death of Irene Silverman."

The judge rejected most of the defense motions to suppress evidence, which included Sante's having possession of Irene's personal house keys, her social security card, and a forged deed to the mansion purporting to transfer ownership to a corporation they had set up with an Antiguan charter. In his decision, Altman said that prosecutors would be allowed to introduce at trial the contents of the black bag recovered at the Plaza Hotel: a loaded gun, hypodermic syringes, ammunition, plastic handcuffs, a stun gun, brass knuckles, a liquid drug that could render a person unconscious, and the notebooks belonging to the Kimeses.

"The evidence that defendants conspired to steal Mrs. Silverman's home was strong," Altman wrote. "All of this evidence, taken together, strongly supports the inference that defendants caused the death of Irene Silverman in order to further their larcenous purpose."

Altman made his decision after having read thousands of pages of grand jury testimony by more than 100 witnesses and reviewing more than 900 police reports, known in police parlance as "DD-5's." After releasing the decision, Altman, in poor health, turned the case over to Judge Rena Uviller.

The decision was a sweeping victory for prosecutors, who could now concentrate on preparing for the pre-trial hearings, while at the same time it was a bitter disappointment to the defense team.

The second blow for the defense came a few days later, on September 15, when Los Angeles prosecutors revealed they had quietly charged Sante and Kenny with murdering David Kazdin. In the criminal complaint issued on August 18, the authorities alleged that while "lying in wait," Kenny shot Kazdin for "financial gain."

In desperation, the mother-and-son felons decided to embark on a telephone campaign to the press covering the criminal court-house in an attempt to manipulate public opinion. They accused District Attorney Robert Morgenthau of bribing 130 witnesses who were about to testify against them, and they attacked the detectives investigating the case, charging they had planted the evidence found in the Lincoln, the black bag, and in apartment 1B. "I want to open an Internet site so people can e-mail me and I can raise funds for my cause," Sante begged her lawyers. "If Hillary and Bill Clinton can do it for their legal defense fund, why can't we?" she argued. "We're being killed by the press and the cops. I have to use the press to my advantage."

In her charismatic, hypnotic way, the same way that got so many people to do her bidding, Sante went to work on the beat reporters who regularly cover the court. She zeroed in on a handful of reporters to use in her propaganda campaign, believing they would go along in convincing people of their innocence. As the case drew closer to the trial date, the momentum picked up, and Sante began making calls at a maniacal pace.

She turned the pay phone a few steps from her jail cell at Rikers Island into a well-oiled publicity machine. By bartering with inmates on her cell block for their pin numbers and paying them off with cigarette money and other commissary goodies, she was able to have non-stop use of the telephone at the jail. When Corrections learned what she was up to, they slapped her with several serious infractions, and her phone privileges were suspended as punishment.

For some reason, Sante took a liking to Sam Maull of the Associated Press. Even though she'd never even met him, she still thought she could relate to him. Sam was the recipient of a call from her to "please save my son, for his sake, help both of us. We're being framed." Sante may have thought she had a sympathetic ear, but Maull was unmoved.

"This case is a travesty of justice," she pleaded to Laura Italiano of the *New York Post*, who was even asked to come to the 12th floor cell area at the courthouse where Sante wanted her to do a story. The gist of the story was that Judge Altman, who had already admonished the Kimeses for holding hands for an hour in his courtroom, was personally interfering in her lawyers' visits by directly calling the 12th floor to learn who she was visiting with, how long they stayed, and whether the mother and son were sitting on separate sides of the cell area.

The story Sante tried pushing on Italiano did not check out, and when the Kimeses were told their facts were all wet, Kenny turned bright red and started shouting uncomplimentary barbs at her. Sante rejected Italiano, decided she never wanted to set eyes on her again, telling her lawyers "she was very pushy, too young, and that she had her own agenda." But basically, it was because Italiano wasn't going along with Sante's attempts to gain control of the media. In a letter Sante wrote her son, she called Italiano "a bitch" for not revealing the sham and lies being told about them.

One reporter Sante never wanted to meet, even at one of her routine "meet and greet" sessions, was Nieman fellow Barbara Ross of the *New York Daily News*. Although she was afraid of Ross, Sante persistently phoned her. "I'm a mom fighting for my son. We're innocent. We need our side to be told," she pleaded. But when Ross wrote articles that upset her, Sante washed her out of her hair. "She's a smart lady, and she ain't going to be sympathetic to my cause," Sante concluded in a conversation with lawyer Matthew Weissman.

Sante liked male reporters, because she believed they were pushovers and felt her seductive presence could work on them. At one point, she considered going after Dareh Gregorian, whom she'd eyed in the courtroom one day, until Sante learned he was a colleague of Laura Italiano's at the *Post*. Instead, she chose Eric Shawn of Fox News as her leading candidate, "because he always took my calls throughout the case, even when he was traveling."

Finally, Sante's search for the ideal reporter to make the public see another side to the Kimes story ended when she began reading David Rohde of the *New York Times*. Sante believed he wrote stories that were more in line with her version of the events surrounding the case. She was also impressed that Rohde won a Pulitzer Prize when he was 28 years old for his coverage of a massacre in Bosnia when he worked at the *Christian Science Monitor*. Because of his war experiences, Sante was convinced that Rohde would be more willing to go out on a limb and fight for them than other reporters. However, Rohde did not buy into her stories and always kept a distance.

Sante thought she'd hit payday when she met the writer of this book, but after a couple of visits to her cell area, she decided I was "too strong a reporter to fall for her baloney" and couldn't be controlled. During one jailhouse visit, Sante reached with her hand through the peephole in the steel bars and grabbed a jeweled crown brooch, which had a two-inch pin fastened to my lapel, and tried ripping it from my dress. "I want that," she demanded. "It will be my good luck piece."

"Sorry, Sante you can't have it. It can be used as a weapon," I said.

Sante sold an interview to Britain's ITV network, a one-hour documentary about the case, in exchange for $7,000 in clothing and other accessories that the producer, Jane Treays, purchased for the Kimeses at Bloomingdale's. The Kimeses wore their new duds for their appearance on *60 Minutes* and throughout the trial. Sante was outfitted in a Chanel light-blue pants suit, accessorized with silk scarves and blouses. Kenny got a Burberry light gray plaid wool suit, an Armani blue blazer, dozens of white button-down shirts, and black jeans. Each of them got two pair of sweatpants.

To satisfy Sante's ego—she insisted she was a size 12—the size 16 labels in the suits and on anything else purchased for her had to be removed and replaced with size 12 tags.

Just days before jury selection was to get underway, Sante wanted a better-looking picture of herself circulated to the news media to replace her 1998 arrest photo. A pool photographer was sent to the 12th floor to snap her picture. Makeup and a scarf were brought to gussy her up so that she wouldn't appear as if she were in jail. Corrections officials were nice enough to arrange for the photo session to take place in a library setting. But instead of posing for pictures, Sante reverted to her old tricks. She snatched the makeup and scarf, stuffed them in a large purse she carried that had once been used to shoplift, balked at having her photo taken, and left the area with the new loot. A Corrections officer intercepted these heisted items, and she was slapped with two more infractions for attempting to steal property.

"We're being killed by the press and the cops"

All through this ordeal, Sante never stopped writing Kenny, with all kinds of advice and instructions. *"We mustn't trust the house press. They are pawns of the police and prosecutors and will do anything for them,"* Sante wrote Kenny. Yet this admonition didn't stop Sante from continuing to write David Rohde pages and pages of letters swearing their innocence and insisting that the case was nothing more than "a big frame" by a dishonest mayor and justice system. Despite her distrust of the reporters covering the court, not a week would go by without reporters getting a lengthy voice mail message from Sante about saving her innocent son. The barrage of calls continued week after week, even though there was a standing gag order signed by Judge Uviller barring her from making calls. Eventually, after a call to Irene Cornell of radio station WCBS got on the air, the judge stripped Sante of her telephone privileges. From then on, she could only call one of her lawyers for the duration of the trial.

Sante was frantic after the judge shut down her lifeline to the outside world. It seemed more important to her than freedom. Every day, she badgered her lawyers to beg the judge to restore her phone privileges, but the judge was firm and didn't budge.

On Thursday, December 8, 1999, Sante and Kenny made their public debut in Judge Rena Unviller's courtroom for the start of pretrial hearings, which would determine whether statements they made to law enforcement officers violated their Miranda rights. For once, she looked spiffy. Jailhouse food was either so dreadful that she couldn't eat it or she had gone on a diet, because Sante no longer had a dumpy, dowdy appearance. She wore a two-piece black pants suit and had made a trip to the prison beauty salon, where an inmate-beautician colored her stark black hair with silver-and-white tones that became progressively grayer during the trial. Kenny wore denim pants, a gray long-sleeved shirt and tie, and sported a modified crew cut. On his middle finger he flashed a ring his father had given him.

The combined Wade-Huntley hearings were held over seven days, and Judge Uviller heard from eighteen New York City detectives and agents from the Federal Bureau of Investigation. The purpose of the hearings was also to determine if the police had in any way unduly led prospective witnesses in seeking identification of the Kimeses during line-ups. In a 28-page decision, issued two weeks before the start of jury selection, the judge granted a defense motion to suppress a statement Sante made to Detective Ed Murray, one of the arresting officers the night of July 5, 1998. She had said she had been a paralegal and knew her rights. Also suppressed was her comment to Detective Tommy Hackett that she might be able to provide information about Irene after speaking with a lawyer. Sante's other statements, including her comments that Irene might be walking her dog, and the fact that she refused to provide pedigree information about herself were not suppressed and were admitted into evidence.

Kenny's motion to suppress statements he made to Agent Emilio Blasse that he did not have a car in the area, his statement to Tommy Hackett about providing information about Irene after consulting a lawyer, and any other statements he made asserting his rights were also granted.

What this meant was that when those detectives and FBI agents testified at the trial, they were not going to be asked those specific questions, and the jury would never know that the Kimeses had indicated a willingness to provide information about Irene's disappearance, but only after they spoke with an attorney. They never supplied police or prosecutors with any useful information about where they dumped Irene's body. "We don't know where this woman is. Wherever she is, I pray to God she's all right," Sante told *60 Minutes*.

19

"Only I can convince the jury of our innocence"

It was a cold, blustery day on January 27, 2000, when the first couple of hundred potential jurors were called to the jury room of the Criminal Courts building at 100 Centre Street in the heart of Chinatown. There, potential jurors waited patiently to be considered to hear the case of the State of New York against Sante and Kenny Kimes. Before the screening process could even get underway, Judge Uviller barred television cameras from the courtroom, saying that under state law she could not give permission for the trial to be broadcast. The Kimeses desperately wanted a national television audience, because Sante felt she could not only convince jurors of her innocence, but could also sway public opinion of her and Kenny's innocence if the case was televised.

One of the few victories the defense could claim was that the jurist turned down a request by prosecutors who wanted an anonymous jury, rejecting the argument that reporters or defense investigators might contact them.

The defense brought in Dr. Arthur Weider, a renowned forensic psychologist, as a jury consultant. The 80-year-old Weider evaluated Lt. William Calley after the 1972 My Lai massacre, developed the Cornell screening questionnaire given to every candidate in the NYPD since 1975, and was involved in developing the Wechsler-Bellevue Adult Intelligence IQ Scale. "I wanted someone with no psychological baggage," Weider said. "I wanted taxi drivers, FedEx drivers, blue-collar workers. I work on the premise that we don't see things as they are but as *we* are. I didn't want them too old or too young," he explained. Weider sat in on all defense strategy sessions with the defendants as the jury was selected and stayed on for the actual trial, observing Sante and Kenny.

The tedious process of screening the jury pool took two weeks. One of the most intensive parts of the process occurred when prospective jurors were called into the deliberation room and faced Sante and Kenny, the lawyers and prosecutors, the judge and Dr. Weider. One by one, the jurors were asked whether the pretrial publicity in the case would influence their decision process. Sante and Kenny were not permitted to speak with them, but that didn't stop the Kimeses from putting on the charm. Sante was all smiles, like a hostess greeting patrons in a restaurant, but at the same time she was very business-like. She knew what she was doing. She wanted an all black or Hispanic jury, because she thought they would be more sympathetic; another reason she had Michael Hardy and José Muniz on her defense team. Kenny gave jurors a boyish grin as if to say, "I'm harmless." When stockbroker Julia Belledonna smiled at Kenny, he was ecstatic. "We're keeping her," Kenny said of the young stockbroker. "If I have to look at Uviller for the next four months, I need something nice to look at," he told José Muniz during the selection process.

"This should prove to be a very interesting and very colorful trial. But it will also be lengthy because there are over 100 witnesses in this case, and you will be asked to examine and search your conscious," Uviller told prospective panel members. As an inducement to becoming a juror, the judge said that, if selected, they wouldn't be called for jury duty again for eight years, a proposition that appealed to the prospects.

The clerk swore in the group, and the judge went through preliminary questions to weed out the panel, asking mundane questions, such as did they have difficulty speaking or understanding English and whether they knew the defendants or lawyers in the case. She described the charges against the Kimes, telling them about Irene's disappearance and that the case was based strictly on circumstantial evidence.

"It is no better, no worse than direct evidence. The absence of a body is not needed for a conviction. It does not decide the case for you one way or another. If the people have met their burden of proof, despite the absence of the body, the only reasonable conclusion to be drawn is that she is dead and the defendants killed her," Uviller told prospective jurors.

Defense lawyers were concerned that her remarks were legally incorrect, because it gave the jury the ability to convict and not consider the absence of the body. The defense felt they were handicapped, because prosecutors sought to weed out panel members who said they could not convict on circumstantial evidence alone. "If you feel a murder charge cannot be proved without a body, that is your opinion, but you cannot serve on this jury," Uviller said.

Although Uviller never mentioned it to jurors, there have been several dozen successful prosecutions of similar cases around the United States in which a conviction was obtained without a body. At least two murder cases in New York State have yielded guilty verdicts without a body in recent years.

Over the next four days, panels of 75 people each filed into the courtroom, filling all of the seats in the room. The judge asked each group the same questions until the search was narrowed from nearly 1,000 people to 100 prospects. Once the pre-trial publicity questions were out of the way, the panel was put through an extensive voir dire process and also handed lists of potential witnesses who might be called to testify to see if any of the prospective jurors knew them. (A voir dire examination occurs when a judge or an attorney questions a prospective juror to determine the qualifications of the juror for jury service.)

The judge, sitting on the bench, looked prim and proper in her black robe, with the fluff of gray that highlighted her hair. As prospective jurors waited to be called, a panel member whispered to a woman that the bespectacled Uviller reminded her "of a nun with a clicker in her hand perched up there." Uviller introduced the panel to the participants in the case, then went through the litany of informing them of the qualities needed to serve: "keep an open mind, reserve judgment, and confine yourself to the evidence."

Finally, on Valentine's Day, the last roadblock to opening statements was past, and the courtroom came alive as 12 jurors—eight women and four men—and six alternates filed into the jury box in the courtroom of Judge Uviller. The Kimes' fate would eventually rest in the hands of an assistant cook at a public school, a telephone technician, a librarian, a stockbroker, a social service specialist, a teacher, a law firm receptionist, a housing authority worker, a salesman, two postal employees, and a woman with a degree in economics.

Without a corpse, confession, drop of blood, or eyewitness, prosecutor Connie Fernandez took a deep breath and went directly for the jugular. Wearing a Tiffany silver, gold, and sapphire heart-shaped art deco pin on the lapel of her black two-piece suit, the lead prosecutor spent three hours outlining for jurors how the Kimes' "arrogance and greed overcame their common sense. They left a trail of bread crumbs for police to follow from California to Las Vegas, from Florida to New York City, and to Irene Silverman's home." Pointing her finger at the defense table, Fernandez turned and said, "Irene Silverman was murdered at the hands of these two people." She told jurors that when they heard all the evidence, they would "come to the conclusion that there is simply no other explanation but that Irene Silverman is dead and that the defendants killed her to get her out of the way. She had to be gotten out of the way. If the defendants could keep Irene Silverman's body from being found, they could buy enough time to complete the [real estate] transfer."

Fernandez went on to tell jurors that the murderous duo had

long planned to steal Irene's townhouse before deciding to kill her and hide the body. She spoke of Sante's many aliases, her calls to title companies to check on liens on the property, how Sante, posing as Irene, tricked a notary into approving a deed that transferred ownership to an offshore shell corporation that Sante controlled. She spoke of how the Kimeses used a rent receipt to forge Irene's signature in numerous forms and spoke of trying to dupe one of Irene's employees to reveal a social security number. She pointed out that in the notebooks, Sante had indicated they knew Irene was about to evict them. Connie described Irene "as an astute judge of character . . . a sharp businesswoman. She knew what she wanted and she knew what she didn't." And what she didn't want was Kenny Kimes in her home. She had become suspicious of Kenny wandering around the mansion and, Fernandez stressed to the jury, his failure to complete a routine credit application and how he hid his face from security monitors when he entered the building. She reminded them that Irene's house keys were among the items found in Kenny's pocket when he was arrested.

"Irene Silverman would never have given those keys to a stranger, let alone to someone she wanted evicted. The only way he would have the key is if he took it from Irene Silverman by force," Fernandez said. The prosecutors made sure jurors were aware that "she hadn't spent a night away from her beloved home in 15 years."

By the time Fernandez went over the main points of the case, reciting for jurors the names of dozens of witnesses who were going to testify, Kenny had turned pale. His gray-haired mother, who wore granny glasses and a white shawl around her shoulders to suggest her innocence, had stopped writing in her notebook and was solemn.

In his opening remarks, Michael Hardy emphasized the importance of remembering, "There is no evidence to support a murder charge . . . prosecutors have a lot of theories. There will be nothing that comes from this witness stand that says the Kimeses are guilty of anything in this case. No body is no body." He argued that police made the Kimeses "scapegoats" because "they're from out of town," that "it has become a trial by ordeal to see if they can float," and that a "timeline" would exonerate them. "There's an ancient proverb that says 'a theory is like mist upon glass, it obscures even the facts.' We will clear that glass and take away the mist so you can see that my client did not commit acts of murder, conspiracy, robbery."

Mel Sachs provided the only banter in opening statements, leaving jurors and the audience in laughter. He told them the prosecutors' case was "a smoke screen," "a house of cards built with a flimsy, shaky, foundation and light as feathers," that it was "filled with red herrings in your path" and "window dressing." "Where's the beef? What this case is about is the quantity, not quality of evidence in living color and stereophonic sound," Sachs continued, characterizing prosecution witnesses as "meaningless," saying they would take the stand just "to dazzle you." Uviller interrupted Sachs an unprecedented 19 times during his 45-minute opening, warning him "to stick with the evidence . . . and not characterize the witnesses."

When Sachs likened the Kimes case to Richard Jewell, who had been falsely accused of planting a bomb during the July 1996 Olympics in Atlanta, and to boxer Hurricane Carter, wrongfully convicted for a triple murder in New Jersey, the exasperated Uviller had had enough and put her foot down. "All right Mr. Sachs, you are through. We are not talking about Richard Jewell, Sacco and Vanzetti, Hurricane Carter, or Abraham Lincoln. Now sit down. You're finished," she sternly ordered, articulating her words in a clear, deliberate voice.

What defense lawyers never bothered to explain was the enormous body of circumstantial evidence against their clients—the aliases, guns, stun gun, wigs, wiretapped tapes of Irene's calls, the forged deed, Irene's late husband's passport, her social security number, and keys.

With opening statements out of the way, the prosecution team was off and running. Day after day, week after week, and month after month, witness after witness took the stand offering evidence that indicated the Kimes' guilt.

There was Mengistu "Mengi" Melese who, over three days on the stand, offered damaging testimony that Irene never left the house unaccompanied and would never willingly have given up her keys.

Ramon Casales, the former superintendent of the mansion for

over 20 years, testified that when Irene disappeared, her keys, glasses, and a red-checkered dress were also missing. Once again, Mel Sachs managed to sneak in a joke by asking Ramon if he was the prosecution's *key* witness. Little did he realize how damning the keys were against his client.

The jurors listened intently to the chilling tape of Irene's voice as Sante tried to get her to give up her social security number; to the testimony of José Alvarez, who spoke about the pair stopping at a New Jersey roadside to discuss disposing of a body; and to the testimony of the real Manuel Guerrero, a homeless man Sante hired, who was found on an Indian reservation in Blackfoot, Idaho. Sante stole his identification, birth certificate, and social security number and used versions of it in New York City to cash the checks for the property taxes on Irene's house and to gain entry into her home. There was another homeless victim, Judy Hyman, who had worked briefly for Sante in Las Vegas and Los Angeles and from whom Sante stole a passport and other identification needed to open a second mailbox in New York City.

There were many other unforgettable witnesses who testified: Don Aoki, Noelle Sweeney, Stan Patterson, Robert McCarren, Nanette Wetowski, Lucy Wilson (she was Irene's friend from Texas), Sonia Baptiste, Helene Pandelakis, Jeff Feig, Max Schorr, Valerie McLeod, Zang Toi, Marta "Aracelis" Rivera, and Carol Hansen—all contributed evidence, testimony that may have appeared insignificant, but in the end provided jurors with tiny pieces of the puzzle that together proved beyond a reasonable doubt that the Kimeses were guilty as charged in the indictment.

For nearly four months, prosecutors laid out for the jury Sante's wild schemes, as she moved from California to Nevada to Florida, to Louisiana, to the Bahamas, and to New York. This included the testimony of Anthony Murphy, a Social Security Administration agent who testified about two phony social security cards that were found on the Kimeses when they were arrested. The cards had been issued in 1998 to two infants in Las Vegas.

The Silver Task Force investigation revealed that the person who had applied for those social security cards could only have done so by applying in person at the regional social security office in Las

Vegas with a birth certificate. In this case, the birth certificate produced was a manufactured birth certificate. There weren't any
records that these two infants were born in New York City or Las
Vegas. When detectives tried tracing the original application, it had
mysteriously disappeared from Social Security Administration files.

"Since we know the Kimeses were in Florida and en route to
New York when someone applied for the cards, the person who
dealt with the Las Vegas social security office had to have been
someone Sante knew and trusted to carry out her wishes,"
Wasielewski said. "The government sent the social security cards to
Sante's mail drop address in Las Vegas and then the Kimeses for-
warded them to the mailbox in New York City that Sante and
Kenny had rented. The cards were among the items found on the
Kimeses the night of their arrest. "We have a good idea who may
have handled the contract for Sante," Wasielewski said.

As the trial headed for the wind-up, Connie Fernandez brought to
the witness stand two of the Silver Task Force detectives who had
played an active role in the two-year investigation, Tommy Hackett
and Danny Rodriguez. Their recitation of the contents of the notebooks was spellbinding. The jury panel would later cite notebooks
as the "glue that put the case together for them," pointing the finger
of guilt at the Kimeses and providing the evidence to convict them.

"Everything they are trying to do to Mrs. Silverman is laid out in
these notebooks," Ann Donnelly told the jury. "If you look at them,
you will see the relentless plan to take Mrs. Silverman's life."

By the time the notebooks were read to jurors, they'd been made
aware of what Sante's abbreviations and obscure entry's meant.
There were notes about weapons to buy, the stun gun, knives,
mace; lists of videos to watch, including *Whispering Death;* and
lists of pamphlets to read: "Document Fraud and Other Crimes"
and "How to Build a Practical Firearms Suppressor." On the day
they moved in, June 14, 1998, Sante's notebook contained an entry
to "change locks/change title/stay packed." From then on, until July
5, the day they murdered Irene, there were detailed "to do" lists
seeking Irene's schedule, the layout of the building, and notes
about the city's complex tax laws. There were entries about finding
out about Irene's household staff and her habits, and ominous

orders to Stan Patterson, who was on his way from Las Vegas, to "give no one information/none . . . and if P comes—nothing. The P, it was explained to the jury, referred to the police. Other entries in the book indicated that Sante was extremely thorough:

Is there a burg[lar] alarm in her apartment? Safe? Buzzer? Get blank checks? Who am I? Ask "I'd like to take a photograph of you" Who was Sam S? Who are her friends? Does she like wine? Try to get a receipt to make 6000 look like for 6 months/ check out rooms/ see if she can cash a check/Look at all rooms/Get all keys/basement? Attic/side exit/ try and get a check/Are we on other side of wall? Get her signature some way/"Could you write your name?"/pack all in Lincoln/ what street to New Jersey? /copy SS [social security] in color/buy garbage bags/paper towels/shower curtain/disinfectant/gloves bacon/broom & mop/send our mail to???/make copies SS #s/open JF [Jeff Feig] account/practice sig/type up deed/keys/ take passports/take SS card for copying/check out Colby [Coby] Foundation? Who attys? Officers?/Who am I? Any illness?/Any exits in her apt?/like movies?/Favorites?/when goes to sleep?/Gets up?/Any friends living in apt?/what kind of music does she like?/flowers favorite?/Get p of a [power of attorney]/pack up papers?/check out trunk/Bove/Muriel Seibert/aff[idavit]/Noelle Sweeney—prepare meet 8:30 at hotel/ do sig[nature]/carbon/roller luggage/who are the good people who know how bad she is? Who can I trust and who would tell me if she's coming into my room? I gave her $16,000/agreement has to say $16,000/get Lincoln/park closely.

However, there was nothing in the notebooks as to where the body was dumped.

Perhaps the most dramatic testimony of all came, ironically, from Irene Silverman herself. As exhibit 44, a secret tape Sante and Kenny Kimes made was played in the absolutely still Manhattan courtroom. Irene's strong, confident voice filled the cavernous room. It brought chills as jurors listened to Irene's high-pitched voice, as if she was right there as she answered the telephone inside the bedroom of her mansion. It was as though the diminutive millionaire's spirit was actually speaking from beyond the grave and pointing her dainty, gracefully manicured fingers at Sante Kimes, who was trying to trick the former ballet dancer into giving up her social security number as part of the plot to steal her fortune.

Sante had a prepared script, written in her own handwriting and found after her arrest in one of the notebooks she kept. She claimed to Irene that she was a representative from Circus Circus casino in Las Vegas, Nevada. "Are you sitting down? I have a wonderful surprise for you," Sante's grating voice was heard telling Irene.

"I am sitting down," the sharp-as-a-tack Irene shot back. "But I'm also wondering what the catch is?"

For those paying close attention to Sante's every word, it seemed clear where she was headed as she tried to score a hit by convincing her pigeon that she had won a free, all-expense paid trip—airplane, hotel, food—for four days to Las Vegas, courtesy of the casino. "There is no catch. It's a campaign we do . . . a random selection . . . we'd love to have you," were Sante's replies to the skeptical Irene, who was reminded at least twice that if she doesn't take advantage of the offer "in the next two months, you lose it."

"I just have a few questions . . . do you drive, ma'am?"

"No," came the terse response from Irene, who was ready to hang up on her caller. Sante promptly made another pitch asking, "So how about a social security number?"

Irene may have been 82 years old, but she certainly was not the gullible old lady Sante and Kenny hoped she would be. She didn't take the bait and did not give it to her. In a matter of seconds, the astute grande dame businesswoman turned the tables on the queen of cons. "I don't know my number," was Irene's cautious bouncy response to her gravel-voiced caller. "You send me the information you have there and if I like the idea, I will give you my social security number."

✖

On May 4, 2000, after 43 days of testimony, 12 weeks of hearing 129 prosecution witnesses, 425 exhibits that had thousands of component document pages attached, and 10,843 pages of transcript, Connie Fernandez stood up and informed the judge and jury that "the prosecution rests."

It was now up to the defense.

The four defense lawyers had chipped in $1,250 to hire Mark Denbeaux, a handwriting expert, to neutralize the testimony of John Osborne, the prosecution expert who never actually proved it was Sante's handwriting in the notebooks. It was Osborne's opinion, however, that the signature on the forged deed, power of attorney, and signatures purporting to be that of Irene Silverman were "tracings. I could not identify them as being the genuine signature of Irene Silverman," he said. The best Denbeaux could do was to argue to the jury that Sante and Kenny weren't the authors of the notebooks and that the scientific community did not accept the field of handwriting analysis.

As the case neared the end, perhaps the most bizarre day of the entire trial came after Judge Uviller ruled on the Sandoval hearing on Friday, May 5. She said that, given Sante's "consistent and persistent life of criminal activity," including "acts of deception," that if she took the witness stand in her own behalf, prosecutors could ask her about her involuntary servitude conviction. "It is clearly a type of conviction . . . that shows her disposition to place her own interest above the interests of society," the judge said. Furthermore, prosecutors could also question Sante about her escape from jail, the documents she forged to have her sentence reduced, the arson of her Hawaii home in 1990, the harassment of Chubb insurance executives, the so-called *E. coli* phony lawsuit in 1997, the Geronimo Way arson in Las Vegas, the use of force to get Robert McCarren to file a false claim, and the theft of the motor home.

The ruling did not leave Sante Kimes a happy camper, but she was determined to testify. She had already written out the speech she intended to read to jurors from the witness stand. The defense asked for time to speak with her privately, and for more than an hour after lunch the lawyers tried to dissuade her from testifying. The meeting took place in an L-shaped anteroom that prisoners pass through before they enter the courtroom. Sante and Kenny were chained to chairs. Four court officers kept the outside door ajar while the lawyers pleaded with Sante, who was demanding to testify, stating repeatedly, "only I can convince the jury of our innocence."

"Sante was totally convinced she could grasp the minds of the jurors and make them believe her version of the events surrounding Irene's death," Matthew Weissman said. "'Kenny can't do it, he's just a college kid,'" she'd emphasize. "Kenny had absolutely no intention of testifying in any event, because he believed he would not be convicted anyway without a body or DNA evidence. His naïveté was appalling to the legal team, who had tried to explain to him that the proof that he believed was lacking in the prosecutors case could be overcome by a good presentation of the circumstantial case."

"These guys are right, mom. You are going to kill us if you go up there. The entire case will be lost and I'll spend the rest of my life in jail," Kenny pleaded, tears running down his cheek.

Sante was unmoved, until Michael Hardy told her he planned to advise the judge that it was his opinion that if she testified it would be against the advice of counsel. "You're on your own out there, and all we're going to do is ask you one question and sit down."

Hardy and Muniz were obviously concerned about perjury and would not be a party to her testimony. "Kenny began to cry and beg his mother not to testify, but it didn't have an impact on Sante at all. She was indifferent to Kenny's babyish pleas, as if she didn't care about what he said or that he was in a highly emotional state," Weissman said.

"Honey, I know what to do here," she said firmly.

Kenny didn't seem to think so. "Mom, please, don't do this. I don't think you grasp how much damage you can cause us in light of the judge's ruling."

"I'm the only one who can convince the jury of our innocence. I'm the only one who can do this."

The only way to prove to Sante that it was detrimental for her to take the stand was to put her through a mock cross-examination. Muniz, who was to have handled her direct examination, started the questioning.

When Muniz posed his first question, she looked wide-eyed at him and innocently asked, "Well, how should I answer that question?" Her eyes gazed intently on the lawyer, pleading for a reply.

"None of us can tell you how to answer these questions," Muniz advised. Later he said, "We knew if she took the stand she would perjure herself. The plan was to ask what happened from June 14 to July 5 . . . and sit down and she would be testifying to a narrative. It wouldn't be a question and answer setting."

Sante would have faced a problem when Ann Donnelly got up to cross-examine her and asked about the slavery conviction. With a jury panel ethnically composed of six blacks, three Hispanics, and three white women, the slavery conviction would have caused a negative impact on the jury. "In short," said Muniz, "she would have been doubly fucked had she testified."

At 2:20 P.M. Sante walked back into the courtroom. Kenny was all smiles. "Your honor, our client wishes to make a statement to the court," Muniz said.

"She is choosing not to testify; is that it?" Uviller asked.

"I'm not sure," Muniz replied.

"Your honor, I would like to just ask—I hope I have the right to ask this question?"

"I will not answer questions, ma'am, but I will hear you."

"I feel this case has been covered up two years and I'm in custody again and want cameras in the courtroom for fairness."

The judge explained that her lawyers had made the application for cameras and had been denied. When Sante asked the judge that she be allowed to speak with the press "to get the truth out," she was reminded that any further applications of this type had to be made through her attorney.

But Sante persisted in further annoying the judge by asking that the prosecutors stop talking and granting interviews to the media. Under the state's Code of Responsibility, prosecutors cannot talk about a case or grant interviews. Notwithstanding what Sante had to say, the Manhattan D.A.'s office has always adhered to this policy, and interviews were not being granted.

The judge had heard enough from Sante. "Thank you, Ms. Kimes. You can be seated."

"No, I am not going. You don't want me to talk, as a result of the Sandoval ruling that you made. More than anything in the world,

I wanted to take that stand. I am this boy's mother, and we are innocent and I did want to take the stand."

"You're free to take the stand."

"I'm afraid of you. I'm afraid of this system. I'm afraid of gossip, the lies that have been fed about my son and me," Sante said, holding up a newspaper dated March 26, 1999, with a headline that read: POLL: COPS OUT OF CONTROL, NEED FEDERAL MONITOR. "I'm afraid of this, that everybody in New York doesn't trust," she said raising her voice several octaves.

"Have a seat ma'am, please," Uviller replied. "Have a seat."

At that point Sante became emotional and began to cry. Facing the packed courtroom she pleaded, "This is a justice system? We're innocent. We are innocent. For God's sake, help us," she sobbed, her voice choking. A court officer forcefully pushed Sante down in the chair.

"Ms. Kimes," the judge said, "if you do not behave yourself, I will exclude you from the courtroom. You are going to follow the rules that everybody follows of civility in this courtroom. If there is another outburst of that nature, that will be your statement to me that you wish to absent yourself from these proceedings. So I'm advising you now, if there is any outburst again of this kind, you will be excluded, and the proceedings will continue in your absence."

After that, Sante stayed seated and resumed writing animatedly in her notebook, while Kenny informed the judge he did not wish to testify.

Sante had a prepared an eight-page, close to 2,000-word handwritten statement she wanted to deliver to jurors, had she taken the witness stand. In it, she insisted that Alan Russell was responsible for getting her to go to Florida, that he had rented the apartment in the Silverman mansion, that Irene wanted the sale of the mansion to be secret, and that she had met Irene in 1994 after the death of Kimes, Sr. All of it, pure fantasy.

This is what Sante planned to tell jurors and the world on May 5, 2000:

"Only I can convince the jury of our innocence"

On June 98 Allan Russell, my lifetime management attorney, legitimately purchased IS apt at 20 E 65 Street, for 6 million plus a deposit of 395,000 in a secret sale from IS. IS has demanded the sale be secret because she did not want her staff and friends to know. Because of promises she had made and that Irene wanted secret sale. previously, she was afraid to tell them she was selling, and simply wanted the money and OUT—AR purchased IS apt in name of one of his Atlantis Corporations (There are 3 Atlantises).

We, K & I Are not the purchaser and not the Atlantis that purchased! AR is! Allan Russell and his staff of 10–15 people were very suspicious of IS because she demanded the sale be secret and all proceedings therein hidden & confidential.

Before the actual purchase, AR sent K & I to do exhaustive search, investigation on IS and the property to assure she was real owner and the property was free & clear. AR was involved in numerous real estate purchases for his many big money offshore corporations & we helped as he directed—AR sent K & I first to LA, then to Wellington and now to New York to research IS purchase and numerous other potential corporate purchases.

IS was trying to sell secretly. IS wanted OUT—to retire, she was discharging staff getting ready for AR to take over—IS sent us on errands, had us locate notaries (secretly) help her get sale thru, keep all secret—At night IS came into 1B & was packing up a lot of her special possessions. She was going to take 1 apt—smallest & pack up her things & put in there.

IS plan was to always keep 1 little apt and to travel—She was getting cosmetic surgery turning over all to new owner. She wanted to be free of all the problems—She didn't want any confrontations—She just wanted out. She couldn't handle she said—needed to travel & retire, but didn't want to face all of them—that's why secret sale!

Help Jury understand—Kenny's a 22 yr old college kid—produce the police sketch—its Joey with oiled down hair—NOT Kenny—This is very very important! It clearly shows IS didn't like Joey & is referring to Joey—"the Manny."

We didn't run into IS until later! I must explain this to jury! Kenny's not the renter—not who they called Manny—Joey rented! Joey didn't like any of them & tried to keep away from all the snoopy staff& IS too—

IS knew & liked us! After Papa had died in 1994, Ralph Pellecchia invited us to N York for holidays. He was wining & dining me to try to gain control of the fortune my husband had left me for investment in Equitable. I brought K & grand kids to NY & Ralph introduced us to IS and Vicarro—we became casual friends & kept in touch—

Later in 97 she told me she wanted to sell, that she was running out of money, too old, and she wanted OUT—to retire! I told Allan Russell, my life management atty & he decided to purchase apt—He sent staff & us there to investigate—He didn't trust IS at all—she demanded the sale be secret not open! So, we all went to research.

Finally, after lots of investigation—AR purchased apt for 6 mil & 395,000 deposit—IS asked me to get notary to secretly come early or late to apt for secret deed, and IS sent Jeff or Courier to get notary Noelle to apt & I know she signed our deeds.

No one knows where IS Is—No crime!

Corrupt NY police have made the worst frame in New York history. In a premeditated frame the police have manufactured a crime and for 22 months have fed the press filthy lies in a premeditated plan to kill my innocent son! We have been beaten, framed and stripped of every constitutional right! Our case is a case of terrifying police and prosecutorial corruption—a system gestapo, out of control! On the very day of disappearance, our able attys have proven the police raided the apt seized contents, and then planted it on us—planted it on us to frame us and kill us, trying to cover up their mistake.

Because there is no body & no evidence, they have planted it and tricked over 100 witnesses to lie and say we are guilty! They have bribed inmates to steal our files to try & sabotage our trial—We must present those incidents to the jury to let them see what this evil & corrupt system is doing—trying to kill innocent mother & son. There is no crime so they are building a mountain of BS witnesses & planting false evidence to wrongly sway a jury & kill us! The jury has to have a candid camera accounting of these terrifying corrupt acts!

All of the business acts we are accused of are not criminal— We were directed by A Russell and IS to assist in the sales transaction—in secret—The jury has to hear this! A viable explanation!

We did not have IS keys or personal anything—all planted— None of her papers or personal stuff in 1B & 1A—planted— The jury has to hear that A Russell is mastermind Buyer & directed all! They have to hear our side—They are drowning in a pool of 135 circumstantial, planted evidence!

There was no criminal intent—we had no criminal intent in the use of Schorr credit card and D. Guerrin got card, said it was her uncle's and had authorized all staff to use it. We had no criminal intent there was no pattern of fraud—We told the waiters it was not our card and gave them our whereabouts! (Jesus at the Pierre)

All of the aliases they say we used (exist) & we were directed to use those names by AR & staff—No crime committed—no pattern of fraud—The jury needs to hear our side of defense to every charge & insinuation. These had viable explanations that only I can tell—distance Kenny as the college kid he is— He only did as he was told.

Not our apt—not our car—we didn't check bag—The jury needs explanation. All the jury is hearing is filthy lies—we have a burden to explain & help the jury see alternatives! In this rare circumstantial case we have a burden to save Kenny's innocent life!

I was directed to keep diaries of all and I did—the ledgers are also

1. Notes dictated to me
2. Notes I took down of other's notes
3. Notes of what staff wanted or said
4. Others have written in ledgers—planted—framed—lots of people's handwriting—
5. We got things FOR them not as them
6. I'm a doodler—I can't remember all notes or meaning!

Like Yea IS probably meant Yea the sale is OK I think.

The jury needs a viable explanation of the ledgers—I can easily prove it to them—otherwise the ledgers not explained are bad—The jury needs explanation here—every word in these ledgers can be explained to our benefit—we must let me explain on the stand—I have prepared carefully for defense & cross questioning—

I gave Kenny dictation a lot for his Books—It all must be explained in context! to jury—

No one knows where IS is

But we must take stand and give jury our side—at least the facts leading to this nightmare and what may have happened! Give the jury alternatives & what our role was in all this—

1. No one knows where She is—We think
2. IS herself may have taken the money & run—not wanting to face her staff & friends
3. Her friends found out and were furious and have hidden her somewhere—
4. Any random thing—anyone in the world could know where she is—

But the police are bribing 100 witnesses to lie & pin it on us and planting evidence on us—

I must take the stand & explain what has happened—give the jury a viable explanation and alternative—we have no motive—AR had no motive when IS disappeared—the sale was halted a lot of money was lost!

1. I was not with or impersonated IS with notary. I believed the deeds authentic and brought Noelle notary to IS as IS requested— We need experts! Or, at least our side explanation to the jury! Put me on the stand—
2. We did not—IS and her phone genius expert taped her own calls—

We must get original tapes and much will prove she & Richard did the phone taping!

3. We did not rob or burglarize a thing—we had keys—all had keys—police went into apt July 5, 98 seized & planted on us!

July 3 she said she was so happy—all was well—She had discharged all—and July 5—AR was sending Stan Patterson to manage & handle the take over! A little party planned—Some of AR's associates at Plaza—everything seemed fine—

DEAD END

We went to get Stan Patterson at Hilton & were briefing him to IS to work with & take over & we got arrested! & the Nightmare Began!

20

"If it walks like a duck, talks like a duck, sounds like a duck, it is a duck"

With summations set to begin May 8, in the 13th week of testimony, Sante sensed it was the end of the line. The weather had turned unusually hot and humid for so early in the season, and the courtroom was sweltering. The unseasonable weather didn't stop the judge from clarifying for the lawyers the instructions she planned to deliver to the jury once closing arguments concluded. But before summations could start, José Muniz notified Judge Uviller that Sante wanted to make a statement to the jury.

The judge explained to Sante that either she could testify and subject herself to cross-examination or she could remain silent. "The choice of this defendant is to either allow her lawyer to deliver that summation or to proceed as her own lawyer, *pro se* (representing herself without the aid of her lawyers), and deliver her own summation with the lawyer making no argument or closing statement to the jury," Uviller said.

Sante conferred with her lawyers and, after an off-the-record discussion with them, Muniz advised the judge that she had elected not to proceed *pro se* and would allow the defense to make the "appropriate" summation.

With that out of the way, Michael Hardy began what was a biting and at times sarcastic six-and-a-half-hour summation that lasted over two days. It started with him placing a 1970 photo of Sante on the monitor to take jurors back in time to when she appeared as an Elizabeth Taylor lookalike. He reminded them not to allow sympathy and concern for Irene to "dictate the verdict" and warned them against blaming the Kimeses as a "convenient scapegoat" for her disappearance.

As the afternoon wore on and the courtroom became increasingly hot and uncomfortable, Hardy's summation became more passionate and fiery. He discounted the importance of the Lincoln's contents and the guns found on the Kimeses. He denounced the police, saying they had not thoroughly investigated the case, neglecting to delve into other suspects who might have had a motive to want Irene to disappear from the face of the earth. He argued that the Coby Foundation Irene set up to honor her mother's needlecraft work stood to gain upon her death, which was simply echoing what Sante had perhaps convinced herself of: that Irene's staff and the Coby Foundation were trying to stop the sale of the building, and so they bumped her off or knew where she was.

Hardy also addressed what he referred to as "the outrageous" testimony of José Alvarez, who testified about Sante and Kenny sleeping together, and that of Roseann Lombardo, the customer service representative at Chase Manhattan Bank who suggested in her testimony that Kenny was a kept man. "It's all to distract you," he said. "Don't fall into the smear tactics. This case is about a mother and son trial. It is a unique case. When in the course of history . . . can we recall a mother and child being on trial together? There is no way that a mother can ever not be concerned about in some way, or cut herself off from, her children," he said quietly.

"If it walks like a duck, talks like a duck . . . it is a duck"

After lunch, with the jury seated and ready to listen to Mel Sachs give his summation, Sante suddenly stood up from the defense table and glared at the judge. "You didn't let Mr. Hardy finish," she said, venom spewing from her mouth.

"Let the jury step out," Uviller hastily ordered.

With jurors out of earshot of the goings-on inside the courtroom, Uviller read Sante the riot act. "If I hear another outburst out of you again, you will leave this courtroom and you will not come back until I am assured by your lawyers that you will not speak out before this jury. If you do, you will be immediately ejected. A single word by you will mean you are ejected." Michael Hardy slapped Sante's hand in an effort to calm her down and signal her to knock it off.

It was now Mel Sachs's turn to speak for Kenny. He began his summation by telling the jury the case "was replete with reasonable doubt" and then repeated the words four times for emphasis. "The case the prosecution presented is like a house of cards . . . that would topple." He attacked witnesses as "unreliable, not trustworthy. It is an insult to your intelligence."

After speaking for more than six hours over two days, Sachs got to the bottom line of his argument pleading with jurors to "be fair to this young man who was not able to make all his own choices in life."

It was now up to the prosecution to speak for the last time. For the next two and a half days, Connie Fernandez and Ann Donnelly went over the evidence, reminding the panel that, contrary to what the defense suggested, Irene did not walk away from everything on July 5. The prosecution conceded that while there were no eyewitnesses, blood, DNA, or body, "the sheer force of the credible, consistent, and incriminating and conclusive evidence that is before you is what you will use to decide if these defendants are guilty."

Fernandez went on to describe the prosecution's version of the crime. "They choked her; they wrapped her up; they took her out and put her in the trunk of that Lincoln Town Car and disposed of her. They robbed her of her personal keys, which were like part of her body, and they burglarized her apartment and peeled away her life. They took her personal possessions. They were arrested with those items within hours of Irene Silverman last being seen alive. They had on them her social security card, which they could only have gotten from her office. Do not reward these defendants just because they were clever enough to dispose of Irene Silverman's body. Remember, to them she was an object, she was an obstacle, she was nothing. To her friends, she was someone who was full of life on the fourth of July," an exhausted Connie Fernandez concluded.

On Monday, May 15, shortly before Judge Uviller was to instruct the jury on the law, the court was informed by an uncle of juror number four, Michael Brown, that he had taken ill during the night and was in the hospital, and it was uncertain as to when he would be released. With the uncertainty of Brown's release, Uviller waited more than two hours before replacing the ailing juror with alternate Michael Alvarez, a librarian. The judge then took over three hours to instruct the jury, explaining reasonable doubt to them and the difference between direct and circumstantial evidence. She went over in detail the specific charges of the indictment, and itemized the elements of each charge needed to convict or acquit the Kimeses of a particular charge.

There was one other obstacle that had to be resolved before the case was to be handed to the jury: Out of the blue, pet psychic Paula Forrester turned up again in the courtroom, claiming to have overheard jurors discussing the case in the ladies' bathroom at the courthouse and when she went down the elevator with them. If true, this might have resulted in a mistrial. Fortunately, the prosecution and defense lawyers and the judge learned of the story, individually questioned the jurors, and found the allegations not true. The concern was that if Forester had waited until after the guilty verdict to inform the defense, which was a possibility, they could have conceivably moved for a mistrial on grounds of jury interference.

At 2:20 P.M. the twelve members of the jury walked past Sante. The alternates were dismissed with the thanks of Judge Uviller. Ella Reape, juror number seven, made eye contact with Sante, who tilted her head sideways trying to establish eye contact with her. "But as we walked to the deliberating room, I could see she had tears in her eyes, like a 'have pity on me' kind of look on her face. She was trying to get me to look at her. Toward the end of the trial, I had noticed she would try and make herself cry when she couldn't control what was happening in the courtroom."

"If it walks like a duck, talks like a duck . . . it is a duck"

The cream-colored deliberating room, down the hallway from Judge Uviller's robing room, was rather non-descript. The furnishings were skimpy: a large, rectangular, conference-style, dark wood table, twelve high-back leather chairs, two bathrooms, a water cooler, an air-conditioning unit, and two windows that faced south overlooking the state's Motor Vehicle Bureau office building.

✖

Once inside the small room, the jurors could discuss the case for the first time.

In extensive interviews, the jurors disclosed their thoughts and observations of what happened during their four days of deliberations. Of the eight women and four men on the panel, only one juror, Raymond Rivera, could not be located after the trial. Two of the jurors who kept in touch with Michael Brown after he was replaced said he indicated to them that he would have voted for conviction, had he remained on the panel.

Brenda Safford had not realized that since she was the first juror selected for the panel back in February, she automatically became the jury foreperson. She had never served on a jury before, but after concluding deliberations, her colleagues said that she handled her new assignment like a pro.

Brenda began by asking her colleagues how they wanted to proceed. Forty minutes later, she sent the first note to the judge. The jury wanted diagrams of apartment 1A and 1B, which Irene and the Kimeses had occupied. They also asked for the eavesdropping tapes, the tape-recording device, and the black bag retrieved from The Plaza Hotel that contained the "FINAL DYNASTY" folder and the forged deed, and pictures of the interiors of the apartments. They also wanted to see the notebooks, "mainly out of curiosity," Ella Reape said. "They had heard so much about the notebooks. There was no rhyme or reason to the request. The jury just wanted everything."

At 6:45 P.M., after deliberating four and a half hours, the panel broke for dinner and was taken to Forlini's restaurant behind the courthouse. They were a jovial bunch, laughing and appearing relaxed to Joe Forlini, one of the owners at the popular Italian restaurant, who observed them during dinner. After dinner, they retired to an area motel for the night. By 10 A.M. the next morning, the jury was fast at work back at the courthouse.

As the person sitting closest to the witness box, Brenda described herself as a witness watcher, carefully observing witness's reactions to questions the prosecutor and defense posed and making a mental note of the reactions of Kenny and his mother to those responses.

Brenda considered José Alvarez's testimony about Kenny dumping the body strong. She also considered significant the testimony of the notaries, Don Aoki, Noelle Sweeney, and Nanette Wetkowski. "I also think José knew more about their plans and what they were up to than he testified in court. He knew more than he told on the witness stand about their sleeping habits.

"Kenny's body language told me a lot. I noticed that he dropped his head and didn't look at Debby, the flight-attendant girlfriend, when she testified. He did everything to avoid making eye contact with her. Sante, on the other hand, was stone-faced. Her lips were tight; she had a taut expression on her face. She tried to scare a chosen few of us on the jury. There was one juror who absolutely wouldn't even look at her anymore. But what got me was Kenny. He'd look at the ceiling; he'd bat his eyes as if in a trance, and I couldn't figure out if he was trying to convey that he was a mental case," Brenda said.

Two jurors weren't going to take anything for granted. Before voting on the eavesdropping counts, they wanted to be shown proof that the Kimeses had the recording device and that the tapes they made actually existed, even though the tapes had been played for them during the trial. Once they were satisfied, the jurors began recording their votes on the five-page verdict sheet on Tuesday, the second day of deliberations, placing guilty votes next to each of the Kimes' 29 eavesdropping counts before moving on to the other charges.

It had been unanimously agreed before voting commenced that the panel would not take a secret ballot, but would always vote on each count by a show of hands after the evidence related to the charge was discussed. Since Brenda was the jury foreperson, she decided to always be the last to vote on a particular count, so as not to appear to be rushing panel members into making a hasty decision. "There was never any pressure put on any juror," Ella said.

The familiar refrain by jurors at voting time was, "Who are we voting on?" If reminded it was Sante, they'd good-naturedly put up two hands as an indication of how they felt—that she was doubly guilty of whatever charge jurors were voting on.

Before turning to the evidence in the case, the jury had a rather long and emotional discussion about Kenny and whether he was a victim of his mother. "He's so young, he never had a life; he had a domineering mother," were phrases most often echoed in the room. Questions arose as to whether Sante had manipulated him. What kind of relationship was there between them? Many in the room felt the relationship went beyond that of a mother and son. Was she in bed with him?

"When I heard José Alvarez testify they were in bed together, I felt the lady is sick," Mamie Johnson, the number six juror said.

The jury's consensus during deliberations was that while Kenny wasn't the mastermind, he definitely had responsibility in it. Vanessa Miller, juror number nine, felt sympathy for him, but pointed out that she was the same age as Kenny. "In the end, I concluded he was very conscious of right and wrong. He had a mind to make up on his own. He was not a child."

One of Kenny's traits Ella remembered while deliberating was the look he gave the judge towards the end of the trial. "For most of the trial, he sat at the defense table acting rather innocent. But when the judge ruled against them, he gave a frightening stare to the judge that was scary. When I saw the expression in his face, I knew he was a murderer. There was no doubt in my mind, from the hatred in his eyes, that this man was capable of murder."

Sante fared no better for many jurors, who observed her giving a witness that "I'm going to kill you if you don't drop dead on the stand right now" look. "She had a look of hate in an attempt to intimidate the witness," Ella said.

Before turning to the evidence in the case, jurors discussed the attachment they had developed to Irene Silverman and the impact

she had on them after having listened to her voice on those eavesdropping tapes, having heard witnesses describe her as vibrant,
and having seen life-size pictures of a smiling woman. "I kept hoping Irene would just walk in through the door and say, 'here I am,'"
Patricia Jones, juror number eight, said. "I had a very heavy attachment to her during those months of the trial and felt the Kimeses
were responsible for her not being there. They killed her, and I had
to say, 'you're guilty.'"

Others on the panel were similarly affected, especially when
Connie Fernandez placed Irene's tiny white slip-on mules on the
jury rail during summations for them to see. The mules were a constant reminder to jurors, not only of Irene's petite size four, but of
how vulnerable she was at the hands of the Kimeses. "It was very
effective," Ella said.

Most of Tuesday was spent going back and forth between the
deliberation room and the courtroom. The jury asked the judge to
re-instruct them on the law regarding possession of a loaded
firearm. Then they wanted a read-back of Detective Ed Wallace's
testimony on whether the guns recovered in the Lincoln were
loaded. After lunch, the jurors submitted another note asking
about the forgery evidence. Then they wanted a read-back of
Nanette Wetkowski's testimony regarding when she informed
Sante that the bank account they shared had been frozen and that
she would be unable to write checks on the account. The testimony
showed Nanette had informed Sante about the bank problem the
weekend of February 13, 1998, which meant that when Sante and
Kenny turned the $14,900-plus check over to James Blackner in
Utah for the Lincoln, they knew it was a bad check and would not
be honored at the bank.

The jurors couldn't wait to begin reading the notebooks, and once
they did, it became easy to figure out what the Kimeses were up to,
Ella said. She suggested that jurors look at the books to determine
what evidence they wanted to find. "I was trying to get people to
focus in on what was evidence in this particular case. But I could-
n't believe how detailed the books were. The Kimeses talked about
fires and the insurance. They documented everything in the books.
They thought they were so clever, but they were really stupid."

"If it walks like a duck, talks like a duck . . . it is a duck"

When jurors began reviewing the notebooks, they weren't looking for any particular information to help convict or acquit them. But what made the notebooks credible was that it was scripted in the Kimes' own handwriting. They planned out what they wanted to say, jurors later said. It was obvious to jurors that Sante was the brains of the operation, but that Kenny assisted her. She believed her own lies, and that's why she had to write everything down in those books.

At the beginning of the trial, jurors observed that both Sante and Kenny took notes non-stop. After a while, Kenny never wrote again, but Sante kept it up. "Kenny must have been told by his lawyers to stop writing, because when the prosecution handwriting expert John Osborne testified, he said that when he tried to get Kenny to give him a sample of his scriptwriting, Kenny claimed he never wrote script, only block letters," Ella said.

The jurors also didn't buy Kenny's explanation that he always held a pen or pencil a peculiar way between his middle fingers. The panel members had actually viewed his handwriting style early on in the trial, when documents were put into evidence. "It was obvious to us that Kenny was trying to avoid giving the expert a specimen of his handwriting for comparison," Ella said.

"The journals without a doubt tied everything together that the prosecution had brought out during the trial," Vanessa Miller said. "Sante was wickedly thorough."

Another area jurors explored was the three-hour time gap on July fifth on the Kimes' cellular phone. The consensus was that they had plenty of time to kill Irene and dispose of her body and could have easily gotten to New Jersey, dumped her body, and gotten back in the time frame the prosecutors suggested. "That was incriminating," Ella said.

"Where was she? Where else could Irene be? Where would this woman be if she weren't murdered? Those were the questions jurors asked in the room. Some jurors voiced the opinion that if Aracelis had gone back to the first floor that day to speak with Irene, that Kenny would have killed her, too," Ella said. It was an interesting observation on the part of jurors, because Joe Reznick had come to the very same conclusion during the investigation of the case.

"If both Irene and Aracelis had turned up missing, our immediate thought would have been that the two women had taken off together," he said.

"In reviewing the notebooks and recalling the testimony, it was the feeling of the jurors that when Kenny called Aracelis the afternoon of the fifth and asked her to clean and change the sheets in apartment 1B because he was going to have a party, his intention was to lure her to the apartment and kill her, knowing that the police might figure that Mrs. Silverman and Aracelis were off somewhere together," Ella said.

"In fact, when we looked in the notebook, there was a notation Sante made in April when she inquired about renting an apartment at the mansion. She wrote there were no cleaning facilities available on Sunday. They knew no one would clean the apartment that day, and the call was merely a ruse to grab Aracelis and leave no witnesses in the building," she said.

"There were also so many other damaging notes in the books about duct tape, plastic bags, a shower curtain, and disinfectant. When someone dies, they lose their bodily fluids, and that's why they needed disinfectant to clean up and the shower curtain to wrap her body in before putting her into plastic bags. They certainly didn't need a shower curtain for the bathroom in apartment 1B, because all of the apartments in the building came equipped with glass-enclosed shower doors," Ella said.

Still another question that jurors had to resolve was why the trunk of the Lincoln was virtually empty. "That made absolutely no sense. In New York, you want to hide valuables in your car, as opposed to the Kimeses, who left them exposed on the rear seat where anyone could grab them," Ella said. She found the notebooks and lists of books about how to commit murder and assassinations suspicious. "One of them was a step-by-step instructional manual on how to become a hit man," Ella said.

"By the time I went through all the evidence, including the tracing of the signatures, I told the other jurors, 'Look, if it walks like a duck, it talks like a duck, it sounds like a duck, it is a duck.' The evidence was just overwhelming. Even without a body, it was obvious," Ella said.

"If it walks like a duck, talks like a duck . . . it is a duck"

Wednesday, May 17, the jurors did some serious voting on the grand larceny, forgery, and weapons possession counts. Many jurors later spoke of the difficulty they had voting Kenny guilty, saying the evidence was there. They went into Irene Silverman's home, they were caught with keys, her social security card, her signature, practicing her signature. It was all very incriminating, jurors said. That afternoon, the jury voted on the murder, robbery, and burglary charges. When they walked into the courtroom that night before heading out for dinner, several jurors could be seen wiping tears from their eyes.

Thursday morning, the jury sent out a note asking for the telephone calls Stan Patterson made from the Hilton Hotel to the Kimes' cell phone; they also wanted their cellular phone records and the calls made to the mansion, as well as a call Mengi made to Irene from Atlanta, Georgia. The defense had tried to suggest to the jury that Mengi might be responsible for Irene's disappearance. Once the jury had that information in hand, it had cleared up a juror's question and they went back to discussing the car again. For nearly two days, the issue of whether the Kimeses stole the car had become a bone of contention. Brenda sent out another note saying they were having difficulty interpreting the law on criminal possession of stolen property. The discussions inside the jury room had become so "ugly and heated" over the car that Brenda turned on the air conditioning unit in the room to cool everyone off. It turned out that some jurors felt the car was stolen; others believed the Kimeses passed a bad check.

Judge Uviller patiently explained the law and indicated to them that perhaps she had confused them in her original charge. She simplified the elements of the charge and went through the definition of knowingly possessing stolen property. When the jury walked out of the room at 12:50 P.M., prosecutor John Carter, a mild-mannered, easy-going gentleman, shook his head in disbelief that the jury could be hung up in reaching a verdict on such a minor charge in the indictment. Out of frustration, he looked at his colleagues and blurted out a four-letter epithet that in polite circles translates as "Screw the car." Everyone in earshot of John's remarks cracked up laughing and went to lunch, while jurors continued to wrestle with the car issue.

Once the judge had explained criminal possession of the car for what seemed to some jurors the umpteenth time, the panel voted on the remaining count regarding the car. The vote was unanimous—guilty. Brenda signed the final note to the judge indicating that a verdict had been reached. Only then did the panel attempt to munch on the lunch that court officers had brought them. No one in the room became emotional until that last note went out that a verdict had been reached. "It was a sad ending," jurors said.

In the end, it was the accumulation of the evidence inside the black bag, the keys, the notebooks with their massive "to do" lists, and the testimony of witnesses like Renee Andrews, the inmate Sante met the first night in jail, who testified that Sante swallowed a piece of paper in the holding cell and saw her flushing other torn papers down the toilet. The testimony of the cellular phone expert, among others, was all "very compelling. It showed they were at the mansion," the jurors said.

Would the jury have voted differently if Sante had taken the witness stand in her own defense? "Oh, God, no. It would have made it worse for her had she testified," was the reaction from jurors.

Brenda Safford pushed the buzzer twice, signaling to the court officers outside the jury room that a verdict had been reached. The sound of the buzzer reverberated to the outside 11th floor courtroom, where a three-and-a-half month trial was about to end for Sante and Kenny Kimes. The jurors had deliberated the case against them for nearly four days. It was also the end of a two-year saga for the Silver Task Force detectives and the four prosecutors.

Shortly before 2 P.M. on May 18, 2000, the spacious marble corridor outside Room 1132 of the Manhattan Criminal Courts building was bustling with the news, as word quickly spread throughout the floor and then the building that the Kimes jury had voted on all 118 counts in the indictment. When court officers opened the locked doors to the 80-seat courtroom, the crowd rushed inside, scrambling for seats.

Seated in the front row of the spectator section, behind the four prosecutors, were Thomas Hackett, Joel Potter, Danny Rodriguez, Tom Ryan, John Schlagler, Anthony Vazquez, and Eugene Wasielewski, the seven detectives from the New York

Police Department that Joseph Reznick had hand-picked to find Silverman's killer.

All eyes were focused on a door to the left of the judge's bench, waiting for the Kimeses to make their appearance in the courtroom. Reznick was like an anxious father waiting for his wife to give birth. He was a few blocks away at Police Headquarters, pacing nervously in his sixth floor office, waiting for his telephone to ring. Wasielewski had promised Reznick he would dial him up on his cellular phone and "tap out" the verdict as it was being read by the foreperson: one tap meant guilty; two taps, not guilty.

At 2:45 that afternoon, a hush fell over the wood-paneled room as the door leading from the holding cell suddenly swung open. A handcuffed Kenny Kimes, appearing grim, ashen, and arrogant, was brought into the courtroom, accompanied by two rugged-looking court officers. The only sound in the room was the unnerving rattle of keys as officers removed his steel cuffs.

"This is *it*," he told lead defense lawyer Mel Sachs, sweating profusely in the air-conditioned room. His co-counsel, Matthew Weissman, was near tears. He knew his client was going down. "It's all right, Matt. You did the best you could," Kenny consoled his young civil attorney, patting him on his back.

Four minutes later, her head shaking nervously from side to side, her dark eyes darting around the room anxiously like a scared, bewildered animal about to be slaughtered, his mother, Sante Kimes, was swiftly seated. Several beefy, no-nonsense court officers pushed her down into a seat at the defense table next to José Muniz. "Mom, we have a verdict. Whatever it is, don't make a scene," Kenny whispered to his stone-faced mother. She looked at him as if she wanted to kill. "It was a look you'd expect her to give people before she blew their brains out," Weissman recalled after the trial.

"We're not going to win this," Sante said matter-of-factly, turning to José Muniz. On the third day of deliberations, Sante could see the handwriting on the wall and seemed resigned to her fate. She leaned forward to José, pursed her lips, and confided, "We're going to get convicted, aren't we?" she asked, munching on her favorite candy bar—Pay Day. He tried reassuring her that the trial record was protected and she had good grounds for an appeal.

By now, a dozen strapping court officers surrounded the Kimeses in the well of the courtroom as other uniformed officers were strategically placed around the room in case of trouble. The tension in the room mounted. The silence was deafening as everyone sat motionless, staring at the two defendants, waiting breathlessly for the jury to come in and let the world know the Kimes' fate.

"Folks, we have received a note from the jury. They have reached a verdict," Judge Uviller said. Uviller then addressed Sante and Kenny: "I do want to make it clear to each of the two defendants, if there is any outburst of any sort, the jury will be asked to leave, the defendants will be removed from the courtroom, and we will continue and complete the verdict without the defendant who creates an outburst. I trust that will not happen," the judge warned them sternly.

"We're ready for the jury," she said, nodding her head to her clerk, George Cartagena, for him to open the door behind which jurors were lined up waiting to enter the courtroom.

✖

At precisely 2:54 P.M., the side door from the jury deliberation room swung open. One by one, the 12-member panel walked to their assigned seats in the jury box, never once glancing at either defendant as they went past the Kimeses, their eyes focused on the green tile floor.

"Look at them. They're going away. Good-bye," a member of the audience was overheard saying as the jury walked to their assigned seats.

Michael Hardy seemed tired and kept looking at the faces of jurors for a glimmer of hope, a sign of encouragement as to how they had voted.

"This is not a good sign. There was no eye contact when the jury entered the courtroom," Kenny observed. "This doesn't look good." Until the prosecution began to introduce the devastating tell-all notebooks into evidence, the defense felt confident that at least three or four jurors on the panel were leaning toward acquittal. But even Richard Backus, the juror the defense believed was in their camp, avoided Sante and Kenny Kimes' gaze. Instead of a thumbs-up nod or signal, Richard hardly gave them a glance.

"The day the notebooks were entered as evidence, Backus stopped winking at us," Weissman recalled. "After that, he would-n't even look at us when he walked by. That was the day, to me, that the case was lost and there was a distinct difference in that jury."

"Ma'am, just remain seated and listen to the clerk, and he will ask you some questions and please respond," the judge told Brenda Safford.

"Madam Forelady, has the jury reached a verdict, yes or no?" George Cartagena asked.

"Yes," replied Safford.

"How say you to the sixth count of the indictment, charging the defendant, Sante Kimes, with the crime of robbery in the first degree; guilty or not guilty?"

"Guilty."

"How say you to the eighth count of the indictment, charging the defendant, Sante Kimes, with the crime of burglary in the first degree, guilty or not guilty?"

"Guilty."

"How say you to the second count of the indictment, charging the defendant, Sante Kimes, with the crime of murder [felony murder robbery], guilty or not guilty?"

"Guilty."

"How say you to the fourth count of the indictment, charging the defendant, Sante Kimes, with the crime of murder, in the second degree [a felony murder burglary], guilty or not guilty?"

"Guilty."

"How say you to the first count of the indictment, charging the defendant, Sante Kimes, with the crime of murder [intentional murder] in the second degree, guilty or not guilty?"

"Guilty."

Brenda's voice grew stronger and louder every time she intoned the word "Guilty."

"Conspiracy? Attempted grand larceny? Criminal possession of stolen property? Eavesdropping? Forgery? Weapons possession? Fraud? Grand larceny?"

"Guilty. Guilty. Guilty. Guilty. Guilty. Guilty. Guilty. Guilty. . . ."

Twenty minutes later, it was over. Brenda had uttered the word "Guilty" 118 times—58 for Sante and 60 for Kenny—as the clerk recorded the jury's decision on each and every count in the indictment.

Wasielewski had tapped "guilty" so many times into the phone that Reznick mistakenly figured the Kimeses had been found not guilty. He dialed Wasielewski back, giving him a "911" signal. When Wasielewski gave him the exact same emergency signal, Reznick rushed to the courthouse in time to learn that it was a clean guilty sweep of the indictment.

"Mom, I love you. It'll be okay. Don't worry. Relax. It's not over yet," Kenny whispered as court officers slapped cuffs behind his back. Kenny said he was not surprised by the verdict. He had confided to Weissman that he knew it was going to be the last time he and his mother would be together again until their sentencing.

Sante sat at the table stoically, in stunned silence, refusing at first to stand and be cuffed. She leaned toward José Muniz and asked, "How could they come back with this verdict?" Michael Hardy just had his hands over his eyes but didn't show any emotion or say anything to his client.

"Once I heard guilty on the burglary and robbery, I knew they were going to find them guilty of everything," Muniz said. Weissman had gotten close to Kenny in the preceding two years and was taking the guilty verdict the hardest. He was stunned. "This is a 25-year-old kid who could have been something so different. To me, Kenny is a special kind of person," he said.

Resting her head on Muniz's shoulder, Sante asked José "to come up to my cell after this to talk about the appeal. And when do I get my telephone privileges back?" is all she wanted to know.*

---

*After Sante's conviction, to show her appreciation for their legal services, the ever-grateful Sante filed disciplinary charges against Jose Muniz and Larry Frost. In one of her perpetual fantasies, she accused them of not only stealing $30,000 that was never in the black bag, but insisted they collaborated with prosecutors and were traitors to her defense. Both Muniz and Frost were ultimately cleared of the charges, after an extensive investigation that cost both men money and time.

"If it walks like a duck, talks like a duck . . . it is a duck"

The judge set a sentencing date of June 27, and the handcuffed Kimeses were swiftly led out the door to their respective holding cells and then to a waiting bus to return them to their Rikers Island jail cells. Once they were out of the room, the crowd in the courtroom erupted into a roar of approval.

The scene inside the courtroom was bedlam as the Silver Task Force detectives; the prosecutors Connie Fernandez, Ann Donnelly, John Carter, and Owen Heimer; and friends of Irene Silverman hugged and kissed. It was time to breathe a sigh of relief that justice had been served, Joe Reznick said. "It was truly the Kimes' dead end."

21

"She's one of a kind ... a monstrous individual, a violent serial killer"

It was only moments after her conviction, as Sante was on her way to the holding cell, that she began screaming that her civil rights had been violated. To lengthen the drama, she "fainted," and when she was "revived," she claimed to court officers she was having a heart attack. But when she heard that Cheryl Fiandaca, a reporter with *Eyewitness News*, and David Rohde of the *New York Times* were waiting in the wings to interview her, Sante made a miraculous recovery. It was, after all, an opportunity to make a grand appearance to start spinning her story.

With lawyers Michael Hardy and José Muniz at her side, Sante was in rare form. She started off doing a one-on-one exclusive with Cheryl, denying her guilt and Kenny's. Predictably, she said they were framed; that the police manufactured the case. She called the verdict "a temporary set-back," said she was "just devastated and praying for justice," and that everyone in the world should look into the case closely. "I was dying to tell the truth, to let people know the truth. I wanted to help in the closing argument," she told reporters. Sante claimed her constitutional rights were violated and spoke of how much she really wanted to talk to the jury. She said that when she spoke to Kenny after the verdict, he told her that he still believed in justice and that they would win on appeal. "To me, they turned it into a witch hunt," she said. She and her wonderful son hadn't done anything; they didn't know where Irene was and, like any good mother, she would fight to her dying breath for her son.

Ever since they were arrested, the buzz around the courthouse was that there were some odd goings-on between mother and son. Kenny always gazed lovingly at his mother, with his piercing green eyes fixed on her, as though he was captivated and in awe of her. Judge Herbert Altman initially observed the pair in his courtroom holding hands in an unusual manner and had to admonish them a number of times about their behavior. "Will you stop that?" Altman snapped at one point during a hearing. He ordered court officers to separate them, and when they were made to sit at opposite ends of the defense table, they vigorously protested the seating arrangements.

"When they first came to court, they held hands for a solid hour. I've seen them stroking and caressing each other in court," Christine Cornell, a courtroom artist, observed.

Defense lawyers who met with them noticed the Kimeses sneaking off to a corner of the room where they would kiss and hold hands. "This was not just the peck on the cheek kind of kiss," Muniz said. Then there was their *60 Minutes* appearance on television, in which Kenny described his mother as "physically beautiful," a remark so out of the ordinary that most young men would never use it in portraying their mother. And when the interview ended abruptly, it was Kenny, not a studio technician, who removed the microphone from his mother's chest. As he unclipped the device, Kenny could be seen gently running his hand across her breast. Not to be overlooked in the incest-mix was the testimony of José

Alvarez, who said he found Sante and Kenny sleeping naked together in the same bed. Roseann Lombardo testified that from the way the Kimeses acted in the bank, she was under the impression that Kenny was Sante's boy toy. The bond between the Kimeses certainly came up during deliberations by jurors, who felt "it was a sick relationship." Finally, in letters between Sante and her son, Kenny addressed his mother as "darling," "you are my soul mate," and "how the fuck are you?" He spoke often about the two of them looking forward to taking long drives in the desert and sitting under the stars drinking wine and talking for hours. That's the kind of talk lovers engage in, not mother and son.

During her interview, Cheryl Fiandaca pressed Sante about allegations that she and Kenny had "an unusual relationship." It was a good question, one that had obviously been on the mind of all those who followed the case.

Sante looked frantic, stunned by the question. Suddenly, she burst into tears. "I slept with him when he was a baby. I held him on my chest in bed with my husband. He was just a baby," she wept as she explained away the strange attachment she had with her adult son.

Dr. Arthur Weider, the defense forensic psychologist who observed the Kimeses throughout the trial, found that Kenny's "sexual attraction toward his mother indicates severe psychopathology." It was his opinion as a trained observer, with 55-years of experience in behavioral science, that there was "evidence of incest-like behavior. It is abnormal for a grown man to share the same bed with his mother in the nude. It exhibits an intense love for his mother," he said.

Weider believes that because of Sante's past as a prostitute, she may have unconsciously sexually abused Kenny as a child, knowing that what she was doing was wrong, but, as a psychopath, lacking feelings of guilt. "It is also possible that if Kenny as a little boy saw Sante engaging in sexual activity with a man, he developed a yen for his mother, and it became an unconscious wish for him to want his mother sexually.

"Essentially, Sante Kimes demonstrates psychopathic personality features with no guilt, conscience, remorse, or empathy. She is typically charming socially, arrogant and 'full of herself,' egoistic, with a superiority complex. She feels everyone is stupid and will do her bidding, and everyone has their price and can be 'paid off.'"

Furthermore, Weider believes that "Mrs. Kimes has a multiple personality disorder, and in order to keep these many aliases orderly, she has to assume their personalities and keep copious notes in her books to retain who is saying what to whom and in order to remember what she said to whom."

In Weider's opinion, Sante is "an actress, and in assuming so many aliases and their personalities, she has had to control and intimidate her supporting actor, namely her son, and convince him of her invincibility. Consequently, they have had a shared relationship in which she has been the Svengali to his Trilby. She writes the scripts and scenarios, and he performs some of the behaviors and is convinced of her invincibility and optimism."

Both mother and son demonstrate paranoid ideation, and they are certain there is a conspiracy against them, Weider said. "They are absolutely convinced they are not at fault nor guilty. Both denial and a lack of insight contribute to make them feel conspired against by everyone. Each believes this to be the 'God's honest truth.' It is ironic that they invoke the Constitution when both have trespassed upon the civil rights of their victims and people whom in general they conned."

Government psychological reports submitted at Sante's slavery sentencing concede she is the "product of an unhappy childhood that included early experiences of sexual victimization. [But] it appears that Mrs. Kimes manipulates others to her own benefit. It seems Mrs. Kimes has little concern for her actions and the impact they have on others."

A defense report submitted at the time by Dr. Verdun Trione, a Las Vegas psychologist, indicated "that Mrs. Kimes sometimes finds it difficult to separate fact from fantasy. This is a person who snaps from time to time. The clinical picture, overtly, is one of repressed anger, rage reactions, resulting in conflicting disorganized social adjustments. There is affective disorder, mingled with . . . anxiety attacks. This is manifested by denial . . . repression, immature and manipulative behaviors." It was Trione's opinion that Sante suffered from "deranged behaviors."

Another court-appointed Las Vegas psychiatrist, Dr. William O'Gorman, wrote that he found Sante to have "poor insight and impulsive, not reflective, judgment."

Sante spent the month after the Silverman conviction working on her appeal. By the time sentencing day rolled around on June 27, she had decided on a bold course of action: She fired her lawyer, José Muniz, whom she had always referred to as "my savior," and accused him publicly of stealing a million-dollar ring she had entrusted to him the first day they had met in July 1998. She also claimed that he had violated the client-attorney privilege by collaborating with prosecutors and turning over defense evidence to them. What made her charge regarding the jewelry even more preposterous was that when Muniz briefly bowed out of the case in October 1998 for four months, he turned the ring—which was at best a semi-precious stone—and four sets of keys she had given to him over to Mel Sachs and got a signed receipt from Mel for the jewelry and the keys. Her purpose in firing José was to make him the fall guy by accusing the lawyer of not providing adequate counsel during the trial. It later backfired on her when the disciplinary committee of the Bar Association reviewed the charges she filed against him and tossed her complaint out the window.

Muniz received a letter from another lawyer, Irving Anolik, shortly before sentencing day, saying that Sante had discharged him. "It seems strange to me that counsel is sending out letters saying she's discharging me . . . if he hasn't even been retained," José told the judge during a bench conference. "That's where we're at," he explained. "There's no sense in me staying here if I'm not wanted," José said. "She's going to go into an outburst," he warned the judge.

During the sidebar conversation between the judge, Muniz, and the other lawyers present, it was finally agreed that before the sentencing proceeding began, Muniz would state that he'd been discharged and ask permission from Uviller to leave. And that's exactly what happened. Muniz walked out of the courtroom, but not before Kenny motioned to speak with him briefly, saying, "You know how Mom is," and thanking him for his services.

"She's one of a kind . . . a monstrous individual"

✖

It was a standing room only crowd that packed the courtroom on sentencing day. Most of the deliberating jurors who could take the day off from work asked Judge Uviller's clerk if seats could be set aside for them.

A sense of anticipation filled the room as the crowd waited for the proceeding to start. The main players, Sante and Kenny, were hustled into the courtroom. They were seated at the defense table and were stunned when they looked at the jury box. Seated in the number one jury seat was Joe Reznick, who headed up the Silver Task Force. Filling up the rest of the juror seats were detectives Eugene Wasielewski, Tommy Hackett, Tony Vazquez, Joel Potter, Danny Rodriguez, John Schlagler, Tommy Ryan, and Tommy Hovagim. It must have been unnerving for the Kimeses to see these detectives, who played a key role in their downfall, staring intently at them throughout the proceeding.

Before arraigning the Kimeses for sentencing, it was necessary for Judge Uviller to put on the record that Sante had been convicted by a jury trial of three counts of murder in the second degree, one count each of robbery, burglary, conspiracy, attempted grand larceny, possession of stolen property and a forged instrument, four counts of gun possession, 16 counts of forgery, and 29 counts of eavesdropping, totaling 58 counts. Kenny was convicted of the identical counts, except that he had 17 forgery counts and two counts of possession of a forged instrument, making it 60 counts.

It was then up to John Carter to summarize for the judge the case against Sante before the judge could mete out the sentence. He began by making it absolutely clear that Sante was a sociopath who was motivated "by simple and naked greed" and that she had long planned the "cold-blooded murder of Irene Silverman." He then spent a few minutes highlighting Sante's scheme to steal the house, repeating the lies she told, the documents she forged, her use of different names, and listing two loaded guns, the date-rape drug, the empty stun box, scream masks, handcuffs, knives, brass knuckles, ammunition, latex gloves, duct tape, and syringes found in the Kimes' possession.

Carter then described Irene's "brutal and heinous" murder and spoke of her many friends. He reiterated that Irene was an "intelligent, vibrant, perceptive, and energetic" woman with a "dynamic personality" who spoke many languages, loved to dance and read, and who led a very active social life.

"There is an image in my mind, Judge, that I have, of the defendants wearing 'Scream' [from the movie *Scream*] masks when they grabbed tiny Irene Silverman, all four-foot-ten,115 pounds, just before they killed her; of Irene Silverman looking at these Scream masks as the last thing she ever saw. What terror she must have felt," he said.

Carter reminded the judge that just hours after the verdict, Sante was spinning her story on television. She managed to give interviews protesting her innocence and accusing police and prosecutors of a frame-up, saying that Irene's home was "a haven of prostitution" where "at night all kinds of men were coming there." She said there was a loud argument the night before she was murdered during a party with three or four "Latin-type" men. John mentioned the federal sentencing after Sante's slavery conviction, when the U.S. Attorney said, "Overall, she has continued to blame everybody else for her criminal behavior. She's shown no remorse for her actions."

"Here we are, fourteen years later, at another sentencing . . . and she continues to blame everybody but herself for her predicament. She will never change. She'll continue to lie. She'll tell the most shameful, nonsensical lies because that's who she is; that's what she does. She'll continue to cheat, steal, and kill anyone who stands between her and whatever her particular goal is at the time. Throughout her life, she has used deceit, threats, violence, manipulation, and murder to profit herself in some manner.

"Every moment of every day of this woman's existence is either about lying to someone, scamming someone, planning a crime, or committing a crime, without any sense of regret or remorse, all without taking any responsibility for her actions or acknowledging her action."

"She's one of a kind . . . a monstrous individual"

Carter characterized Kenny as "a willing and active participant in the murder" of Irene. "The fact is, Judge, she has such little regard for even him that she has allowed and encouraged her son to participate in murder here and elsewhere. Sante Kimes is a unique individual. She's one of a kind. Thank God. She's a monstrous individual, a violent serial killer and career criminal who should be sentenced to the maximum allowed by law . . . so that there won't be even the slightest possibility that she could ever freely walk our streets and prey on people again."

Assistant District Attorney Owen Heimer was next up, reminding the judge of how Kenny Kimes killed Irene Silverman. "On the morning of Sunday, July 5, 1998, Kenneth Kimes walked in stocking feet past the open door of Irene Silverman's office, and he saw her sitting there. Then Kenneth Kimes returned to apartment 1B and lay in wait. When Irene Silverman walked down the hall and over to the elevator door, Kenneth Kimes opened the door to 1B, pulled her inside, and killed her. He strangled her; he snuffed the life out of her with his bare hands. It took no more than a minute or two, which perhaps was not a long time to him, but must have been an eternity of horror to Irene Silverman."

Heimer spoke of how, after killing Irene, Kenny reached into her pocket and took her personal keys and put those in his pocket, then put her lifeless body into heavy-duty garbage bags and bound those bags into a tight package with duct tape, leaving a wad of duct tape in a trash can with his fingerprints all over it. He then stuffed Irene into a large nylon duffle bag, put the bag on a luggage cart, wheeled it out of the apartment to the empty trunk of the car, and drove away.

Heimer told of Kenny retrieving the Lincoln from a parking garage on July fourth and loading the back seat of that car "up to the ceiling with his and his mother's belongings as they moved out of apartment 1B and emptied whatever was in the trunk into the back seat. "The trunk had to be empty because that's where, the next day, he was going to put the body of Irene Silverman," Heimer said.

As part of the sentencing procedure, victims or a family member of the victim are invited by the Court to offer what is referred to as a "victim's impact statement." Irene's only living relative, her second cousin in Los Angeles, Despy Mallas, sent the judge such a statement, which was read into the record by prosecutor Connie Fernandez. In Mallas's statement, she spoke about the cold-blooded murder the Kimeses planned. "Your cries of innocence fall on deaf ears. You couldn't even begin to step into my cousin's shoes. You took away a beautiful human being to satisfy your insatiable, selfish greed. You left me and others who loved Irene with nothing but contempt, anger, and hatred toward the both of you. Her loss is a loss to all who knew and loved her. Your loss today is your freedom. With your incarceration, we will be assured, as a free and civil society, that you will never, never walk free again to continue in your evil ways."

It was now up to Michael Hardy to say a few compassionate words about Sante before the defendant herself could take center stage and plead for mercy. Hardy started off by saying that it was "a difficult moment" for himself and "a difficult case, because there was no body," and as a result it becomes a precedent-setting case. "After listening to some of the statements by the prosecution . . . you wonder, how do you represent someone who is despised by the world, despised by humanity. And who rises to the level that you ask? Is Mrs. Kimes a Hitler? Is she a Mussolini? Is she a Jack the Ripper? Is she this historical criminal that will one day belong side by side in some wax museum with other famous criminals? She is a mother, your honor. Many have said that she has allowed her son to kill. Again, she denies that either she or her son had anything to do with the murder of Irene Silverman," he said as he went on pleading with the judge to not impose a sentence of over 100 years. The lawyer stressed that given Sante's age, any sentence was tantamount "to a death sentence . . . unless this case is reversed, she will never see the light of day and will never walk alive outside of a prison," he said.

Hardy then informed the judge that Sante wanted to make a statement.

"You can stand right there, Mrs. Kimes," the judge said, as Sante started to walk from the defense table toward the podium behind the prosecutors.

Sante began by saying she was standing "before the American people and God" pleading "to every living mother in this world. I'm here to defend my son. I don't care about myself. All the lies you've heard are not true." She droned on about her "wonderful marriage" to Kimes, Sr., "the wealthiest man in the world" and how they had everything. "My pleasant, wonderful son would not hurt a fly," she said. Glaring at the prosecutors, sitting to her right, Sante turned towards them saying, "I hope all of your children will suffer the way you have made this innocent kid suffer."

At this point Judge Uviller stopped Sante short. "Mrs. Kimes, please address the Court. You are not addressing anyone else in the courtroom."

Sante pleaded with the judge "not to make it complicated" for her and went on to assail "this court, an out of control system that made a mistake . . . and arrested us on a little check charge that I didn't write, and they decided to pin a murder on some innocent people." She then took off about "a dark day for justice," how their "precious constitutional civil rights had been trampled" . . . and that "they planted and planted and planted evidence to fool and mislead a jury. Frankly, I have to be honest. If I were our jury, I would have convicted us," she said.

She became very emotional at that point, turned again to the prosecutors and inadvertently blurted out, "You didn't want to win this—I mean, you didn't want to lose this case," Sante said, correcting herself. "No one has told the truth in this case. My attorney has literally let me down and sold me out and was intentionally inadequate," she said referring to José Muniz. "My own attorney . . . induced by the district attorney has lied and violated the attorney-client relationship. He has divulged false information, which undermined our ability to defend ourselves, and he's virtually precluded our ability to take the stand, which would have proved our innocence." She also begged the judge "to direct Mr. Muniz to return over a million dollars worth of valuable jewelry which he's withholding from me. And to advise my other attorney, Alan Russell, to release over two hundred and fifty million dollars . . . which he will not give me, which has rendered me and my son indigent. They promised a strong defense, but at the last minute, after promising forty-five witnesses . . . that would prove our innocence, they produced nothing . . . to an already brainwashed jury [prevented] from hearing the truth."

Sante next turned her attention to the judge, saying that through-out the trial she was "hostile and prejudiced against me and my son. I begged you to permit me to take the stand and participate in clos-ing arguments." She accused Uviller of conspiring to "allow these prosecutors to address evidence against me which was . . . very irrelevant. I was stopped from taking the stand and from partici-pating in my own defense."

Again, Sante faced the audience, her voice cracking as if she were about to cry, and pleaded, "Everyone in this planet, there is no crime. Don't be fooled like the jury. Don't be misled by gossip and slander. The record clearly reflects a diabolical frame by one of the most corrupt law enforcement systems in this United States, a frame in which the system, the police, the prosecutors, assisted by my own attorney, manufactured a crime, and produced a B horror movie.

"The only murderers in this case, your honor, are these prosecu-tors who are murdering our Constitution."

Sante rattled on, claiming that Irene Silverman "was a friend of mine that I met in 1994" and saying how she, Sante, had gotten "very interested in longevity, and I met a man named Ralph at—"

Kenny knew where his mother was headed and frantically tried cutting her off. "Mom, Mom, Mom, Mom, one second please," he begged, interrupting her four times as she ignored his pleas.

She barreled ahead and began shooting off her mouth about how Ralph had introduced her to Irene, and that she had invited her to New York. "I came for Christmas and met with Irene; liked her, very funny, and we became friends."

As a result of Kenny's constant interruptions, Sante became dis-tracted and appeared bewildered, perhaps unsure of how to pro-ceed. She stopped talking long enough to have an off-the-record discussion with Kenny as the rest of the courtroom and the Judge waited for Sante to continue talking.

"Please, Mrs. Kimes, address the Court. Your son will have his time."

For a moment, Sante seemed undecided as to what to do. "I don't want to endanger my appeal. I'm only trying to give the truth . . . to speak . . . the truth," she hesitantly told Uviller.

"It's all on the record, Mom. Everything you say is on the record," Kenny pleaded, trying to get her to stop speaking.

"Can you tell me if that is true?" she asked the judge.

"You are here to speak, Mrs. Kimes. No one has interfered with your right to be heard. Please continue."

"It will not interfere with my appeal?" she asked again.

"I'm not saying that. I will make no assurance."

"Kenny, I got to talk now," she told her son.

But no sooner was Sante discussing her "life manager, Alan Russell," and saying he was interested in Irene's apartment and went to see her, Kenny was back, imploring her to go on to another subject. "Mom. Mom. Please, I'm asking you, Mom."

"Okay," she said.

"Mom, you don't realize, this is evidence. By giving evidence you impair—"

"My son is concerned I'm giving evidence. I'm sure I don't want to do anything that would, you know, do that. I wish your Honor could tell me if in telling the truth here if that is hurting . . . can you not tell me?" she asked.

"You have a capable attorney," the judge informed her. "They are here to advise you. I am not here to advise you."

Sante still didn't know when to stop. She persisted, trying to give her version as to why there was a legitimate reason she came to New York. By now, Kenny was obviously frustrated and he cried out, "Jesus Christ . . . please."

"The truth has got to come out," she replied, and after another brief off-the-record discussion with Michael Hardy, she went on proclaiming her innocence and attacking the remarks John Carter made to the judge. When she started talking about her government cooperation and why she couldn't use her name, it was Michael Hardy who was concerned over what Sante was saying in court.

"I just want the record to reflect that I have on several occasions advised my client that I believe her statement is sufficient and I am advising her again now on the record that her statements have been heard by the court. It's in her interest to terminate her statement at this point," he said.

"Let me just say, Mr. Hardy, that I completely reject any innuendo with regard to you or to Mr. Muniz and any assertions that she's cast upon your professionalism or your integrity. So, rest assured that there is no merit to it and I reject it completely," the judge said.

Again, Sante wanted the last word, insisting that Muniz "withheld valuable jewelry" from her and that she "has proof of that."

"Just move on to the issue of sentence, Ms. Kimes," the judge said, sounding annoyed. "We have a long day ahead of us."

When it appeared she was again talking about "everybody rattling" her, Kenny seemed to have also had it with his mother. "Mom, stop, Mom, oh, Jesus," he again cried out.

The judge gave Sante another fifteen minutes to finish her remarks, telling her she had given her more time than other speakers. Sante protested she couldn't do it in that time. "You've had two and a half years," Uviller replied angrily.

"Mom, can I just ask you a question?"

"No, honey, I've got to talk now," she told her son.

With that, Sante was off and running. Once again, she blasted the judge for being prejudiced against her, for allegedly precluding her access to her lawyers, for threatening to handcuff her and throw her into solitary if she used the telephone or wrote a note to her lawyers; then she reverted to her familiar theme that they were framed, sold out by the system and José Muniz. She claimed Irene's will was a forgery, but the deed conveying the mansion to The Atlantis Group was real; that there is no proof, no crime, and they didn't rent "that apartment. If you don't save my son . . . it's going to be your son next or your daughter."

Sante would have gone on speaking, but Judge Uviller had heard enough. "All right, Mrs. Kimes, your performance—I mean, your statement is concluded," the judge said to the thunderous applause of everyone in the courtroom. Her monologue had run 55 minutes.

It was soon to be Kenny's turn to speak his mind to the judge. First, Mel Sachs had to go through the formality of giving his reasons why the judge should show leniency for his client. For once, Sachs was brief and to the point: Kenny did not choose his parents, Sachs explained, and asked Uviller to show understanding when he is sentenced. "Your honor, the supposed sins of a mother should not be visited on the child," he pleaded. Sachs reflected that Kenny didn't have the chance that Kenny's father did "and having the mother that he had." He asked the judge to "see him for who he is and know what he had experienced. Anything that he did is a far cry from murder. Maybe he didn't deserve the way he grew up and not having the love and support and care that others here have been able to receive. At least, he deserves to be treated with fairness."

Kenny spoke to the judge for 25 minutes. He opened his somewhat disjointed statement by addressing the detectives sitting in the jury box, "My mom is scared. She's scared of you guys. Of all of you sitting there." Then looking at the judge, he added, "No offense, but you're spooky. Your honor, you're a little scary, too." Having gotten that out of his system, he blasted Uviller for her "lack of legal professionalism" and "legal manners" because of her earlier remark about Sante's "performance" at the conclusion of her sentencing comments. He continued Sante's barrage against the police and the alleged manufacturing of the evidence against them. He mentioned how they had wanted Court TV to televise the trial.

Several times, Kenny turned to speak to the audience and Uviller constantly reminded him to address her. "I'm not trying to give you a cry story. I'm not trying to say that we are angelic. You can't say that I'm bullshitting you."

He then got to what was bothering him and he held up what he said was a police document to the court and to the audience saying that the "issue of Shawn Little" destroyed his defense.

"Halfway through the trial, Kenny began focusing his exclusive attention on Shawn Little because he was aware that Little would be one of the main witnesses against him at the Los Angeles murder trial," Matthew Weissman explained. "Kenny was obsessed with this single NYPD document that contained Shawn Little's name and the term 'suspect' in one of the columns. Kenny's interpretation of this document was false, in that the document merely reflected the individuals whose fingerprints were compared with those found in the mansion."

No prints belonging to Shawn Little were ever found in Irene's home, the Town Car, or in any of the personal belongings of the Kimeses. Silver Task Force detectives confirmed that Little had never been to New York City and was in California the entire time Sante and Kenny were in the city at Irene's home.

Kenny insisted that the notebooks didn't prove murder. In continuing, Kenny began to curse, and the judge admonished him, directing him to "control your language."

"Your honor, I will be soft-spoken, and I won't use any four-letter words," he promised. "We're not dealing with misdemeanors here and, unfortunately, I won't be able to see that fair side of you, because I know you're going to throw the book at us, no matter what. So, on a personal level, your Honor, respectfully, it's been interesting. But I wish it could have been respectfully interesting," he added as he took his seat.

It was time for the main event. Judge Uviller leaned forward in her chair. She started off recalling Irene Silverman as a lively, irrepressible, generous woman. "It is sad indeed that this spirited and intelligent woman became known to New Yorkers only through the circumstances of her death.

"In many ways Mrs. Silverman embodied the best of this city. She was curious and energetic. She had a wide circle of developed friends. She was interested in the buzz of New York, and had, not withstanding her years, a great appetite for life."

The judge spoke of Irene as "a woman of substantial wealth," whose home and heart were open to people from all walks of life. "In her beautiful mansion . . . she entertained together the artists, the butcher, the housekeeper, and the banker." Judge Uviller highlighted many of those who admired and loved Irene, mentioning Mengi, Ramon, Noel, Valerie, Aracelis, and others. "They were Mrs. Silverman's family," she said and made reference to the many letters of tribute she had received about Irene from friends expressing their grief.

Finally, Judge Uviller got down to what everyone in the courtroom was waiting to hear—what she would say about the defendants. She started with "It is galling to speak of Sante Kimes in the same breath as Irene Silverman, [but] I turn now to the matter of sentencing.

"Sante Kimes is surely the most degenerate defendant who has ever appeared in this courtroom, and her degeneracy extends even to the willful corruption of her own son. Her protestations of concern for him, like her protestations of her own innocence, are as false as any bad check she has ever passed. They are the self-serving blather of an intractable con artist.

"Sante Kimes would have sacrificed her own son in an instant in order to further her own perverse ends. It is clear that Ms. Kimes has spent virtually all of her life plotting and scheming, exploiting, manipulating, and preying upon the vulnerable and the gullible at every opportunity."

Uviller contrasted the characters of Irene and Sante. "Just as Mrs. Silverman reached out to the strong, the talented, and the honest, Sante Kimes targeted the weak, naïve, and vulnerable. It really comes as no surprise that she is one of the rare people in this century to have been convicted of slavery.

"Sante Kimes has lived a life of criminal calculation. However, when she came to our city, Sante Kimes made several miscalculations. First, she misread Mrs. Silverman as just another easy mark. What a colossal misjudgment. Next, Sante Kimes . . . sorely underestimated this City's law enforcement capabilities. However often she may have eluded punishment elsewhere for her sordid crimes, this defendant did not count on the perseverance and professionalism of the New York City police officers who helped bring her to justice. They are commended for the excellence of their work in this case.

"And finally, Sante Kimes has grossly overestimated her own cleverness. The staggering stupidity of a criminal keeping a detailed to-do list added one more extraordinary note to this bizarre case."

At the start, the judge said she thought Kenny was "just the vacuous dupe of his malevolent mother, deserving of some pity as another of her victims, whose universe has been controlled from birth by a sociopath.

"However, as this trial proceeded and Kenneth Kimes could be observed arrogantly chatting and smirking through the accumulating evidence, it became clear that he has evolved into a criminal as dangerous as Sante Kimes. He, too, has become a remorseless predator, a proverbial chip off the old block. I care not how Sante Kimes became who she is or why Kenneth Kimes was unable to resist her. In the end, evil is indeed banal," the judge said. "There is no doubt that the jury's verdict is correct, in every respect."

Uviller made mention of the fact that Irene's body has never been recovered, but that it didn't mean the Kimeses would be rewarded "for their deviousness in being able to conceal and dispose of it." She also observed that in her many years on the bench, she always found it "difficult" and a "painful obligation" to sentence a defendant, "no matter how grievous the crime. It is sad to say that in this case, it is not painful.

"The sentence I impose now in the case of Sante Kimes is a matter of just desserts, designed to reflect the unremitting malevolence of this woman, even though, because of her age, she will serve only a fraction of it.

"For Kenneth Kimes, the sentence is geared toward his permanent incapacitation. His casual will to violence, together with his youth, require that he never be released from confinement."

With those parting words, Judge Rena Uviller sentenced Sante to 127⅔ years to life in prison and Kenny to 130 years to life in prison.

After more than three hours it was all over. Sante and Kenny were cuffed and swiftly herded out of the courtroom. The judge went back to chambers, and prosecutors and police milled around inside the well of the courtroom smiling, hugging one another, and relaxing for the first time in two years, before heading over to Forlini's Restaurant to celebrate.

✖

A few days later, Matthew Weissman met with Kenny one last time, shortly before Kenny was transferred upstate to the Clinton Penitentiary in Danamora, New York. It was a rather solemn visit for both of them. They knew they would not be seeing each other again for a long time. Hanging over Kenny's head now was the murder trial of David Kazdin in Los Angeles, where prosecutors had yet to decide whether to seek the death penalty.

"You know, Kenny, there's another way out of this. There's still time to tell where Mrs. Silverman is," Matthew hinted cautiously, choking to get the words out of his mouth.

Kenny merely gazed at Matthew and snapped, "Ask Shawn Little."

Epilogue

One week after Sante was sentenced, she was back in the news again when a fellow inmate reported that was she plotting to escape. Evidently, Sante had tried to recruit the inmate in her attempt to break out by hiding in a crawl space below the bus that would take her from the Rikers Island jail to the Manhattan Courthouse. How Sante was going to accomplish this scheme was never made clear.

Because Sante had briefly escaped federal custody before her slavery trial in December 1985, and because of this information, whether it was true or not, New York Corrections officials weren't going to take any chances with their high-profile prisoner. They put restrictions on her movements and refused to allow her to leave Rikers Island until she was transferred under a heavy escort to the Bedford Hills Correctional Facility in nearby Westchester County on July 12, 2000. "Whenever we hear the 'E' word we take precautions," said Tom Antenen, the Corrections spokesman.

Nothing could deter Sante from continuing to defy the rules of the institution. She enlisted another inmate to sneak a three-page letter out of Rikers Island to her friend, Carolene Davis, "the daughter she never had," in Santa Barbara, instructing her to *"tear this* [letter] *up. Keep Secret."* Sante asked Carolene to become her publicity agent and set up books, movies, and television contracts for her.

> *You have clout. You can line up interviews with us personally. Get $. Use your maiden name. Call International Creative Mgmt.—Wilshire Blvd, Los Angeles—Get them on your side for media everything.*
>
> *Please honey, save innocent Kenny! We also need very secretly (careful) to get Security Title loan file that AR escrowed and directed on Sahara—on Geronimo house. AR directed the loan at Security Title on Geronimo—closed Jan. 11, 1998. Loan was from Ocwen Loan Co to David Kazdin. (just in name only.)*

Sante asks Carolene to get copies of the escrow and instructs her to:

> *act like you have buyers and need property profile. Help us secretly—the truth is all there if you can get it.*
>
> *With you, God and truth we will xpose this terrifying frame. Please, you are the only one we trust. Don't let that bastard and corrupt framing police kill innocent Kenny.*

Sante ends the letter by again appealing to Carolene to line up book and movie deals.

> *The real truth of this terrifying frame is the dynamic story, not the lies and filth everyone is lying about! Tell ICM I want*

to deal on THE DYNAMITE TRUTH the world is waiting to hear.

It would also be great to get an internet page on 'Kimes—The Real Truth.' You can even bid on the internet—There's a Matt Drudge gossip internet columnist who might be a big help—Try anything . . . All my love & trust.

Sante signed the letter *"Mom."*

Sante's days at the Rose M. Singer Center, the only female facility among Rikers Island's 10 jails, where she was housed with 1,400 other women, were about to come to an end. For months, she'd badgered Mel Sachs to set up an interview for her and Kenny with CNN's Larry King, so she and Kenny could appear on national television and profess their innocence. Because of her reported escape plan, the Corrections Department insisted on stringent precautions for the interview at the jail and said that King would have to interview the Kimeses separately. Under exceptionally heavy security, Sante was brought handcuffed and shackled to a trailer at the far end of the 415-acre island, where the program was taped.

The interview aired July 19, a week after her transfer to New York's only maximum state correctional facility for women, in Bedford Hills, New York. It was vintage Sante, as she went through her usual litany with King of knowing Irene since 1994, that they had become "social friends," that Irene called her in 1996 and "was worried and wanted to sell her house," and knew Sante had connections and could help her.

She didn't rent apartment 1B, she and Kenny never had Irene's keys or guns or syringes, and the arrest "over a little car thing" was caused by a bookkeeper who wrote the check that bounced. She accused the police and prosecutors of planting all the evidence against them and called Judge Uviller "totally biased, unfair. The judge is really the worst guilty person in all of this." At least a half dozen times, in her response to King when he asked her specific questions about the evidence in the case, Sante would plead with him "to just read those transcripts," and he would see how all the evidence was planted on them.

Finally, even Larry King couldn't take her protestations any longer. "But Sante, Sante, if I'm reading the same thing the jury had, and you said if you were on the jury, you would have convicted, what am I going to learn?" King asked incredulously.

Sante's reply was to simply spin her tired web around and around in circles, trying to convince him how she had wanted to bring out the truth but was gagged. By the time Kenny appeared on the program, he was an angry young man who had become hostile and bitter, and his message was rather anticlimatic.

Kenny was transferred into state custody on July 11. After undergoing a brief orientation, he was sent to the Clinton Correctional Facility in Dannemora, New York, near the Canadian border, one of the oldest penitentiaries in the state, built in 1845 and housing more than 2,800 hard-core inmates. Initially placed in the general population, Kenny was moved a few weeks later to a more secure area after a couple of seasoned inmates reportedly beat and sexually abused him.

On September 17, two days after Maria Zone, a Court TV reporter, conducted a pre-interview with Sante at Bedford Hills for a planned documentary about her and Kenny, Sante was disciplined for being out of place after she had signed out of her housing unit for one location and was found in another. A hearing on September 25 led to the loss of 30 days of phone privileges for those infractions, which for Sante was a catastrophic tragedy. It meant she couldn't have access to the outside world and would be unable to have any kind of telephone communication with her son.

On October 10, Zone and her camera and sound crew arrived back at Dannemora at 10:00 A.M. and began setting up for the on-camera interview with Kenny to be held in the visiting room. Around 2:15 P.M., Kenny got up to use a bathroom while Zone headed in the opposite direction to buy bottled water from a vending machine.

When Zone and Kenny returned to the table to finish the interview, Kenny suddenly grabbed the reporter, spun her around so that her back was against his chest, and then, with his arm wrapped around her shoulder, he pushed a pen against the reporter's neck. With the pen still pressed to her neck, he dragged her across the room to a corner.

An officer observing the interview pushed the alarm button and called for help. Officers immediately responded, as well as the prison's crisis intervention unit, consisting of trained negotiators.

"Back off," Kenny ordered the security personnel and crew from Court TV. And that's exactly what they did.

A little more than four hours later, Kenny was distracted long enough to separate him from the reporter. He was wrestled to the floor, where he was subdued and placed in restraints before being moved to the facility's disciplinary housing unit. For the most part, Zone was shaken but unhurt. Kenny had told hostage negotiators his plan in seizing the reporter was to force New York State Governor George Pataki to deny a request from California Governor Gray Davis that his mother be extradited to face the death penalty in Kazdin's murder.

Because both Sante and Kenny were considered escape risks, Sante was moved to the disciplinary housing unit during the hostage incident as a security precaution. Officers searched her cell and found a pen that had been altered at the top to form a hand grip, which they suspect a young woman by the name of Tina Barrett smuggled into the prison for Sante. Barrett had attended the trial daily with her mother and after Sante's conviction struck up a correspondence with her. Barrett met with Sante behind bars at Bedford Hills, and during one of her visits, authorities suspect that Barrett gave Sante a pen, which inmates are banned from possessing under Correction Department regulations.

The Inspector General's office of the Corrections Department began an investigation into how Sante got the pen, and although Barrett and her mother were never specifically charged, because they were Sante's only visitors during the time period, they were subsequently banned from ever visiting her.

The murderous Kimeses were back in the news again on October 21, when Governor Pataki signed the papers that set in motion the extradition of the mother and son, transferring them to Los Angeles. "These murderers must be held accountable for each and every one of their vile acts," he said.

Two days later, the Corrections Department socked it to the Kimeses. Kenny was found guilty of violent conduct, violating direct orders, making threats, assault, and possession of a weapon. He was sentenced to eight years in solitary confinement, and his mother was given six months for having violated prison rules.

"A discipline of eight years is a very long one," Commissioner Glenn S. Goord said, "given that only six percent of inmates receive sanctions exceeding five years. It speaks to our policy of 'no-tolerance' when it comes to prison assaults." One quarter of all such sanctions are for less than the six months Sante received, he said.

As a result of violating prison rules, both Sante and Kenny lost such privileges as receiving packages from outside sources, the ability to make purchases at the prison commissary, and the use of telephones to make collect-only calls. Those inmates confined to the "hole" are housed in separate cells from the general population with no contact between the two groups. They are kept in their cells around the clock, except for one hour of daily outdoor exercise, legal and medical visits, and one non-legal visit a week.

Sante managed to get into still more hot water. Her six months in solitary were supposed to end on April 9, 2001, but her time was extended when Corrections officials tacked on another 180 days for stashing contraband, namely stockpiling pills, which she was probably going to use to make herself ill enough to require a transfer to the prison infirmary, where she could plot her escape.

One month after the hostage incident, Kenny was back in the spotlight. In a stunning jailhouse admission to Detectives Tommy Hackett and Danny Rodriguez, he claimed he'd dumped Irene's body in a ditch by a building under construction in New Jersey and placed debris on top to prevent discovery of his grisly package.

On November 14, handcuffed and shackled, a bearded Kenny, looking like Ted Kaczynski, was brought down from his Clinton solitary cell to meet with Los Angeles detectives English and Cox about the Kazdin case.

The unusual meeting took place in a conference room at the State Corrections Academy in Albany, New York, about 185 miles south of the prison. The New York detectives met with Kenny after Los Angeles detectives were through with him. Hackett suggested to Kenny that if he told how he got rid of Irene's body, they might be able to shorten his solitary sentence and make life better for him. Kenny initially played games with them and the detectives were about to leave when he revealed the gory details.

"He said that he put Irene's body in the trunk of the Lincoln, drove down Fifth Avenue to the Holland Tunnel to New Jersey, headed south until he saw an excavation site alongside a building under construction, dumped Irene in the ditch, and covered the body with dirt and debris," Hackett said.

The burial site was somewhere near water, and Kenny said the trip took 90 minutes from Irene's mansion to where he dumped the body and then back to the town house. He claimed he couldn't pinpoint the exact town and was vague as to the site, because it was so long ago. Kenny said he just drove around and found this construction site. When detectives pressed him for specifics as to how Irene died, Kenny merely shrugged his shoulders and said, "What difference does it make how she died?"

Kenny went back to the hole at Clinton, and Hackett, Rodriguez, and members of the Tactical Assist Response Unit (TARU) spent days driving up and down the Jersey coast shooting video and still photos of every imaginable site where Kenny could possibly have dumped the body. When they went to show Kenny the photos, he refused to talk with them. "It was all a ploy," Hackett said.

However, 10, 20, 50, or more years from now, should Irene's body surface, there will be a way to identify her. Resting on a secure shelf at the police laboratory are Irene's hairbrush and toothbrush, found in her apartment at the mansion. The items have undergone extensive DNA testing and only await a comparison when and if Irene's body is ever found.

Searching for Irene's body was put on hold, Chief Reznick said, after Kenny was extradited to Los Angeles on March 20, 2001, for the Kazdin murder. His mother continued to challenge her extradition until June, when she also threw in the towel and admitted defeat. Her mind-boggling delaying tactics included a claim that she was 90 percent deaf and 95 percent visually impaired. She even demanded that a Corrections guard keep the overhead lights on in her cellblock because she was "legally blind." Her final stall before being shipped to Los Angeles was to insist that state officials prove that she was the Sante Kimes mentioned in the extradition warrant.

In Los Angeles, prosecutor Eleanor Hunter continues preparing for the murder trial of Kenny and Sante, in which she will seek the death penalty for the pair. Prosecutors in New York were unable to seek the death penalty for the Kimeses because, under New York state law, only the actual killer can be charged with first degree murder during a felony or intentional murder.

Since Silverman's body was not found, there was no way to determine whether Sante or Kenny murdered her, the prosecutor said. Without a body or direct proof of how she was killed, it is not surprising that prosecutors could not prove which defendant killed Silverman.

After the preliminary hearing, the next step will be the trial itself in 2002. Among those set to testify against the Kimeses will be Shawn Little, Stan Patterson, Robert McCarren, Nanette Wetkowski, Judy Hyman, Dawn Guerin, and Daniella Scaramuzza. Those infamous notebooks that they kept, with such sinister notations as "DK is out of the picture, DK is no more," will once again be the focus of attention by a jury.

One of the biggest surprise prosecution witnesses will no doubt be Kent Walker, Sante's son from her second marriage, who went on national television (*Dateline*, NBC, April 24, 2001) to reveal that Kenny had admitted to the murders of David Kazdin and Irene Silverman.

"You're going to have to turn state's evidence . . . and you've got to be willing to cooperate," Kent claims he told his half brother during a jailhouse visit. Kenny reportedly agreed, saying, "I'm willing to cooperate."

Kent has also come under scrutiny by Los Angeles detectives because of his remarks about the death of Kenneth Kimes, Sr. In a television interview, Kent indicated that shortly before Kimes, Sr., died of an aneurysm, the real-estate developer confided to him that

Sante was poisoning him, a suspicion members of the Kimes family had long held.

"That makes him an accomplice to my uncle's death," a Kimes nephew said, speaking for the family. "Why didn't Kent go to the police and report the matter? Why didn't he call Linda or Andrew or contact Ken's brother? Why did Kent cover up Uncle Ken's death to the coroner and give false information on the death certificate that allowed his mother and Kenny to loot the estate for years? And why didn't he help my uncle escape from Sante's clutches if he knew she was poisoning him? Kent let it happen."

The nephew also points out that Kent claims that he overheard his mother and Kimes, Sr., argue in a car while driving in Los Angeles about what he now suspects is the murder of Elmer Holmgren, a disbarred lawyer who vanished in 1991. According to Kent, both Sante and Ken, Sr., accused each other of the murder. "There's no way my uncle would have participated in a murder," the Kimes nephew said. "Sante killed him. That may have been her first murder. If my uncle suspected that Holmgren was speaking with the authorities about the fire in Hawaii, he would more than likely have bought his way out of a jam by giving the guy money to shut him up if he was threatening."

In June 2001, Kent called Matthew Weissman and asked that he and the other defense lawyers not put in a claim for legal services against the estate of Kenneth Kimes, Sr., for services rendered in the two years they represented Sante and Kenny in their joint defense. "It will only hurt Kenny," Kent told Weissman. But the lawyer suspects that Kent, who has been visiting Kenny at the Los Angeles jail on a regular basis, is now his half brother's guardian and wants to oversee Kenny's portion of the estate.

Sante and Kenny—the Odd Couple, the Grifters, Con Artists, Mommie Deadliest, Mommie & Clyde—still capture the front pages of the tabloids for a case that is believed to have cost New York police and prosecutors upwards of five million dollars to bring to justice.

Joseph Reznick was promoted to deputy Chief of Detectives and is assigned to the Bronx. Detectives Joel Potter, Eugene Wasielewski, Danny Rodriguez, John Schlagler and Tony Vazquez have all retired.

A few days after the Kimeses were sentenced, John Carter, an assistant district attorney for the past 13 years, was appointed a criminal court judge by New York City Mayor Rudolph Giuliani. Owen Heimer, another member of the prosecution team, was made chief of the Rackets Bureau in the Manhattan District Attorney's office. Ann Donnelly and Connie Fernandez are staying where they are, prosecuting career criminals.

The defense lawyers have also gone back into a routine of doing what they do best—defending clients accused of crimes. But they offered some observations and remembrances of their notorious clients.

In the two years that Matthew Weissman was involved in the Kimes case, he found Kenny "compassionate and very gifted," but led astray by his mother. He concurs with defense psychologist Arthur Weider that Sante molested Kenny as a child, although Kenny never accused his mother of molesting him. Both Weissman and José Muniz observed that the pair were "always close . . . a little bit beyond what we might have had with our mothers," said Weissman. "They always acted like lovers more than mother and son."

"His mother is twisted and turned him into a devil, a serial killer," Muniz said. "He would never discuss his mother with us. It was as if she didn't exist. It was almost as if when he was with us, he was human. He'd relate his experiences in the Caribbean, partying with young women. He was like any other kid you'd meet at college or on vacation, talking of the good times, and he'd say, 'José, when this is over, we'll go down to the Bahamas and party.' You didn't feel like he was bullshitting you.

"Kenny was very different from Sante. When she told you about going to the Bahamas, you felt it was total garbage. But when Kenny said it, you believed that he was sincere.

"When Kenny grabbed your hand, you felt warmth from it. When Sante felt my hand, there was a tremendous difference. It felt like my hand was being held by a witch," Muniz said.

"The other thing Sante did when she grabbed your hand is look at you dead in the eye, and you had to look her back in the eye. If you looked away, she felt you were lying. That's why it was always important to look at her."

Mel Sachs found the Kimes case "fascinating" and called it "the case of the millennium." He reckons the reason why the defense couldn't succeed in convincing the jury of their innocence was because "the court of public opinion seeped into the courtroom. There was a prevailing public sentiment that Sante and Kenny were responsible for the disappearance and death of Irene." He felt that there was much hearsay admitted that allowed the Kimeses to be convicted based upon character assassination. "It was never proven that Irene was in fact dead, and there wasn't any proof of good hard reliable evidence connecting them to her disappearance.

"The evidence in the notebooks that Sante and Kenny filled out was devastating to both of them, and clearly the jury found the notebooks significant during deliberations. But the acts they committed are a far cry from murder."

Michael Hardy's supporters are promoting his run for Manhattan District Attorney. Of his former client, Hardy summed it up by saying, "Sante Kimes believes in living life her way. She's like the old Frank Sinatra song, 'My Way.' And she'll keep on doing it her way, even if it means spending the rest of her life in prison."

A detective who had been guarding the mansion adopted Irene Silverman's prize boxer, Georgie; he is now living the life of a spoiled country dog in upstate New York. Interestingly, after Irene disappeared, detectives observed that the animal, which had always had free rein of the house, would stop short at the threshold to apartment 1B and refuse to go into the apartment.

Mengi is still the caretaker at the townhouse, although it is virtually empty of furnishings. The Bank of New York has cataloged Irene's prize possessions and will ultimately sell them at auction. Marta Aracelis Rivera, Ramon Casales, Noel Rodriguez, and Valerie McLeod have all moved on to new endeavors, some even working for Irene's former guests. Jeff Feig can still be found at the Feathered Nest, and the directors of the Coby Foundation have put the mansion up for sale for a cool $11 million. Judge Uviller still maintains a heavy caseload, presiding over a variety of criminal cases.

As for the courthouse itself, nothing much has changed. The elevators still don't work properly, and the smell of bacon continues to permeate the lobby as one enters the building. But what goes on inside those courtrooms changes 24–7.

A new murder case has captured the imagination and headlines at the Manhattan Criminal Court: that of three young men accused of the grisly killing of a tenant for his apartment in a housing project—which just goes to prove what my colleague, Chris Michaud at Reuters, says, "Getting a place to live in New York City can be murder."

APPENDIX A

The Kimes' Letters

The following are excerpts of lengthy letters that Sante and Kenny exchanged with each other; with Kent Walker, Sante's older son and Kenny's half brother; with Nanette Wetkowski, her personal notary public; and with her friend Carolene Davis; and during the two years the Kimeses were "guests" of New York City authorities. The letters, many of which are repetitive, highlight plots, schemes, their inner thoughts, and alibis. Spelling, punctuation, abbreviations, and grammar have not been changed.

JULY 10, 1998—SANTE TO KENNY:

My mom's heart & soul is always with you. I will keep preparing daily summaries so we can get our defense clear and ready. I think the cops in LA traced a certain kind of gun to Stan & he blamed us to save his rear. Honey this disappearance of this crazy madam is in no way could be blamed on us. That old woman had a lot of enemies. She was so mean & filthy minded. . . . They're looking for a Spanish man—probably José or? Or who? That has nothing to do with us. Maybe she took off because she was broke.

The LA thing is just as unbelievable—Kazden was a friend. If they have a tape of you calling him—so what? I don't know where we were, but I think in Las Vegas or I can't remember. They believe we nailed Kazden because we got $ from a loan.

Yea! Just on news—police not charging with murder. They finally wised up. Now maybe they will get the real criminal. I sure love you ole green eyes. I am with you every minute. I love you Tiger! Urgent you wire $ to K's [Kent's] acct— no other choice. He is trying to help. He knows we are innocent. He says he can get loan on land—so great! Our attys are really great. They have heart, but we have nothing to pay them. Because the case is so in media it's a great opportunity for an atty to get a big name for himself. We have done nothing wrong. Why don't they go out and persecute other people who just traded a car—came to New York & tried to get going on a loan deal & business.

Try to get money safe—our attys will win this. LA is a entrapment. Millions of people could have gotten DK. We need Kent's help NOW. Call him all the time. I will leave messages in code part of. The police went to see Kt—asked about who were 8 or 9 names? He told them nothing. They will see Nan too because of LA. I am trying to call her—she needs to be quiet.

I'm trying to get a time schedule. If you are in doubt, just write back what do I remember—so you are so right to confirm with me—in this nightmare— its very confusing and devastating—we will help each other remember.

JULY 12, 1998—SANTE TO KENNY:

You are so young & to have this nightmare attack on you when you are so young and innocent is so life shattering. Get bail—you first. We have been so abused of our rights. I believe all they are doing is illegal. Entrapment—Set up by snitch. The little car case is civil. DK not conned out of anything. DK had so many enemies. LA is pure nothing—circumstantial. Papers in car ledgers or copies of woman's signature. So what? The toys—so what—they don't prove anything. & they were Stan's. Should we do anything about hotel? Papers were for loan?

Maybe Kent is best. I'm talking to Kent & Carson. Even Lynn. We need them now—people may try to interview them—my God! They are going through your computer. I don't think we need a PR agent—too much $. They are practically burying us with slander. Kent knows all. Kent key on outside to watch over all. K says you have not called him. We need him now.

JULY 13, 1998—SANTE TO KENNY:

My Wonderful Son. All we did was rent an apt. What else do you remember? Financing on Irene's bldg. [IS] crazy unable to run a successful apt. She [IS] was broke now. You can't get a loan on a bldg if owner disappears. IS negligee—no panties—pranced. So many Cubans & odd guys. And which Cuban cleaned our up car—they had keys & was in it if they try to plant anything— we must prove it's a sabotage because it is.

July 13, 1998—Sante to Kenny:

Watch for planted evidence. Get Kent here. Protect all to Kent. I will prepare, He is director and can sell get a loan or first—Call Kent at home—get him here to protect. We have always had to use aliases because of cooperation. Attys— they have to take your direction. We will have Kt take care of mail & storage.

Stan as a snitch & informer can be stricken, his testimony was entrap- ment—illegal—He CYA'd to protect himself. My life is mostly lived & its been great—I had you! Your life just beginning—fight & we will win. Kent has to help and control our holdings. Never trust but we must have Kent now. Kent transfer now protect before they seize. DNA plant.

July 13, 1998—Sante to Kenny:

I pleaded with Kent to come NOW to protect our assets & titles. He can become director of A.G. Ltd. &transfer, sell or get a loan. But HE—not attys or anyone— He needs to come NOW. I can sign for BU or MG for Atlantis & Kent can be a director. Wr $ to Kent's acct. He would protect more than anyone at this time. He is family. Try to get him here before they seize. Kent needs to find back up NY counsel if our attys won't get investigator—we have to find someone who will give collateral on land & wire $ to Kent. There is no time—we are being framed.

July 14, 1998— Sante to Kenny:

My son—my hero—my heart. Read these notes—truth. the woman disap- peared at 11—who sez! We can prove at hotel, then walking park, then Italian restaurant, then Hilton at 3—arrested at 4, is that your memory? We may have some problems. A witch hunt. Be careful with $ if we have to we will use land as collateral. I have tried to get Kent here it would help transfer. I am worried they will "plant" evidence. It's all filthy lies.

July 15, 1998—Sante to Kenny:

We have a wonderful new attorney replacing Matthew—he is a homicide spe- cialist. He & José will win for us. I believe in them.

July 17, 1998 Sante to Kenny:

Kenny my soul! Fight! Fight!

Plan every minute. Know nothing of toys. Prepare witness list for LA—who can prove where we were & our defense. Help N I told Kent to pay her this month for normal duties as usual . . . she can cash my SS check . . . Joey put in 2 bags black case in our car for Stan. About 2 weeks ago Joey, Stan's friend put Stan's stuff in our car. Joey was dark and like a Mexican cowboy type—smaller—from Bronx. Do all U can to get Mel to set up these meetings now before the gun thing or Feds take the case—we must meet now!

July 17, 1998—Sante to Nan Wetkowsky:

We love you. We are innocent. No one had done anything wrong. Don't be intimidated or frightened by authorities. Don't talk so it can be turned. DK authorized you to notarize docs for years—never a problem. You *never* did anything wrong as a notary. Don't talk or be forced into saying what they are trying to set up. Honey, its hell—but we will win this simply because we have done nothing wrong. Your little Ken calls out to you, bless him, he's being so strong. We have wonderful attys. Mel Sachs is so upset about the entrapment & unjust burning at the stake. He will win. He's famous & never takes a case he doesn't win.

David is the only one who could at this time say he didn't sign papers or tell you to notarize. He did this for years! *No one else in the world can dare say you didn't notarize rightfully.* We were friends altho he was having so much trouble with daughter, girlfriend, money—I was shocked when I heard he's gone. Don't be intimidated. Don't believe a thing you read it's all sensational lying media. Barbara Walters is fairer. She wants to interview us, but I can't say a word now— all is silence. Then the truth will come out.

More lying creeps behind this. . . .

July 25, 1998 Sante to Ken:

We were taking Stan's toy to him—he was moving here. This week be strong. They will be charging us as expected. They have nothing but gossip & entrapment. The exact same is true in LA. There are lots of attys who want the notoriety. I must know Mel is on for keeps. We have always told them no more cash—land is collateral. They will become very very famous over our trial and benefit greatly. It's frozen. We can give written promise to pay. The media will pay millions. Time Magazine is calling Kent. We must take advantage of the newsworthiness of this—it's huge! The attys will become world famous over this case—that's worth **BIG BUCKS**. Maybe we should get a PR company. We need the press! I hear Johnny Cochrane is interested in the case. BS about handcuffs. I use them to hold luggage together. Mel & José committed to us. Handcuffs used for holding luggage together. Get media to tell our side daily. They want to know who we really are. Close your eyes—the future will be bright. Never tell anyone my true ID unless I say yes in person—that's for the future at the right time. I will protect & fight for you forever. You are wonderful.

August 3, 1998—Sante to Nan:

Allen responsible for all of loan. We have millions in damages coming. Continue as normal and be secretive.

August 8, 1998—Sante to Nan:

Be careful & silent. Notarize David's signature. Pay yourself. My $10,000 white mink coat—you have it as an early birthday present. We know nothing of the fire.

August 23, 1998—Kenny to Sante:

How are you my sweet? I saw in an article yesterday something about cops freezing Bermuda and are now in the process of freezing Antigua. I think they may go after Cayman after Antigua and discover Nan's account, but so what. It may bring Nan into the media though and that may un—nerve her. Well, know this our faces will be known forever. I just want to hold your little hand & have a beautiful dinner with you. How exciting.

August 24, 1998—Kenny to Sante:

Just got off the phone with Kent . . . Shallow man like ½ inch. He thought also we were on the news to much. I enjoy our little picnics! Deep chats. I pretend we are on couch drinking nice red wine & having one of our deep 1 on 1's. Mama dear confuscious say; Mama—san & Kenny—boy are doing OK.

August 25, 1998—Kenny to Sante:

What's shakin'? When this is done we are going to C. I am going to go on a strict diet of rum, coke, cigars, and women until the doctor tells me am close to exhaustion.

August 29, 1998—Kenny to Sante:

How the fuck are ya! Well mom we have made all the front pages [local, foreign, spanish, russian] for the past three days. I am now going into an overview of all the issues: we need a progress report for FL/UT/NV/CA. The only future problems we face are: Murder charges in NY, fraud on title apt, murder in CA, why we were in NY, time frame for the credit card fraud. Mom be O so careful! Hide your notes. People will go in your cell and read them. Be cool and sly. We are getting support & sympathy. We are no part of Atlantis. We don't have to be! WE have our own companies: KMI & XCL in Nassau!

I was with you & Nan & Kent March 11–14th, I know and remember because it was around the time of my birthday. We spent those 2 weeks w/ our close friends in NV.

Think about time frame for July 5th! *Who when how who and what* . . . we can probably dismiss the credit card issue . . . One last thing . . . I never said that that would be a great place to get rid of something "as in the burrial area, that is what José had said—Also he 1st said I never said anything [we never] about a plot murder or anything weird. Well momma how are you? Hang in their and stay strong we are winning big time. All of the things the cops are saying are contradictory and self defeating. They are completely shitting on themselves. Never spazz out. Always be even and in command. Are you getting along w/ the girls? I have a suspicion that you are not. We have the best civil cases we will have books, movies, interviews. Our dreams are in closer grasp than ever, because of the situation. The media will be dying to hear our side of it! We will start the new Kimes chapter and I will assume the role you and father have created for me. Protect your health so that you may help me and protect the new generation that is coming. I only have you left momma. In Aeternum [Forever].

September 1, 1998—Kenny to Sante:

I think, "I know," we are soul mates you and me. Realize that because of our circumstance we are entitled to the riches of Babylon. At least you can really rest and think in jail.

September 2, 1998—Kenny to Sante:

I like the morning in prison much more than the evenings. How are you my darling? Weakness is the worst enemy. Don't worry about LA, "even if SL came forth that would not be enough! Their needs to be hard evidence & he needs to have someone back up what he says! Its dead. Ha Ha. Also the only 3 things we have to worry about are 1. Fed gun charges—which we will win its all SP. 2. Time extension of 30 more days for Utah (and no more that's the max! [THIS IS A NON ISSUE]) 3. Time extension on credit card matter (not a felony!) Nothing else can bite us in the ass. Also the thing on you in Florida –the charge was not in your name! Don't worry about that! José was a little slick yesterday w/ his questions about C. I didn't like it.

September 3, 1998—Kenny to Sante:

How are you dearest? Dawn is our focus. Has she been approached? Is she staying quiet? We will try to get Dawn. Why would she say we gave her $ for guns? You are so damn cute. Don't worry about me. I am strong and fine. Nothing but you can ever hurt me. Mom just realize that all of these hardships that we currently are facing are a blessing in disguise because we will have fame & fortune after we win this. SP is hated by all—feds—wife—and the media already has a bad boy file on him. We could potentially trick Dawn into saying some things about him to Mel & Les. We think his own wife has it in for him and his own children. I am so happy that I will get to see you tomorrow and see your beautiful face and hold your strong warm little hands. I think that I would turn to ice were it not for your warm grip thawing my cold hands out. You are so warm and fantastic. It's never dull for us mom, is it, always an experience and an adventure. We are winning and will win over-all.

SEPTEMBER 4, 1998—KENNY TO SANTE:

Our blood—DNA if your suspicions are positive this DNA test will prove in one day that we are related. One problem is that if we are not, this will confirm we are or are not related. W/ this their is no way to play games. (But we could get our own DNA person and run a private test and if test is good use it, if not don't use it.) All that is needed is some hair from any of the relatives of that family How do we get hair? One big issue is Dawn. She is the only weak link on everything. Do you think that she is playing witness? Her involvement may be more harmful to SP and her than to us! I sure love you mom, Your such a cutie. You know to them we must be like legendary adventurers travelling @ the speed of light. They can grow and share our strength with us. Even from prison we are in their daily thoughts and lives. Think of it. Lynn and Kent must have thought, "Thank God, now they will be away from influencing them," but now we are in their home on the TV the phone, the radio, magazines. Hell, the way the kids watch TV they probably see more of us than they see their mom and dad! I bet you now that the bitch will start to turn the TV off and tell the kids they should read more. Those kids love us and now they will always respect us. Please go over my letters and go over the key points for review. Our case will make world history. Mel will be super famous. Please don't be too affectionate w/ him, it makes him nervous. Don't worry when he gives us his bill you won't like him nearly as much as now. I love him for his brilliance, but realize he does not care about us @ all. His love is only w/ the case and the benefit it will bring him, that is all. Don't be hurt by this, but I must tell you my feelings for I am the only one who sees all and loves you. When you gave him the kiss on the cheek he didn't respond and he hesitated w/ his return of your affection.

SEPTEMBER 5, 1998—KENNY TO SANTE:

We will have the most famous case in history. books, money fame. This is our time . . . Dawn weak link Your such a cutie. I wish we could be together right now having drinks, food, & fun. Our case will make world history. We are going to be stars! Please don't be affectionate with him it makes him nervous. . . . *never tell him that you love him again.* Trust me, Mel is one of the coldest hearted people I have ever met. Between you and me he is more cold blooded than a snake, but he is our best defense.

SEPTEMBER 6, 1998—KENNY TO SANTE:

Momma, If we are charged (and I have no idea anymore, because we have them "DA" in a very bad position) it will be murder and possibly fraud as well, or just one of the two.

I think we should have the court case televised! But to be honest we know nothing until we are charged. We don't know shit until we see all of our demons. But know this, we are beginning to become very powerful and we will BLOW AWAY anything they throw at us. Don't worry about UT/LA/or FL, all of our battles are in NY and we have all bases covered.

SEPTEMBER 6, 1998—KENNY TO SANTE:

How the fuck are you? It was great talking to you yesterday, you sounded great as you should. I feel great myself. I worked out this morning and had a great lunch. That judge was fantastic. I hope that he will take all of our cases. You know if we go to court again and those bastards try to keep us from holding hands again, I am going to ask the judge if I can hold your hand. Okay I just had a cookie and finished taking a nap. So, mom, Friday was fantastic. You know the cops hated it that you and me were so exuberant. That one lady cop who took you away was angry w/ our happiness. You should start thinking of our plans outside of prison. We will hopefully have our freedom back w/in the next month or 2 and we should do everything we can to protect it. We can't blend in like we used to ever again, and I strongly feel that we should get the fuck outta here fast when we have a chance. I have one more hour until I can call my best friend in the world! Have you spoken w/ Kent—be careful.

SEPTEMBER 7, 1998—KENNY TO SANTE:

I had a relaxing day, reading a book, napping and so forth. I was thinking of you "as I always do" and I always feel that when I look into your eyes, I see two things A] myself as a child and us playing all the time, and B] the soul of a fun loving child 'kid.' I just want so bad to hug you and get out of the US. I am always thinking about big C and how happy we both were there. I am curious, the UT thing is what is holding us, but is the NY credit card thing holding us in any way? It doesn't seem like it is. Don't forget that the bastards are going to make us do a line up on Thursday.

September 31, 1998—Sante to Carolene Davis:

Hi my little daughter. We are surviving in hell. We will win. I'm sure you know how innocent we are. Is there any justice for a mother & son? Is there any justice in the US? Also could you fax him the C.V. Narasimhan first on the property. Please do this *very secretly*. Be careful—don't talk to a soul until you call Matthew & we know its OK. Any news at all on property . . . please keep a close watch OK? Don't worry you will be rewarded—there is so much good coming—but we have to be so quiet & not talk now. Never mention business—its confidential. Don't even tell anyone you've heard from us, its best not to. We are totally innocent honey we were framed!

Fall 1998—Sante to Nan:

Your little Irish son is fighting like only the Irish can. These are all lies—a set up triggered by Stan Patterson. It is worse than hell in here. Silence now honey. Don't be intimidated. They have nothing. Pay yourself. Do this very confidentially—just like what you have for years. Don't talk. Don't be afraid. Mel Sachs is like a God. Brilliant. I talked to Kent—he's been hounded, too. If you could go see him . . . he will give you the $.

October 30, 1998—Sante to Kenny:

Let me handle Mel & Les. Rehearse every day in your mind our defense on the 2 cases. Go through every detail. Never let it fade. I do this even naming the witnesses—time & entire defense. Honey, my hero, here is my summary of where we are and what we need to do. Mel wants all the glory. We need more than lead atty Mel to survive and do real paper work & actual work. I have started Moreno on land, get money in Freeport. We have to get out of this crooked system no matter what. We will try anything. We need to scream out to the media. NOW is time. We know what to say. It won't hurt our trials at all. Moreno should get ahold of Barbara Walters etc. It's too quiet. The public wants us. My son is hero—young just a student, who gave up education to try to save Mom & family from GC attackers! We did not rent apt. We did not do deed & we certainly did not kill anyone! Framed. I am you! I will always be the same. I am fine. You are my life. If you are OK—I'm OK. I want you out—any way necessary—no limit. Protect our fortune secretly. Read this every day. Rehearse in your mind the LA defense and the NY defense—timing, etc. We will win. Read & review this 1 zillion times a week.

November 4, 1998—Sante to Kenny:

My Precious Leprechaun! Top o the world to ye me wee super laddie! Bless your courageous wonderful Irish spirit, heart & soul. Thank you God for giving me the most wonderful superhuman Son that will ever be. Thank you my dearest soul son for being my son! Listen to me with your heart. Thank God we got it down pat about my attorney Allan Russell! It fits like a glove. I am just an unsophisticated Mom. You just a college kid weren't even there. Your little mom was bilked of all her fortune. Poor David was your Mom's friend—you never even met him!

November 26, 1998—Sante to Kenny:

Ho my Son! Gobbles of love. Honey tear this up after you read it—#1 is get out—Friday was a rare opportunity. That nice lady—so nice to us after ct & elevator close by. She let us secretly talk for 5 minutes! & no cuffs! Wow! Best time is after court. Think please! Opportunities are rare! So risky! Seize the moment! Always carry anything of importance you might need. One never knows when opportunity will knock. Be ready for anything. Friday could have happened—for both maybe. Elevator is key, I think—opinion? Best if we could just get you out! Whatever it takes. I need to know the best floors? If Friday happens again we might luck out. Hide anywhere! Can you find out layout & what's on floors? Do you have ANY officers who are really friendly and love $. These are just ideas. Never stop scheming & planning. Wish I knew the floor plans! Tear this up now my precious son! I think a cab & then to a big dept store if possible. Lots of people. Go to bedding dept—get under bed—wait til closed—do they have dogs or metal detectors? They have everything you need—clothes, food, weapons? Then when mob rush is on mingle and & walk out. Get disguised—find an identity. Do whatever it takes. If we ever make it— don't wait for me if something happens. Get out—start a dynasty! I sure wish we had toys. Never stop scheming. Please tear this up! I sure love you!

November 27, 1998—Sante to Kenny:

The Bottom Line is: we are innocent. Framed by police & guilty informants trying to save themselves. We were just guests trying to please our manager. There was weird stuff going on always at apt—lady was drunk—all kinds of strange things—questionable people. Please read honey—Study—Now we have to get Mel clued and prepare our witness list again.

December 1998—Sante to Kenny:

Honey. New plan. Cover your back. The framing police you can bet have all phone records at Wellington apt for April & May and probably cellular calls made in New York. So all we know is we didn't do any of it. They did—that's simple. None of the guns were ours.

December 21, 1998—Sante to Kenny:

Hi Beloved Son! Snookums! Here's the key to win—Distance All the way defense. Not our apt. Not our car. Not us they are trying to get. No real evidence—all presumed.

December 25, 1998—Sante to Kenny:

Merry Christmas to my wonderful son!

Christmas is here my precious Son—
This year, blue victory, next fun!
Everyone's waiting for presents galore
This luckiest mother already has more!
Blessed is your mother because she has you!
No other has a son so true!

My heart's your present, and all the stars—are twinkling & waiting for King Karam on Mars!

I promise after we win every day will be Christmas for the rest of your & your childrens & wife's lives!

Undated letter—Sante to Kenny:

Honey—My Life! I don't want to worry you, I just want to protect you as only a mom would & the facts are: Mel has done nothing for 5 months. He talks. We are endangered, really endangered & we must file to recuse & venue. We must get our motions done—for God's sake the Judge is in collusion with the DA! Jdg Altman has allowed DA to unseal bag when it was sealed by Judge Alderman! He's letting the DA do just about anything he wants. The judge has unfairly denied bail. Altman has threatened our counsel with, "you're going to be in jail like your clients!" Our counsel tried to diplomatically ask judge to recuse himself. He refused. He was so emotional about it he was shaking!

There's no body—we don't know if she's dead or where she is. Could have been anyone. Can't eliminate reasonable possibility she is alive. Mom did not conceal she was at apt—just wasn't there much—always sightseeing. Odd apt. Odd goings on. Mom did not impersonate IS. Not even there.

Our difficult issues, I call them "stickies," like the ID.

1. The sticky stuff they have MG ID with your pic,
2. My ledgers,
3. Corporate Atlantis papers in car,
4. Nan—they have blank forms she notarized,
5. the unsealed bag—Joey out it there,
6. the deed—I think its real. We didn't do the deed,
7. the PO boxes and cellular application. They will have handwriting experts. You errand boy, went for FOR not AS M Guerro & Dr. Nick.

They are trying to sway jury with a mountain of presumed things. We have to give jury an explanation.

We must take stand. Jury has to understand, to counter brain washing. WE have to get rid of this judge before all. Scream to media. We have to get different venue. Mel will fight this. He wants Manhattan to star in. Kenny, venue is how we will get new judge!

There is an evil cover up going on by city: They are covering an embarrassment. The city knows the apt was an old failing brothel—run by old has been Madam, IS! City knew trying to bury truth & any link! There is no crime. It is the worst travesty ever in NY. Just like Diallo.

Undated—Kenny to Sante:

Do you know I love you totally and completely. It is so fantastic how our defense keeps getting more and more powerful. We need to handle a few more issues and then we will be almost unbeatable. Finish Altman, get court date, handle NV then its our win all the way. I am worried about how you are trying to bring Nan in w/ Allan Russel . . . leave it alone keep it simple or you will fuck up. I don't understand why you so foolishly & stupidly keep telling about Allan. Stop. I will not participate and you confuse the issue and endanger my life. All we need are alibis. No more Allan Russel he will destroy you. Our enemy is SL focus. Easy.

Undated—Sante to Kenny:

The way she ran around like a crazy prostitute negligées & no panties—strutting around—maybe one of those Cubans did it . . . that old madam had so many enemies and Mafia friends. What an atrocity trying to involve us.

She was an old prostitute and was in a lot of unethical stuff—like running a "ho" house. He said she was really nutty and lost things and still thought she was a queen. She talked filthy about her maid and others servicing the men in rooms. She was in debt ruining the place. He said she had Mafia connections. The place was a whore house—full of Mexicans, sick men at nite for a couple of hours.

On July 4, there was a party & she & others loud and drunk. On Sunday . . . was in her nightie & no panties going up & down the elevator. We left and never saw again. We had drinks at Plaza and lunch at little italian restaurant. We went to meet Stan at Hilton (we believe he set us up for cop arrest). In short we have no idea what happened to her. I had papers on my person because we were try-ing to help Jeff get a loan. That big party. Her goings on. It's all entrapment honey. The truth will come out. Stan never gave us the guns before DK—it was after. Be strong—use this horrible set up for a book someday. DK thing is a joke! Keep in touch with Kent—he knows we are innocent.

JANUARY 1, 1999—SANTE TO KENNY:

Help me today. Urgent. Let me lead don't disagree. We have to go into action, but we must TRICK everyone about the Las Vegas trip. They don't care about LA defense. They are New York—so we must outsmart them & say ? must get to L. Vegas *for New York* defense & kind of just keep LA alibi in background. I agree with you LA is more serious! So let me trick them & order them to get to L Vegas. Help me trick them all.

Nan W. is in Vegas. She is crucial—the notary & we need [secretly get LA alibi] to get with her and try to assure she's on our side.

Between U & me, I am worried *most* about LA too. Eric said LA is more seri-ous simply because they have a BODY—a child can see that.

JANUARY 9, 1999—SANTE TO KENNY:

I'm excited Matthew . . . got Norman Seigel! The Norman Seigel! New York Civil Liberties Union! He's THE civil rights leader! He can help us so much. All of our civil rts are being denied.

JANUARY 11, 1999—SANTE TO KENNY:

Bottom line is you know nothing—just a student. SP all the way. They are con-fusing you with Joey the Limp! It's Joey they saw in apt. We must take stand. You never took IS keys. We need to rehearse with attys & Les— they don't have it straight. Don't sign or believe anyone. I am you.

JANUARY 26–29, 1999—KENNY'S DIARY:

We have confirmation that the FBI are not going to make any attempts for us, and we are almost certain that LA is not going to go forward.

January 30, 1999—Kenny's Diary:

I want nothing more than to regain freedom & get the hell out of the US forever. To wake..be able to step outside onto the beach with the sun shining & the ocean calling knowing that my mom is safe nearby. I wish we were back in Cuba driving around in those old ancient cars. O Lord what does the future hold for us? will most likely burn all my past bridges so the new future will be one completely foreign to me. I am entirely sick of the US so it will be other places from now on. One doesn't truly live unless they are adventuring or venturing out.

February 2, 1999—Kenny's Diary:

Just getting ready for interview. Also the word is over that I am the "celebrity" I am everyone's #1 topic, inmates and officers alike.

February 8, 1999—Kenny's Diary:

Kent is making a statement a negative one? On us. I have to see that to believe it. I can't understand why Kent would do such a thing, could it be for $, or could this just be hype?

February 10, 1999—Kenny's Diary:

The news is that my brother has gone to one of the tabloid $ TV groups & did a paid interview whereby he put mom down, I was numb. I couldn't believe that he would sell mom out. Kent being scared for his life from mom? Come on! I am very ashamed of what Kent has done, maybe his wife forced him to go on for the $. Any respect I had for him has blown away. I miss you Cuba.

March 26, 1999—Kenny's Diary:

I am lying on my bed smoking a swisher and just thinking away . . . a memory of me mom and dad @ a little boondock hotel in Costa Rica . . . .during a massive lightning storm . . . sitting drinking luscious rum drinks . . . dad smoking a havana, the smell of rain, ozone, and havana smoke—the scent of dreams & romance. When this is all over Cuba will be their [sic] and so will me & mom. Our legacy is just begun and I swore to myself to bring the family back to greatness. I miss mom and dad so much—our little trio—we were family & friends—like bullshit buddies. O dad now I have your shoes to fill.

May 3, 1999—Kenny's Diary:

The bus drive to Rikers was torture, Being able to see & smell freedom, people doing as they please, restaurants, bars, beautiful women, being able to drive . . . all robbed from me & mom.

May 11, 1999—Kenny's Diary:

I went to Manhattan w/ my best friend on earth my mom! By the Lucia and grace of God we were together on the bus, right next to each other. My soul was well fed with this time spent w/ her.

Undated June 1999—Sante to Kenny:

Kenny, My beloved Son! Sweetheart Please read this. It's important, then flush! We must have same stories. For 11 mths our story has been & should continue to be Your Mom got involved over Govt. Cooperation. The govt did not help as promised. The pursuers found us & trying to kill us. (There is proof of this-). We must show why we acted secretly and had to have secret identities— Running for our lives. After I lost Papa I fell into control of evil crooked group—Joey Lusitas—very important. He was your age, looked same like you but had a permanent limp. He rented apt—they are confusing you with him. This has been our defense for the entire time. Don't change it. It's perfect. It opens the door to all kinds of suspects! They have a mountain of seized files— we must have a reasonable defense & we do have.

Your strategy of SL is just fine. Even better. After we find his July 5 whereabouts you can proceed with this genius strategy of the blood being Shawns. *[NYPD Silver Task Force detectives interviewed Shawn Little and confirmed that he was working in California prior to and including July 5, 1998 and was never in New York City.]*

We don't have to rule out Joey Lusitas. We've had him on for ten months. He's perfect. We know he can't be disproven! Joey could be there when you ran over and got the parking ticket. You thought you saw SL (back of his head) parking car—Joey said—here's parking ticket and bag we checked at Plaza for Stan. (They thought SP was going over to Plaza, see?). That way you can involve SL but in case he has iron clad alibi you think you saw back of his head & you have Joey for further proof & of course Joey can never be disproven! Don't change our defense.

Joey has to remain. They have those tapes and she refers to M.G. (reservation made in name of M.G. by SP). I have always represented that Joey was SP's buddy from the Bronx. Honey expect anything! Seize every opportunity. Get tough with Matthew. Demand he bring copies. He lies & does nothing! Our goal. Get to Court, get new judge. Get Bail! Get Alibi W taped—then protect & keep secret!

A moment to tell you how much your Mom adores you! All I care about is YOU OUT! Please my precious son—say to Matt (and Mel) get on Ball!

UNDATED JULY 1999—SANTE TO KENNY:

All attorneys working on Recusal. Push this honey. Today we attack on recusal! All we have to do is get rid of this judge—*Whatever it takes!* I am trying to get Sydney Shelton [sic] to do the Big Book. Hope he's not too old. He is a superb writer. If we could talk him to the Book. Let's try. Honey, take care. I am starting on the little paperback. Prologue will be about Hackett beating us & saying Fuck the Constitution. Chapters will be The Frame, Hackett, IS? Mafia et cetera—all before trial. We gain truth and let them know it's not us! Kind of a mystery suspense of what could have happened. The prime suspects? Let public figure out. I love you!

JULY 13, 1999—SANTE TO KENNY:

My Soul Son! We will make this a win week. Just never forget, I am you. Your life & future are my life's dedication—whatever it takes. We will win. We have our alibi witness. Witness has to be T L Ced. This witness has to be guarded & babied like an incubator baby. Keep this witness secret like no other! I want to talk to you about creeps rotten bastards—You are the main heir! I'm sure we can work this to advantage. There is a marriage certificate & *you are* the heir. That rotten filthy Linda goes for your money—Never! We may find out about more money—it may open Pandora's Box. She can't be executor B of A (Bank of America) was executor of old will—then Papa wrote new will in 1993 (Secret) so we win in the future. It's yours whatever there is.

Honey, the apt was a failing old whorehouse. Even Mel said it was a house and Mafia too. You can proceed with SL blood strategy but know *Joey stays in. It helps!* We must show when they play tapes of Irene that she's talking Joey thinking he's Manny Guerro—*not you.* Remember Irene knew us & liked us. Ralph P had introduced us 4 years before. All Joey does is help you if Shawn comes up with July 5 alibi & Joey is essential to 1, we did not rent—2. you aren't M.G. renting., It was Joey. 3. IS is putting Joey down, it's not you. She knew you. She puts down the rentor with a limp calls him a criminal! 4. We weren't there on July 1 & 2 in the morning. We were driving back from Wellington in Joey's white Chevy. Joey is Key and he can never refute. He can never come forward. Can never be disproved. *[Joey could never come forward or be disproven because according to NYPD Silver Task Force investigation he never existed and is a figment of Sante's imagination.]*

All attys have the above story. Don't change it. They have to believe it and we must never change it. The more staff SP has the better—The more possible suspects the better *but Joey is key to all our defense & can never be disproven. Don't change this!* All attys have been told this—don't make us look like liars. The more suspects & doubt the better. You can be just as effective introducing SL & blood but stick to our original story—Joey Lusitas is just key. José (A) saw him in Florida. Never change that.

About Atlantis—you say police got records in Antigua—so the worst they have is your picture on M.G. ID. You were told to act for MG. That does not mean you were Atlantis or had any interest in Atlantis. You knew about it but didn't own it and had no financial interest. You just did what the big guys told you to do as errand boy.

JULY 18, 1999—KENNY'S DIARY:

Michael Hardy is joining our team . . . fantastically skilled and empathetic lawyers.

JULY 19, 1999—SANTE TO KENNY:

Sweetheart, If you can think of any good friend alibi in LA witnesses. If you can think of any friends in Vegas who will remember seeing you on March 13 Friday And March 14, Saturday write them a letter [saying] "Hi—thinking of you, need your help—hope you remember—I remember because important date in my family. We have others who are helping too, remember etc etc. I'm in hell, being framed but we are winning. I know you will help . . ."

We can stop LA trouble and Nan needs background help on her past notary work. She can link AR & DK to Atlantis! I have some papers she notarized. Thank God I got those papers from the (A.H! Matthew.). N can also help prove we weren't Atlantis. Alibis are an automatic win!

JULY 20, 1999—KENNY'S DIARY:

O Jesus, I called Mels office . . . We have a new judge! Its official Altman is off of our case! While I was speaking to mom I began stuttering, then my voice totally failed. Anyone is better. I know that our legal team is ecstatic!

JULY 20, 1999—SANTE TO KENNY:

There are no words. It was mostly your efforts (some mine) that we got rid of Altman! I cried for joy. Thank you God! Now we must attack. We must be sure that Judge Uviller is fair & not just a buddy of Judge Altman & that Altman didn't self appoint .

JULY 22, 1999—SANTE TO KENNY:

A miracle! It's confirmed March 13 (day DK was done in). We were with her in Vegas (as 5 others will also). She needs to remember & see key papers which will refresh her memory on papers she notarized. She was overjoyed to hear me & cried!

JULY 26, 1999—KENNY TO SANTE:

Dear Mom, Well I have been very busy. I wrote a scad of letters to people in NV. I have about 10 people who I think are dependable and that can be counted on. Also we must get the days right. MUST so let's find out! I think M[arch] 12-13. Can't fuck this.

Wow! I just talked to a cop in here on the 12th floor and asked him about our new judge! They are all saying she is great & fair! They said that on a 1–10 basis (10 fair, 1 bad) Altman was a 2 and our new judge Uviller is an 8! This judge has thrown out big cases for legal reasons before. We are finally on the right track! Thank God.

I love you. How are you? Stay strong and feel up. We need to begin our new relationship w/Uviller very smoothly. We should try to be kind and friendly to her—feed the ego. Now w/NV. I can think of strong alibis for us, Name of that import place that sold the great wines and chocolates. Cost plus? Remember we would go in their and hunt around @ all the crazy stuff they had-you like their soap! We could dam well get our alibi list up to 14 or 15 people. Lets see if CA will want to touch us then with 15 including you. I am happy CA [California] has left N alone. See SP & SL didn't know shit. Only RM knew a tiny bit about N. Also the insurance investigation tape of him will destroy all his credibility so he's out. We'll address this down the road but lets get out NV situation set up! We need to know the exact date these bastards are saying DK was killed!

JULY 27, 1999—KENNY TO SANTE:

If things don't change we drop all of these fuckers and go with Mike & Eric. I am not going to put up with anymore. José needs to get photos of the Lincoln windows showing how dark and go to parking garage and photo all other cars to see if windows are left open. Also letter to LA for confirming date as to when DK? Mel seems to have done nothing. I want it in writing what Mel did or did-n't do! And if Mel doesn't provide—he's out (2 weeks). Our guys are lying stalling to us. It may be time to let go of Mel. No court date, no papers and no meeting . . . then Mel goes OUT and we let Mike lead. Let's get 20 alibis in NV and destroy CA! Remember Maccaroni Grittle by the Merryl Lynch building across from Palace. We knew alot of people in their (manager, waiter, waitress.

Dark hair, long, she was slim and tall wore blue long sleeve shirt. Southern man w/blue eyes and let us make drinks in bar.)

UNDATED AUGUST 1999—SANTE TO KENNY:

NY Defense set in stone. We must have alternative defense explanation. First defense—Justice is injustice. No crime, no body, no evidence & our alibis but they have 125 bribed lying witnesses. 2nd Defense—Leave open the door for many possibilities. AR rented apt Joey Lusitas staff on June 14, 98 at noon in name of Transamerica—NOT US!—AR & staff did lots of business with IS & LA, Wellington—We were guests—AR ran all. IS knew & liked us—from 94, All are suspects to IS disappearance. Anyone in New York! We did not have IS things on us! All planted by Vasquez after IS disappeared.

We need to get all alibi witnesses! And be over prepared in these multiple frames. THIS IS SET IN STONE.

AUGUST 28, 1999—SANTE TO KENNY:

Kenny My Soulmate Son. Hi Honey. It's 8:30 Saturday nite. I'm relaxing in my room writing to the lite of my life whose future is my dream. We have won! They have NADA. We have to be completely transferred out of Riker's [sic]—totally! The DA has a year of control in here & would love to destroy & silence us. They know we are going to win! They will do anything! Because of my secret witness cooperation & the media & stolen files exposing this to enemies here, we must be transferred out of Riker's. There is a tidal wave of bribed cellmates. The DA wields too much power. It's life safety!

We need to defend & put on our own & show Mike's brilliant strategy—that we are framed. We got involved with underworld creeps. Then we walked innocently into a whorehouse with loud mouthed old madam. You need to be distanced—just a young college kid. Police have made worst unjust mistake in history.

AUGUST 29, 1999—SANTE TO KENNY:

Now my precious one NOW we must be the fire, the spirit. After a year lots of people get worn out! NEVER. Even keep sense of humor! We are winning. We are superhuman—we must be. Mike & Eric—our saviors! Need to be unequivocally backed, praised, helped, they must know we love them. Mike needs TLC. They are our champions of justice. Did you know Rev Al was stabbed 10 years ago? Rev Al is a symbol of justice as is Hardy. Cheerlead! Praise! Scream innocence. Injustice—Set up, Framed! Justice will be restored by Michael, Rev Al, Eric. Mike's strategy is genius. The jury has to believe our emotional story—its much better than theirs.

Even tho we would NEVER take detector tests I understand lots of people fail when innocent—nerves, etc. Our innocence is embedded in my soul.

This is not a murder case. It's a disappearance. There's no fraud. JF is very important—he turned in missing person almost before she's disappeared. This is a dream case attorneys pray for all their lives! It has it all—justice restored—framed.

AUGUST 30, 1999—SANTE TO KENNY:

Lead the way to victory—cheers! My super human son! Treat Mike & Eric like Gods. They are super! They are the hope. Mike will win with the SECRET in court! Study Mike's secret defense!! His eyes lite up! Without it, I know he would NOT have taken case. BACK HIM EVERY SEC . . . this largest injustice ever—framed by evil system. That's his defense!

UNDATED SEPTEMBER 1999—SANTE TO KENNY:

Kenny My Soul mate Son—LA Set up Frame! The NYPD have coerced LA to charge us—further frame & set up. Have we been indicted? I believe best to go to trial NY first. Expect anything.

SANTE TO KENNY:

Honey Pie—End of Attack Day. I'm OK! Read my notes. Key is Michael happy confident with his SECRET defense. I want you at Fed Housing. Honey the DA is behind the solitary infractions scam, trying to silence us! DA is trying to kill us they know we are going to win.

NOVEMBER 24, 1999—SANTE TO KENNY:

My Dearest Son. Happy Thanksgiving. I have more to be thankful for this year than any other in my life. Here's what I am so thankful for—You! And you & you. The strong, most loyal, super human son ever borne by any woman. Bless you!

We are going to win! You need to read my ever answer [to the indictment]. If I give it to you today . . . guard it with your life. It's the win. Its our *completely viable explanation* for the mountain of charges hurled at us. Study it . . . every attorney needs a copy of these answers I have prepared. It's our defense. It's the case.

Demand priority from all! Scream! We must have sessions! Demand *Investigation*! Mike needs to come more! *All* attorneys must read my answers to Indictment! *You* need to study it carefully—I've spent hours on it. Ask Mike what needs to be done. Once I finish answers to indictment they have their defense—word by word!

Never tie down dates with SL & always place him with Joey for back up. We need to distance you.

NOVEMBER 28, 1999—SANTE TO KENNY:

Dearest Kenny. Honey I have finished answering ever # on the indictment. It's the win. The gist of it is Not us!

But remember—we did not rent apt. We were in Hoboken til 4pm on Sunday. We were guests. We weren't with notaries and we have alibis where we were on July 5, 98. Could not use our i.d.s. IS knew us & liked us from 94. For ID secrecy you used M. Guerro with your ID on a Florida ID because of GC. You—errand boy. You went *for* Dr. Nick, not *as*. We just took orders. There was just lots of deals going on—at nite too. Joey & Eva in apt a lot—all had keys.

Sweetheart I am sitting here on 12th floor dying to see you. I never leave your side. God Bless my kid. I'm fine! Thank God I got the indictment all done! Attys need to read it. They need to rehearse & get briefed. Don't get clothes. Cici will & attys will share cost! We must save $ LA is in the future. Save every penny.

Always remember the rules. The same-ness. We could never use Kimes.

NOVEMBER 30, 1999—SANTE TO KENNY:

We have to get LA atty! & alibis somehow. I have been in criminal trials— Believe me, if we can possibly it would be good to take stand. The England people liked us. But they have to strike my priors or I can't.

Get your commissary $ built up—when they take us to LA we need our little survival $ Think ahead!

Don't believe Mel! Don't be lulled! Always be ready. Have a defense whether we use it or not!! The attys must ..actually review my answers. I can tell by their questions they need to do their homework. You can't be overprepared! Trust Mom! Don't be pacified—the more they pacify you the less the attys do!

Juries are emotional. They will like us—are more & more like a kid—we aren't geniuses.

Remember—they have your passport—it may or will show trips to Barbados? Antigua? That's OK. That could have been another of AR's staff travelling with your passport. Dig?

How can I make you understand? You must understand & you don't! The DA is going on a mountain of BS charges QUANTITY! To try to sway a jury— even if you think they can't use it—Listen! So far our case has been all things Mel and the others said would not happen! Like suppression never happened and the new judge went along with it! We must have ready a viable explanation to all the charges. Just in case.

Somehow we have to get CC to Vegas & say its all for NY defense—I'm thinking about the future. They [NY lawyers] aren't!!

DEAD END

DECEMBER 20, 1999—SANTE TO KENNY:

If the judge follows the written law—no contest. What filthy liars—They had a World War III militia on us by July 5 eve. Cover-up. Just in case judge doesn't rule for us we must have back up alternative defense. I want LA associate counsel. Think ahead.

UNDATED DECEMBER 1999—SANTE TO KENNY:

Sweetheart My Son! Kenny did you see N.Y. key witness more than once? Think. They will try & confuse him & get him to break down & say how could he remember it was July 5. We were there. We must give him help & reasonable reasons we & he could remember: Here they are:

We were at Hotel just once? Hope so. They are trying to say you picked up notaries there? Think. I hope we only saw Key witness once. It helps. Key witness remember (& we remember) it was day after the 4th. We both had hangovers. Up late watching fireworks. We told him we had been up late & were crackered out. We told him we loved New York and were going to meet our manager who was coming from Las Vegas & may be his corporation could give him a job! This automatically proves the 5th. The key he remembers day after 4th & we said we had hangovers. I remember as we left we said we were going to meet Stan. Can we say only there once?

Back to Las Vegas Alibis. Did we drive Lincoln in—yes. Drove in Wednesday. You drove! The motor home was already over at Dave's right. We left LA about 1 PM. Got to Vegas about 7 or 8 Wed. nite. Went to motor home, then on to meet Nan next day! Thursday. Any suggestions. Maybe best to say we were at Daves nite of March 11, Wed.,March 12, Thursday & March 13 Friday! Covers it all, more logical. We drove Wednesday , got to Dave's Wednes nite about 7 or 8, March 11. March 12, Thurs. Got up went to meet Nan, went to Pony. March 13, Friday, got up, went to meet Nan, went to Pony, then Saturday we also picked up mail at Ponys. We might bring in Care[olene Davis] Wed—we'll see. The above are our best witnesses. We must give witnesses an easy explanation of why they remember. Our key is March 13 Kenian's birthdate. N & Pony routine, always did that. Always went to St. Viators to say prayer on March 13. Remember we did.

Cici also needs to help Nan (when in Vegas) in something else. I got the profile on S. Maria land & thank god I got papers showing the AKI transfer to Atlantis! N notarized it. This is very important because on the stand or even on tape she can confirm we are not Atlantis—that a R. Tanis, a man from Mexico City signed it over to Atlantis—NOT US—Very important. She needs help! To refresh her memory. Cici will show her the deed. Then I will also give her the Grant Deed when Papa deeded me the Santa Maria land! She and a Don were witnesses & Paige notarized. This is important too—Remember the creeps. Cici needs to become friends, give Nan confidence & help! *[Cici McNair, a defense investigators never met or interviewed Nan during her January 2000 trip to Las Vegas searching for witnesses.]*

Remember Kazdin took N's ledger book of notarized acts she had notarized—that's important. Just as long as she doesn't say we took it, right. The key is for N to say DK signed & she notarized—sometimes AR signed for DK. He handled the loan. But you me or Nan never signed for DK or anyone! AR or the real people did. They may be able to prove DK didn't actually sign some papers because he was not in town. Then AR signed them. Not us or not Nan—DK told Nan it was OK for AR to sign. When N went to grand jury they asked her about papers she notarized that were blank. Answer is we traveled and SP, etc said get some notarized before. We just took orders. She didn't hurt us at G. Jury.

CHRISTMAS 1999—SANTE TO KENNY:

Merry Christmas, my cherished son! You are the best Christmas present anyone ever had—and I give you this Christmas all the love, commitment and heart and soul—and our win is coming. Honey, I want you to read this letter. Study it. Remember, your Mom has been thru trials before. Everything I have predicted has come true!

The key is they have *nothing*—so they are trying to lynch us. This is a modern day lynching attempt—sensationalism & LIES to cover the truth—Framed from Day 1—No crime—To cover they set us up and try to convict us on lies, planted witnesses—They know they have made the worst mistake in history. You know what they are going to try to do.

They will bring in 125 lying, coerced, bribed witnesses to influence the jury. This is QUANTITY brainwashing Bullshit—But don't kid yourself. They will try to sway the jury—witness after witness—that they are contaminating & rewarding & suggesting too—We CANNOT ignore the QUANTITY Frame. We must have a viable explanation to offer to the jury. These 125 witnesses are going to LIE and paint us as monsters—True—it's irrelevant—but with 125 witnesses taking stand-it could *sway if we don't have a viable explanation. And we will have one!*

The creeps—G.C. [Government Cooperation], only we were running. We have to defend. We must have a reasonable defense. Believe me, 125 liars must be explained. The jury has to have a reasonable explanation. Never forget this.

Even if you don't agree—know this-the D.A.'s whole case is QUANTITY LIES. We must fight and show we are victimized too. They even took your Camaro—the loan $—30 million in CD's.

It's the Hitler tell a Big lie. The bigger lie, the better and they are using bribed, coerced people who are all lying to do us in.

DECEMBER 1999—SANTE TO KENNY:

Here's a Christmas Poem for the most wonderful son who ever lived & the best Christmas present a mother ever had—God Bless you, dearest one! My Hero, My Brave Heart!

Twas the night before Christmas and all thru the cell
Not a creature was stirring, not even in jell!
The inmates were smuggled so deep in their beds,
where visions of justice plums dances in their heads.
When all of a sudden, there arose such a clatter—
Ken sprang from his bed to see what was the matter—
The moon on the bars of new fallen snow
Revealed to my Kenny all he knew and wanted to know-
And he could hear Santa and Justice laughing—Ho Ho . . . ! How Ho!
Thru the windows came Santa full of good cheer—
He spoke yes a word and went straight to his work—
He twinkled & danced and said *Justice is here!*
And then with a nod & laying a finger aside of his nose,
out the gates he rose & rose!!
But I heard him exclaim as he flew out of sight!
Merry Christmas dear Kenny and to you a good life!

P.S. The stockings were filled with Justice, Joy & good cheer—And victory that's coming this 2000th New Year!

And lovely little grandchildren that soon will be here!

My most cherished son, I am with you heart & soul this Christmas and every minute. God Bless you this Christmas and surround you with love and joy & protection—all your dreams come true!

JANUARY 1, 2000—SANTE TO KENNY:

My awesome son. I love you! OK we are at countdown! 3 weeks! We need every minute of our atty meetings. Only 3 weeks [to start of trial]. We all need to rehearse our strategy to this lynching mob—this travesty. I can't wait to see what lies the 125 have been contaminated to say by this framing DA!

Honey, don't buy me any more clothes. We have to stash away $ for LA or we will be without. I'm going to prepare a mock up of where I think our worst problem areas are—like the ID pic[ture] of you. Cici has to prove why we use aliases—GC!

They are trying to assassinate our character with lies & lying witnesses. We need to be ready! We need to distance you—a college boy—dumb—not brilliant—OK & let your hair grow. It makes you look so college—you just did errands & used id's given you by AR staff!

I talked to Mike briefly. They are getting ready for 3 month trial—yea! We need assoc. LA counsel NOW—each atty should have one so we have a LA team that NY atty can work with! Now my super hero—Please *EAT, REST. We must feel great for trial! We are going to win this travesty! But expect every dirty trick in the book—every dirty surprise!* They are trying to kill us with lies because they have nothing!

I have a friend who will cut my hair if we can get to beauty parlor. She's a professional hair cutter—I'll keep trying. I think of you every minute and want to be your hero too. I'm your Mom—I must get you free. NO MATTER what it TAKES! Be careful on phones. This is a heinous—filthy scum maggot we are fighting—capable of anything.

JANUARY 1, 2000—SANTE TO KENNY:

2000 is Our Year! New Year's Resolution!!

Because I have been blessed with the most wonderful son in the world—I resolve for our Winning 2000th year the following resolutions never to be broken—into eternity!

- I will become 1,000 x's more spirited and I will become a master of strength for my son!
- I will do everything humanly possible to protect my son FIRST, above all! For he is the dynasty maker—All of this persecution has only made him *more* of the superhuman he already is.
- I will do whatever it takes to free my Kenny & urge him to *seize* any opportunity *ANY* to get out of this evil Gestapo country—*whatever it takes!*
- I will convince Kenny *NOT* to worry about me or leaving me. He is the future. He will lead the way. He is the HOPE! I cannot do the thing he can do-He is the Star, *THE one!* He is the future! I will convince him that no matter what it takes to be free—*do it* & don't worry about me. His flying guarantees he can help. In here, he can't do the millions of.
- I will prepare my beloved Kenny if we are separated to not worry. *We are soulmates.* I mean when they take us to LA or we are separated—not to worry. We are prepared! I will work up a complete *LA Defense summary*—our defense for Kenny by middle of January! Including—Associate LA counsel and interns so when we get there we are not without help.

Long before our arrest on July 5, 98, we were being set up and framed. Huge homicide force—under ruse of car thing. Then comes Police on July 5, 98 declare us guilty & IS is homicide, Vasquez seized all illegally on July 5, 98. Anything they say they found on us was planted!

UNDATED JANUARY 2000—SANTE TO KENNY:

Honey, My Light—Do you know how special—how superhuman you are? It's really awesome. Hell is temporary. We must get you out no matter what! Whatever it takes. Fly! Another girl escaped here—wow! I want you to promise me you seize every opportunity. You are the dynasty. Never worry about me. When you are free, then my heart & soul are free! It's all SPIRIT and genius and sometimes even humor & its getting help from all—never taking No for an answer. No spelled backwards is ON. Ha! They say Castro in jail for 14 years became the genius there—a superhuman power.

JANUARY 3, 2000—SANTE TO KENNY:

Oh honey, our alibis are so urgent! That lying bastard homicide Det. Vasquez lied at the hearing. They proclaimed homicide on July 5, 98 & said Kimes did it to the world!! Filthy Bastards! We have 3 1/2 weeks until the trial. We must focus now. I'm going to limit my reading to one hour before I go to sleep—I must help guide attys I'm almost thru with our witness list. I still believe we maybe should be ready to take stand. Every case I won I took stand!

Before I forget. Please nix forever, the plan to return to New York. I want your solemn oath. F the system. Never get involved here! I'm glad you have ideas. Super! But promise the going back to NY is OUT. NY is worse than Communist China Kenny. We want to disappear on foreign land & start your dynasty! The secret is to get AWAY from NY. Don't scare me!

Can you feel my hand in yours. It will always be there. Let your hair grow. Get fatter.

JANUARY 3, 2000—SANTE TO KENNY:

Well, my dearest. Thank God holidays are gone. Now lets attack! Now we know that Det. Vasquez and the lynch mob system invaded the apartment on July 5, 98 & illegally searched 1B & this is where they seized everything & proclaimed the Kimes did it when the poor lady had been gone only hours!! They proclaimed to world—fed frenzy to the media, lies, our names & proclaimed it a homicide. They did it all. They are building a Mt. Everest Mountain of Shit. We have to have in the Wings an alternative defense. In otherwords, don't rely on Justice.

JANUARY 6, 2000—SANTE TO KENNY:

My honey bunny. My Gift! My precious Son!. Every breath I have is for you. You are my life. I am carefully working on my body language presence. See what you think.1. My hair. 2. Body language specifically my "jerking my hands or showing bad emotions, & 3. Your coldness or "mean look." You are a young handsome wonderful college boy. Never endanger that look of innocence & youth and irish friendliness. You have such great features—Large & handsome—keep your eyes so soft & kind—Don't let hard or cruel looks come out of those eyes. Look like the young kiddish, sweet handsome likeable college kid. "Soften"—think of Carson [Kent Walker's child]. Look at jury as you would Carson & I. You must practice—Relax your face-don't get that hard mean cold stare on. And your hair is almost more important than mine. The longer & more curls the better. You need lots of hair because you are big featured & headed. Lots of hair gives you a college young look.

Also I think its OK to show some emotion—like sadness, unhappiness—shock (at lies). A lot of times you read in paper—the defendant was cold showed no compassion—we are human, not robots. The key is to show good emotions & softness & vulnerability & hope—Never anger! Or physical anything—just like a sweet little beaten puppy—loving and maybe even a little frightened sweet puppy who needs help. The jury has to like us & feel sorry for us & think we look just like what we are—a caring mom's and a young sweet college boy! Don't look cold, mean, demanding or mad-right? Or too smart—Now Body language of hands—always in lap or on desk—never any hands to face or whispers secret—all calm and show-not jerky actions-never combative! Always soft-sweet.

I will get my hair to look neater. I also think if we look sad & almost ready to cry when we hear the lies & look like we need help-is great—it's the truth. Hands should be quiet—never too much motion. Be a sweet puppy, scared, not a German shepherd.

January 10, 2000—Sante to Kenny:

My precious hero kid! We have little time before trial! It's our year to triumph. Thank you for being you & never wavering, never complaining and all the incredible thoughtful things you have done in the inferno. There are no words! Honey, I am prioritizing on BODY LANGUAGE & looks. I'm practicing—your hair looks better & better, let it grow, you look so much younger & kiddish & your sweetness is showing. No cold looks! I'm fixing my eyebrows & getting ready. I'm a puppy, a sweet little puppy & so are you—Rehearse in front mirror—every day. The key is being a kid and so nice & kidlike. Just a college kid. Watch your eyes. Keep soft and kind. Never angry.

Me? I'm becoming very soft-nothing jerky-never any anger! Sweetness, a grandma—old. I practice every day & yes being sweet to all guards. They must see us as a sweet young kid and a older grandma—not geniuses.

January 12, 2000—Sante to Kenny:

Urgent. Get as much $ as possible in commissary! Don't tell Matt you have any. We need to take $ to LA or we are stranded. Won't be able to use phones. When we talk we must be the SAME. This is Key. The Secret. Explains the frame & coverup. Did not want to be linked to brothel. Boy I sure love you. Sic em! Les always supposed to work free. He agreed to work with Mel. Work on body language & looks. Your hair gets better & better. How do you like my eyebrows? I love you more than life itself.

January 13, 2000—Sante to Kenny:

Thank God we have our stories the same. We need LA alibis. Just 1 or 2. If we are separated. Brace yourself. Fight. Keep list of all your good buddies & prepare a secret plan. When they transfer us in 4 or 5 months they take everything. I just want you to be prepared.

January 14, 2000—Sante to Kenny:

There's going to be a little problem coming because José wants to do opening statement but Mike should so I'm going to just be cool & just let it happen! Mike thinks they will try & say we were going over some bridge. We had alibis. He said they may try toll bridge liars or videos. My answer is a NO but we didn't have car. Everyone had keys. So you see honey—we win here. We must show no crime & fight 125 bribed witnesses too.

Never write any letters in your handwriting to potential witnesses. Type or have someone copy or dictate a letter in other handwriting. Please.

January 14, 2000—Sante to Kenny:

How is your suit. I know how wonderful you will look like a loveable handsome college kid! I love you so much. I am so dedicated to you. Don't ever get down! Just fight and use them all. Just be careful. I'm so enraged that you have to go thru this! We've got to get you out! one way or other. People & buddies will help especially if they think you've got millions frozen & hidden. I'm doing a summary—total of that case for LA.

God we have to be so strong. I am because of you. I never allow myself to get down or too worried. The answer is Spirit. I'm working on Body language. This girl is going to style my hair Monday. Please let your hair grow & look younger. Don't look smart. We are just an average nice young student & Mom & grandmom who got in with the wrong people. So practice body language. Sleep. Stock up on commissary $. Lead the team. Con the hell out of them.

January 17, 2000—Sante to Kenny:

This is a heart to heart from your Mom's heart. The Dunes books are wonderful—very deep. I know the Preacher is Paul. Always there with his beloved kids, a parents love—separation was necessary to prepare for future generations. I want to tell you this—my dearest one. You must always forge ahead—*protect you first. Fly.* Don't worrying about me hold you back. I am OK. It's you we need to turn heaven & earth to get out. At my age I can't even think of the things you could. Concentrate on flying any way you can. I could do just as well fighting these trials alone. If there's any possibility to fly, grab it! When you are free. I am free! Use everyone in your path to a dynasty even Kent. He owes, boy does he owe. I think they are in Oceanside. You can always reach him thru Kerby. *Never trust him.* He'd turn you in—But you may need $—whatever it takes to survive. If you are going to be free . . . be ready for separations. You live, I live. Always carry important #s on you. Always expect anything. If separated—know we are one—Fly. Use everyone—Con them! Get out of U.S. Do whatever it takes. You are one in a trillion. You have to con & manipulate & get your life free & SECRET!

Keep stroking Les, say "we love him, he's the genius." Just play him-stroke him . . . just keep telling him, OK. (I think he's a SOB but we have to stroke & be cool.)

JANUARY 20, 2000—SANTE TO KENNY:

Trial in one week. Practice body language all the time. Look 19, kiddish, sweet & friendly, never show anger or smartness. I have great vibes for trial. We must cheerlead team. We need all of them—stroke-nothing negative. I think Les stopped because he got Puffy case. What a bastard. I'm stroking him—pleading. I really HATE him.

JANUARY 23, 2000—SANTE TO KENNY:

Our victory begins I hold your hand and I swear to do this: 1. Practice beautiful calm and innocence. Sweetness grandmother Karma! 2. Comb hair back & keep neat & away from face. 3. Dress neat & look neat & nice. 4. Use beautiful body language. I will look & act like a lovely sweet grandmother innocent and who loves her innocent son! I will move gracefully & calmly & not act nervous or jerk my hands or appear nervous. 5. Make my hero son proud of me & proud of my body language & presence. 6 Get stronger and stronger for my hero son! 7. Help attys in trial. 8 Prepare for LA—Carefully. . . . Thursday is our Big Beginning. The jury will see that wonderful young irish kid. It's so important. I got this cane for :dizziness" & heart trouble. It will help I think.

JANUARY 25, 2000—SANTE TO KENNY:

Hello my soulmate son. It's a new day. We are going to win. I have the most wonderful son in the planet!. OK here's my check list for today. Know that I love you and bless you! Mike's defense is great. There's no crime. The card? We had authorization. Joey & Eva used it at Channel Store—we may have used it a couple of times to eat. At Pierre Hotel where we ate—we told them it was not our card, a friend's uncle, and any problem we would pay cash—No criminal intent.

I'm working with my hair—going to curl it a little. Is it OK—and every minute I practice body language. Watch me today. How am I doing? Your hair looks better & better. Can you coax it to curl a little in front. Don't look smart & stern. Look friendly & like a kid. I must look like a grandma—sweet & average.

Kenny, I love you my Tinkertoy Hero son! U will never know how much! Can't wait for Thursday. Jury selection is so important!

I think Nan's being told by police, lies—cooperate or she goes to jail. Yes, she is probably is enemy. She's in up to her neck. We can really see how traitor she is. I'm writing up questions for Mel to ask her like did she know DK? Or has her Bank acct been frozen or has she been coerced by police? Think about this, OK?

JANUARY 27, 2000 (FIRST DAY OF JURY SELECTION)—SANTE TO KENNY:

All the Best! All luck! My precious. Wow! Our first day of our win! Bless our victory! Free my beloved Kenny. Spirit! Optimism. The win is coming. We are the spirit of victory, a symbol of justice for all framed and oppressed people in this evil corrupt system who has committed the worst injustice. We are twins to Diallo—only they are trying to kill my son [by] premeditated frame! I am with you. We are on the road to victory! *[Four NYPD police officers were cleared of all charges in February 2000 stemming from the shooting death of Amadou Diallo, an unarmed man who was hit by 19 of 41 bullets fired at him on Feb. 4, 1999 in the vestibule of his Bronx apartment by the officers. The incident prompted widespread protests of what many said was heavy-handed police tactics.]*

JANUARY 30, 2000—SANTE TO KENNY:

We need to get [N.Y.] Times updated on our frame. Say how would they like to be accused of murder & have the Mayor of New York come out hours after disappearance & say Kimes guilty! It's time we give interviews or talk to press solely on frame. Get cameras. All we want is truth & to stop cover up & secrecy . . . so media & public can see truth. We need to speak up! And the attys need to scream to Jdg [Judge]—how can we defend with all this sealed documents!!! We aren't grifters. I have no violence record, you have no record. There is no crime. Vasquez stripped all within hours of disappearance to cover up any link with elected official. American public needs to know! *[Irene Silverman disappeared July 5, 1998. It was not until July 7th that detectives at the 19th precinct and the Silver Task Force learned of the Kimes. Detective Vasquez was never at the Silverman home until later that week.]*

Tell me if you OK my presence today. It's great luck our case is running parallel to Diallo. I finished Children of Dune—WOW! It's great reading—deep—deep—lots of truth in *thinking,* the voice, total mind control over others—It's all about the awesome control of the mind—the power of the brain—can do anything—right?

May 2000—Kenny to Kent:

I do appreciate your loyalty, but you did say some unfamily like things about me and mom. All you are doing now is upsetting us, and especially your fragile mother who is trying hard to stay strong and fight her case. You mentioned that you really want to help. You could send the $5000 you spent of your mother's SS money. Cut a check to Matthew. $5000 or was it more? That would be a good indicator of how true your intentions are. This would be a good beginning and is much needed. Our best wishes to Lynn and the children.

"BIBLE" DATED SUNDAY, AUGUST 28, 1999—SANTE TO KENNY:

My dearest Beloved Son! BIBLE!
Here's our Bible!
Keep this list! Its our Bible! *Please* Memorize on your heart & *Brain*, honey!

1. No matter what. Protect you! Seize any opportunity! This country is evil—
Fly anyway you can—Don't worry about me—The greatest win is *you* out—
Be strong! Carry on! Become a Fidel Castro! Fight—*You* are young—Keep
strong! Get stronger!
2. We MUST get transferred!—Problem—There is no federal housing for women
in New York—only for men—Both of us—a fair judge has to put us where we
are safe! The DA has infiltrated Rikers, and has control—you must get out of
Rikers. The attorneys can take a sealed order to fair judge—a tidal wave of
inmates out to destroy & bill us! I have written the order up for Eric—using
Media leaks of government cooperation & more—Any place but *Rikers!*
3. If they put me in Bing—*scream*—Get me out to Eric—Eric's home # is
431- – – – –. (Don't overuse!) –In Bing I only come out 1 hr. a day & can only
call at that time—*Our Mon Wed Friday meetings* will save us! We must be
able to communicate—Eric can get me out in court—The infraction is illegal—But it will be Eric who will go to court & get me out—Matthew is a
joke! Yet we need him if only he is a body— at our meetings so we can see
each other! This is all the DA trying to silence—Scream to Eric—They are
trying to silence us—They know we are going to win with you & Michael—

The evil system wants us silenced because they are *involved* !!! Eric can get infraction off in Court. Tell him hurry! Mysterious death in Bing—There is an investigation— THE SCERET

4. Michael & Eric are undisputed LEAD—They are our SAVIORS They hate the system—BACK them! It's WHY they took the case! They have the story of lies! And we have ours! They have nada, only lies—our story has to be better! More & it is believable! Does not have to be ironclad—Just suggestion

Keep & study.
Kenny you can go to Federal housing at Brooklyn
RID court
Read this Memorize—It's why we have Mike! A win! Mike's secret The Win! The Secret Defense!
Our win! Mike's win! Our story true US Their frame & Lies!
All this adds up for Michael! Defense—His eyes shine!
—IS told me she could bury [many elected officials] with what she knows! She said all men are Feds! Think with their dicks—
—The day we were arrested = the day J Feig made our missing person report— police stripped apt to get rid of any link to [elected officials] & VIP johns even took computer roller!
—Rudy comes out on TV—1 day later & says we are guilty!
—Posters put up say we are guilty
—We (I) hear Hackett in hall when beating me—he says, "Jesus, that's [name deleted] friend that old Madam!"
—I remember SP saying IS told him she was friends of Bigwheels—boasting about her power!
—I remember dining & waiting for IS & a friend at a Paradise Club—they were looking for "girls"—whores to help—I waited in car. They may remember— the hos—whores in there—
—City records & taxes will prove IS illegal & did not pay taxes—or payroll! She old madam—drunk has been—threatening to a lot of important people—

And more & more—
So Mike has his secret defense—Never change it—it's the win & why Mike took the case! Its very possible! Much more so than their lying story! And it's emotional—the jury has to have a reasonable answer to the system frame! And this is it! Mike believes in us—
Back this with all your heart & soul! Its our true story—even without Debby—it will fly! Its better than theirs! It explains the frame, the cover up— Its our win Add to it if you can!
Michael are *estatic* [sic]—Mike will hit every paper in the world –Mom & son innocent—

Honey—

—You must distance *you*! Just a college kid—Errand boy—

—The worst is your ID with M Guero name—Every answer you could not use Kimes. [Name deleted] always used friends ID's—MG existed! Sent to Nassau to protect & house maintainance—sometimes he took off—But [name deleted] always used his or other buddies names.

—We went to Chase for MG not as—they could not find MG Just did what told.

—Don't forget hustlers! You saw them a little—Joey the Limp *more*—We did not rent—also that Jap notary—He has been at apt. week earlier—new job, IS—Joey—You saw him week earlier—

—You never saw *Noel* at Palace—mistaken—you in Wellington

—We have our NY alibi—Tie down with Michael's inves,

—We must get to L Vegas & get LA alibis & help LA Mike handles!

—We need to scream Innocent More to Mike—Scream [name deleted] is behind this! But only to Mike & Eric—not to other do nothings—Make Mike believe in us Light his fire! He's the win!

Innocent Mom & son vs. evil system and old madam & brothel!

Then honey we must Praise and Back Michael and Action Network all the Way—*He is Lead* He will fill the courtroom with Backer—people for justice—We have been beaten, stripped of every civil & constitutional right, framed, entrapped

The bastards have seized a mountain of papers as records illegally gotten to the biased judge! We *must*—I repeat must—*fight* with Mike's Secret Defense—it is reasonable—it explains it all—the evil frames & why to a jury—& that Jury will love it! Mike must use his secret defense! It's our win!

Everytime you see Mike scream framed by evil system—Believe me—they know it's the win! *Never* change it! Or we would lose Michael—He loves this—they are champions against the evil system—It explains *all* to a jury—We have to have a defense! Its perfect, *there* & very logical—even if a juror *wonders* about it—we win!

All the "staff" can be proven *liars on stand*—are lying for police! Never forget they are confusing you with *Joey the Limp* (who IS hates & refers to on tapes) IS knew & liked you—

Always BACK Mike—He rarely takes cases—they have to be dynamite wins! It took 8 months to get him! The Secret defense is the case of the Century!

I have to also keep offering the land, the gift—anything—He believes in us—they fight! They are our lives!

(All suggestions, investigative leads, innuendo, gossip, and salacious details were thoroughly investigated by the defense, Hardy says. There was no secret defense as Sante claims. "The defense of the Kimeses was the defense presented at trial by the Kimes' lawyers, and while questions were asked of witnesses to establish that the mansion may have been used for illicit purposes, the jury rejected that theory.

"Obviously, if there was a connection between Mayor Giuliani and Irene Silverman, that would have been sensational and clearly something we would have wholeheartedly pursued," Hardy said. *"The defense never sought to call or subpoena the mayor, because to do so would have been irresponsible in light of the evidence that the defense had in its possession.")*

ALIBI FOR DAVID KAZDIN DEFENSE

Sante to Kenny —
   I ♥ U more than life more than there is or stars!

March 12, Thursday
1. *Nan—lunch McGoos*—11ish AM at McGoos
2. *Dave Munoz*— at his house in motor home had Lincoln & motor home—left motor home there 2 or 3 times—stayed on it at his house more than once in front! Also saw his mom & daughter
3. *Pony Ex*—Stan & Steve—got mail *in afternoon*—always we picked up mail—always Hopefully Stan & Steve both will verify—
4. *Tony & Lenny*—Thursday about 6pm stopped by had drinks socialized there about hour
5. Chevrys Restaurant—(the Manager) in *the afternoon*—let us use the phones & sent faxes for us—We sat in back by pay phones—Invited him to Caribbean—Kind of used area like a little office We very friendly invited him to Caribbean! He knew it was important for we were sending—helped us
6. Christy at McGoo's—*11ish* at *restaurant*

March 13 Friday
1. *Nan*—11:30ish late brunch at McGoo's
2. *Dave Munoz* at his house staying on motor home—
3. *Pony Express*—Stan & Steve picked up mail as always—routine
4. *Christie* at McGoo's—11ish
5. *7-11* lady afternoon—

Saturday March 14—
1. Caroline?
2. Dave Munoz stopped at his house on motor home
3. Pony—picked up mail as usual before 2 pm.

Have the witnesses, read our letters to them—assure them won't be bothered—advise keep silent—our innocent lives depend on—charm & assure them assure our witnesses we have back up witnesses—*TLC*

APPENDIX C

The Investigators

The arrest and conviction of Sante and Kenny Kimes was due to the highly skilled investigative work of many law enforcement agencies. Among them were the Silver Task Force of the New York Police Department and the prosecution team at the Manhattan District Attorney's office of Robert Morgenthau.

NEW YORK POLICE DEPARTMENT

Deputy Inspector Joseph Reznick (Now Chief of Detectives, Bronx County)

Capt. Warren Curry
Sgt. Andy Dietz
Sgt. Gene Wasielewski
Det. Tom Bidell
Det. John Flynn
Det. Tom Hartnett
Det. John Olshaw
Det. Randy Rocca
Det. José Rosario
Det. John Schlagler
Det. Jimmy Turnbull
Det. Gregory Yovane

Sgt. Jerry Beyrodt
Sgt. Bobby Maas
Det. Joe Arigoni
Det. Reggie Britt
Det. Tom Hackett
Det. Tom Hovagim
Det. Joel Potter
Det. Danny Rodriguez
Det. Tom Ryan
Det. Jimmy Torrellas
Det. Tony Vazquez

The Investigators

THE MANHATTAN DISTRICT ATTORNEY'S OFFICE

DEPUTY BUREAU CHIEF & SENIOR TRIAL COUNSEL
Assistant District Attorney (ADA) Connie Fernandez, Lead Kimes Prosecutor
Senior Trial Attorney, ADA John Carter
Senior Trial Attorney, ADA Ann Donnelly
Chief of Fraud Bureau, ADA Owen Heimer

NEW YORK CITY DISTRICT ATTORNEY'S DETECTIVE SQUAD
Joseph Roman

TRIAL ASSISTANTS
Mary Kanigher	Stella Eng
Amy Hsu	Margaret Morales

PHOTOGRAPHER
Laura Badger

VIDEO UNIT
Mike Mannion	Eddie Marcano
Minerva Tineo	Vito Ciarmella

DESIGN ENGINEER
Marie Ventianque

The following United States government and law enforcement agencies also contributed their talents to the Kimes investigation:

FINGERPRINT, BALLISTICS, CHEMIST DIVISION
Det. Charles Koch	Det. Sean Walsh
David Fleischer	Nanishi Agarwal
Nagy Bekhit	Det. Daniel Perruza

CRIME SCENE UNIT
Det. Thomas Deutsch	Det. Karen Engdahl

JOINT FBI/NYPD TASK FORCE
Det. Edward Murray	Det. Michael Ryan
Edward Wallace	

CHIEF MEDICAL EXAMINER'S OFFICE
Dr. Marina Stajic

AGENTS OF THE FEDERAL BUREAU OF INVESTIGATION

David Stone   Emillio Blasse
Wilfred Baptiste   Christopher Aquilino
Kevin Irwin   Thomas Moore
Philip Swabsin

LOS ANGELES POLICE DEPARTMENT

Det. Dennis English   Det. Bill Cox
Det. Ted Ball (Ret.)   Det. Brian Carr

LAS VEGAS METROPOLITAN POLICE DEPARTMENT

Det. Jimmy Vaccaro

OTHER AGENCIES

Manhattan South Homicide Unit
NYPD Aviation Unit
NYPD Canine Unit
Emergency Medical Service
New York State Canine Unit
Port Authority of New York & New Jersey
NYPD Warrant Squad
Secret Service
Bureau of Alcohol, Tobacco, and Firearms
Social Security Administration
Immigration and Naturalization Service
Department of State
Baton Rouge, Louisiana, Police Department
New Orleans, Louisiana, Parish Sheriffs Department
Palm Beach, Florida, Police Department
Miami, Florida, Police Department
Belle Glade, Florida, Police Department
Manalapan, Florida, Police Department
Ramapo, New Jersey, Rescue Association
Royal Bahamian Police Department

APPENDIX D

The Kimes Trial

February 22
    4. James Blackner—Utah Lincoln car dealer
    5. Jean Paoa—Wells Fargo Bank
    6. Dennis Garrett—Utah driver who drove Green Lincoln to LA to Kimes
    7. Ramon Casales—Superintendent of Silverman mansion

February 24
    Ramon Casales

February 25
    Ramon Casales
    8. Elizabeth Howlett—Palm Beach condo
    9. Carina Qureshi—Palm Beach condo where wallet ID stolen
    10. Eileen Elms—title searches, Florida, tape conversation
    11. Dr. Athanassios Tsoukas—(video testimony) his missing ID from wallet

February 28
    Dr. Tsoukas (video testimony)
    12. Jean Gerber—Salvation Army from Florida, telephone records, Sante
    asks her to get medication in Bahamas for 82-year-old woman
    13. José Alvarez—Hired by Sante in Florida to drive car to NY & do errands

February 29
    José Alvarez
    14. Detective Robert Lerner—made copies of tapes

March 2
    15. Lisa Sagolia—dancer, Silverman friend, eavesdropping tape
    16. Collette Villemin—Silverman friend, French, eavesdropping tape
    17. Beverly Feingold—real estate
    18. George Dessaro—bar, Schorr credit card
    19. Ralph Pellechia—New Jersey financial advisor, met Sante in Nevada,
    1994
    20. Janet Sangekar—former secretary to Ralph Pellechia
    21. Rudy Vaccari—butcher, Silverman friend
    22. Fred Stafford—Manhattan D.A., tapes

March 3
    23. Don Aoki—notary, refused to notarize, no ID
    24. Kirk Lynch—parking garage manager (East Side)
    25. Christopher Acuna—parking attendant
    26. Jane Duval—Use of Schorr credit card by SK
    27. Juan Frias—eavesdropping drop

March 6
28. Greg Lenert—eavesdropping tape, producer, writer
29. Chandler Evans—eavesdropping tape
30. Valerie McLeod—I. S. staff

March 7
Valerie McLeod
31. Neil Kleinhandler—lawyer (SK used name Judy Hylan)
32. May Lazaro—Postal Express on Third Ave., Kenny used ID of Dr. Tony Tsoukas to open account
33. Norman Massre—computer store salesman, sold cell phone to Kimes
34. Howard Pitter—real-estate agent tape

March 9
35. Noelle Sweeney—notarized a deed
36. Janine Vendetto—Salvation Army Supervisor, Long Island City; Sante asked for worker
37. Glenn Hutchinson—Homeless man from Salvation Army, called Sante about job

March 10
38. Nydia Morales—eavesdropping tape, friend of Noel Rodriguez
39. Mary Urrico—new insurance requested by Silverman for mansion
40. Noel Rodriguez—Silverman staff, maintenance
41. Salmon Salha—Park Lane hotel waiter, Schorr credit card
42. Lesbia Mendez—eavesdropping tape
43. Bob McVeety—fraud investigator, Schorr credit card

March 13
44. Deborah Montagner—Kenny's girlfriend
45. Peter Jacobson—TV producer, writer, resident at mansion
46. Richard Stadler—Silverman friend, telephone repair
47. Anthony Murphy—social security agent, Silverman social security forgery

March 14
Anthony Murphy
48. Melba Rodriguez—Silverman staffer at mansion
49. Roseann Lombardo—Chase Manhattan Bank, Dept. of Finance
50. Detective Charles Koch—ballistics
51. Detective Sean Walsh—ballistics

March 16

52. Gerard Connell—Bell Atlantic (now Verizon), telephone calls, Silverman mansion & Hilton Hotel
53. Marta Aracellis Rivera—Silverman's weekend companion

March 17

Marta Aracellis Rivera

March 20

54. Elleni Mulu—Mengi friend in Virginia
55. Manuel (Manny) Guerrero—homeless man found by Sante in shelter
56. Robert McCaffen—homeless man hired by Sante
57. Nanette Wetkowski—Sante's friend and personal notary

March 21

Nanette Wetkowski (cross examination)
58. Ronald Butler—Sam Silverman son
59. Gary Sutcliffe—AT&T Wireless, cell sites and where Sante made calls
60. Gabriela Casales—eavesdropping tape, wife of Ramon

March 23

Gary Sutcliffe (cross-examination)
61. Lucy Wilson—Silverman friend from Texas
62. John Kirtley—resident at Silverman mansion
63. Judy Hyman—Sante hired her from homeless shelter in Nevada.
64. Detective Edward Murray—arrested Kimes 7/5/98

March 27

Detective Murray
65. Patrick Leempoel—eavesdropping tape, Silverman resident
66. Detective Michael Ryan—arrested Kimes 7/5/98

March 28

Detective Ryan
67. Stan Patterson—handyman/driver/ID'd Kimes 7/5/98

March 30

68. Elizabeth Huntington—Valerie McLeod friend
69. Sonja Baptiste—Line Overseas Management (LOM), Bermuda off-shore account set up by the Kimeses
70. Detective Edward Wallace—crime scene, Lincoln Town Car

March 31
> Detective Edward Wallace
71. David Stone—FBI Supervisor, Joint Task Force, 7/5/98
72. Wilfred Batiste—FBI/NYPD Task Force case agent

April 3
73. Helen Pandelakis—Greek friend, last to speak to Silverman, 11:45 A.M., 7/5/98
74. Despy Mallas—Silverman cousin from Los Angeles
75. Elva Shkreli—fashion designer, spoke with Silverman 7/5; also at 7/4 party
76. Susana Bono—real estate agent, at house 6/19 with Jordanian royalty
77. Alex Genova—met Kimeses on 6/14/98, Puerto Rican parade
78. Emillio Blasse—FBI, Joint Task Force, arrested Kimeses 7/5/98
79. Phillip John—W. 44th St. garage where Kenny parked car 6:40 P.M., 7/5
80. David Fleischer—NYPD chemist

April 4
81. Ramon Casales, Jr.—son of Ramon Casales, eavesdropping tape
82. Jeff Feig—Irene Silverman assistant

April 6
> Jeff Feig
83. Max Schorr—forged credit card used by Kimes
84. Dereje Hailegorghis—Mengi friend, phone calls, Georgia 7/3 & 7/6
> Alex Genova—recalled as witness
85. Nicola Ramsey—AirTrans Airways, Mengi ticket
86. Eva Papakostopoulos—maid, staff at Silverman mansion

April 7
> Eva Papakostopoulos
87. Marjorie Opio—sales clerk, Gracious Home department store
88. Kirn McLeod—Valerie's daughter, spoke with Kenny on phone
89. Gus Mavroudis—Silverman accountant
90. Lettie Eason—Lawyer Title Co., NYC, ID, Kenny
91. Dr. Marina Stajic—medical examiner's office, toxicologist
92. Eddy Hiraldo—eavesdropping tape, friend of Aracellis
93. Nancy Haddock—Bank of New York, Silverman investments

April 10
> Nancy Haddock
94. Larry Frost—defense investigator, black bag

95. Detective Thomas Deutsch—Crime Scene Unit
96. Detective Karen Engdahl—Crime Scene Unit
97. Christopher Bruno—attorney, Lawyers Title Co.

April 11
98. Zang Toi—fashion designer, close friend of Silverman
99. Jesus Delgado—waiter
100. Vernon Vergara—travel agent, Sante bought NYC ticket for SP
101. Detective Mark Rawdon—evidence collection/apt. 1B
102. Martina Martinez—eavesdropping tape, Aracellis sister
103. Waheed Gill—Plaza Hotel bellman, black bag
104. José Lopez—Plaza Hotel captain, black bag
105. Robert Pantekas—Plaza Hotel bellman, gave black bag to Frost

April 13
106. Renee Andrews—inmate, Central Booking, encounter with Sante
107. Police Officer John Cafarella—effects on body, stun gun
108. Sgt. Robert Maas—NYPD lineup of the Kimeses
109. Dr. John Merriam—Silverman eye doctor
110. Robert Hammer—real-estate agent, 3 E. 65th St.

April 14
111. Barbara Cohen—Chase Manhattan Bank, Kimeses finance check
112. Dr. Sanford Friedman—Silverman internist
113. Maritza Casales—eavesdropping tape
114. Detective Thomas Hackett—Silver Task Force detective, only detective to interview Sante

April 17
Detective Hackett
115. Manishi Agarwal—NYPD fingerprint expert
116. Nagy Bekhit—NYPD criminologist, fingerprint
117. Luigi Palazzo—owner of café next door to Silverman mansion
118. Detective Daniel Perruzza—latent print examiner

April 24
Detective Perruzza
119. Carolyn Clark—Milbank Tweed law firm, Silverman will

April 25
Carolyn Clark
120. Paula DelNunzio—real-estate townhouse specialist
121. Dr. Ronald Castellini—Silverman resident, not at mansion 7/5/98

122. Elizabeth Camp—Bank of New York, trust officer
123. Detective John Flynn—shower curtain
124. Detective Vito Ciaramella—District Attorney squad, tape

April 27
125. Detective Anthony Vazquez—Silver Task Force, Manhattan North Homicide
126. Detective Daniel Rodriguez—Silver Task Force, Manhattan North Homicide

April 28
    Detective Rodriguez
127. John Osborne—handwriting expert
Sandoval hearing, preliminary jury charge, stipulations (no jury)

May 2
    John Osborne
128. Sgt. Eugene Wasielewski—Silver Task Force, Manhattan North Homicide
129. Carol Hansen—attended party at Silverman mansion, 7/4/98, calls to Silverman & Aracellis 7/5, eavesdropping tape

May 3
Court hearing (jury not present) to bar press at Sandoval hearing

May 4
    Carol Hansen—Silverman friend recalled
Prosecution rests

DEFENSE WITNESSES

May 4
    1. Mark Denbeaux—handwriting expert

May 5
Stipulations, motion to dismiss, Sante outburst
Defense rests

CLOSING ARGUMNENTS

May 8
Michael Hardy, defense (Sante)

May 9
Michael Hardy, defense (Sante)
Mel Sachs, defense (Kenny)

May 10
Mel Sachs, defense (Kenny)
Connie Fernandez, prosecution

May 11
Connie Fernandez, prosecution
Ann Donnelly, prosecution

May 12
Ann Donnelly, prosecution
Connie Fernandez, prosecution

CHARGE TO JURY

May 15
Judge Uviller

JURY DELIBERATIONS

May 15–18

VERDICT

May 18

SANTE AND KENNY KIMES SENTENCING

June 27

APPENDIX E

The Kimes Chronology

July 24, 1934—Sante Singhrs born. (Also claimed on other documents that she was born in 1937, 1939, and 1944.)

1935—Sante; her parents, Mary Van Horn Singhrs and Prame Singhrs; her older sister, Prema; and her brother, Karam, move to California.

1937—The Singhrs family returns to Oklahoma City and remains in Oklahoma until 1940.

1939—Younger sister of Sante, named Retha, born.

1940—Father, Prame, dies and family returns to Los Angeles.

1944—Sante accused of stealing cheese.

1945—Adopted by Mary and Edwin Chambers, Carson City, Nevada. Sante claims Edwin raped her from age 11 until she was about 16.

1946—Meets Ed Walker.

1948—Enters Carson City High School, graduates June 6, 1952.

1950—At age 16 Sante is arrested for shoplifting in Carson City, Nevada.

1953-54—In Reno, Nevada, then Sacramento, California, takes typing, writing classes.

May 9, 1956—Marries Lee Powers in Carson City.

1957—Divorces Powers.

November 9,1957—Marries Ed Walker.

Feb. 12, 1961—Arrested for petty larceny, age 26. Pleads guilty, fined $131.25 or 12½ days jail; pays fine.

Sept. 26, 1963—Kent Walker born. (She also claims Kent born in 1962.)

Dec. 29, 1965—Arrested, grand theft, property, at age 31 in Los Angeles.

Dec. 30, 1965—Arrested, grand theft, auto, Los Angeles.

Jan. 3, 1966—Arrested, grand theft, property, Beverly Hills. Pleads guilty on 5/2/66. Placed on three years probation, $200.00 fine, $20 penalty assessment.

May 1, 1967—Separates from Ed Walker.

Nov. 27, 1967—Files for divorce.

Nov. 11, 1968—Arrested, non-sufficient funds, checks, Glendale, California. Case dismissed on 3/3/69 for lack of prosecution.

Nov. 25, 1968—Arrested, grand theft, property, Riverside, California.

Jan. 9, 1968—Divorces Walker; final degree awarded Dec. 8,1969.

1969—Mary Chambers dies of cancer at age 69.

1970—Meets Kenneth Kimes, Sr.

1971—Claims she married Kimes, Sr., in (a) Tijuana and (b) Mexico City (no official record of marriage or license).

April 26, 1972—Arrested on six counts of credit card forgery; grand theft, auto; minor traffic offenses at age 37 in Santa Ana, California. Forgeries case dismissed April 4, 1973. Grand theft, auto, dismissed May 22, 1973.

Aug. 10, 1972—Arrested theft, grand theft, in Palm Springs at age 38.

Feb. 26, 1974—Sante and Kimes, Sr., crash Blair House formal party hosted by Vice President Gerald Ford and wife, Betty. They go on to crash several other Washington, D.C., functions that night.

Sept. 27, 1974—Arrested, grand theft, Newport Beach, California, of an art object, at age 40. The victim of the crime identified Sante. In Sante's car was a jacket identified by victim as stolen property. Convicted June 26, 1975. Sante pled guilty to receiving stolen property, 24 months probation, $250.00 fine; charges of grand theft and burglary dismissed.

1974—Seeks abortion.

March 24, 1975—Kenneth Karam "Kenny" Kimes born.

1976—Sante's mother dies

April 18, 1978—Fire at Sante and Kimes, Sr., 271A Portlock Road home overlooking Diamond Head in Hawaii. Causes about $18,000 damage. No one charged with arson.

Feb. 5, 1980—Arrested and charged with stealing a mink coat at the Mayflower Hotel, Washington, D.C., at age 45. Also arrested and charged with grand and petty larceny was Kimes, Sr. On March 12, both are named in a two-count indictment.

July 11, 1980—Mink trial begins.

Sept. 15, 1980—Kenneth Kimes, Sr., buys five-bedroom, four-bathroom home at 2121 Geronimo Way in Las Vegas.

1980—Edward Chambers dies of a stroke, age 81.

April 5, 1981—Sante claims she renewed vows with Kimes, Sr., in Las Vegas at the World Famous Chapel of the Bells, reporting at the time to federal officers that two children were born from this relationship. Kenny, then age 10, and Kenian, then age 4. Marriage certificate deemed a forgery in 2000.

Nov. 20, 1981—Arrested, grand larceny, at age 47 in Las Vegas. Sante identified as suspect in theft of grand piano. On Oct. 26, 1981, piano recovered after it was noticed being offered for sale in a newspaper ad. Case was dismissed on June 1, 1983.

March 13, 1982—Claims to have given birth to son Kenian, whom she says was given up for adoption, alternately either in Mexico or Texas.

March 20, 1982—Received a citation for petty larceny in Las Vegas after being observed in a local department store placing several items of merchandise in her purse and exiting the store without paying for the merchandise. Case dismissed February 18, 1983.

Dec. 27, 1982—Arrested under bench warrant and charged with kidnapping, robbery, false imprisonment, and grand larceny in Las Vegas at age 48. On Dec. 22, 1981, Anaheim Police were sent to Mecca Hotel (owned by Kimes, Sr.). The victim, a maid, said she was propositioned by one of three suspects at Mecca Hotel to perform work for her. Victim allegedly was held in room of suspects, her purse containing $2,000 taken and not returned. Victim was made to clean up the room and iron clothes, and was not allowed to make phone calls or inform her husband of her whereabouts.

July 18, 1985—Found guilty of grand larceny, stealing mink.

Aug. 3, 1985—Sante arrested on slavery charges in San Diego, California, at age 51. Charged with conspiracy, involuntary servitude, transportation of illegal aliens, and aiding and abetting.

Aug. 8, 1985—Sante and Kenneth Kimes named in a 17-count indictment on slavery charges; Sante remanded, no bail.

Dec. 26, 1985—Sante removed from federal facility to a jail ward for medical evaluation.

Dec. 30, 1985—Escapes from prison hospital in Nevada.

Jan. 3, 1986—Apprehended.

Feb. 28, 1986—Found guilty of slavery charges.

May 15, 1986—Sentenced, three years federal prison.

Dec. 11, 1989—Released from federal prison.

July 1990—Elmer Ambrose Holmgren, a lawyer who had fallen on hard times, answers want ad placed by Sante and Kimes, Sr. They put him on retainer as house counsel.

August 1990—Sante asks Holmgren to torch Hawaii home for $3,000.

Sept. 16, 1990—Portlock Road home goes up in flames—arson. Holmgren goes to Las Vegas, calls Sante, who instructs him he will find money under front seat of parked car.

January 1991—Holmgren, still in Las Vegas, secretly records confession to Alcohol, Tobacco, and Firearms agents about arson and agrees to wear a wire and gather taped evidence against Sante.

February 1991—Holmgren advises ATF agents in a telephone call to them in Hawaii from Santa Barbara, California, that the sting would be delayed. Holmgren's family, friends, and ATF never hear from him again. ATF agents believe Sante found the number that Holmgren telephoned, because agents recall receiving a phone call at their Honolulu office from an unidentified woman who only asked for the name of the office she was speaking with. Sante has not been charged with arson or Holmgren's disappearance.

March 28, 1994—Kenneth Kimes, Sr., dies; Kent Walker supplies phony information to the coroner, thus allowing Sante to hide Kimes's death.

September 1995—Kenny enrolls at University of California, Santa Barbara.

Late 1996—Linda and Andrew Kimes learn that their father died two years earlier.

September 4, 1996—Syed Bilal Ahmed, a banker, disappears after dining with Sante and Kenny at the Androsia Restaurant in Nassau, the Bahamas.

January 23, 1998—Documents arrive at David Kazdin's Granada Hills, California, home from mortgage lender Ocwen Federal Bank in West Palm Beach, Florida, that he owes $280,000 on a 30-year mortgage on Kimes's Geronimo Way home. Kazdin makes inquiries, and Sante's name pops up from the lender, advising him that the check had already been mailed to Wetkowski's Wells Fargo account.

January 31, 1998—A suspicious blaze, deemed arson, destroys the Kimes home at 2121 Geronimo Way.

February 1998—Sante and Kenny, using the names Sandy and Manny Guerrin, rent a home at 3221 Elvido Drive in Bel Air Estate, California. A homeless man, Robert McCarren, whom they call Robert Carro, moves in.

Mid-February 1998—Sante orders a 1997 Lincoln Town Car from Parkway Motors in Cedar City, Utah, and has it delivered to them at the Beverly Wilshire Hotel on February 27 by driver Dennis Garrett. Sante trades in a 1993 silver Lincoln and gives Garrett a Wells Fargo check for $14,973.50. Check later bounces.

March 13, 1998—David Kazdin murdered. His body is found in a Dumpster the next day near Los Angeles International Airport. Family and friends of Kazdin suspect the Kimeses and advise Los Angeles detectives to question Sante and Kenny. The Kimeses are already en route to Palm

Beach, Florida, stopping briefly in Las Vegas to pick up another homeless person from a shelter before going on to Baton Rouge, Louisiana, where they order another Motor Home that is to be delivered to them in Florida.

April–June 1998—Kimeses stay at Polo Club, Wellington, near Palm Beach, Florida.

Early June 1998—The Kimeses purchase a stun gun and eventually leave for New York City with another down-and-outer, José Alvarez, whom they hire to clean and drive the car.

June 14, 1998—Sante and Kenny arrive in New York City. Kenny checks into 20 East 65th Street, the home of Irene Silverman, and moves into apartment 1B, which he has rented under the name Manny Guerin for $6,000 for one month. They soon begin to eavesdrop on Silverman and her staff.

July 5, 1998—Irene Silverman disappears. She is reported missing around 6:00 P.M. At 7:00 P.M., Sante and Kenny are arrested by the NYPD/FBI Joint Fugitive Task Force near the Hilton Hotel on a warrant from Utah. Irene Silverman's personal property found on the Kimeses, but it is not until July 7 that a connection between the Kimeses and Silverman is made by a task force detective.

July 6, 1998—Kenny Kimes is arraigned, bail denied.

July 7, 1998—Sante Kimes is arraigned, bail denied. Defense lawyers José Muniz and Matthew Weissman appear for both defendants.

July 14, 1998—Defense lawyer Mel Sachs enters the case.

July 24, 1998—Lineup of Sante and Kenny at district attorney's office. The black bag that Sante checked at the Plaza Hotel is turned over to prosecutors. The forged deed to the Silverman mansion and a .22-caliber handgun are among the items found in the bag.

July 31, 1998—Sante and Kenny are indicted for using a forged credit card in the name of Max Schoor, fraudulently charging nearly $700 on the card.

July–November 1998—Sante and Kenny are denied bail 13 times by nine judges.

Dec. 16, 1998—Sante and Kenny are indicted on 84 counts, including second degree murder, burglary, robbery, fraud, weapons possession, and eavesdropping.

January 4, 1999—Sante and Kenny are arraigned. Both plead not guilty.

July 22, 1999—Defense lawyers Michael Hardy and Eric Seifert enter the case.

Dec. 8–Dec. 20, 1999—Pretrial hearings take place.

January 27, 2000—Jury selection begins.

February 14–15, 2000—Opening statements and witness testimony begins.

May 18, 2000—Sante and Kenny are found guilty of all charges.

June 27, 2000—Sante and Kenny are sentenced to a combined 257⅔ years in prison.

March 2001—Kenny is extradited to Los Angeles to face charges stemming from the murder of David Kazdin. He could face the death penalty.

June 2001—Sante is extradited to Los Angeles to face charges stemming from the murder of David Kazdin. She could face the death penalty.

Dec. 7, 2001—Judge sets a date for the preliminary hearing. The trial begins in 2002.

Acknowledgments and Sources

This book is a comprehensive, in-depth account of the criminal career of Sante Kimes, a cold-blooded, calculating killer who lived according to her own mad rules. The book reveals how she masterminded a cross-country trail of fraud, high-tech thievery and murder, and trained her young son, Kenny, as her personal assassin.

The book is based on extensive interviews conducted with more than 200 people and on my observations of the Kimeses since first meeting them in July 1998, when I began covering the mother-and-son con artist team after their arrest in New York City.

Statements by police officers; FBI and Alcohol, Tobacco, and Firearms agents; as well as statements by Nanette Wetkowski, Robert McCarren, Stan Patterson, Edward Walker and his son, Kent Walker; among others mentioned in the book, come from grand jury testimony, the preliminary hearing, trial transcripts, and official police reports of the investigation, or from numerous personal interviews with officials.

During the course of my research, I obtained previously undisclosed material that shed light on the Kimes family. Among the documents I utilized was Sante's federal pre-sentence report from April 1986, prepared by the United States Probation Office before she was sentenced on her slavery and escape convictions, which described in detail her prior arrests, her personal and family history including her education, and physical, mental and emotional reactions. In writing the book, I also relied on a 31-page Alternative Sentencing Resources report prepared by a San Diego consulting firm hired by Sante, in which 18 people, from personal friends to her ex-husband, Edward Walker, son Kent, a Las Vegas psychologist, and even Sante herself were interviewed.

The quotations of Sante and Kenny come from trial transcripts or private conversations the pair had with other people who came in contact with them and heard the remarks. In writing the book, I had full access to the official record, including memoranda of both the prosecution and defense and written statements by witnesses.

The investigation into the murder of millionaire widow Irene Silverman was one of the most intensive and exhaustive probes by New York City police in recent history. It was conducted by the most experienced, diligent, and dedicated detectives assigned to Manhattan. Together with the four prosecutors from the New York County District Attorney's office, they all gave up their vacations and weekends during the summers of 1998 and 1999 to investigate Silverman's disappearance and bring to justice the pair that murdered her.

I am deeply grateful to former Police Commissioner Howard Safir and Deputy Police Commissioner for Public Information Marilyn Mode, who provided invaluable assistance in helping me to have unfettered access to the Silver Task Force and other departmental agencies investigating the case. I want to especially thank "my heroes," who generously gave me hundreds of hours of their time, providing insight into how they solved the case: Deputy Chief Joseph Reznick, Joel Potter, Danny Rodriguez, John Schlagler, Tony Vazquez, and Eugene (Gene) Wasielewski of Manhattan North Homicide Squad, and the three detectives from the 19th Precinct, Tommy Hackett, Tom Ryan and Tom Hovagim. Special thanks also to former Police Commissioner Bernard Kerik, who was the Correction Commissioner while the Kimeses were held in New York City and who, when asked about Sante's stay as his "guest" at Rikers Island, said, "She was a pain in the ass."

While the detectives investigated the tell-tale clues left behind by the Kimeses, it was the "fearless fantastic" four prosecutors—Connie Fernandez, Ann Donnelly, John Carter and Owen Heimer—who did a brilliant job of leaving nothing to chance and putting together a dynamite case that led to the conviction of Sante and Kenny Kimes. Stella Eng, Amy Hsu, Margaret Morales, and Mary Kanigher are also owed a special thank you for their help in bringing about the conviction.

It is a tribute to Robert Morgenthau, the nation's dean of prosecutors, that in his 27 years in office, he has developed a staff that has the expertise to vigorously and effectively oversee a complex and daring prosecution of this kind. Few other prosecutors would have had the confidence or skill to pursue a case that had no body, no blood, and no DNA or physical forensics. Despite his heavy workload as both a prosecutor and civic leader, he found the time to give me legal information about a case that had become a national and international drama. A special thanks also to Morgenthau's top deputies, James Kindler, Daniel Castleman, and Nancy Ryan, his secretary Ida Van Lindt, and his press staff, headed by the able Barbara Thompson, and her staff, Wayne Brison, Gloria Montealegre, Sherry Hunter, Eileen Romaniello and Julie Nunez-Reyes, who were gracious with their time and extremely supportive in digging up documents.

Thank you's also go to members of the NYPD/FBI Joint Warrant Task Force, notably detectives Edward Murray and Michael Ryan, and FBI agents David Stone, Emillio Blasse, and Wilfred Baptiste.

I am also indebted to Deputy Correction Commissioner for Public Information Sandy Smith and her predecessor, Tom Antenen; John Mohan; Tom McCarthy, the Warden at the Rikers Island Rose M. Singer Center facility; Jacqueline Thomas-Andrews; and Correction Officer Wyellene Woodruff, among others, for their insight and thoughts about the Kimeses, and in arranging extensive jailhouse interviews with them during the two years Sante and Kenny spent with the New York City Correction Department.

The three Manhattan Supreme Court Judges—Herbert Adlerberg, Herbert Altman and Rena Uviller—who ultimately presided over the Kimes trial are all to be commended for their wisdom and their patience as the case made its way through the judicial system. The lengthy pre-trial and trial process went smoothly owing to Captain Emil Catalano and his court officers Gerry Monahan, Dawn DelCioppo, Robert Mulligan, Randy Hendricks, Nick Zubrick, Barbara DeRosa, Mike Mainolfi and Bob Schmidt. David Bookstaver at the Office of Court Administration superbly organized the courtroom logistics and made it easier to cover such a lengthy trial.

I am most indebted and appreciative for the generous time the Kimes jury and alternates afforded me, so that I could understand how they went about the difficult task of determining the guilt or innocence of the Kimeses. My deepest gratitude goes to those jurors and alternates who shared their thoughts for the book: Brenda Safford, Patricia Jones, Ella Reape, Mamie Johnson, Vanessa Miller, Robert Hernandez, Michael Alvarez, Richard Backus, Michelle Holmes, Bebe Bridges, Raymond Rivera, Julia Belladonna, Michael Brown, Joan Abbott, Alice Berick, Carol Anderson and Sharon Jackson.

The members of the defense team—José Muniz, Matthew Weissman, Michael Hardy and Mel Sachs—all offered incredible impressions of the Kimeses, and I am deeply appreciative of the time they spent with me in reconstructing key points of the case. I also owe a debt of gratitude to their investigative staff, Les Levine, Larry Frost and Cici McNair, for providing me with background information, pictures, and other documents. A special thank you also to paralegals Pablo Rodriguez, Adam Silvera and Rosario Torres for their unfailing help.

My book research into the Kimes' shenanigans and their convoluted real-estate deals was clarified with the assistance of two Los Angeles lawyers, Jill Rosenthal and Bob Eroen, and I am most appreciative for their valuable help. I would also like to thank the real Kenneth Kimes family, many of whom have asked not to be identified because they are still fearful of Sante and her entourage.

In writing the book, I relied on interviews with former business associates of Kenneth Kimes, Sr., his neighbors, school chums, various Kimes family members, army buddies and their spouses, former employees, attorneys, bankers, bartenders, restaurant managers, and others who contributed information about Sante and her bizarre relationship with Ken Kimes.

In Los Angeles I want to especially thank detectives Dennis English and Bill Cox; Eleanor Hunter, deputy district attorney; and Sandi Gibbons, public affairs officer, for their help in dissecting the David Kazdin case. Also, my thanks go to Carolene and Tim Davis, Alan and Trish Katje, Larry Haile, and Irene DeVito for sharing their accounts of Sante and Kenny with me.

In Washington I am indebted to Katy Hunt, who tracked down documents at the Library of Congress, and to Charlotte Hays of the *Washington Post*, who recalled her encounter with Sante during the mink caper.

In Hawaii, a big thank you to Beverly Bates-Stone, who recalled many of Sante's wild exploits while living in Honolulu, and to Stuart Ho and Jeffrey Portnoy and to the many others who asked to remain anonymous. In Las Vegas, researchers at the Clarks County Library and *Las Vegas Review-Journal* were most helpful in digging up details of Sante's slavery trial. Detective Jimmy Vaccaro helped in reconstructing the events with Stan Patterson. I am also indebted to Kenny's friends Neil Huffey, Kira Wirges, and Vittorio Rahd for generously offering their remembrances and photos of Kenny.

Brian Basore of the Oklahoma City Historical Society was most helpful in providing detailed information about Sante and her family during her early life in the 1930s. Ken Hawkins was most generous in sharing his investigative talents on the disappearance of banker Bilal Ahmed in the Bahamas, and I thank him.

I am particularly indebted to those who loved Irene Silverman, including her many friends, such as Teru Graves and her husband, Richard; Florence Barrack; Zang Toi; and Norma Eberhardt Dauphin, who shared with me a lifetime of memories with Irene.

Thank you also to my friend Barbara Halpern and my in-laws Miriam and Roger Bilyeu, who put me up as a houseguest during my research forays into the Los Angeles area. And to neighbors Mike and Elaine DeLuca for caring for Lois Lane and Clark Kent, my two cats, during those frequent out of town trips.

At Reuters, many many thanks go to Patrick Rizzo, Grant McCool, Chris Michaud, Toni Reinhold, and Arthur Spiegelman, not only for their wise counsel but for being extremely supportive of the book project as it unfolded and for encouraging me to write this book. I am particularly grateful and want to especially thank the ever-savvy Ellen Wulfhorst for her guidance and ideas—she got me through the rough spots. And thanks, too, to Peter Morgan, Mike Segar, and Jeff Christensen for photos.

My friend Suzie Schlomann was incredible. She gave me insight in dealing with the Kimeses and spent many hours skillfully organizing the voluminous documents and letters I used to write this book.

The legal commentary offered by Enid Gerling, the "dean" of courthouse defense lawyers, was priceless and refreshing, and I thank her for her brilliant analysis of the legal system.

Steve Somerstein, who provided me with constant legal explanations, was always available whenever I called with a question. He was truly a gem with his time, and I am more than appreciative. Dr. Arthur Weider and Dr. Katherine Sundstrom helped me understand why Sante Kimes behaved as she did. And I thank them.

My newspaper colleagues at the Manhattan Criminal Court building were superb and invaluable as the book project progressed. My thanks and appreciation to Dareh Gregorian, Laura Italiano, Ann Bollinger, court legend Mike Pearl and Kiernan Crowley of the *New York Post*; Sal Arena, John Marzulli, Joe Barefoot, Mike Lipack and Charlie Rudman of the *New York Daily News*; Samuel Maull of the Associated Press; Juliet Papa, Carol D'Auria, and Stan Brooks of Radio Station WINS; Mary Gay Taylor at CBS Radio; John Sullivan, James Barron and Julian Barnes of the *New York Times*, and Patricia Hurtado of *Newsday*.

Three very special colleagues went beyond the call of friendship. My deepest thanks to David Rohde of the *New York Times*, who not only kept me on the straight and narrow path during the two years before the Kimes went to trial and gave me thoughtful analysis of the book, but he, more than anyone, is responsible for recommending me to my publisher, George de Kay at M. Evans and Company, Inc. Then there are my two brilliant and witty closest friends who sit alongside me in the crowded pressroom—Barbara Ross of the *New York Daily News* and Irene Cornell of WCBS Radio. These two loving women have had the patience of Job and have good-naturedly moaned and groaned every time I spoke the name Kimes. Thank you Ross (her pet name in the pressroom) and Irene for putting up with me all these years.

My thanks also to producer Richard Greenberg at *Dateline*, Andrew Holland at *American Justice;* Stephanie Tomasky at *Biography;* Jane Treays at the London, England, channel ITN; Mike Sheenan and Eric Shawn at *Fox*

News. I also want to express my appreciation to my colleagues at Court TV; to David Diaz, Lou Young, John Slattery, Pablo Guzman, and Michael O'Looney at WCBS-TV; Jonathan Dienst and Tim Minton at WNBC-TV; John Miller and Cheryl Fiandaca at WABC-TV; Mary Murphy, Rosemary Gomez, Julian Phillips, Barry Cunningham, Ellen Marks and Pauline Liu at WB-11 News; Rebecca Spitz and Gigi Stone at New York News 1; and courtroom artists Christine Cornell and Jane Rosenberg for their astute observations of Sante and Kenny.

Charles Salzberg was truly magnificent in editing and improving this book, and I am eternally grateful for his sensitive hand in fine-tuning the manuscript.

My agent, Mimi Strong of the Marianne Strong Literary Agency, was unswerving in her enthusiasm about the project from the moment she read the proposal and graciously opened many doors to me, including access to many of Irene Silverman's friends. Mimi, a former journalist, was a hands-on agent and was involved in every aspect of the project. She and her assistant, Mai Wong, were very supportive throughout the project.

My publisher, George de Kay, deserves kudos. He has been truly very supportive of *Dead End.* I owe him a deep debt of gratitude and thanks for not only his wise counsel but in steering the project and giving me confidence, support, and enthusiasm for the book. I truly appreciate his hard work and that of his staff: Harry McCullough and Marc Baller. Thank you everyone at M. Evans and Company.

Finally, I would like to thank my sister Selma, my cousins, my in-laws, nieces and nephews, grandchildren, my many friends, and Heidi and Christopher, who mean so much to me and for encouraging me to write the book. If I overlooked birthdays and holidays over the last two years as I researched and wrote this book, my apologies, but thank you for always being there for me when I needed you the most.

Jeanne King

Index

335

About the Author

Award-winning journalist Jeanne King began her coverage of Irene Silverman's diappearance and murder on July 6, 1998, the day after the crime was committed. She lived the case daily from that date through June 27, 2000, when Sante and Kenny Kimes were sentenced to serve a total of 257⅔ years in jail.

Jeanne King has been covering crime and courts for over 30 years, starting with the retrial in 1966 of Dr. Sam Sheppard, who was accused of murdering his wife Marilyn.

Among the sensational trials she has covered for Reuters since 1980 are the trials of Joel Steinberg, accused of murdering his adopted daughter; the Howard Beach and Bensonhurst cases; the trials of the teenagers accused of the vicious beating and rape of a Central Park jogger; and the trials of John Gotti and Leona Helmsley.

In 1994, she won the prestigious Newswoman's Club Deadline Award for her breaking exclusive story—and a 24 hour beat—about how one of the defendants in the World Trade Center bombing agreed to testify for the prosecution. The story, written against deadline, was an industry-wide beat and received major play in newspapers and on radio and television.